Equip Your Mind with the Word of God

A Guide to Life-Transforming Bible Verses

As for God, his way is perfect; the word of the LORD is flawless.
He is a shield for all who take refuge in him.

2 Samuel 22:31

After Jesus said this, he looked toward heaven and prayed: "Father, the time
has come. Glorify your Son, that your Son may glorify you. . . .
Sanctify them by the truth; your word is truth.

John 17:1, 17

All Scripture is God-breathed and is useful for teaching, rebuking, correcting and
training in righteousness, so that the man of God may be thoroughly equipped
for every good work.

2 Timothy 3:16–17

For the word of God is living and active. Sharper than any double-edged sword,
it penetrates even to dividing soul and spirit, joints and marrow; it judges the
thoughts and attitudes of the heart.

Hebrews 4:12

And we also thank God continually because, when you received the word of God,
which you heard from us, you accepted it not as the word of men, but as
it actually is, the word of God, which is at work in you who believe.

1 Thessalonians 2:13

He replied, "Blessed rather are those who hear the word of God and obey it."

Luke 11:28

Do your best to present yourself to God as one approved, a workman who does not need to be ashamed and who correctly handles the word of truth.

2 Timothy 2:15

How can a young man keep his way pure? By living according to your word.
I seek you with all my heart; do not let me stray from your commands.
I have hidden your word in my heart that I might not sin against you.

Psalm 119:9–11

Teach me, O Lord, to follow your decrees; then I will keep them to the end. Give me understanding, and I will keep your law and obey it with all my heart. Direct me in the path of your commands, for there I find delight. Turn my heart toward your statutes and not toward selfish gain. Turn my eyes away from worthless things; preserve my life according to your word.

Psalm 119:33–37

For everything that was written in the past was written to teach us,
so that through endurance and the encouragement of the Scriptures
we might have hope.

Romans 15:4

May the God of hope fill you with all joy and peace as you trust in him,
so that you may overflow with hope by the power of the Holy Spirit.

Romans 15:13

Equip Your Mind
with the Word of God

Volume 1
Foundational Truths for Living

NIV® Edition

Barney O. Browne

MindEquip
www.mindequip.com

Equip Your Mind with the Word of God
Volume 1
Foundational Truths for Living
NIV® Edition

ISBN: 978-0-9801399-0-7

Cover design and inside illustrations by Daniel Williams

This book may be ordered from the MindEquip website below.

MindEquip
www.mindequip.com

Contents

Section 3   What the Bible Says About Human Beings

Appendices

Dedication

To Jesus Christ
My Lord
My Savior
The Messiah
The Son of God
The Lamb of God
The First and the Last
The Alpha and the Omega
The Beginning and the End
The King of Kings and Lord of Lords

For to us a child is born, to us a son is given, and the government will be on his shoulders. And he will be called Wonderful Counselor, Mighty God, Everlasting Father, Prince of Peace.

Isaiah 9:6

Surely he took up our infirmities and carried our sorrows, yet we considered him stricken by God, smitten by him, and afflicted. But he was pierced for our transgressions, he was crushed for our iniquities; the punishment that brought us peace was upon him, and by his wounds we are healed. We all, like sheep, have gone astray, each of us has turned to his own way; and the LORD has laid on him the iniquity of us all.

Isaiah 53:4–6

As soon as Jesus was baptized, he went up out of the water. At that moment heaven was opened, and he saw the Spirit of God descending like a dove and lighting on him. And a voice from heaven said, "This is my Son, whom I love; with him I am well pleased."

Matthew 3:16–17

"Not everyone who says to me, 'Lord, Lord,' will enter the kingdom of heaven, but only he who does the will of my Father who is in heaven.

Matthew 7:21

"Come to me, all you who are weary and burdened, and I will give you rest. Take my yoke upon you and learn from me, for I am gentle and humble in heart, and you will find rest for your souls. For my yoke is easy and my burden is light."

Matthew 11:28–30

Then Jesus came to them and said, "All authority in heaven and on earth has been given to me. Therefore go and make disciples of all nations, baptizing them in the name of the Father and of the Son and of the Holy Spirit, and teaching them to obey everything I have commanded you. And surely I am with you always, to the very end of the age."

Matthew 28:18–20

For the Son of Man came to seek and to save what was lost."

Luke 19:10

He said to them, "This is what I told you while I was still with you: Everything must be fulfilled that is written about me in the Law of Moses, the Prophets and the Psalms." Then he opened their minds so they could understand the Scriptures. He told them, "This is what is written: The Christ will suffer and rise from the dead on the third day, and repentance and forgiveness of sins will be preached in his name to all nations, beginning at Jerusalem. You are witnesses of these things. I am going to send you what my Father has promised; but stay in the city until you have been clothed with power from on high."

Luke 24:44–48

The next day John saw Jesus coming toward him and said, "Look, the Lamb of God, who takes away the sin of the world!

John 1:29

"For God so loved the world that he gave his one and only Son, that whoever believes in him shall not perish but have eternal life. For God did not send his Son into the world to condemn the world, but to save the world through him. Whoever believes in him is not condemned, but whoever does not believe stands condemned already because he has not believed in the name of God's one and only Son.

John 3:16–18

Whoever believes in the Son has eternal life, but whoever rejects the Son will not see life, for God's wrath remains on him."

John 3:36

For I have come down from heaven not to do my will but to do the will of him who sent me. And this is the will of him who sent me, that I shall lose none of all that he has given me, but raise them up at the last day. For my Father's will is that everyone who looks to the Son and believes in him shall have eternal life, and I will raise him up at the last day."

John 6:38–40

When Jesus spoke again to the people, he said, "I am the light of the world. Whoever follows me will never walk in darkness, but will have the light of life."

John 8:12

"You are a king, then!" said Pilate. Jesus answered, "You are right in saying I am a king. In fact, for this reason I was born, and for this I came into the world, to testify to the truth. Everyone on the side of truth listens to me."

John 18:37

But whatever was to my profit I now consider loss for the sake of Christ. What is more, I consider everything a loss compared to the surpassing greatness of knowing Christ Jesus my Lord, for whose sake I have lost all things. I consider them rubbish, that I may gain Christ and be found in him, not having a righteousness of my own that comes from the law, but that which is through faith in Christ—the righteousness that comes from God and is by faith.

Philippians 3:7–9

When I saw him, I fell at his feet as though dead. Then he placed his right hand on me and said: "Do not be afraid. I am the First and the Last. I am the Living One; I was dead, and behold I am alive for ever and ever! And I hold the keys of death and Hades.

Revelation 1:17–18

Preface

At the age of forty I became a Christian and began to study the Bible. Slowly but surely my view of the Bible began to change. I came to the realization that the Bible was much more than I originally thought it to be. I became aware of the overwhelming evidence proving beyond any reasonable doubt that the Bible is truly of supernatural origin and that its content has been almost perfectly preserved from ancient times to the present. I learned that although we are separated from the original manuscripts of the Bible by thousands of years, cultural differences, and language differences, we have available to us reliable and accurate Bibles that communicate what God wants us to know.

The following evidences convinced me that the Bible is truly the Word of God:

1. *Regarding integrity*: Although the Bible was written by approximately forty individuals over a period of more than 1,500 years, its consistent message, verifiable accuracy, and timeless wisdom clearly reflect integrity of design. This amazing feat is not something that human beings could accomplish without God's divine involvement.

2. *Regarding science*: Though not a book on science, the Bible's teachings are consistent with what we observe in the physical world around us. Neither biblical creation nor the theory of evolution has been proven by science. However, new discoveries that are scientifically verifiable are far more consistent with the Bible's account of creation than with the theory of evolution. Appendix 5 looks deeper into the scientifically outdated theory of evolution that continues to be widely promoted and vehemently defended in our culture.

3. *Regarding human beings*: The more that I study the Bible, observe people, and look within myself, the more that I discover that the Bible explains human nature and behavior far more accurately than man's wisdom does.

4. *Regarding predictive prophecy*: Only the Bible accurately describes events hundreds and sometimes thousands of years before they occur. The Bible's prophecies fall into two categories: those that have already been fulfilled and those that have yet to be fulfilled. Unlike the prophecies of man, none of the Bible's prophecies have been proven wrong. Only someone who is not

bound by the dimension of time as we are and who is able to see the future could have authored the hundreds of precisely fulfilled prophecies of the Bible. God is that someone. He tells us in the book of Isaiah:

> "Remember the former things, those of long ago; I am God, and there is no other; I am God, and there is none like me. I make known the end from the beginning, from ancient times, what is still to come. I say: My purpose will stand, and I will do all that I please. From the east I summon a bird of prey; from a far-off land, a man to fulfill my purpose. What I have said, that will I bring about; what I have planned, that will I do." *Isaiah 46:9–11*

5. *Regarding archeology*: Again and again new discoveries demonstrate the accuracy of the Bible's accounts of historical people, places, and events. Because of the Bible's proven accuracy, many archeologists rely on the Bible to guide them to sites of historical interest.

6. *Regarding wisdom*: The more that I trust the Bible's teachings, the more that I realize that the Bible provides the best framework for understanding this world, human nature, myself, and what to expect in life. The more that I observe and experience how life on earth really works, the more apparent it is that the wisdom of the Bible is far superior to the wisdom of man.

God uses the above evidences to authenticate His involvement in authoring the Bible and to demonstrate the Bible's accuracy and trustworthiness. When I finally realized these things, I made the decision that I would strive to trust what the Bible says beyond the wisdom of this world and even beyond my own thinking. Although I was a skeptic when I originally began investigating the Bible, I gradually discovered, and continue to experience, that the Bible is fully trustworthy.

Realizing the trustworthiness of the Bible and committing my life to the Lord Jesus Christ has been life-transforming for me in several ways:

• *First*, the Bible taught me about myself, God, how God views sin (the breaking of His laws), and His great love for me and all people. I have found that the Bible's teachings about human beings are fully consistent with the reality that I observe in the world around me and within me. I cannot say the same for those ideas of man that are contrary to the Bible. God demonstrated His amazing love for us when He sent His Son, Jesus Christ, into the world to pay the full penalty for our sins. The Bible clearly teaches that in order to spend eternity with God we each must place our faith in the Lord Jesus Christ, repent of our sins, and become obedient to Jesus Christ. Realizing these truths changed how I viewed everything.

- *Second*, I learned that the Bible presents a picture of reality—God's *big picture*—that is consistent with the real world and explains, in a coherent way, all that I observe and experience in life. This biblical way of approaching and understanding the world—a *biblical worldview*—allows one to make sense out of this imperfect and trouble-filled reality in which we live. It also allows true followers of Jesus Christ to be joyful, thankful, and hopeful in the midst of troubles because God's big picture—true reality—does not end with our physical death.

- *Third*, I learned that for those who choose to put their faith in and follow the Lord Jesus Christ, there is a confident expectation that God will fulfill His promises regarding eternal life with Him. God has been faithful in keeping His promises and fulfilling His prophecies in the past. Christ-followers can trust that God will be true to His Word in keeping all that He has promised them. They can also be confident that God, in His perfect timing, will bring to pass His yet-unfulfilled prophecies.

- *Fourth*, I learned that the Bible contains everything we need for living our lives in the way that God knows is best, both for us and for the people whose lives we touch. We each must decide whom we will trust for wisdom and guidance. I have observed, experienced, and finally learned that any worldly wisdom that is contrary to the Bible leads to foolishness and is harmful to one's soul. I now strive to trust the Bible above the wisdom of this world and above my own thinking.

This book did not start with a vision to publish a book. It began with a problem. A major struggle I faced as I began studying the Bible and applying it to my life involved my memory. I was continually losing track of many Bible verses that I wanted to remember and apply. This book began as a personal project to help me learn and apply those Bible verses that had special meaning to me. I found it very helpful to use my personal computer as a tool to help me topically organize, retrieve, review, and study my growing collection of Bible verses. The next step was to print a loose-leaf paper version of my Bible-verse collection. This allowed me to easily read and meditate on the Bible verses I had collected. Although my family and some friends expressed interest in what I had assembled, I did not seriously consider the publishing path. My plan was simply to continue adding verses and topics to aid me in my Bible study. If left to myself, this is where my Bible-verse collection would be today.

Looking back, I believe that God worked through life's circumstances, my family, and several friends to change my thinking and provide me with the encouragement, support, help, and prayers that made another path possible. During the summer of 2002 my wife, Heidi, and I made the decision to turn my Bible-verse collection into a self-published book. Our plan was to publish a book that presented Bible verses in a format that could be used in a variety of ways. I have listed many of these ways on the back cover of this book. Our desire is that many people will find this book to be a valuable companion to their Bibles and that it will help them to develop a biblical worldview and to grow in spiritual maturity—thinking and living more like Jesus Christ and less like this world.

Barney Browne
April 2009

If you would like to send me your comments
regarding this book, please go to my website below
and select the *Contact* tab near the top of the screen.

Thank you.
Barney Browne

MindEquip
www.mindequip.com

Acknowledgments

I am very thankful for the many Christians who encouraged and supported us during this long and challenging adventure into the unknown. There were many times when the light at the end of the tunnel did not seem to be getting any closer. I am especially grateful to the following people for playing important roles in making this *Equip Your Mind with the Word of God* book series a reality. It is because of their prayers, encouragement, support, guidance, suggestions, and patience that I was able to complete this book.

Heidi Browne—My devoted wife and best friend, who convinced me to shift gears and set out to self-publish this book series. I am eternally grateful for her encouragement, ideas, hard work, sacrifices, patience, and editing support that continue to this day. Heidi is truly a Proverbs 31 woman and it is a privilege to share this mission with her.

Dr. David Stampfl—My friend and ministry partner, who shared Heidi's and my vision for this book series almost from the day we decided to follow the self-publishing path. Dave provided the friendship, encouragement, wisdom, guidance, and support throughout this long-term project that enabled me to stay the course.

Our children, Erik, Heather, and Holly—Now adults, they have been very supportive and encouraging throughout this project. They have all shared ideas and insights with me that I found valuable in the development of this book series. During the late 1990's while my daughters were still living at home I gave them a copy of the Bible-verse reference binder that I had assembled for my personal use. Both Heather and Holly expressed how helpful this reference was in connecting them with life-transforming Bible verses at that stage of their lives. They used it as both a Bible-verse reference and as a devotional book. This was well before our decision to self-publish a book. However, the fact that our teenagers found this Bible-verse reference relevant to their lives was a significant factor in our decision to move forward with a self-published book.

Daniel Williams—My friend, who worked closely with me as he developed the book covers and inside graphics for this book. I greatly appreciate Dan's creativity, graphic design skills, initiative, and passion for a design that truly reflects the purpose of this book. I am also thankful for Dan's valuable suggestions regarding other aspects of this book.

The Reverend Michael R. Williams—My friend, whose Bible teaching and insightful conversations further developed my understanding of the Bible and how to apply it to everyday thinking and living. I am also very thankful for Mike's valuable guidance and suggestions during the early development of the chapter introductions.

William Magoon—My friend, who continually lifted up this book project and my family in prayer, provided regular encouragement, and helped with supporting this project.

Richard Barkow—My friend and cousin, who, upon hearing of this book project, was led to bless us with his encouragement, prayers, and support.

Connie Stampfl—My friend, for her helpful suggestions regarding the section and chapter introductions.

Mary Booker—My friend, for her helpful suggestions of the front pages and the chapter pages containing Bible verses.

Dawn Jeffers—From Raven Tree Press, whose suggestions to employ chapter introductions and the use of graphics guided my early design decisions. I am grateful for her wise advice regarding self-publishing.

David Bergsland—My digital publishing mentor, who was instrumental in helping me learn about digital publishing and Adobe® InDesign® software. It was through David that I learned about the elements of typography and the importance of "readability" in page design. David is the author of several excellent books on these topics.

Pastor Jim Bomkamp—My friend, for his valuable insights and editing suggestions during the final year of this book project.

I am grateful to the many others, too numerous to name, who have encouraged me and prayed for the success of this book project.

Introduction

Welcome to the *Equip Your Mind with the Word of God* book series. Each book in this series presents Bible verses within topics that are of utmost importance to every human being. The goal of each chapter's page design is to present Scripture text that is easy on the eyes to read, encourages focusing and meditating on the Scripture paragraphs, and has ample space for personal notes. These design features enable this book to be used as a topical Bible-verse reference, as a devotional book, or as a small-group Bible-study resource. My desire is that this book will be a helpful window into the timeless truths of the Word of God.

The primary goal of this Introduction is to define several important terms and concepts. Accurately understanding these terms and concepts is foundational to understanding and properly applying the truths found within this book.

The God of the Bible

This book, Volume 1, focuses on what the Bible says about itself, God, and human beings. When I use the word *God* with a capital "G" in this book, I am always referring to the one true God, the God of the Bible. His attributes are clearly revealed throughout the Bible. Section 2 of this book focuses on what the Bible says about God. In this world it is quite common for people to use the word *God* to refer to someone other than the God of the Bible. If the attributes of the one they are referring to as *God* are the same as God's attributes as presented in the Bible, then they are in fact speaking about the God of the Bible. If, on the other hand, the attributes are not the same, then when they use the word *God* they are in reality speaking about someone else. For this reason, it is very important in our communications with others that we clarify what we mean when we use the word *God*.

The Lord Jesus Christ

In this book I often refer to Jesus Christ as the *Lord Jesus Christ* to acknowledge His ruling position over all creation. *Noah Webster's 1828 First Edition of the American Dictionary of the English Language*[1] first defines *Lord* as follows: "*1. A master; a person possessing supreme power and authority; a ruler; a governor.*" Christians view Jesus Christ not only as their Savior, but also as their Lord and Master.

The following Bible verses help us to understand how God wants us to view the Lordship of Jesus Christ:

> In the past God spoke to our forefathers through the prophets at many times and in various ways, but in these last days he has spoken to us by his Son, whom he appointed heir of all things, and through whom he made the universe. The Son is the radiance of God's glory and the exact representation of his being, sustaining all things by his powerful word. After he had provided purification for sins, he sat down at the right hand of the Majesty in heaven. *Hebrews 1:1–3*

> On his robe and on his thigh he has this name written: KING OF KINGS AND LORD OF LORDS. *Revelation 19:16*

Terms Referring to the Word of God

For the benefit of those who are new to reading the Bible, I need to mention the different terms often used to refer to the *Word of God*. In this book the following terms are used interchangeably: *Bible, Scriptures, Word of God, God's Word*, and *His Word*. When I refer to several adjacent verses, I interchangeably use the terms *Bible verses* or *Bible passage*.

Wisdom of God vs. Wisdom of This World

The terms *wisdom of God, wisdom of this world*, and *wisdom of man* are used frequently throughout this book. I use the phrase *wisdom of God* to refer to God's principles, ways, and wisdom as presented in the Bible. I use the phrases *wisdom of this world* and *wisdom of man* interchangeably. These refer to man's ideas, reasonings, and speculations that conflict with God's principles, ways, and wisdom. The word *world*, when used in the context of the wisdom of this world, refers to the secular and ungodly thinking of mankind and cultures throughout history. At any point in time our thinking will be based on either the wisdom of God or the wisdom of this world. Many problems, temptations, and difficult choices that Christians face in life can be avoided by trusting in the wisdom of God found in the Bible rather than trusting in the wisdom of this world.

Avoid Confusion Regarding the Term Christian

Although the term *Christian* is widely used in our culture today, it often means different things to different people. This can lead to wrong assumptions, misguided communications, and wrong conclusions. The consequences of this can be serious. To avoid such problems in this book, I differentiate between two terms: *Christian* and *professing Christian*. I consider *Christians* to be a subset within the broader group of *professing Christians*.

What I Mean by the Term *Christian* (including *Bible-Based Christian*, *Biblical Christian*, and *Christ-Follower*)

When I use the terms *Christian, Bible-based Christian, biblical Christian,* and *Christ-follower* in this book, I mean a committed follower of the Lord Jesus Christ according to the Bible. I use these terms interchangeably. The Bible tells us the following about those who have placed their faith in the Lord Jesus Christ:

1. **Christians** are people whose hearts were convicted and humbled when they heard the clear Gospel message of Jesus Christ and came to the realization that they had sinned against the holy God of the Bible. Sin is the breaking of God's laws, and every sin is a sin against God.

   > Therefore no one will be declared righteous in his sight by observing the law; rather, through the law we become conscious of sin. *Romans 3:20*

   > As for you, you were dead in your transgressions and sins, in which you used to live when you followed the ways of this world and of the ruler of the kingdom of the air, the spirit who is now at work in those who are disobedient. All of us also lived among them at one time, gratifying the cravings of our sinful nature and following its desires and thoughts. Like the rest, we were by nature objects of wrath. *Ephesians 2:1–3*

   > Everyone who sins breaks the law; in fact, sin is lawlessness. But you know that he appeared so that he might take away our sins. And in him is no sin. No one who lives in him keeps on sinning. No one who continues to sin has either seen him or known him. *1 John 3:4–6*

   > Who can say, "I have kept my heart pure; I am clean and without sin"? *Proverbs 20:9*

If we claim to be without sin, we deceive ourselves and the truth is not in us. If we confess our sins, he is faithful and just and will forgive us our sins and purify us from all unrighteousness. If we claim we have not sinned, we make him out to be a liar and his word has no place in our lives. *1 John 1:8–10*

This righteousness from God comes through faith in Jesus Christ to all who believe. There is no difference, for all have sinned and fall short of the glory of God, and are justified freely by his grace through the redemption that came by Christ Jesus. *Romans 3:22–24*

But the Scripture declares that the whole world is a prisoner of sin, so that what was promised, being given through faith in Jesus Christ, might be given to those who believe. *Galatians 3:22*

Surely he took up our infirmities and carried our sorrows, yet we considered him stricken by God, smitten by him, and afflicted. But he was pierced for our transgressions, he was crushed for our iniquities; the punishment that brought us peace was upon him, and by his wounds we are healed. We all, like sheep, have gone astray, each of us has turned to his own way; and the LORD has laid on him the iniquity of us all. *Isaiah 53:4–6*

2. **Christians** understand and admit that because they have sinned against the holy God of the Bible, they deserve the just punishment for their sins—physical and spiritual death. Spiritual death means separation from God.

    The heart is deceitful above all things and beyond cure. Who can understand it? "I the LORD search the heart and examine the mind, to reward a man according to his conduct, according to what his deeds deserve." *Jeremiah 17:9–10*

    Have mercy on me, O God, according to your unfailing love; according to your great compassion blot out my transgressions. Wash away all my iniquity and cleanse me from my sin. For I know my transgressions, and my sin is always before me. Against you, you only, have I sinned and done what is evil in your sight, so that you are proved right when you speak and justified when you judge. *Psalm 51:1–4*

If we deliberately keep on sinning after we have received the knowledge of the truth, no sacrifice for sins is left, but only a fearful expectation of judgment and of raging fire that will consume the enemies of God. *Hebrews 10:26–27*

"For God so loved the world that he gave his one and only Son, that whoever believes in him shall not perish but have eternal life. For God did not send his Son into the world to condemn the world, but to save the world through him. Whoever believes in him is not condemned, but whoever does not believe stands condemned already because he has not believed in the name of God's one and only Son. *John 3:16–18*

Whoever believes in the Son has eternal life, but whoever rejects the Son will not see life, for God's wrath remains on him." *John 3:36*

But he continued, "You are from below; I am from above. You are of this world; I am not of this world. I told you that you would die in your sins; if you do not believe that I am the one I claim to be, you will indeed die in your sins." *John 8:23–24*

3. **Christians** are individuals who humbly ask God to forgive them for their sins. They experience godly sorrow (deep sorrow for sinning against the holy, righteous, and loving God of the Bible). They also experience worldly sorrow (sorrow for the earthly consequences that they must face and for the troubles and pain that they have caused other people to experience). However, it is their godly sorrow that moves them to truly repent.

If we claim to be without sin, we deceive ourselves and the truth is not in us. If we confess our sins, he is faithful and just and will forgive us our sins and purify us from all unrighteousness. If we claim we have not sinned, we make him out to be a liar and his word has no place in our lives. *1 John 1:8–10*

Who can discern his errors? Forgive my hidden faults. Keep your servant also from willful sins; may they not rule over me. Then will I be blameless, innocent of great transgression. May the words of my mouth and the meditation of my heart be pleasing in your sight, O LORD, my Rock and my Redeemer. *Psalm 19:12–14*

Even if I caused you sorrow by my letter, I do not regret it. Though I did regret it—I see that my letter hurt you, but only for a little while—yet now I am happy, not because you were made sorry, but because your sorrow led you to repentance. For you became sorrowful as God intended and so were not harmed in any way by us. Godly sorrow brings repentance that leads to salvation and leaves no regret, but worldly sorrow brings death. *2 Corinthians 7:8–10*

4. **Christians** go beyond asking for forgiveness. They willingly repent of their sins because God calls them to repent, because they experience godly sorrow, because through the Holy Spirit they have the power to repent, and because they truly desire to honor and serve God in how they live their lives. To repent means to experience a change of heart and mind that results in turning away from sin and becoming obedient to the Lord Jesus Christ. Genuine repentance always results in an observable change in a person's life.

   "Now, brothers, I know that you acted in ignorance, as did your leaders. But this is how God fulfilled what he had foretold through all the prophets, saying that his Christ would suffer. Repent, then, and turn to God, so that your sins may be wiped out, that times of refreshing may come from the Lord, and that he may send the Christ, who has been appointed for you—even Jesus. He must remain in heaven until the time comes for God to restore everything, as he promised long ago through his holy prophets. *Acts 3:17–21*

   "Therefore since we are God's offspring, we should not think that the divine being is like gold or silver or stone—an image made by man's design and skill. In the past God overlooked such ignorance, but now he commands all people everywhere to repent. For he has set a day when he will judge the world with justice by the man he has appointed. He has given proof of this to all men by raising him from the dead." *Acts 17:29–31*

5. **Christians** believe that Jesus Christ is God in human form. He always was, is, and will be holy and without sin.

Everyone who sins breaks the law; in fact, sin is lawlessness. But you know that he appeared so that he might take away our sins. And in him is no sin. No one who lives in him keeps on sinning. No one who continues to sin has either seen him or known him. *1 John 3:4–6*

God made him who had no sin to be sin for us, so that in him we might become the righteousness of God. *2 Corinthians 5:21*

Jesus answered, "I did tell you, but you do not believe. The miracles I do in my Father's name speak for me, but you do not believe because you are not my sheep. My sheep listen to my voice; I know them, and they follow me. I give them eternal life, and they shall never perish; no one can snatch them out of my hand. My Father, who has given them to me, is greater than all; no one can snatch them out of my Father's hand. I and the Father are one." *John 10:25–30*

6. **Christians** believe that Jesus Christ is their sin-bearer, Savior, and Lord. Out of love, He took their sins upon Himself when He went to the cross. Jesus Christ then received the full punishment for the sins of the world—the wrath of God against sin—thereby paying the full penalty for our past, present, and future sins. Those who repent of their sins and place their faith in the Lord Jesus Christ are spiritually reborn, freed from the eternal penalty for their sins, and promised eternal live in heaven with God.

> Surely he took up our infirmities and carried our sorrows, yet we considered him stricken by God, smitten by him, and afflicted. But he was pierced for our transgressions, he was crushed for our iniquities; the punishment that brought us peace was upon him, and by his wounds we are healed. We all, like sheep, have gone astray, each of us has turned to his own way; and the LORD has laid on him the iniquity of us all. *Isaiah 53:4–6*

> This is how God showed his love among us: He sent his one and only Son into the world that we might live through him. This is love: not that we loved God, but that he loved us and sent his Son as an atoning sacrifice for our sins. Dear friends, since God so loved us, we also ought to love one another. *1 John 4:9–11*

Therefore, there is now no condemnation for those who are in Christ Jesus, because through Christ Jesus the law of the Spirit of life set me free from the law of sin and death. *Romans 8:1–2*

The next day John saw Jesus coming toward him and said, "Look, the Lamb of God, who takes away the sin of the world! *John 1:29*

But God demonstrates his own love for us in this: While we were still sinners, Christ died for us. *Romans 5:8*

That if you confess with your mouth, "Jesus is Lord," and believe in your heart that God raised him from the dead, you will be saved. For it is with your heart that you believe and are justified, and it is with your mouth that you confess and are saved. As the Scripture says, "Anyone who trusts in him will never be put to shame." *Romans 10:9–11*

Since you call on a Father who judges each man's work impartially, live your lives as strangers here in reverent fear. For you know that it was not with perishable things such as silver or gold that you were redeemed from the empty way of life handed down to you from your forefathers, but with the precious blood of Christ, a lamb without blemish or defect. He was chosen before the creation of the world, but was revealed in these last times for your sake. Through him you believe in God, who raised him from the dead and glorified him, and so your faith and hope are in God. *1 Peter 1:17–21*

On his robe and on his thigh he has this name written: KING OF KINGS AND LORD OF LORDS. *Revelation 19:16*

7. **Christians** believe that after Jesus Christ physically died on the cross He was physically resurrected by God.

    "We are going up to Jerusalem," he said, "and the Son of Man will be betrayed to the chief priests and teachers of the law. They will condemn him to death and will hand him over to the Gentiles, who will mock him and spit on him, flog him and kill him. Three days later he will rise." *Mark 10:33–34*

A week later his disciples were in the house again, and Thomas was with them. Though the doors were locked, Jesus came and stood among them and said, "Peace be with you!" Then he said to Thomas, "Put your finger here; see my hands. Reach out your hand and put it into my side. Stop doubting and believe." *John 20:26–27*

For what I received I passed on to you as of first importance: that Christ died for our sins according to the Scriptures, that he was buried, that he was raised on the third day according to the Scriptures, and that he appeared to Peter, and then to the Twelve. *1 Corinthians 15:3–5*

I pray also that the eyes of your heart may be enlightened in order that you may know the hope to which he has called you, the riches of his glorious inheritance in the saints, and his incomparably great power for us who believe. That power is like the working of his mighty strength, which he exerted in Christ when he raised him from the dead and seated him at his right hand in the heavenly realms, far above all rule and authority, power and dominion, and every title that can be given, not only in the present age but also in the one to come. And God placed all things under his feet and appointed him to be head over everything for the church, which is his body, the fullness of him who fills everything in every way. *Ephesians 1:18–23*

Since, then, you have been raised with Christ, set your hearts on things above, where Christ is seated at the right hand of God. Set your minds on things above, not on earthly things. *Colossians 3:1–2*

In the past God spoke to our forefathers through the prophets at many times and in various ways, but in these last days he has spoken to us by his Son, whom he appointed heir of all things, and through whom he made the universe. The Son is the radiance of God's glory and the exact representation of his being, sustaining all things by his powerful word. After he had provided purification for sins, he sat down at the right hand of the Majesty in heaven. *Hebrews 1:1–3*

Let us fix our eyes on Jesus, the author and perfecter of our faith, who for the joy set before him endured the cross, scorning its shame, and sat down at the right hand of the throne of God. *Hebrews 12:2*

8. **Christians** trust the Bible when it proclaims that the Lord Jesus Christ alone can rescue them from the eternal consequences of sinning against God. They believe that they are saved by God's grace alone through faith in Jesus Christ. They realize that there is nothing they can do to avoid God's judgment for their sins except to repent of their sins and place their faith in Jesus Christ as their personal Savior and Lord.

> Whoever believes in the Son has eternal life, but whoever rejects the Son will not see life, for God's wrath remains on him." *John 3:36*

> But he continued, "You are from below; I am from above. You are of this world; I am not of this world. I told you that you would die in your sins; if you do not believe that I am the one I claim to be, you will indeed die in your sins." *John 8:23–24*

> Jesus answered, "I am the way and the truth and the life. No one comes to the Father except through me. *John 14:6*

> But because of his great love for us, God, who is rich in mercy, made us alive with Christ even when we were dead in transgressions—it is by grace you have been saved. *Ephesians 2:4–5*

> For it is by grace you have been saved, through faith—and this not from yourselves, it is the gift of God—not by works, so that no one can boast. For we are God's workmanship, created in Christ Jesus to do good works, which God prepared in advance for us to do. *Eph. 2:8–10*

> You know that I have not hesitated to preach anything that would be helpful to you but have taught you publicly and from house to house. I have declared to both Jews and Greeks that they must turn to God in repentance and have faith in our Lord Jesus. *Acts 20:20–21*

9. **Christians** are spiritually reborn when they experience godly sorrow, repent of their sins, and place their faith in Jesus Christ alone as their personal Savior and Lord.

> In reply Jesus declared, "I tell you the truth, no one can see the kingdom of God unless he is born again." *John 3:3*

And you also were included in Christ when you heard the word of truth, the gospel of your salvation. Having believed, you were marked in him with a seal, the promised Holy Spirit, who is a deposit guaranteeing our inheritance until the redemption of those who are God's possession—to the praise of his glory. *Ephesians 1:13–14*

For you have been born again, not of perishable seed, but of imperishable, through the living and enduring word of God. For, "All men are like grass, and all their glory is like the flowers of the field; the grass withers and the flowers fall, but the word of the Lord stands forever." And this is the word that was preached to you. *1 Peter 1:23–25*

10. **Christians** acknowledge the Lordship of Jesus Christ and strive to honor and obey Him with how they live their lives.

Trust in the LORD with all your heart and lean not on your own understanding; in all your ways acknowledge him, and he will make your paths straight. *Proverbs 3:5–6*

Has not my hand made all these things, and so they came into being?" declares the LORD. "This is the one I esteem: he who is humble and contrite in spirit, and trembles at my word. *Isaiah 66:2*

Then Jesus said to his disciples, "If anyone would come after me, he must deny himself and take up his cross and follow me. *Matthew 16:24*

Moreover, the Father judges no one, but has entrusted all judgment to the Son, that all may honor the Son just as they honor the Father. He who does not honor the Son does not honor the Father, who sent him. *John 5:22–23*

"If you love me, you will obey what I command. *John 14:15*

Then Jesus came to them and said, "All authority in heaven and on earth has been given to me. Therefore go and make disciples of all nations, baptizing them in the name of the Father and of the Son and of the Holy Spirit, and teaching them to obey everything I have commanded you. And surely I am with you always, to the very end of the age." *Matthew 28:18–20*

> Submit yourselves, then, to God. Resist the devil, and he will flee from you. Come near to God and he will come near to you. Wash your hands, you sinners, and purify your hearts, you double-minded. *James 4:7–8*

> So then, just as you received Christ Jesus as Lord, continue to live in him, rooted and built up in him, strengthened in the faith as you were taught, and overflowing with thankfulness. *Colossians 2:6–7*

> But in your hearts set apart Christ as Lord. *1 Peter 3:15a*

What I Mean by the Term *Professing Christian*

When I use the term *professing Christian* in this book, I mean anyone who professes or claims to be a Christian, whether or not he or she actually is a spiritually reborn follower of Jesus Christ as previously described. Many professing Christians are, in fact, Christians. Other professing Christians know that they are not Christians but are unwilling to admit it. Then there are professing Christians who sincerely believe that they are Christians, when in reality they are not. This usually happens because they have relied on the opinions of men rather than on the Word of God for their understanding of what it means to be a follower of Jesus Christ.

Know for Sure Whether You Are a Christian—a Christ-Follower

If you think you are a Christian but find that some of the previously listed characteristics of a biblical Christian are foreign to you, now is the time to be sure that you have a right relationship with God. When we face Him after this life, He will hold each one of us accountable for our own relationship with Jesus Christ. God knows our hearts and whether we have truly placed our faith in Jesus Christ as Savior, repented of our sins, and submitted ourselves to His Lordship. May the following words of Jesus not apply to you on judgment day:

> "Not everyone who says to me, 'Lord, Lord,' will enter the kingdom of heaven, but only he who does the will of my Father who is in heaven. Many will say to me on that day, 'Lord, Lord, did we not prophesy in your name, and in your name drive out demons and perform many miracles?' Then I will tell them plainly, 'I never knew you. Away from me, you evildoers!' *Matthew 7:21–23*

If you have doubts as to whether you have a right relationship with the Lord Jesus Christ, find out what the Bible says and trust it above the wisdom of this world. Review the ten items listed in the subtopic: "What I Mean by the Term *Christian* (including *Bible-Based Christian*, *Biblical Christian*, and *Christ-Follower*)" on page 3 of this Introduction. As you do, meditate on the Scriptures presented underneath each of the ten points. Make sure that you understand the meaning of each of these verses. The book of 1 John in the Bible is also helpful for understanding what a right relationship with the Lord Jesus Christ looks like in a Christian's life. Then test your heart using the Bible and ask God to reveal to you where you stand with Him. Seek advice from spiritually mature Christians and ask for supporting Scriptures. Test everything against what the Bible says.

What I Mean by the Term *Spiritual Maturity*

Throughout this book, when I use the term *spiritual maturity* I mean Christlikeness or Christlike character. *Spiritual maturity* applies to Christians. Growing in *spiritual maturity* means thinking and living more like Jesus Christ and less like this world. *Spiritual maturity* involves growing in our understanding of God's attributes and the true nature of the human heart. It requires ongoing repenting of sins because Christians still struggle with sin while in this life. It involves walking in humility, denying self, and glorifying God. Growing in *spiritual maturity* requires increasingly trusting, revering, accurately understanding, and obeying the Word of God. The following Bible verses provide insights and guidance for growing in *spiritual maturity*—Christlikeness:

> Has not my hand made all these things, and so they came into being?" declares the LORD. "This is the one I esteem: he who is humble and contrite in spirit, and trembles at my word. *Isaiah 66:2*

> Jesus replied, "If anyone loves me, he will obey my teaching. My Father will love him, and we will come to him and make our home with him. *John 14:23*

> Therefore, I urge you, brothers, in view of God's mercy, to offer your bodies as living sacrifices, holy and pleasing to God—this is your spiritual act of worship. Do not conform any longer to the pattern of this world, but be transformed by the renewing of your mind. Then you will be able to test and approve what God's will is—his good, pleasing and perfect will. *Romans 12:1–2*

It was he who gave some to be apostles, some to be prophets, some to be evangelists, and some to be pastors and teachers, to prepare God's people for works of service, so that the body of Christ may be built up until we all reach unity in the faith and in the knowledge of the Son of God and become mature, attaining to the whole measure of the fullness of Christ. *Ephesians 4:11–13*

Do your best to present yourself to God as one approved, a workman who does not need to be ashamed and who correctly handles the word of truth. *2 Timothy 2:15*

For the word of God is living and active. Sharper than any double-edged sword, it penetrates even to dividing soul and spirit, joints and marrow; it judges the thoughts and attitudes of the heart. Nothing in all creation is hidden from God's sight. Everything is uncovered and laid bare before the eyes of him to whom we must give account. *Hebrews 4:12–13*

Therefore, dear friends, since you already know this, be on your guard so that you may not be carried away by the error of lawless men and fall from your secure position. But grow in the grace and knowledge of our Lord and Savior Jesus Christ. To him be glory both now and forever! Amen. *2 Peter 3:17–18*

We know that we have come to know him if we obey his commands. The man who says, "I know him," but does not do what he commands is a liar, and the truth is not in him. But if anyone obeys his word, God's love is truly made complete in him. This is how we know we are in him: Whoever claims to live in him must walk as Jesus did. *1 John 2:3–6*

This is love for God: to obey his commands. And his commands are not burdensome, *1 John 5:3*

When Christians first step into a saving faith in Jesus Christ they are beginning a lifelong journey of understanding the attributes of God, knowing Him better, unlearning false beliefs, trusting the Word of God, loving God more than worldly treasures, being obedient to God, and denying self to glorify God. Our moment-by-moment choices will always affect these dimensions of our Christian life, one way or the other. Our choices will always impact our growth in *spiritual maturity*. To the extent that we trust, rely on, revere, and obey the Bible rather than the wisdom of this world we will honor God and grow in *spiritual maturity*.

As we grow in *spiritual maturity* we will increasingly experience the fruits of the Holy Spirit:

> But the fruit of the Spirit is love, joy, peace, patience, kindness, goodness, faithfulness, gentleness and self-control. Against such things there is no law. Those who belong to Christ Jesus have crucified the sinful nature with its passions and desires. Since we live by the Spirit, let us keep in step with the Spirit. *Galatians 5:22–25*

The less *spiritually mature* a Christian is the more he or she will be trusting in self and the wisdom of this world rather than in the Bible. This leads away from experiencing the fruit of the Spirit and toward sin. Equipping your mind with the Word of God as described in Appendices 1–3 will help you to grow in *spiritual maturity.*

Be Sure to Accurately Handle the Word of God

As you explore the chapters within this book, you may find that you are already quite familiar with the Bible verses presented. Some of you already have an accurate understanding of what God is saying through these verses. Others of you will likely encounter Bible verses that are unfamiliar to you. When this happens, please keep in mind the importance of discovering what God is actually saying in the verse or verses.

There is widespread confusion today because many people are careless in their reading and studying of the Bible. The danger is when people think that they understand God's principles and wisdom when in reality they are trusting in the foolish ideas of men. Be diligent in making sure that the foundation upon which your thinking is based is a solid one. As your foundation goes, so goes your thinking. There have been times in my Christian life when I assumed that my understanding of a Bible verse was accurate even though I had not yet studied it. However, when I studied the verse in context with the surrounding and related Scripture, I discovered that it actually meant something else or something deeper. I learned that I needed to be more diligent in my handling of the Word of God. It is very important to God that Christians accurately understand and properly apply the words of Scripture. This is God's admonition to us in 2 Timothy 2:15: *"Do your best to present yourself to God as one approved, a workman who does not need to be ashamed and who correctly handles the word of truth."*

If you come across verses in this book that you have not yet studied, I encourage you to make it a point to look them up in your Bible. This is important because it enables you to view the Bible verse or passage in its biblical context. Reading Scripture in context is an important part of accurately understanding the meaning of the verses as intended by the author. Since all Scripture is inspired by God, He is the ultimate author of the Bible. It is His intended meaning that we seek to understand when we read the Bible. In addition, God often uses a single verse or passage to teach us at multiple levels and on multiple subjects. Sometimes this will not become apparent unless we read the Bible verse or passage in its context. In addition, it is very helpful to utilize the cross-references in your Bible or those in a separate cross-reference resource such as the *Treasury of Scripture Knowledge*[2]. You will often find that the verse you are studying is cross-referenced with other related verses in the Bible. Exploring these related verses often leads to a more thorough understanding of the original verse being studied and can lead to other rewarding insights as well. Be sure to use your Bible!

Please note, I am not saying that you should never open this book unless you can immediately look up these verses in your Bible. However, I do recommend that you develop a system that enables you to accurately handle God's Word. One approach is to make a small mark next to those verses in this book that you have not previously studied. If you don't have enough time at the moment, reserve time later in the day or week to look up these marked verses in your Bible. Whatever method you use, the important thing is to remain faithful to God's directive in 2 Timothy 2:15 to correctly handle the word of truth.

About the Chapter Introductions

As you read my chapter introductions you will notice that some of the same comments appear in multiple chapters. I have done this intentionally to allow the message of each chapter introduction to be independent of the other chapter introductions. My goal is that this book may be opened to any chapter, in any order, even after extended periods of time, and the chapter introduction will help prepare the reader for the chapter's Bible verses. In addition, this book is intended for a wide range of readers of all ages, including many who are new to the Bible. My hope is that this approach to chapter introductions will enhance the value of this book across its many applications and its wide variety of readers.

My comments in the chapter introductions and in the appendices reflect my perspectives and insights based on my current understanding of the Bible.

Please keep in mind that I am not a Bible scholar. Rather, I am one who has learned to trust the Bible through the faithful teaching of many Bible teachers who themselves truly trust the Bible. In addition, my confidence and trust in the Bible has grown through my own study of the Bible and through my coming to realize that the Bible explains the world we live in and human beings far better than any other source. I acknowledge that I am continually learning what the Bible says and how to properly apply it to my life. I definitely do not have all the answers. That is why I continue to study the Bible and look to it above all else to find out how God wants me to view Him, this world, others, and myself. Please use my comments at the beginning of each chapter simply as starting points to introduce the chapter's topic. What is of primary importance is what God is saying through the Bible verses that are the essence of each chapter.

About the Quoted Bible Verses and Their Punctuation

I have chosen to use the following conventions when quoting Bible verses in this book. All quoted Bible verses are presented with their punctuation as it appears in the Bible. Those verses which are quoted within a paragraph, including their original punctuation marks, are enclosed within extra quotation marks. The verses themselves, along with all other quoted material embedded within text paragraphs, are italicized for readability. Those verses which are quoted as indented, stand-alone paragraphs are not enclosed in extra quotation marks. Their punctuation reflects exactly what is in the Bible. Where my quoted verse or passage represents only a portion of a quote in the Bible, you may notice quotation marks in the beginning of the quoted verse but not at the end. This indicates that the actual quote continues into the next Bible verse, which was beyond what I chose to include in my book. For those verses that are quoted as stand-alone paragraphs, only the verse address is italicized. Finally, I have chosen to not split quoted Bible verses or passages across page boundaries. I want each quoted Bible verse or passage to be fully visible on a single page. It is my hope that these conventions will enhance the readability of this book.

Overview of the Appendices

I would like to introduce you to the appendices in the back of this book. The title of this book—*Equip Your Mind with the Word of God*—is worded as a call to personal action. It is partially based upon the following Bible verses:

All Scripture is God-breathed and is useful for teaching, rebuking, correcting and training in righteousness, so that the man of God may be thoroughly equipped for every good work. *2 Timothy 3:16–17*

Therefore put on the full armor of God, so that when the day of evil comes, you may be able to stand your ground, and after you have done everything, to stand. Stand firm then, with the belt of truth buckled around your waist, with the breastplate of righteousness in place, and with your feet fitted with the readiness that comes from the gospel of peace. In addition to all this, take up the shield of faith, with which you can extinguish all the flaming arrows of the evil one. Take the helmet of salvation and the sword of the Spirit, which is the word of God. And pray in the Spirit on all occasions with all kinds of prayers and requests. With this in mind, be alert and always keep on praying for all the saints. *Ephesians 6:13–18*

I have included the following appendices for three reasons. First, I want to encourage all who read this book to be increasingly committed to equipping their minds with the Word of God. Second, I have designed these appendices with the goal of helping people equip their minds with the Word of God. Third, I hope that these appendices will be a useful resource to help readers protect themselves from self deception and from the deception that is so prevalent in the world around us. Both kinds of deception work to undermine people's trust in the Bible. This leads to havoc in people's lives, in families, and in nations. For these reasons I encourage you to explore each of these appendices.

> *Appendix 1: What It Means to Equip Your Mind with the Word of God—* I share my perspective on this subject by answering five questions.

> *Appendix 2: Why It Is Important to Equip Your Mind with the Word of God—*This appendix presents ten reasons why Christians should want their minds to be equipped with the Word of God.

> *Appendix 3: How to Equip Your Mind with the Word of God—*In this appendix you will find eighteen action items to help you to successfully equip your mind with the Word of God.

> *Appendix 4: How the Word of God Can Teach You—*Here you will find a list of ten ways that the Holy Spirit can use the Word of God in your life. In addition, this appendix presents a practical example of just one of the many ways that God can use His Word to equip and fortify your

mind with important biblical truths and principles. I explain how viewing and meditating on a theme-based collection of Bible verses can grow your understanding of the Bible's timeless truths. Seven theme-based collections of Bible verses from this and future volumes of this book series are included as usable examples.

Appendix 5: Do Not Be Misled by Darwin's Theory of Evolution—Why would I include a discussion on the theory of evolution in a Bible-verse reference book? The reason is because Darwin's theory of evolution has been used very effectively since 1859 to undermine people's confidence in the Bible. In this appendix you will learn why the theory of evolution is scientifically outdated and why believing in evolution is just as faith-based as believing in the Genesis account of creation. In addition, I share with you several valuable tools and resources. These can help you to discover for yourself why the biblical creation account is consistent with the physical evidence and why the theory of evolution is not.

Appendix 6: Trusting the Bible—A Self-Test for Christians—This appendix is intended for everyone who proclaims to trust the Bible. An introduction briefly introduces and positions the "Self-Test." The test itself is labeled *Thirty Important Questions*. It is designed to help Christians to better understand to what extent they are allowing the Word of God to guide their thoughts, words, and actions. This "Self-Test" questionnaire is designed to be used individually or within a small-group setting.

This Book is Another Window into the Bible

Please consider this book to be another window into the Word of God. Please do not allow this book to take time away from your regular reading and studying of the Bible. Rather, may this book encourage you to read and study the Bible even more. It is my hope that this book will help you to discover more of God's timeless truths, equip your mind with them, and share them with others.

Section 1

The Bible

The Bible claims to be the actual Word of God. It teaches us about the holy God of the Bible, the human beings He created, and this world we live in. The Bible teaches us about God's love for us, man's sinful nature, the consequences of sin, and God's loving provision for bringing repentant human beings into an eternal relationship with Him. It explains the reality of heaven and hell, angels and demons, the widespread evil in this fallen world, and the great spiritual battle for the heart, mind, and soul of every human being. The Bible teaches us about the Lord Jesus Christ and His earthly mission to offer salvation to mankind. It gives us wisdom for living that is timeless and far wiser than the wisdom of man. The Bible teaches that God's Word is true and stands forever. Jesus prayed to God the Father in John 17:17b: *"your word is truth."*

Many people in our culture, including some who call themselves Christians, do not believe much of what the Bible says. Up until the age of forty, I believed that the Bible was simply a mixture of ancient history, myths, rigid rules, outdated values, human wisdom, and wishful thinking. When I finally began to earnestly study the Bible and investigate the evidence for its reliability, I realized how wrong I had been. The more that I study the Bible the more that I find it to be trustworthy.

God—the all-knowing, all-powerful, Creator of the universe—calls us to trust in Him and in His Word. It is then that we can begin to understand the holiness, righteousness, justice, and love of God. The Bible reveals to us our sin nature and how God views sin—the breaking of His laws. It teaches us how sinful people can be forgiven by God and welcomed into heaven if they put their faith in Jesus Christ who has paid the just penalty for their sins. Only by trusting the Bible's teachings can you truly come to know the loving God who created you. I pray that this book will help you to view God, yourself, other people, this world, life's troubles, and salvation through the lens of the Bible—the Word of God.

Chapter 1

What the Bible Says About Itself

**All Scripture is God-breathed and is useful for teaching,
rebuking, correcting and training in righteousness, . . .**
2 Timothy 3:16

In the verse above, God is telling us that all Scripture—the entire Bible—is God-breathed. Although men wrote the words of the Bible, they were supernaturally directed by the Holy Spirit to pen what God wanted them to write. God wants us to confidently believe what the Bible says about itself—that it is truly the Word of God. Then the Holy Spirit will use the Bible to open the eyes of our understanding, transform our lives, and draw us deeper into a loving relationship with Him for eternity.

How we view and treat the Bible will significantly influence our understanding of God and our relationship with Him. It will determine how we view ourselves and other people. Our trust in the Bible will determine how we view this world and our understanding of how life on earth works. Our attitude toward the Bible will be foundational to how we make moment-by-moment choices. How we view and treat the Bible will determine the direction of our lives, how we touch the lives of everyone within our sphere of influence, and the role we allow God to have in our lives. This chapter presents Bible verses that tell us how God wants us to understand and view His Word.

Do not add to what I command you and do not subtract from it, but keep the commands of the LORD your God that I give you.

Deuteronomy 4:2

Love the LORD your God with all your heart and with all your soul and with all your strength. These commandments that I give you today are to be upon your hearts. Impress them on your children. Talk about them when you sit at home and when you walk along the road, when you lie down and when you get up.

Deuteronomy 6:5–7

**the word of the LORD
is flawless.**

He humbled you, causing you to hunger and then feeding you with manna, which neither you nor your fathers had known, to teach you that man does not live on bread alone but on every word that comes from the mouth of the LORD.

Deuteronomy 8:3

"As for God, his way is perfect; the word of the LORD is flawless. He is a shield for all who take refuge in him.

2 Samuel 22:31

And the words of the LORD are flawless, like silver refined in a furnace of clay, purified seven times.

Psalm 12:6

As for God, his way is perfect; the word of the LORD is flawless. He is a shield for all who take refuge in him.

Psalm 18:30

The law of the LORD is perfect, reviving the soul. The statutes of the LORD are trustworthy, making wise the simple. The precepts of the LORD are right, giving joy to the heart. The commands of the LORD are radiant, giving light to the eyes. The fear of the LORD is pure, enduring forever. The ordinances of the LORD are sure and altogether righteous. They are more precious than gold, than much pure gold; they are sweeter than honey, than honey from the comb. By them is your servant warned; in keeping them there is great reward.

Psalm 19:7–11

For the word of the Lord is right and true; he is faithful in all he does. The Lord loves righteousness and justice; the earth is full of his unfailing love.

Psalm 33:4–5

**For the word
of the Lord
is right and true;**

Blessed are they whose ways are blameless, who walk according to the law of the LORD. Blessed are they who keep his statutes and seek him with all their heart.

Psalm 119:1–2

Your word, O LORD, is eternal; it stands firm in the heavens. Your faithfulness continues through all generations; you established the earth, and it endures. Your laws endure to this day, for all things serve you.

Psalm 119:89–91

Your word is a lamp to my feet and a light for my path.

Psalm 119:105

The unfolding of your words gives light; it gives understanding to the simple.

Psalm 119:130

Righteous are you, O LORD, and your laws are right. The statutes you have laid down are righteous; they are fully trustworthy.

Psalm 119:137–138

Your righteousness is everlasting and your law is true.

Psalm 119:142

All your words are true; all your righteous laws are eternal.

Your statutes are forever right; give me understanding that I may live.

Psalm 119:144

Yet you are near, O LORD, and all your commands are true. Long ago I learned from your statutes that you established them to last forever.

Psalm 119:151–152

All your words are true; all your righteous laws are eternal.

Psalm 119:160

I will bow down toward your holy temple and will praise your name for your love and your faithfulness, for you have exalted above all things your name and your word.

Psalm 138:2

"To you, O men, I call out; I raise my voice to all mankind.
You who are simple, gain prudence; you who are foolish,
gain understanding. Listen, for I have worthy things to
say; I open my lips to speak what is right. My mouth speaks
what is true, for my lips detest wickedness. All the words
of my mouth are just; none of them is crooked or perverse.
To the discerning all of them are right; they are faultless to
those who have knowledge. Choose my instruction instead
of silver, knowledge rather than choice gold, for wisdom
is more precious than rubies, and nothing you desire can
compare with her.

Proverbs 8:4–11

Where there is no revelation, the people cast off restraint;
but blessed is he who keeps the law.

Proverbs 29:18

**The grass withers
and the flowers fall,
but the word of our God
stands forever."**

"Every word of God is flawless; he is a shield to those who
take refuge in him. Do not add to his words, or he will
rebuke you and prove you a liar.

Proverbs 30:5–6

The grass withers and the flowers fall, but the word of our
God stands forever."

Isaiah 40:8

As the rain and the snow come down from heaven, and do
not return to it without watering the earth and making it
bud and flourish, so that it yields seed for the sower and
bread for the eater, so is my word that goes out from my
mouth: It will not return to me empty, but will accomplish
what I desire and achieve the purpose for which I sent it.

Isaiah 55:10–11

Jesus answered, "It is written: 'Man does not live on bread alone, but on every word that comes from the mouth of God.' "

Matthew 4:4

"Do not think that I have come to abolish the Law or the Prophets; I have not come to abolish them but to fulfill them. I tell you the truth, until heaven and earth disappear, not the smallest letter, not the least stroke of a pen, will by any means disappear from the Law until everything is accomplished.

Matthew 5:17–18

Jesus replied, "You are in error because you do not know the Scriptures or the power of God.

"Therefore everyone who hears these words of mine and puts them into practice is like a wise man who built his house on the rock. The rain came down, the streams rose, and the winds blew and beat against that house; yet it did not fall, because it had its foundation on the rock.

Matthew 7:24–25

But everyone who hears these words of mine and does not put them into practice is like a foolish man who built his house on sand. The rain came down, the streams rose, and the winds blew and beat against that house, and it fell with a great crash."

Matthew 7:26–27

Jesus replied, "You are in error because you do not know the Scriptures or the power of God.

Matthew 22:29

Heaven and earth will pass away, but my words will
never pass away.

Matthew 24:35

If anyone is ashamed of me and my words in this
adulterous and sinful generation, the Son of Man will be
ashamed of him when he comes in his Father's glory with
the holy angels."

Mark 8:38

Jesus replied, "Are you not in error because you do not
know the Scriptures or the power of God?

Mark 12:24

The devil said to him, "If you are the Son of God, tell this
stone to become bread." Jesus answered, "It is written: 'Man
does not live on bread alone.' "

Luke 4:3–4

**Heaven and earth
will pass away,
but my words
will never pass away.**

"Why do you call me, 'Lord, Lord,' and do not do what I
say? I will show you what he is like who comes to me and
hears my words and puts them into practice. He is like a
man building a house, who dug down deep and laid the
foundation on rock. When a flood came, the torrent struck
that house but could not shake it, because it was well built.

Luke 6:46–48

But the one who hears my words and does not put them
into practice is like a man who built a house on the ground
without a foundation. The moment the torrent struck that
house, it collapsed and its destruction was complete."

Luke 6:49

He replied, "Blessed rather are those who hear the word of God and obey it."

Luke 11:28

He said to them, "How foolish you are, and how slow of heart to believe all that the prophets have spoken! Did not the Christ have to suffer these things and then enter his glory?" And beginning with Moses and all the Prophets, he explained to them what was said in all the Scriptures concerning himself.

Luke 24:25–27

In the beginning was the Word, and the Word was with God, and the Word was God.

He said to them, "This is what I told you while I was still with you: Everything must be fulfilled that is written about me in the Law of Moses, the Prophets and the Psalms." Then he opened their minds so they could understand the Scriptures. He told them, "This is what is written: The Christ will suffer and rise from the dead on the third day, and repentance and forgiveness of sins will be preached in his name to all nations, beginning at Jerusalem. You are witnesses of these things. I am going to send you what my Father has promised; but stay in the city until you have been clothed with power from on high."

Luke 24:44–48

In the beginning was the Word, and the Word was with God, and the Word was God. He was with God in the beginning. Through him all things were made; without him nothing was made that has been made. In him was life, and that life was the light of men. The light shines in the darkness, but the darkness has not understood it.

John 1:1–5

If you believed Moses, you would believe me, for he wrote about me. But since you do not believe what he wrote, how are you going to believe what I say?"

John 5:46–47

"You do not want to leave too, do you?" Jesus asked the Twelve. Simon Peter answered him, "Lord, to whom shall we go? You have the words of eternal life.

John 6:67–68

"As for the person who hears my words but does not keep them, I do not judge him. For I did not come to judge the world, but to save it. There is a judge for the one who rejects me and does not accept my words; that very word which I spoke will condemn him at the last day. For I did not speak of my own accord, but the Father who sent me commanded me what to say and how to say it. I know that his command leads to eternal life. So whatever I say is just what the Father has told me to say."

John 12:47–50

Sanctify them by the truth; your word is truth.

After Jesus said this, he looked toward heaven and prayed: "Father, the time has come. Glorify your Son, that your Son may glorify you. . . . Sanctify them by the truth; your word is truth.

John 17:1, 17

Now the Bereans were of more noble character than the Thessalonians, for they received the message with great eagerness and examined the Scriptures every day to see if what Paul said was true.

Acts 17:11

Consequently, faith comes from hearing the message, and the message is heard through the word of Christ.

Romans 10:17

For everything that was written in the past was written to teach us, so that through endurance and the encouragement of the Scriptures we might have hope.

Romans 15:4

We have not received the spirit of the world but the Spirit who is from God, that we may understand what God has freely given us. This is what we speak, not in words taught us by human wisdom but in words taught by the Spirit, expressing spiritual truths in spiritual words.

1 Corinthians 2:12–13

Therefore, since through God's mercy we have this ministry, we do not lose heart. Rather, we have renounced secret and shameful ways; we do not use deception, nor do we distort the word of God. On the contrary, by setting forth the truth plainly we commend ourselves to every man's conscience in the sight of God.

2 Corinthians 4:1–2

And we also thank God continually because, when you received the word of God, which you heard from us, you accepted it not as the word of men, but as it actually is, the word of God, which is at work in you who believe.

1 Thessalonians 2:13

Consequently, faith comes from hearing the message, and the message is heard through the word of Christ.

Be joyful always; pray continually; give thanks in all circumstances, for this is God's will for you in Christ Jesus. Do not put out the Spirit's fire; do not treat prophecies with contempt. Test everything. Hold on to the good. Avoid every kind of evil.

1 Thessalonians 5:16–22

All Scripture is God-breathed and is useful for teaching, rebuking, correcting and training in righteousness, so that the man of God may be thoroughly equipped for every good work.

2 Timothy 3:16–17

For the word of God is living and active. Sharper than any double-edged sword, it penetrates even to dividing soul and spirit, joints and marrow; it judges the thoughts and attitudes of the heart.

Hebrews 4:12

For the word of God is living and active.
. . .
it judges the thoughts and attitudes of the heart.

For you have been born again, not of perishable seed, but of imperishable, through the living and enduring word of God. For, "All men are like grass, and all their glory is like the flowers of the field; the grass withers and the flowers fall, but the word of the Lord stands forever." And this is the word that was preached to you.

1 Peter 1:23–25

And we have the word of the prophets made more certain, and you will do well to pay attention to it, as to a light shining in a dark place, until the day dawns and the morning star rises in your hearts.

2 Peter 1:19

Above all, you must understand that no prophecy of Scripture came about by the prophet's own interpretation. For prophecy never had its origin in the will of man, but men spoke from God as they were carried along by the Holy Spirit.

2 Peter 1:20–21

The revelation of Jesus Christ, which God gave him to show his servants what must soon take place. He made it known by sending his angel to his servant John, who testifies to everything he saw—that is, the word of God and the testimony of Jesus Christ. Blessed is the one who reads the words of this prophecy, and blessed are those who hear it and take to heart what is written in it, because the time is near.

Revelation 1:1–3

Blessed is the one who reads the words of this prophecy, and blessed are those who hear it and take to heart what is written in it,

Then the angel said to me, "Write: 'Blessed are those who are invited to the wedding supper of the Lamb!'" And he added, "These are the true words of God." At this I fell at his feet to worship him. But he said to me, "Do not do it! I am a fellow servant with you and with your brothers who hold to the testimony of Jesus. Worship God! For the testimony of Jesus is the spirit of prophecy."

Revelation 19:9–10

I warn everyone who hears the words of the prophecy of this book: If anyone adds anything to them, God will add to him the plagues described in this book. And if anyone takes words away from this book of prophecy, God will take away from him his share in the tree of life and in the holy city, which are described in this book.

Revelation 22:18–19

Chapter 2

The Wisdom and Power of God's Word

All your words are true; all your righteous laws are eternal.
Psalm 119:160

God has given us minds to reason with and amazing physical senses for experiencing and exploring our world. With these we are able to gain knowledge and wisdom regarding many things in life. However, in spite of man's extensive accumulated knowledge, it is clear that there are many areas where man's understanding is very limited. A few examples include: why the laws of nature are what they are, exactly how life functions at all levels, the complexity of the human mind, and the origin of DNA.

Man's wisdom is also very limited. As humans, we have a tendency to believe that our accomplishments are the result of our own efforts apart from God. Our tendency is also to trust our own thinking and that of "experts" above the Word of God. A truly wise person humbly recognizes that his or her abilities come from God and that God's wisdom is far beyond man's wisdom. A truly wise Christian is one who earnestly studies the Bible, prays for God's guidance, and then uses the Bible to test his or her thinking. For such a Christian, God then uses His Word to reveal His truth, impart His wisdom, and provide guidance for everyday living in this imperfect world.

The Bible not only contains God's truth and wisdom, but also is powerful in that God uses Scripture to accomplish amazing things in the lives of people. God uses His Word to reveal to people how they have sinned against Him by breaking His laws and what the penalty is for their sins. God uses the Bible to introduce people to the Lord Jesus Christ and to explain to them how they can be saved through Him. God uses His Word in the lives of Christians to teach, rebuke, correct, equip, strengthen, guide, protect, comfort, transform, mature, and bless them. To what extent are you allowing God to do these amazing things in your life through His Word?

"As for God, his way is perfect; the word of the LORD is flawless. He is a shield for all who take refuge in him.

2 Samuel 22:31

And the words of the LORD are flawless, like silver refined in a furnace of clay, purified seven times.

Psalm 12:6

As for God, his way is perfect; the word of the LORD is flawless. He is a shield for all who take refuge in him.

Psalm 18:30

The law of the LORD is perfect, reviving the soul.

The law of the LORD is perfect, reviving the soul. The statutes of the LORD are trustworthy, making wise the simple. The precepts of the LORD are right, giving joy to the heart. The commands of the LORD are radiant, giving light to the eyes. The fear of the LORD is pure, enduring forever. The ordinances of the LORD are sure and altogether righteous. They are more precious than gold, than much pure gold; they are sweeter than honey, than honey from the comb. By them is your servant warned; in keeping them there is great reward.

Psalm 19:7–11

Your word, O LORD, is eternal; it stands firm in the heavens. Your faithfulness continues through all generations; you established the earth, and it endures. Your laws endure to this day, for all things serve you.

Psalm 119:89–91

Oh, how I love your law! I meditate on it all day long. Your commands make me wiser than my enemies, for they are ever with me. I have more insight than all my teachers, for I meditate on your statutes. I have more understanding than the elders, for I obey your precepts. I have kept my feet from every evil path so that I might obey your word. I have not departed from your laws, for you yourself have taught me. How sweet are your words to my taste, sweeter than honey to my mouth! I gain understanding from your precepts; therefore I hate every wrong path. Your word is a lamp to my feet and a light for my path.

Psalm 119:97–105

The unfolding of your words gives light; it gives understanding to the simple.

Psalm 119:130

The unfolding of your words gives light; it gives understanding to the simple.

Righteous are you, O LORD, and your laws are right. The statutes you have laid down are righteous; they are fully trustworthy.

Psalm 119:137–138

Yet you are near, O LORD, and all your commands are true. Long ago I learned from your statutes that you established them to last forever.

Psalm 119:151–152

All your words are true; all your righteous laws are eternal.

Psalm 119:160

I will bow down toward your holy temple and will praise your name for your love and your faithfulness, for you have exalted above all things your name and your word.

Psalm 138:2

By the word of the Lord were the heavens made, their starry host by the breath of his mouth. He gathers the waters of the sea into jars; he puts the deep into storehouses. Let all the earth fear the Lord; let all the people of the world revere him. For he spoke, and it came to be; he commanded, and it stood firm.

Psalm 33:6–9

By the word of the Lord were the heavens made,

For the LORD gives wisdom, and from his mouth come knowledge and understanding. He holds victory in store for the upright, he is a shield to those whose walk is blameless, for he guards the course of the just and protects the way of his faithful ones. Then you will understand what is right and just and fair—every good path. For wisdom will enter your heart, and knowledge will be pleasant to your soul. Discretion will protect you, and understanding will guard you.

Proverbs 2:6–11

My son, preserve sound judgment and discernment, do not let them out of your sight; they will be life for you, an ornament to grace your neck. Then you will go on your way in safety, and your foot will not stumble; when you lie down, you will not be afraid; when you lie down, your sleep will be sweet. Have no fear of sudden disaster or of the ruin that overtakes the wicked, for the LORD will be your confidence and will keep your foot from being snared.

Proverbs 3:21–26

My son, keep your father's commands and do not forsake
your mother's teaching. Bind them upon your heart forever;
fasten them around your neck. When you walk, they will
guide you; when you sleep, they will watch over you; when
you awake, they will speak to you. For these commands
are a lamp, this teaching is a light, and the corrections of
discipline are the way to life,

Proverbs 6:20–23

"Every word of God is flawless; he is a shield to those who
take refuge in him. Do not add to his words, or he will
rebuke you and prove you a liar.

Proverbs 30:5–6

The grass withers and the flowers fall, but the word of our
God stands forever."

Isaiah 40:8

**Every word of God
is flawless;
he is a shield to those
who take refuge in him.**

As the rain and the snow come down from heaven, and do
not return to it without watering the earth and making it
bud and flourish, so that it yields seed for the sower and
bread for the eater, so is my word that goes out from my
mouth: It will not return to me empty, but will accomplish
what I desire and achieve the purpose for which I sent it.

Isaiah 55:10–11

Jesus answered, "It is written: 'Man does not live on
bread alone, but on every word that comes from the
mouth of God.' "

Matthew 4:4

"Do not think that I have come to abolish the Law or the Prophets; I have not come to abolish them but to fulfill them. I tell you the truth, until heaven and earth disappear, not the smallest letter, not the least stroke of a pen, will by any means disappear from the Law until everything is accomplished.

Matthew 5:17–18

"Therefore everyone who hears these words of mine and puts them into practice is like a wise man who built his house on the rock. The rain came down, the streams rose, and the winds blew and beat against that house; yet it did not fall, because it had its foundation on the rock.

Matthew 7:24–25

Heaven and earth will pass away, but my words will never pass away.

But everyone who hears these words of mine and does not put them into practice is like a foolish man who built his house on sand. The rain came down, the streams rose, and the winds blew and beat against that house, and it fell with a great crash."

Matthew 7:26–27

Jesus replied, "You are in error because you do not know the Scriptures or the power of God.

Matthew 22:29

Heaven and earth will pass away, but my words will never pass away.

Matthew 24:35

Jesus replied, "Are you not in error because you do not know the Scriptures or the power of God?

Mark 12:24

"Why do you call me, 'Lord, Lord,' and do not do what I say? I will show you what he is like who comes to me and hears my words and puts them into practice. He is like a man building a house, who dug down deep and laid the foundation on rock. When a flood came, the torrent struck that house but could not shake it, because it was well built.

Luke 6:46–48

But the one who hears my words and does not put them into practice is like a man who built a house on the ground without a foundation. The moment the torrent struck that house, it collapsed and its destruction was complete."

Luke 6:49

Everything must be fulfilled that is written about me in the Law of Moses, the Prophets and the Psalm."

He said to them, "This is what I told you while I was still with you: Everything must be fulfilled that is written about me in the Law of Moses, the Prophets and the Psalms." Then he opened their minds so they could understand the Scriptures. He told them, "This is what is written: The Christ will suffer and rise from the dead on the third day, and repentance and forgiveness of sins will be preached in his name to all nations, beginning at Jerusalem. You are witnesses of these things. I am going to send you what my Father has promised; but stay in the city until you have been clothed with power from on high."

Luke 24:44–48

In the beginning was the Word, and the Word was with God, and the Word was God. He was with God in the beginning. Through him all things were made; without him nothing was made that has been made. In him was life, and that life was the light of men. The light shines in the darkness, but the darkness has not understood it.

John 1:1–5

"As for the person who hears my words but does not keep them, I do not judge him. For I did not come to judge the world, but to save it. There is a judge for the one who rejects me and does not accept my words; that very word which I spoke will condemn him at the last day. For I did not speak of my own accord, but the Father who sent me commanded me what to say and how to say it. I know that his command leads to eternal life. So whatever I say is just what the Father has told me to say."

John 12:47–50

Consequently, faith comes from hearing the message, and the message is heard through the word of Christ.

Romans 10:17

For Christ did not send me to baptize, but to preach the gospel—not with words of human wisdom, lest the cross of Christ be emptied of its power.

1 Corinthians 1:17

My message and my preaching were not with wise and persuasive words, but with a demonstration of the Spirit's power, so that your faith might not rest on men's wisdom, but on God's power.

1 Corinthians 2:4–5

In the beginning was the Word, and the Word was with God, and the Word was God.

Let the peace of Christ rule in your hearts, since as members of one body you were called to peace. And be thankful. Let the word of Christ dwell in you richly as you teach and admonish one another with all wisdom, and as you sing Psalms, hymns and spiritual songs with gratitude in your hearts to God. And whatever you do, whether in word or deed, do it all in the name of the Lord Jesus, giving thanks to God the Father through him.

Colossians 3:15–17

But as for you, continue in what you have learned and have become convinced of, because you know those from whom you learned it, and how from infancy you have known the holy Scriptures, which are able to make you wise for salvation through faith in Christ Jesus.

2 Timothy 3:14–15

All Scripture is God-breathed and is useful for teaching, rebuking, correcting and training in righteousness,

All Scripture is God-breathed and is useful for teaching, rebuking, correcting and training in righteousness, so that the man of God may be thoroughly equipped for every good work.

2 Timothy 3:16–17

In the presence of God and of Christ Jesus, who will judge the living and the dead, and in view of his appearing and his kingdom, I give you this charge: Preach the Word; be prepared in season and out of season; correct, rebuke and encourage—with great patience and careful instruction.

2 Timothy 4:1–2

For the word of God is living and active. Sharper than any double-edged sword, it penetrates even to dividing soul and spirit, joints and marrow; it judges the thoughts and attitudes of the heart.

Hebrews 4:12

By faith we understand that the universe was formed at God's command, so that what is seen was not made out of what was visible.

Hebrews 11:3

For the word of God is living and active.

For you have been born again, not of perishable seed, but of imperishable, through the living and enduring word of God. For, "All men are like grass, and all their glory is like the flowers of the field; the grass withers and the flowers fall, but the word of the Lord stands forever." And this is the word that was preached to you.

1 Peter 1:23–25

Chapter 3

The Sufficiency of God's Word

**His divine power has given us everything we need for life
and godliness through our knowledge of him who called us
by his own glory and goodness.**

2 Peter 1:3

In the verse above, God is proclaiming to us that He has made available to Christians everything they need for life and godliness. This includes, but is not limited to, God's mercy and grace, the Lord Jesus Christ, the Holy Spirit who dwells in all Christians, the fruits of the Spirit, the armor of God, the Bible, and prayer. Through these, God teaches, rebukes, corrects, equips, strengthens, guides, protects, comforts, encourages, transforms, matures, and blesses Christians.

God's Word contains all the truth and wisdom we need for living our lives in a way that is pleasing to Him. There are some subjects about which the Bible does not speak. However, where the Bible does speak about a subject, God calls Christians to trust what it says. We may at times find that a Bible passage is confusing, counterintuitive, or simply a message that we do not want to hear. However, nowhere in God's Word are we told that this justifies trusting the wisdom of this world or our own feelings above trusting the Bible. We may at times need help from spiritually mature Christians in understanding what the Bible means or in applying it correctly to our lives. Be sure to seek help from those who truly take the Bible seriously, who revere it, and who handle it faithfully and accurately. May the verses in this chapter lead you to trust the Word of God above the wisdom of man.

Love the LORD your God with all your heart and with all your soul and with all your strength. These commandments that I give you today are to be upon your hearts. Impress them on your children. Talk about them when you sit at home and when you walk along the road, when you lie down and when you get up.

Deuteronomy 6:5–7

Do not let this Book of the Law depart from your mouth; meditate on it day and night, so that you may be careful to do everything written in it. Then you will be prosperous and successful. Have I not commanded you? Be strong and courageous. Do not be terrified; do not be discouraged, for the LORD your God will be with you wherever you go."

Joshua 1:8–9

**As for God,
his way is perfect;
the word of the LORD
is flawless.
He is a shield for all
who take refuge in him.**

"As for God, his way is perfect; the word of the LORD is flawless. He is a shield for all who take refuge in him.

2 Samuel 22:31

"To God belong wisdom and power; counsel and understanding are his.

Job 12:13

And the words of the LORD are flawless, like silver refined in a furnace of clay, purified seven times.

Psalm 12:6

As for God, his way is perfect; the word of the LORD is flawless. He is a shield for all who take refuge in him.

Psalm 18:30

The law of the LORD is perfect, reviving the soul. The statutes of the LORD are trustworthy, making wise the simple. The precepts of the LORD are right, giving joy to the heart. The commands of the LORD are radiant, giving light to the eyes. The fear of the LORD is pure, enduring forever. The ordinances of the LORD are sure and altogether righteous. They are more precious than gold, than much pure gold; they are sweeter than honey, than honey from the comb. By them is your servant warned; in keeping them there is great reward.

Psalm 19:7–11

The mouth of the righteous man utters wisdom, and his tongue speaks what is just. The law of his God is in his heart; his feet do not slip.

Psalm 37:30–31

It is better to take refuge in the LORD than to trust in man.

It is better to take refuge in the LORD than to trust in man. It is better to take refuge in the LORD than to trust in princes.

Psalm 118:8–9

Blessed are they whose ways are blameless, who walk according to the law of the LORD. Blessed are they who keep his statutes and seek him with all their heart.

Psalm 119:1–2

How can a young man keep his way pure? By living according to your word. I seek you with all my heart; do not let me stray from your commands. I have hidden your word in my heart that I might not sin against you. Praise be to you, O LORD; teach me your decrees. With my lips I recount all the laws that come from your mouth. I rejoice in following your statutes as one rejoices in great riches. I meditate on your precepts and consider your ways. I delight in your decrees; I will not neglect your word.

Psalm 119:9–16

Your statutes are my delight; they are my counselors.

Psalm 119:24

I run in the path of your commands, for you have set my heart free.

I am laid low in the dust; preserve my life according to your word. I recounted my ways and you answered me; teach me your decrees. Let me understand the teaching of your precepts; then I will meditate on your wonders. My soul is weary with sorrow; strengthen me according to your word. Keep me from deceitful ways; be gracious to me through your law. I have chosen the way of truth; I have set my heart on your laws. I hold fast to your statutes, O LORD; do not let me be put to shame. I run in the path of your commands, for you have set my heart free.

Psalm 119:25–32

Do good to your servant according to your word, O LORD. Teach me knowledge and good judgment, for I believe in your commands. Before I was afflicted I went astray, but now I obey your word. You are good, and what you do is good; teach me your decrees.

Psalm 119:65–68

Though the arrogant have smeared me with lies, I keep your precepts with all my heart. Their hearts are callous and unfeeling, but I delight in your law. It was good for me to be afflicted so that I might learn your decrees. The law from your mouth is more precious to me than thousands of pieces of silver and gold.

Psalm 119:69–72

Your word, O LORD, is eternal; it stands firm in the heavens. Your faithfulness continues through all generations; you established the earth, and it endures. Your laws endure to this day, for all things serve you.

Psalm 119:89–91

Oh, how I love your law! I meditate on it all day long. Your commands make me wiser than my enemies, for they are ever with me. I have more insight than all my teachers, for I meditate on your statutes. I have more understanding than the elders, for I obey your precepts. I have kept my feet from every evil path so that I might obey your word. I have not departed from your laws, for you yourself have taught me. How sweet are your words to my taste, sweeter than honey to my mouth! I gain understanding from your precepts; therefore I hate every wrong path. Your word is a lamp to my feet and a light for my path.

Psalm 119:97–105

Your word is a lamp to my feet and a light for my path.

Your word is a lamp to my feet and a light for my path.

Psalm 119:105

The unfolding of your words gives light; it gives understanding to the simple.

Psalm 119:130

Righteous are you, O LORD, and your laws are right. The statutes you have laid down are righteous; they are fully trustworthy.

Psalm 119:137–138

Your righteousness is everlasting and your law is true.

Psalm 119:142

Yet you are near, O LORD, and all your commands are true. Long ago I learned from your statutes that you established them to last forever.

Psalm 119:151–152

Yet you are near, O LORD, and all your commands are true.

All your words are true; all your righteous laws are eternal.

Psalm 119:160

My son, if you accept my words and store up my commands within you, turning your ear to wisdom and applying your heart to understanding, and if you call out for insight and cry aloud for understanding, and if you look for it as for silver and search for it as for hidden treasure, then you will understand the fear of the LORD and find the knowledge of God. For the LORD gives wisdom, and from his mouth come knowledge and understanding. He holds victory in store for the upright, he is a shield to those whose walk is blameless, for he guards the course of the just and protects the way of his faithful ones. Then you will understand what is right and just and fair—every good path. For wisdom will enter your heart, and knowledge will be pleasant to your soul. Discretion will protect you, and understanding will guard you.

Proverbs 2:1–11

My son, preserve sound judgment and discernment, do
not let them out of your sight; they will be life for you, an
ornament to grace your neck. Then you will go on your
way in safety, and your foot will not stumble; when you lie
down, you will not be afraid; when you lie down, your sleep
will be sweet. Have no fear of sudden disaster or of the
ruin that overtakes the wicked, for the LORD will be your
confidence and will keep your foot from being snared.

Proverbs 3:21–26

Whoever gives heed to instruction prospers, and blessed is
he who trusts in the LORD.

Proverbs 16:20

"Every word of God is flawless; he is a shield to those who
take refuge in him. Do not add to his words, or he will
rebuke you and prove you a liar.

Proverbs 30:5–6

**Every word of God
is flawless;
he is a shield to those
who take refuge in him.**

Jesus answered, "It is written: 'Man does not live on bread
alone, but on every word that comes from the mouth
of God.' "

Matthew 4:4

"Therefore everyone who hears these words of mine and
puts them into practice is like a wise man who built his
house on the rock. The rain came down, the streams rose,
and the winds blew and beat against that house; yet it did
not fall, because it had its foundation on the rock.

Matthew 7:24–25

But everyone who hears these words of mine and does not put them into practice is like a foolish man who built his house on sand. The rain came down, the streams rose, and the winds blew and beat against that house, and it fell with a great crash."

Matthew 7:26–27

"Why do you call me, 'Lord, Lord,' and do not do what I say? I will show you what he is like who comes to me and hears my words and puts them into practice. He is like a man building a house, who dug down deep and laid the foundation on rock. When a flood came, the torrent struck that house but could not shake it, because it was well built.

Luke 6:46–48

In the beginning was the Word, and the Word was with God, and the Word was God.

But the one who hears my words and does not put them into practice is like a man who built a house on the ground without a foundation. The moment the torrent struck that house, it collapsed and its destruction was complete."

Luke 6:49

In the beginning was the Word, and the Word was with God, and the Word was God. He was with God in the beginning. Through him all things were made; without him nothing was made that has been made. In him was life, and that life was the light of men. The light shines in the darkness, but the darkness has not understood it.

John 1:1–5

After Jesus said this, he looked toward heaven and prayed: "Father, the time has come. Glorify your Son, that your Son may glorify you. . . . I have given them your word and the world has hated them, for they are not of the world any more than I am of the world. My prayer is not that you take them out of the world but that you protect them from the evil one. They are not of the world, even as I am not of it. Sanctify them by the truth; your word is truth. As you sent me into the world, I have sent them into the world. For them I sanctify myself, that they too may be truly sanctified. "My prayer is not for them alone. I pray also for those who will believe in me through their message, that all of them may be one, Father, just as you are in me and I am in you. May they also be in us so that the world may believe that you have sent me.

John 17:1; 14–21

**Sanctify them
by the truth;
your word is truth.**

Consequently, faith comes from hearing the message, and the message is heard through the word of Christ.

Romans 10:17

For everything that was written in the past was written to teach us, so that through endurance and the encouragement of the Scriptures we might have hope.

Romans 15:4

Not that we are competent in ourselves to claim anything for ourselves, but our competence comes from God.

2 Corinthians 3:5

Let the peace of Christ rule in your hearts, since as members of one body you were called to peace. And be thankful. Let the word of Christ dwell in you richly as you teach and admonish one another with all wisdom, and as you sing Psalms, hymns and spiritual songs with gratitude in your hearts to God. And whatever you do, whether in word or deed, do it all in the name of the Lord Jesus, giving thanks to God the Father through him.

Colossians 3:15–17

All Scripture is God-breathed and is useful for teaching, rebuking, correcting and training in righteousness,

Although I hope to come to you soon, I am writing you these instructions so that, if I am delayed, you will know how people ought to conduct themselves in God's household, which is the church of the living God, the pillar and foundation of the truth.

1 Timothy 3:14–15

But as for you, continue in what you have learned and have become convinced of, because you know those from whom you learned it, and how from infancy you have known the holy Scriptures, which are able to make you wise for salvation through faith in Christ Jesus.

2 Timothy 3:14–15

All Scripture is God-breathed and is useful for teaching, rebuking, correcting and training in righteousness, so that the man of God may be thoroughly equipped for every good work.

2 Timothy 3:16–17

For the word of God is living and active. Sharper than any double-edged sword, it penetrates even to dividing soul and spirit, joints and marrow; it judges the thoughts and attitudes of the heart.

Hebrews 4:12

Therefore, get rid of all moral filth and the evil that is so prevalent and humbly accept the word planted in you, which can save you. Do not merely listen to the word, and so deceive yourselves. Do what it says.

James 1:21–22

Grace and peace be yours in abundance through the knowledge of God and of Jesus our Lord. His divine power has given us everything we need for life and godliness through our knowledge of him who called us by his own glory and goodness. Through these he has given us his very great and precious promises, so that through them you may participate in the divine nature and escape the corruption in the world caused by evil desires.

2 Peter 1:2–4

His divine power has given us everything we need for life and godliness

Chapter 4

Trusting and Obeying God's Word

This is love for God: to obey his commands. And his commands are not burdensome,

1 John 5:3

The Bible verses in this chapter represent a call to every person to trust and obey the Bible. God, through the Bible, reveals to us who He is and what He stands for. He reveals to us His love for us, His values, His standards, His commands, His wisdom, and His desire for what is best for us. God tells us in the Bible how He wants us to view and treat His Word. He provides ample evidence that the Bible is, in fact, the Word of God and that it is true and accurate. I have listed some excellent resources in Appendix 5, item 10 for those who would like to explore the evidences supporting the trustworthiness of the Bible.

God reveals to us through the Bible everything we need to know in order to become Christians—spiritually reborn followers of the Lord Jesus Christ (I further explain what I mean by the term *Christian* in the introduction to this book). God clearly states in the Bible how He wants Christians to view Him, love Him, love others, and live their lives. If we truly desire to know God more fully, serve Him more faithfully, and glorify Him in how we live our lives, then we need to earnestly trust, study, and obey the Word of God. May God use the verses in this chapter to draw you closer to Him.

See, I am setting before you today a blessing and a curse—the blessing if you obey the commands of the LORD your God that I am giving you today; the curse if you disobey the commands of the LORD your God and turn from the way that I command you today by following other gods, which you have not known.

Deuteronomy 11:26–28

Now what I am commanding you today is not too difficult for you or beyond your reach. It is not up in heaven, so that you have to ask, "Who will ascend into heaven to get it and proclaim it to us so we may obey it?" Nor is it beyond the sea, so that you have to ask, "Who will cross the sea to get it and proclaim it to us so we may obey it?" No, the word is very near you; it is in your mouth and in your heart so you may obey it.

Deuteronomy 30:11–14

The LORD confides in those who fear him; he makes his covenant known to them.

Who, then, is the man that fears the LORD? He will instruct him in the way chosen for him. He will spend his days in prosperity, and his descendants will inherit the land. The LORD confides in those who fear him; he makes his covenant known to them.

Psalm 25:12–14

I desire to do your will, O my God; your law is within my heart."

Psalm 40:8

In God, whose word I praise, in the LORD, whose word I praise—in God I trust; I will not be afraid. What can man do to me?

Psalms 56:10–11

I am laid low in the dust; preserve my life according to your word. I recounted my ways and you answered me; teach me your decrees. Let me understand the teaching of your precepts; then I will meditate on your wonders. My soul is weary with sorrow; strengthen me according to your word. Keep me from deceitful ways; be gracious to me through your law. I have chosen the way of truth; I have set my heart on your laws. I hold fast to your statutes, O LORD; do not let me be put to shame. I run in the path of your commands, for you have set my heart free.

Psalm 119:25–32

Oh, how I love your law! I meditate on it all day long. Your commands make me wiser than my enemies, for they are ever with me. I have more insight than all my teachers, for I meditate on your statutes. I have more understanding than the elders, for I obey your precepts. I have kept my feet from every evil path so that I might obey your word. I have not departed from your laws, for you yourself have taught me. How sweet are your words to my taste, sweeter than honey to my mouth! I gain understanding from your precepts; therefore I hate every wrong path. Your word is a lamp to my feet and a light for my path.

Psalm 119:97–105

I have chosen the way of truth; I have set my heart on your laws.

Your statutes are my heritage forever; they are the joy of my heart. My heart is set on keeping your decrees to the very end.

Psalm 119:111–112

You reject all who stray from your decrees, for their deceitfulness is in vain. All the wicked of the earth you discard like dross; therefore I love your statutes. My flesh trembles in fear of you; I stand in awe of your laws.

Psalm 119:118–120

I am your servant; give me discernment that I may understand your statutes.

Psalm 119:125

Because I love your commands more than gold, more than pure gold, and because I consider all your precepts right, I hate every wrong path.

Psalm 119:127–128

**Your statutes
are forever right;
give me understanding
that I may live.**

Your statutes are wonderful; therefore I obey them.

Psalm 119:129

Your statutes are forever right; give me understanding that I may live.

Psalm 119:144

I wait for your salvation, O LORD, and I follow your commands. I obey your statutes, for I love them greatly. I obey your precepts and your statutes, for all my ways are known to you.

Psalm 119:166–168

For the LORD gives wisdom, and from his mouth come knowledge and understanding. He holds victory in store for the upright, he is a shield to those whose walk is blameless, for he guards the course of the just and protects the way of his faithful ones. Then you will understand what is right and just and fair—every good path. For wisdom will enter your heart, and knowledge will be pleasant to your soul. Discretion will protect you, and understanding will guard you.

Proverbs 2:6–11

Trust in the LORD with all your heart and lean not on your own understanding; in all your ways acknowledge him, and he will make your paths straight.

Proverbs 3:5–6

My son, preserve sound judgment and discernment, do not let them out of your sight; they will be life for you, an ornament to grace your neck. Then you will go on your way in safety, and your foot will not stumble; when you lie down, you will not be afraid; when you lie down, your sleep will be sweet. Have no fear of sudden disaster or of the ruin that overtakes the wicked, for the LORD will be your confidence and will keep your foot from being snared.

Proverbs 3:21–26

Trust in the LORD with all your heart and lean not on your own understanding; in all your ways acknowledge him, and he will make your paths straight.

My son, keep your father's commands and do not forsake your mother's teaching. Bind them upon your heart forever; fasten them around your neck. When you walk, they will guide you; when you sleep, they will watch over you; when you awake, they will speak to you. For these commands are a lamp, this teaching is a light, and the corrections of discipline are the way to life,

Proverbs 6:20–23

My son, keep my words and store up my commands within you. Keep my commands and you will live; guard my teachings as the apple of your eye. Bind them on your fingers; write them on the tablet of your heart.

Proverbs 7:1–3

For these commands are a lamp, this teaching is a light, and the corrections of discipline are the way to life,

He who heeds discipline shows the way to life, but whoever ignores correction leads others astray.

Proverbs 10:17

He who scorns instruction will pay for it, but he who respects a command is rewarded.

Proverbs 13:13

Whoever gives heed to instruction prospers, and blessed is he who trusts in the LORD.

Proverbs 16:20

Has not my hand made all these things, and so they came into being?" declares the LORD. "This is the one I esteem: he who is humble and contrite in spirit, and trembles at my word.

Isaiah 66:2

Jesus answered, "It is written: 'Man does not live on bread alone, but on every word that comes from the mouth of God.' "

Matthew 4:4

"Do not think that I have come to abolish the Law or the Prophets; I have not come to abolish them but to fulfill them. I tell you the truth, until heaven and earth disappear, not the smallest letter, not the least stroke of a pen, will by any means disappear from the Law until everything is accomplished.

Matthew 5:17–18

"Therefore everyone who hears these words of mine and puts them into practice is like a wise man who built his house on the rock. The rain came down, the streams rose, and the winds blew and beat against that house; yet it did not fall, because it had its foundation on the rock.

Matthew 7:24–25

Jesus replied, "You are in error because you do not know the Scriptures or the power of God.

Jesus replied, "You are in error because you do not know the Scriptures or the power of God.

Matthew 22:29

Jesus replied, "Are you not in error because you do not know the Scriptures or the power of God?

Mark 12:24

"Why do you call me, 'Lord, Lord,' and do not do what I say? I will show you what he is like who comes to me and hears my words and puts them into practice. He is like a man building a house, who dug down deep and laid the foundation on rock. When a flood came, the torrent struck that house but could not shake it, because it was well built.

Luke 6:46–48

He said to them, "How foolish you are, and how slow of heart to believe all that the prophets have spoken! Did not the Christ have to suffer these things and then enter his glory?" And beginning with Moses and all the Prophets, he explained to them what was said in all the Scriptures concerning himself.

Luke 24:25–27

"Why do you call me, 'Lord, Lord,' and do not do what I say?

If you believed Moses, you would believe me, for he wrote about me. But since you do not believe what he wrote, how are you going to believe what I say?"

John 5:46–47

"If you love me, you will obey what I command.

John 14:15

"I am the true vine, and my Father is the gardener. He cuts off every branch in me that bears no fruit, while every branch that does bear fruit he prunes so that it will be even more fruitful. You are already clean because of the word I have spoken to you. Remain in me, and I will remain in you. No branch can bear fruit by itself; it must remain in the vine. Neither can you bear fruit unless you remain in me.

John 15:1–4

"I am the vine; you are the branches. If a man remains in me and I in him, he will bear much fruit; apart from me you can do nothing.

John 15:5

Now the Bereans were of more noble character than the Thessalonians, for they received the message with great eagerness and examined the Scriptures every day to see if what Paul said was true.

Acts 17:11

For everything that was written in the past was written to teach us, so that through endurance and the encouragement of the Scriptures we might have hope.

Romans 15:4

so that through endurance and the encouragement of the Scriptures we might have hope.

I urge you, brothers, to watch out for those who cause divisions and put obstacles in your way that are contrary to the teaching you have learned. Keep away from them. For such people are not serving our Lord Christ, but their own appetites. By smooth talk and flattery they deceive the minds of naive people.

Romans 16:17–18

And we also thank God continually because, when you received the word of God, which you heard from us, you accepted it not as the word of men, but as it actually is, the word of God, which is at work in you who believe.

1 Thessalonians 2:13

Don't let anyone look down on you because you are young, but set an example for the believers in speech, in life, in love, in faith and in purity. Until I come, devote yourself to the public reading of Scripture, to preaching and to teaching. Do not neglect your gift, which was given you through a prophetic message when the body of elders laid their hands on you. Be diligent in these matters; give yourself wholly to them, so that everyone may see your progress. Watch your life and doctrine closely. Persevere in them, because if you do, you will save both yourself and your hearers.

1 Timothy 4:12–16

Do your best to present yourself to God as one approved, a workman who does not need to be ashamed and who correctly handles the word of truth.

What you heard from me, keep as the pattern of sound teaching, with faith and love in Christ Jesus. Guard the good deposit that was entrusted to you—guard it with the help of the Holy Spirit who lives in us.

2 Timothy 1:13–14

Do your best to present yourself to God as one approved, a workman who does not need to be ashamed and who correctly handles the word of truth.

2 Timothy 2:15

But as for you, continue in what you have learned and have become convinced of, because you know those from whom you learned it, and how from infancy you have known the holy Scriptures, which are able to make you wise for salvation through faith in Christ Jesus.

2 Timothy 3:14–15

Now faith is being sure of what we hope for and certain
of what we do not see. This is what the ancients were
commended for. By faith we understand that the universe
was formed at God's command, so that what is seen was not
made out of what was visible.

Hebrews 11:1–3

Therefore, get rid of all moral filth and the evil that is so
prevalent and humbly accept the word planted in you,
which can save you. Do not merely listen to the word, and
so deceive yourselves. Do what it says.

James 1:21–22

But the man who looks intently into the perfect law that
gives freedom, and continues to do this, not forgetting
what he has heard, but doing it—he will be blessed in
what he does.

James 1:25

**Do not merely
listen to the word,
and so deceive
yourselves.
Do what it says.**

And we have the word of the prophets made more certain,
and you will do well to pay attention to it, as to a light
shining in a dark place, until the day dawns and the
morning star rises in your hearts.

2 Peter 1:19

Above all, you must understand that no prophecy of
Scripture came about by the prophet's own interpretation.
For prophecy never had its origin in the will of man, but
men spoke from God as they were carried along by the
Holy Spirit.

2 Peter 1:20–21

We know that we have come to know him if we obey his commands. The man who says, "I know him," but does not do what he commands is a liar, and the truth is not in him. But if anyone obeys his word, God's love is truly made complete in him. This is how we know we are in him: Whoever claims to live in him must walk as Jesus did.

1 John 2:3–6

This is love for God: to obey his commands. And his commands are not burdensome,

1 John 5:3

We know that we have come to know him if we obey his commands.

It gave me great joy to have some brothers come and tell about your faithfulness to the truth and how you continue to walk in the truth. I have no greater joy than to hear that my children are walking in the truth.

3 John 3–4

The revelation of Jesus Christ, which God gave him to show his servants what must soon take place. He made it known by sending his angel to his servant John, who testifies to everything he saw—that is, the word of God and the testimony of Jesus Christ. Blessed is the one who reads the words of this prophecy, and blessed are those who hear it and take to heart what is written in it, because the time is near.

Revelation 1:1–3

Section 2

What the Bible Says About God

    The God of Christianity is the God of the Bible. Throughout the Bible God teaches us about His character traits, His values, His standards, His laws, His power, and the nature and extent of His love for all people. God reveals to us in the Bible the kind of personal relationship that He desires to have with every human being for eternity.

    The "God of the Old Testament" is the same as the "God of the New Testament". God is unchanging, and His character traits are consistently reflected in both the Old and New Testaments of the Bible.

    Many people claim to know and follow God. However, if what they believe about God contradicts what He says about Himself in the Bible, then in reality they are following something else or someone else. It is unreasonable and self-deceiving for people to consider themselves followers of the God of the Bible and then to base their understanding of God on alternative sources that contradict the Bible.

    Do you desire to know who the God of the Bible really is? Do you desire to enter into a personal relationship with your Creator for eternity even if it means submitting your life to Jesus Christ? Are you already a spiritually reborn follower of Jesus Christ who desires to more faithfully honor, serve, and represent Him? If you answered yes to any of these questions, then it is essential that you trust what God says about Himself in the Bible. It is my desire that the chapters in this section will be helpful to everyone who truly desires to know God better and draw closer to Him.

Chapter 5

God—The Father

"This is what the LORD says—Israel's King and Redeemer, the LORD Almighty: I am the first and I am the last; apart from me there is no God.

Isaiah 44:6

God the Father is one of the three divine persons of the Trinity that make up the three-in-one God. In the following verses, Jesus Christ refers to God as both His Father and our Father in heaven:

But when you pray, go into your room, close the door and pray to your Father, who is unseen. Then your Father, who sees what is done in secret, will reward you. And when you pray, do not keep on babbling like pagans, for they think they will be heard because of their many words. Do not be like them, for your Father knows what you need before you ask him. *Matthew 6:6–8*

Jesus replied, "If anyone loves me, he will obey my teaching. My Father will love him, and we will come to him and make our home with him. He who does not love me will not obey my teaching. These words you hear are not my own; they belong to the Father who sent me. *John 14:23–24*

Jesus said, "Do not hold on to me, for I have not yet returned to the Father. Go instead to my brothers and tell them, 'I am returning to my Father and your Father, to my God and your God.'" *John 20:17*

God wants you to know Him for who He really is. Only then will you have a right relationship with Him that is pleasing to Him. He has clearly revealed Himself to mankind through the Bible. God calls us to trust what the Bible says about Him regardless of what the world's philosophies say. May the Bible verses in this chapter be helpful to you as you grow in your understanding of God the Father and in your relationship with Him.

For great is the Lord and most worthy of praise; he is to be feared above all gods. For all the gods of the nations are idols, but the Lord made the heavens. Splendor and majesty are before him; strength and glory are in his sanctuary.

Psalm 96:4–6

Know that the LORD is God. It is he who made us, and we are his; we are his people, the sheep of his pasture.

Psalm 100:3

This is what the LORD says . . . I am the first and I am the last; apart from me there is no God.

The LORD is compassionate and gracious, slow to anger, abounding in love. He will not always accuse, nor will he harbor his anger forever; he does not treat us as our sins deserve or repay us according to our iniquities. For as high as the heavens are above the earth, so great is his love for those who fear him; as far as the east is from the west, so far has he removed our transgressions from us. As a father has compassion on his children, so the LORD has compassion on those who fear him;

Psalm 103:8–13

"This is what the LORD says—Israel's King and Redeemer, the LORD Almighty: I am the first and I am the last; apart from me there is no God.

Isaiah 44:6

As soon as Jesus was baptized, he went up out of the water. At that moment heaven was opened, and he saw the Spirit of God descending like a dove and lighting on him. And a voice from heaven said, "This is my Son, whom I love; with him I am well pleased."

Matthew 3:16–17

"You have heard that it was said, 'Love your neighbor and hate your enemy.' But I tell you: Love your enemies: and pray for those who persecute you, that you may be sons of your Father in heaven. He causes his sun to rise on the evil and the good, and sends rain on the righteous and the unrighteous. If you love those who love you, what reward will you get? Are not even the tax collectors doing that? And if you greet only your brothers, what are you doing more than others? Do not even pagans do that? Be perfect, therefore, as your heavenly Father is perfect.

Matthew 5:43–48

"This, then, is how you should pray: "'Our Father in heaven, hallowed be your name, your kingdom come, your will be done on earth as it is in heaven. Give us today our daily bread. Forgive us our debts, as we also have forgiven our debtors. And lead us not into temptation, but deliver us from the evil one.

Matthew 6:9–13

"This, then, is how you should pray: "'Our Father in heaven, hallowed be your name,

"Not everyone who says to me, 'Lord, Lord,' will enter the kingdom of heaven, but only he who does the will of my Father who is in heaven.

Matthew 7:21

"Whoever acknowledges me before men, I will also acknowledge him before my Father in heaven. But whoever disowns me before men, I will disown him before my Father in heaven.

Matthew 10:32–33

At that time Jesus said, "I praise you, Father, Lord of heaven and earth, because you have hidden these things from the wise and learned, and revealed them to little children. Yes, Father, for this was your good pleasure. "All things have been committed to me by my Father. No one knows the Son except the Father, and no one knows the Father except the Son and those to whom the Son chooses to reveal him.

Matthew 11:25–27

And when you stand praying, if you hold anything against anyone, forgive him, so that your Father in heaven may forgive you your sins."

Mark 11:25

God is spirit, and his worshipers must worship in spirit and in truth."

At that time Jesus, full of joy through the Holy Spirit, said, "I praise you, Father, Lord of heaven and earth, because you have hidden these things from the wise and learned, and revealed them to little children. Yes, Father, for this was your good pleasure.

Luke 10:21

Yet a time is coming and has now come when the true worshipers will worship the Father in spirit and truth, for they are the kind of worshipers the Father seeks. God is spirit, and his worshipers must worship in spirit and in truth."

John 4:23–24

Jesus said to them, "My Father is always at his work to this very day, and I, too, am working."

John 5:17

For I have come down from heaven not to do my will but to do the will of him who sent me. And this is the will of him who sent me, that I shall lose none of all that he has given me, but raise them up at the last day. For my Father's will is that everyone who looks to the Son and believes in him shall have eternal life, and I will raise him up at the last day."

John 6:38–40

Jesus answered, "I did tell you, but you do not believe. The miracles I do in my Father's name speak for me, but you do not believe because you are not my sheep. My sheep listen to my voice; I know them, and they follow me. I give them eternal life, and they shall never perish; no one can snatch them out of my hand. My Father, who has given them to me, is greater than all; no one can snatch them out of my Father's hand. I and the Father are one."

John 10:25–30

Jesus answered,

. . .

"I and the Father are one."

Jesus knew that the Father had put all things under his power, and that he had come from God and was returning to God;

John 13:3

"Do not let your hearts be troubled. Trust in God; trust also in me. In my Father's house are many rooms; if it were not so, I would have told you. I am going there to prepare a place for you. And if I go and prepare a place for you, I will come back and take you to be with me that you also may be where I am.

John 14:1–3

Jesus answered, "I am the way and the truth and the life. No one comes to the Father except through me.

John 14:6

Whoever has my commands and obeys them, he is the one who loves me. He who loves me will be loved by my Father, and I too will love him and show myself to him."

John 14:21

Jesus answered, "I am the way and the truth and the life. No one comes to the Father except through me.

Jesus replied, "If anyone loves me, he will obey my teaching. My Father will love him, and we will come to him and make our home with him. He who does not love me will not obey my teaching. These words you hear are not my own; they belong to the Father who sent me.

John 14:23–24

"I am the true vine, and my Father is the gardener. He cuts off every branch in me that bears no fruit, while every branch that does bear fruit he prunes so that it will be even more fruitful. You are already clean because of the word I have spoken to you. Remain in me, and I will remain in you. No branch can bear fruit by itself; it must remain in the vine. Neither can you bear fruit unless you remain in me.

John 15:1–4

"I am the vine; you are the branches. If a man remains in me and I in him, he will bear much fruit; apart from me you can do nothing. If anyone does not remain in me, he is like a branch that is thrown away and withers; such branches are picked up, thrown into the fire and burned. If you remain in me and my words remain in you, ask whatever you wish, and it will be given you. This is to my Father's glory, that you bear much fruit, showing yourselves to be my disciples.

John 15:5–8

"As the Father has loved me, so have I loved you. Now remain in my love. If you obey my commands, you will remain in my love, just as I have obeyed my Father's commands and remain in his love. I have told you this so that my joy may be in you and that your joy may be complete.

John 15:9–11

This is to my Father's glory, that you bear much fruit, showing yourselves to be my disciples.

"When the Counselor comes, whom I will send to you from the Father, the Spirit of truth who goes out from the Father, he will testify about me.

John 15:26

After Jesus said this, he looked toward heaven and prayed: "Father, the time has come. Glorify your Son, that your Son may glorify you. For you granted him authority over all people that he might give eternal life to all those you have given him. Now this is eternal life: that they may know you, the only true God, and Jesus Christ, whom you have sent. I have brought you glory on earth by completing the work you gave me to do. And now, Father, glorify me in your presence with the glory I had with you before the world began.

John 17:1–5

Now this is eternal life: that they may know you, the only true God, and Jesus Christ, whom you have sent.

Jesus said, "Do not hold on to me, for I have not yet returned to the Father. Go instead to my brothers and tell them, 'I am returning to my Father and your Father, to my God and your God.'"

John 20:17

yet for us there is but one God, the Father, from whom all things came and for whom we live; and there is but one Lord, Jesus Christ, through whom all things came and through whom we live.

1 Corinthians 8:6

Grace and peace to you from God our Father and the Lord Jesus Christ, who gave himself for our sins to rescue us from the present evil age, according to the will of our God and Father, to whom be glory for ever and ever. Amen.

Galatians 1:3–5

There is one body and one Spirit—just as you were called
to one hope when you were called—one Lord, one faith,
one baptism; one God and Father of all, who is over all and
through all and in all.

Ephesians 4:4–6

Let the peace of Christ rule in your hearts, since as
members of one body you were called to peace. And be
thankful. Let the word of Christ dwell in you richly as you
teach and admonish one another with all wisdom, and as
you sing Psalms, hymns and spiritual songs with gratitude
in your hearts to God. And whatever you do, whether in
word or deed, do it all in the name of the Lord Jesus, giving
thanks to God the Father through him.

Colossians 3:15–17

**Every good and perfect
gift is from above,
coming down
from the Father
of the heavenly lights,
who does not change
like shifting shadows.**

Don't be deceived, my dear brothers. Every good and
perfect gift is from above, coming down from the Father
of the heavenly lights, who does not change like shifting
shadows. He chose to give us birth through the word of
truth, that we might be a kind of firstfruits of all he created.

James 1:16–18

To God's elect, strangers in the world, scattered throughout
Pontus, Galatia, Cappadocia, Asia and Bithynia, who
have been chosen according to the foreknowledge of God
the Father, through the sanctifying work of the Spirit, for
obedience to Jesus Christ and sprinkling by his blood:
Grace and peace be yours in abundance.

1 Peter 1:1–2

We know that we are children of God, and that the whole world is under the control of the evil one. We know also that the Son of God has come and has given us understanding, so that we may know him who is true. And we are in him who is true—even in his Son Jesus Christ. He is the true God and eternal life.

1 John 5:19–20

**We know
that we are
children of God,**

• • •

**He is the true God
and eternal life.**

Chapter 6

God—Jesus Christ

For what I received I passed on to you as of first importance: that Christ died for our sins according to the Scriptures, that he was buried, that he was raised on the third day according to the Scriptures, and that he appeared to Peter, and then to the Twelve.

1 Corinthians 15:3–5

The following three questions are perhaps the most important questions that a human being can ask:

1. Who is Jesus Christ?
2. What does the Lord Jesus Christ desire for me and from me?
3. What role will I allow the Lord Jesus Christ to have in my life?

Questions 1 and 2 are not asking for people's opinions. They represent a call to discover the truth—the unchanging reality—about Jesus Christ. They cannot be correctly answered by relying on human feelings or wishful thinking. The true answers to these two questions do not come from within you but from outside of you. God has already answered these questions for you in the Bible. Do not believe any answers to questions 1 and 2 that differ from what the Bible says. God's Word alone is the source of truth regarding Jesus Christ.

Question 3 is different from questions 1 and 2 in that the answer comes from within you. How you decide to answer question 3 will depend upon the current condition of your spiritual heart. Your answer to question 3 will determine the direction of your life and will significantly affect all those in your sphere of influence. How you answer question 3 will determine whether Jesus Christ will someday say to you, "Welcome into my kingdom," or whether He will say to you "I never knew you! Depart from me!" This chapter will help you to answer questions 1 and 2 accurately so that you may view question 3 from a foundation of truth. The Creator God of the universe allows you to answer question 3 any way you choose. May you choose wisely.

For to us a child is born, to us a son is given, and the government will be on his shoulders. And he will be called Wonderful Counselor, Mighty God, Everlasting Father, Prince of Peace.

Isaiah 9:6

A shoot will come up from the stump of Jesse; from his roots a Branch will bear fruit. The Spirit of the LORD will rest on him—the Spirit of wisdom and of understanding, the Spirit of counsel and of power, the Spirit of knowledge and of the fear of the LORD—and he will delight in the fear of the LORD. He will not judge by what he sees with his eyes, or decide by what he hears with his ears;

Isaiah 11:1–3

And he will be called Wonderful Counselor, Mighty God, Everlasting Father, Prince of Peace.

So this is what the Sovereign LORD says: "See, I lay a stone in Zion, a tested stone, a precious cornerstone for a sure foundation; the one who trusts will never be dismayed. I will make justice the measuring line and righteousness the plumb line; hail will sweep away your refuge, the lie, and water will overflow your hiding place.

Isaiah 28:16–17

The Sovereign LORD has opened my ears, and I have not been rebellious; I have not drawn back. I offered my back to those who beat me, my cheeks to those who pulled out my beard; I did not hide my face from mocking and spitting. Because the Sovereign LORD helps me, I will not be disgraced. Therefore have I set my face like flint, and I know I will not be put to shame.

Isaiah 50:5–7

See, my servant will act wisely; he will be raised and lifted
up and highly exalted. Just as there were many who were
appalled at him—his appearance was so disfigured
beyond that of any man and his form marred beyond
human likeness—

Isaiah 52:13–14

He grew up before him like a tender shoot, and like a
root out of dry ground. He had no beauty or majesty
to attract us to him, nothing in his appearance that we
should desire him. He was despised and rejected by men,
a man of sorrows, and familiar with suffering. Like one
from whom men hide their faces he was despised, and we
esteemed him not.

Isaiah 53:2–3

**and the LORD
has laid on him
the iniquity of us all.**

Surely he took up our infirmities and carried our sorrows,
yet we considered him stricken by God, smitten by him,
and afflicted. But he was pierced for our transgressions,
he was crushed for our iniquities; the punishment that
brought us peace was upon him, and by his wounds we are
healed. We all, like sheep, have gone astray, each of us has
turned to his own way; and the LORD has laid on him the
iniquity of us all.

Isaiah 53:4–6

He was oppressed and afflicted, yet he did not open his mouth; he was led like a lamb to the slaughter, and as a sheep before her shearers is silent, so he did not open his mouth. By oppression and judgment he was taken away. And who can speak of his descendants? For he was cut off from the land of the living; for the transgression of my people he was stricken. He was assigned a grave with the wicked, and with the rich in his death, though he had done no violence, nor was any deceit in his mouth.

Isaiah 53:7–9

And a voice from heaven said, "This is my Son, whom I love; with him I am well pleased."

Yet it was the LORD's will to crush him and cause him to suffer, and though the LORD makes his life a guilt offering, he will see his offspring and prolong his days, and the will of the LORD will prosper in his hand. After the suffering of his soul, he will see the light of life and be satisfied; by his knowledge my righteous servant will justify many, and he will bear their iniquities. Therefore I will give him a portion among the great, and he will divide the spoils with the strong, because he poured out his life unto death, and was numbered with the transgressors. For he bore the sin of many, and made intercession for the transgressors.

Isaiah 53:10–12

As soon as Jesus was baptized, he went up out of the water. At that moment heaven was opened, and he saw the Spirit of God descending like a dove and lighting on him. And a voice from heaven said, "This is my Son, whom I love; with him I am well pleased."

Matthew 3:16–17

"Do not think that I have come to abolish the Law or the
Prophets; I have not come to abolish them but to fulfill
them. I tell you the truth, until heaven and earth disappear,
not the smallest letter, not the least stroke of a pen, will
by any means disappear from the Law until everything
is accomplished.

Matthew 5:17–18

"Whoever acknowledges me before men, I will also
acknowledge him before my Father in heaven. But whoever
disowns me before men, I will disown him before my Father
in heaven.

Matthew 10:32–33

At that time Jesus said, "I praise you, Father, Lord of heaven
and earth, because you have hidden these things from the
wise and learned, and revealed them to little children. Yes,
Father, for this was your good pleasure. "All things have
been committed to me by my Father. No one knows the
Son except the Father, and no one knows the Father except
the Son and those to whom the Son chooses to reveal him.

Matthew 11:25–27

**Take my yoke
upon you
and learn from me,
for I am gentle
and humble in heart,
and you will find
rest for your souls.**

"Come to me, all you who are weary and burdened, and
I will give you rest. Take my yoke upon you and learn
from me, for I am gentle and humble in heart, and you
will find rest for your souls. For my yoke is easy and my
burden is light."

Matthew 11:28–30

85

From that time on Jesus began to explain to his disciples that he must go to Jerusalem and suffer many things at the hands of the elders, chief priests and teachers of the law, and that he must be killed and on the third day be raised to life. Peter took him aside and began to rebuke him. "Never, Lord!" he said. "This shall never happen to you!" Jesus turned and said to Peter, "Get behind me, Satan! You are a stumbling block to me; you do not have in mind the things of God, but the things of men."

Matthew 16:21–23

"If anyone would come after me, he must deny himself and take up his cross and follow me.

Then Jesus said to his disciples, "If anyone would come after me, he must deny himself and take up his cross and follow me. For whoever wants to save his life will lose it, but whoever loses his life for me will find it. What good will it be for a man if he gains the whole world, yet forfeits his soul? Or what can a man give in exchange for his soul?

Matthew 16:24–26

"When the Son of Man comes in his glory, and all the angels with him, he will sit on his throne in heavenly glory. All the nations will be gathered before him, and he will separate the people one from another as a shepherd separates the sheep from the goats. He will put the sheep on his right and the goats on his left. "Then the King will say to those on his right, 'Come, you who are blessed by my Father; take your inheritance, the kingdom prepared for you since the creation of the world.

Matthew 25:31–34

Then Jesus came to them and said, "All authority in heaven and on earth has been given to me. Therefore go and make disciples of all nations, baptizing them in the name of the Father and of the Son and of the Holy Spirit, and teaching them to obey everything I have commanded you. And surely I am with you always, to the very end of the age."

Matthew 28:18–20

Then he called the crowd to him along with his disciples and said: "If anyone would come after me, he must deny himself and take up his cross and follow me. For whoever wants to save his life will lose it, but whoever loses his life for me and for the gospel will save it. What good is it for a man to gain the whole world, yet forfeit his soul? Or what can a man give in exchange for his soul?

Mark 8:34–37

He took a little child and had him stand among them. Taking him in his arms, he said to them, "Whoever welcomes one of these little children in my name welcomes me; and whoever welcomes me does not welcome me but the one who sent me."

Mark 9:36–37

But the angel said to them, "Do not be afraid. I bring you good news of great joy that will be for all the people. Today in the town of David a Savior has been born to you; he is Christ the Lord. This will be a sign to you: You will find a baby wrapped in cloths and lying in a manger."

Luke 2:10–12

Then Jesus came to them and said, "All authority in heaven and on earth has been given to me.

Then he said to them all: "If anyone would come after me, he must deny himself and take up his cross daily and follow me. For whoever wants to save his life will lose it, but whoever loses his life for me will save it. What good is it for a man to gain the whole world, and yet lose or forfeit his very self?

Luke 9:23–25

"All things have been committed to me by my Father. No one knows who the Son is except the Father, and no one knows who the Father is except the Son and those to whom the Son chooses to reveal him."

Luke 10:22

'The Son of Man must be delivered into the hands of sinful men, be crucified and on the third day be raised again.'"

Do you think I came to bring peace on earth? No, I tell you, but division.

Luke 12:51

For the Son of Man came to seek and to save what was lost."

Luke 19:10

He is not here; he has risen! Remember how he told you, while he was still with you in Galilee: 'The Son of Man must be delivered into the hands of sinful men, be crucified and on the third day be raised again.'"

Luke 24:6–7

He said to them, "This is what I told you while I was still
with you: Everything must be fulfilled that is written about
me in the Law of Moses, the Prophets and the Psalms."
Then he opened their minds so they could understand the
Scriptures. He told them, "This is what is written: The
Christ will suffer and rise from the dead on the third day,
and repentance and forgiveness of sins will be preached in
his name to all nations, beginning at Jerusalem. You are
witnesses of these things. I am going to send you what my
Father has promised; but stay in the city until you have
been clothed with power from on high."

Luke 24:44–48

In the beginning was the Word, and the Word was with
God, and the Word was God. He was with God in the
beginning. Through him all things were made; without
him nothing was made that has been made. In him was life,
and that life was the light of men. The light shines in the
darkness, but the darkness has not understood it.

John 1:1–5

**In the beginning
was the Word,
and the Word
was with God,
and the Word
was God.**

. . .

**The Word
became flesh
and made his dwelling
among us.**

He was in the world, and though the world was made
through him, the world did not recognize him. He came to
that which was his own, but his own did not receive him.

John 1:10–11

The Word became flesh and made his dwelling among us.
We have seen his glory, the glory of the One and Only, who
came from the Father, full of grace and truth.

John 1:14

The next day John saw Jesus coming toward him and said, "Look, the Lamb of God, who takes away the sin of the world!

John 1:29

"For God so loved the world that he gave his one and only Son, that whoever believes in him shall not perish but have eternal life.

John 3:16

For God did not send his Son into the world to condemn the world, but to save the world through him.

John 3:17

Whoever believes in the Son has eternal life, but whoever rejects the Son will not see life, for God's wrath remains on him."

Whoever believes in him is not condemned, but whoever does not believe stands condemned already because he has not believed in the name of God's one and only Son.

John 3:18

For the one whom God has sent speaks the words of God, for God gives the Spirit without limit. The Father loves the Son and has placed everything in his hands. Whoever believes in the Son has eternal life, but whoever rejects the Son will not see life, for God's wrath remains on him."

John 3:34–36

The woman said, "I know that Messiah" (called Christ) "is coming. When he comes, he will explain everything to us." Then Jesus declared, "I who speak to you am he."

John 4:25–26

Moreover, the Father judges no one, but has entrusted all judgment to the Son, that all may honor the Son just as they honor the Father. He who does not honor the Son does not honor the Father, who sent him.

John 5:22–23

By myself I can do nothing; I judge only as I hear, and my judgment is just, for I seek not to please myself but him who sent me.

John 5:30

If you believed Moses, you would believe me, for he wrote about me. But since you do not believe what he wrote, how are you going to believe what I say?"

John 5:46–47

If you believed Moses, you would believe me, for he wrote about me. But since you do not believe what he wrote, how are you going to believe what I say?"

For I have come down from heaven not to do my will but to do the will of him who sent me. And this is the will of him who sent me, that I shall lose none of all that he has given me, but raise them up at the last day. For my Father's will is that everyone who looks to the Son and believes in him shall have eternal life, and I will raise him up at the last day."

John 6:38–40

"No one can come to me unless the Father who sent me draws him, and I will raise him up at the last day. It is written in the Prophets: 'They will all be taught by God.' Everyone who listens to the Father and learns from him comes to me. No one has seen the Father except the one who is from God; only he has seen the Father.

John 6:44–46

I tell you the truth, he who believes has everlasting life. I am the bread of life.

John 6:47–48

I am the living bread that came down from heaven. If anyone eats of this bread, he will live forever. This bread is my flesh, which I will give for the life of the world." Then the Jews began to argue sharply among themselves, "How can this man give us his flesh to eat?" Jesus said to them, "I tell you the truth, unless you eat the flesh of the Son of Man and drink his blood, you have no life in you. Whoever eats my flesh and drinks my blood has eternal life, and I will raise him up at the last day. For my flesh is real food and my blood is real drink. Whoever eats my flesh and drinks my blood remains in me, and I in him.

John 6:51–56

The Spirit gives life; the flesh counts for nothing. The words I have spoken to you are spirit and they are life.

The Spirit gives life; the flesh counts for nothing. The words I have spoken to you are spirit and they are life. Yet there are some of you who do not believe." For Jesus had known from the beginning which of them did not believe and who would betray him. He went on to say, "This is why I told you that no one can come to me unless the Father has enabled him."

John 6:63–65

Jesus answered, "My teaching is not my own. It comes from him who sent me. If anyone chooses to do God's will, he will find out whether my teaching comes from God or whether I speak on my own. He who speaks on his own does so to gain honor for himself, but he who works for the honor of the one who sent him is a man of truth; there is nothing false about him.

John 7:16–18

On the last and greatest day of the Feast, Jesus stood and said in a loud voice, "If anyone is thirsty, let him come to me and drink. Whoever believes in me, as the Scripture has said, streams of living water will flow from within him." By this he meant the Spirit, whom those who believed in him were later to receive. Up to that time the Spirit had not been given, since Jesus had not yet been glorified.

John 7:37–39

When Jesus spoke again to the people, he said, "I am the light of the world. Whoever follows me will never walk in darkness, but will have the light of life."

John 8:12

"I am the light of the world. Whoever follows me will never walk in darkness, but will have the light of life."

But he continued, "You are from below; I am from above. You are of this world; I am not of this world. I told you that you would die in your sins; if you do not believe that I am the one I claim to be, you will indeed die in your sins." "Who are you?" they asked. "Just what I have been claiming all along," Jesus replied.

John 8:23–25

Jesus said to them, "If God were your Father, you would love me, for I came from God and now am here. I have not come on my own; but he sent me.

John 8:42

"You are not yet fifty years old," the Jews said to him, "and you have seen Abraham!" "I tell you the truth," Jesus answered, "before Abraham was born, I am!" At this, they picked up stones to stone him, but Jesus hid himself, slipping away from the temple grounds.

John 8:57–59

I am the gate; whoever enters through me will be saved. He will come in and go out, and find pasture.

John 10:9

The reason my Father loves me is that I lay down my life—only to take it up again. No one takes it from me, but I lay it down of my own accord. I have authority to lay it down and authority to take it up again. This command I received from my Father."

John 10:17–18

**Jesus said to her,
"I am the resurrection
and the life.
He who believes in me
will live,
even though he dies;**

Jesus answered, "I did tell you, but you do not believe. The miracles I do in my Father's name speak for me, but you do not believe because you are not my sheep. My sheep listen to my voice; I know them, and they follow me. I give them eternal life, and they shall never perish; no one can snatch them out of my hand. My Father, who has given them to me, is greater than all; no one can snatch them out of my Father's hand. I and the Father are one."

John 10:25–30

Jesus said to her, "I am the resurrection and the life. He who believes in me will live, even though he dies; and whoever lives and believes in me will never die. Do you believe this?" "Yes, Lord," she told him, "I believe that you are the Christ, the Son of God, who was to come into the world."

John 11:25–27

Jesus replied, "The hour has come for the Son of Man to be glorified. I tell you the truth, unless a kernel of wheat falls to the ground and dies, it remains only a single seed. But if it dies, it produces many seeds. The man who loves his life will lose it, while the man who hates his life in this world will keep it for eternal life. Whoever serves me must follow me; and where I am, my servant also will be. My Father will honor the one who serves me.

John 12:23–26

I have come into the world as a light, so that no one who believes in me should stay in darkness.

John 12:46

"As for the person who hears my words but does not keep them, I do not judge him. For I did not come to judge the world, but to save it. There is a judge for the one who rejects me and does not accept my words; that very word which I spoke will condemn him at the last day. For I did not speak of my own accord, but the Father who sent me commanded me what to say and how to say it. I know that his command leads to eternal life. So whatever I say is just what the Father has told me to say."

John 12:47–50

I have come into the world as a light, so that no one who believes in me should stay in darkness.

Jesus knew that the Father had put all things under his power, and that he had come from God and was returning to God;

John 13:3

Now that I, your Lord and Teacher, have washed your feet, you also should wash one another's feet. I have set you an example that you should do as I have done for you.

John 13:14–15

"Do not let your hearts be troubled. Trust in God; trust also in me. In my Father's house are many rooms; if it were not so, I would have told you. I am going there to prepare a place for you. And if I go and prepare a place for you, I will come back and take you to be with me that you also may be where I am.

John 14:1–3

Jesus answered, "I am the way and the truth and the life. No one comes to the Father except through me.

Jesus answered, "I am the way and the truth and the life. No one comes to the Father except through me.

John 14:6

Jesus replied, "If anyone loves me, he will obey my teaching. My Father will love him, and we will come to him and make our home with him. He who does not love me will not obey my teaching. These words you hear are not my own; they belong to the Father who sent me.

John 14:23–24

but the world must learn that I love the Father and that I do exactly what my Father has commanded me. "Come now; let us leave.

John 14:31

"I am the true vine, and my Father is the gardener. He cuts off every branch in me that bears no fruit, while every branch that does bear fruit he prunes so that it will be even more fruitful. You are already clean because of the word I have spoken to you. Remain in me, and I will remain in you. No branch can bear fruit by itself; it must remain in the vine. Neither can you bear fruit unless you remain in me.

John 15:1–4

"I am the vine; you are the branches. If a man remains in me and I in him, he will bear much fruit; apart from me you can do nothing. If anyone does not remain in me, he is like a branch that is thrown away and withers; such branches are picked up, thrown into the fire and burned. If you remain in me and my words remain in you, ask whatever you wish, and it will be given you. This is to my Father's glory, that you bear much fruit, showing yourselves to be my disciples.

John 15:5–8

**I am the vine;
you are the branches.
If a man remains in me
and I in him,
he will bear
much fruit;
apart from me
you can do nothing.**

I came from the Father and entered the world; now I am leaving the world and going back to the Father."

John 16:28

After Jesus said this, he looked toward heaven and prayed: "Father, the time has come. Glorify your Son, that your Son may glorify you. For you granted him authority over all people that he might give eternal life to all those you have given him. Now this is eternal life: that they may know you, the only true God, and Jesus Christ, whom you have sent. I have brought you glory on earth by completing the work you gave me to do. And now, Father, glorify me in your presence with the glory I had with you before the world began.

John 17:1–5

**In fact,
for this reason
I was born,
and for this I came
into the world,
to testify to the truth.
Everyone
on the side of truth
listens to me."**

I will remain in the world no longer, but they are still in the world, and I am coming to you. Holy Father, protect them by the power of your name—the name you gave me—so that they may be one as we are one.

John 17:11

Jesus said, "My kingdom is not of this world. If it were, my servants would fight to prevent my arrest by the Jews. But now my kingdom is from another place."

John 18:36

"You are a king, then!" said Pilate. Jesus answered, "You are right in saying I am a king. In fact, for this reason I was born, and for this I came into the world, to testify to the truth. Everyone on the side of truth listens to me."

John 18:37

Jesus did many other miraculous signs in the presence
of his disciples, which are not recorded in this book.
But these are written that you may believe that Jesus is
the Christ, the Son of God, and that by believing you
may have life in his name.

John 20:30–31

Then Peter, filled with the Holy Spirit, said to them:
"Rulers and elders of the people! If we are being called to
account today for an act of kindness shown to a cripple
and are asked how he was healed, then know this, you and
all the people of Israel: It is by the name of Jesus Christ of
Nazareth, whom you crucified but whom God raised
from the dead, that this man stands before you healed.
He is "'the stone you builders rejected, which has become
the capstone.' Salvation is found in no one else, for there
is no other name under heaven given to men by which we
must be saved."

Acts 4:8–12

**Salvation is found
in no one else,
for there is no other
name under heaven
given to men
by which
we must be saved."**

For the wages of sin is death, but the gift of God is eternal
life in Christ Jesus our Lord.

Romans 6:23

You, however, are controlled not by the sinful nature but by
the Spirit, if the Spirit of God lives in you. And if anyone
does not have the Spirit of Christ, he does not belong to
Christ. But if Christ is in you, your body is dead because of
sin, yet your spirit is alive because of righteousness. And if
the Spirit of him who raised Jesus from the dead is living in
you, he who raised Christ from the dead will also give life
to your mortal bodies through his Spirit, who lives in you.

Romans 8:9–11

That if you confess with your mouth, "Jesus is Lord," and believe in your heart that God raised him from the dead, you will be saved. For it is with your heart that you believe and are justified, and it is with your mouth that you confess and are saved. As the Scripture says, "Anyone who trusts in him will never be put to shame."

Romans 10:9–11

Jews demand miraculous signs and Greeks look for wisdom, but we preach Christ crucified: a stumbling block to Jews and foolishness to Gentiles, but to those whom God has called, both Jews and Greeks, Christ the power of God and the wisdom of God. For the foolishness of God is wiser than man's wisdom, and the weakness of God is stronger than man's strength.

1 Corinthians 1:22–25

of first importance: that Christ died for our sins according to the Scriptures, that he was buried, that he was raised on the third day according to the Scriptures,

yet for us there is but one God, the Father, from whom all things came and for whom we live; and there is but one Lord, Jesus Christ, through whom all things came and through whom we live.

1 Corinthians 8:6

For what I received I passed on to you as of first importance: that Christ died for our sins according to the Scriptures, that he was buried, that he was raised on the third day according to the Scriptures, and that he appeared to Peter, and then to the Twelve.

1 Corinthians 15:3–5

For Christ's love compels us, because we are convinced that one died for all, and therefore all died. And he died for all, that those who live should no longer live for themselves but for him who died for them and was raised again. So from now on we regard no one from a worldly point of view. Though we once regarded Christ in this way, we do so no longer. Therefore, if anyone is in Christ, he is a new creation; the old has gone, the new has come!

2 Corinthians 5:14–17

God made him who had no sin to be sin for us, so that in him we might become the righteousness of God.

2 Corinthians 5:21

God made him who had no sin to be sin for us, so that in him we might become the righteousness of God.

Grace and peace to you from God our Father and the Lord Jesus Christ, who gave himself for our sins to rescue us from the present evil age, according to the will of our God and Father, to whom be glory for ever and ever. Amen.

Galatians 1:3–5

I have been crucified with Christ and I no longer live, but Christ lives in me. The life I live in the body, I live by faith in the Son of God, who loved me and gave himself for me. I do not set aside the grace of God, for if righteousness could be gained through the law, Christ died for nothing!"

Galatians 2:20–21

In him we have redemption through his blood, the forgiveness of sins, in accordance with the riches of God's grace that he lavished on us with all wisdom and understanding. And he made known to us the mystery of his will according to his good pleasure, which he purposed in Christ,

Ephesians 1:7–9

Consequently, you are no longer foreigners and aliens, but fellow citizens with God's people and members of God's household, built on the foundation of the apostles and prophets, with Christ Jesus himself as the chief cornerstone. In him the whole building is joined together and rises to become a holy temple in the Lord. And in him you too are being built together to become a dwelling in which God lives by his Spirit.

Ephesians 2:19–22

But our citizenship is in heaven. And we eagerly await a Savior from there, the Lord Jesus Christ,

Your attitude should be the same as that of Christ Jesus: Who, being in very nature God, did not consider equality with God something to be grasped, but made himself nothing, taking the very nature of a servant, being made in human likeness. And being found in appearance as a man, he humbled himself and became obedient to death—even death on a cross! Therefore God exalted him to the highest place and gave him the name that is above every name,

Philippians 2:5–9

But our citizenship is in heaven. And we eagerly await a Savior from there, the Lord Jesus Christ, who, by the power that enables him to bring everything under his control, will transform our lowly bodies so that they will be like his glorious body.

Philippians 3:20–21

He is the image of the invisible God, the firstborn over all creation. For by him all things were created: things in heaven and on earth, visible and invisible, whether thrones or powers or rulers or authorities; all things were created by him and for him.

Colossians 1:15–17

And he is the head of the body, the church; he is the beginning and the firstborn from among the dead, so that in everything he might have the supremacy. For God was pleased to have all his fullness dwell in him, and through him to reconcile to himself all things, whether things on earth or things in heaven, by making peace through his blood, shed on the cross.

Colossians 1:18–20

For by him all things were created: things in heaven and on earth, visible and invisible,

Once you were alienated from God and were enemies in your minds because of your evil behavior. But now he has reconciled you by Christ's physical body through death to present you holy in his sight, without blemish and free from accusation—if you continue in your faith, established and firm, not moved from the hope held out in the gospel. This is the gospel that you heard and that has been proclaimed to every creature under heaven, and of which I, Paul, have become a servant.

Colossians 1:21–23

My purpose is that they may be encouraged in heart and united in love, so that they may have the full riches of complete understanding, in order that they may know the mystery of God, namely, Christ, in whom are hidden all the treasures of wisdom and knowledge. I tell you this so that no one may deceive you by fine-sounding arguments.

Colossians 2:2–4

For in Christ all the fullness of the Deity lives in bodily form, and you have been given fullness in Christ, who is the head over every power and authority.

Colossians 2:9–10

Let the peace of Christ rule in your hearts, since as members of one body you were called to peace. And be thankful. Let the word of Christ dwell in you richly as you teach and admonish one another with all wisdom, and as you sing Psalms, hymns and spiritual songs with gratitude in your hearts to God. And whatever you do, whether in word or deed, do it all in the name of the Lord Jesus, giving thanks to God the Father through him.

Colossians 3:15–17

For in Christ all the fullness of the Deity lives in bodily form,

Here is a trustworthy saying that deserves full acceptance: Christ Jesus came into the world to save sinners—of whom I am the worst. But for that very reason I was shown mercy so that in me, the worst of sinners, Christ Jesus might display his unlimited patience as an example for those who would believe on him and receive eternal life.

1 Timothy 1:15–16

This is good, and pleases God our Savior, who wants all men to be saved and to come to a knowledge of the truth. For there is one God and one mediator between God and men, the man Christ Jesus, who gave himself as a ransom for all men—the testimony given in its proper time.

1 Timothy 2:3–6

For the grace of God that brings salvation has appeared to all men. It teaches us to say "No" to ungodliness and worldly passions, and to live self-controlled, upright and godly lives in this present age, while we wait for the blessed hope—the glorious appearing of our great God and Savior, Jesus Christ, who gave himself for us to redeem us from all wickedness and to purify for himself a people that are his very own, eager to do what is good. These, then, are the things you should teach. Encourage and rebuke with all authority. Do not let anyone despise you.

Titus 2:11–15

In the past God spoke to our forefathers through the prophets at many times and in various ways, but in these last days he has spoken to us by his Son, whom he appointed heir of all things, and through whom he made the universe. The Son is the radiance of God's glory and the exact representation of his being, sustaining all things by his powerful word. After he had provided purification for sins, he sat down at the right hand of the Majesty in heaven.

Hebrews 1:1–3

The Son is the radiance of God's glory and the exact representation of his being, sustaining all things by his powerful word.

But when this priest had offered for all time one sacrifice for sins, he sat down at the right hand of God. Since that time he waits for his enemies to be made his footstool, because by one sacrifice he has made perfect forever those who are being made holy. The Holy Spirit also testifies to us about this. First he says: "This is the covenant I will make with them after that time, says the Lord. I will put my laws in their hearts, and I will write them on their minds." Then he adds: "Their sins and lawless acts I will remember no more." And where these have been forgiven, there is no longer any sacrifice for sin.

Hebrews 10:12–18

Jesus Christ is the same yesterday and today and forever.

Hebrews 13:8

For you know that it was not with perishable things such as silver or gold that you were redeemed from the empty way of life handed down to you from your forefathers, but with the precious blood of Christ, a lamb without blemish or defect. He was chosen before the creation of the world, but was revealed in these last times for your sake. Through him you believe in God, who raised him from the dead and glorified him, and so your faith and hope are in God.

1 Peter 1:18–21

Jesus Christ is the same yesterday and today and forever.

As you come to him, the living Stone—rejected by men but chosen by God and precious to him—you also, like living stones, are being built into a spiritual house to be a holy priesthood, offering spiritual sacrifices acceptable to God through Jesus Christ.

1 Peter 2:4–5

To this you were called, because Christ suffered for you, leaving you an example, that you should follow in his steps. "He committed no sin, and no deceit was found in his mouth."

1 Peter 2:21–22

When they hurled their insults at him, he did not retaliate; when he suffered, he made no threats. Instead, he entrusted himself to him who judges justly. He himself bore our sins in his body on the tree, so that we might die to sins and live for righteousness; by his wounds you have been healed. For you were like sheep going astray, but now you have returned to the Shepherd and Overseer of your souls.

1 Peter 2:23–25

This is the message we have heard from him and declare to you: God is light; in him there is no darkness at all. If we claim to have fellowship with him yet walk in the darkness, we lie and do not live by the truth. But if we walk in the light, as he is in the light, we have fellowship with one another, and the blood of Jesus, his Son, purifies us from all sin.

1 John 1:5–7

But if we walk in the light, as he is in the light, we have fellowship with one another, and the blood of Jesus, his Son, purifies us from all sin.

My dear children, I write this to you so that you will not sin. But if anybody does sin, we have one who speaks to the Father in our defense—Jesus Christ, the Righteous One. He is the atoning sacrifice for our sins, and not only for ours but also for the sins of the whole world.

1 John 2:1–2

Everyone who sins breaks the law; in fact, sin is lawlessness. But you know that he appeared so that he might take away our sins. And in him is no sin. No one who lives in him keeps on sinning. No one who continues to sin has either seen him or known him.

1 John 3:4–6

This is how God showed his love among us: He sent his one and only Son into the world that we might live through him. This is love: not that we loved God, but that he loved us and sent his Son as an atoning sacrifice for our sins. Dear friends, since God so loved us, we also ought to love one another.

1 John 4:9–11

No one has ever seen God; but if we love one another, God lives in us and his love is made complete in us. We know that we live in him and he in us, because he has given us of his Spirit. And we have seen and testify that the Father has sent his Son to be the Savior of the world. If anyone acknowledges that Jesus is the Son of God, God lives in him and he in God.

1 John 4:12–15

**"Do not be afraid.
I am the First
and the Last.
I am the Living One;
I was dead,
and behold
I am alive
for ever and ever!**

When I saw him, I fell at his feet as though dead. Then he placed his right hand on me and said: "Do not be afraid. I am the First and the Last. I am the Living One; I was dead, and behold I am alive for ever and ever! And I hold the keys of death and Hades.

Revelation 1:17–18

Those whom I love I rebuke and discipline. So be earnest, and repent. Here I am! I stand at the door and knock. If anyone hears my voice and opens the door, I will come in and eat with him, and he with me.

Revelation 3:19–20

I saw heaven standing open and there before me was a white horse, whose rider is called Faithful and True. With justice he judges and makes war. His eyes are like blazing fire, and on his head are many crowns. He has a name written on him that no one knows but he himself. He is dressed in a robe dipped in blood, and his name is the Word of God. The armies of heaven were following him, riding on white horses and dressed in fine linen, white and clean. Out of his mouth comes a sharp sword with which to strike down the nations. "He will rule them with an iron scepter." He treads the winepress of the fury of the wrath of God Almighty. On his robe and on his thigh he has this name written: KING OF KINGS AND LORD OF LORDS.

Revelation 19:11–16

"Behold, I am coming soon! My reward is with me, and I will give to everyone according to what he has done. I am the Alpha and the Omega, the First and the Last, the Beginning and the End. "Blessed are those who wash their robes, that they may have the right to the tree of life and may go through the gates into the city. Outside are the dogs, those who practice magic arts, the sexually immoral, the murderers, the idolaters and everyone who loves and practices falsehood.

Revelation 22:12–15

I am the Alpha and the Omega, the First and the Last, the Beginning and the End.

Chapter 7

God—The Holy Spirit

But whenever anyone turns to the Lord, the veil is taken away. Now the Lord is the Spirit, and where the Spirit of the Lord is, there is freedom.

2 Corinthians 3:16–17

The Holy Spirit is one of the three divine persons of the Trinity that is God. Like God the Father, the Holy Spirit does not have a physical body. A major ministry of the Holy Spirit is to draw people to God. In addition, the Bible tells us that the Holy Spirit comes to live within those people who put their faith in and follow Jesus Christ as their sin-bearer, their Savior, and the Lord of their lives. For these individuals, the Holy Spirit has another ministry—being their counselor, teacher, comforter, helper, and strength.

The Bible tells us that the Holy Spirit is a vital part of a Christian's life and being. It is therefore important that we grow in an accurate understanding of the Holy Spirit. Since we cannot learn about the Holy Spirit with our five senses, we must rely on something else. Our own wishful thinking or trusting the opinions of others that are contrary to the Bible are not reliable sources for learning about the Holy Spirit. If you are a Christian, your understanding of the Holy Spirit must be based on the Bible.

As you read the verses in this chapter, ask God to teach you what He wants you to know about the Holy Spirit. Then, it is important for you to read, study, and meditate on the Word of God. First, the Bible will teach you about the Holy Spirit. Second, the Holy Spirit will speak to you through the Word of God. Know that the Holy Spirit will never prompt you to do something that is in conflict with what the Bible says. Know also that the Holy Spirit will not force you to be obedient to God against your will. Beware of making choices that ignore or reject the Holy Spirit's leading in your life. Pray that God would help you to make moment-by-moment choices that invite the Holy Spirit to guide you, teach you, empower you, help you, encourage you, and protect you.

Create in me a pure heart, O God, and renew a steadfast spirit within me. Do not cast me from your presence or take your Holy Spirit from me. Restore to me the joy of your salvation and grant me a willing spirit, to sustain me.

Psalm 51:10–12

A shoot will come up from the stump of Jesse; from his roots a Branch will bear fruit. The Spirit of the LORD will rest on him—the Spirit of wisdom and of understanding, the Spirit of counsel and of power, the Spirit of knowledge and of the fear of the LORD—and he will delight in the fear of the LORD. He will not judge by what he sees with his eyes, or decide by what he hears with his ears;

Isaiah 11:1–3

And I will put my Spirit in you and move you to follow my decrees and be careful to keep my laws.

I will give you a new heart and put a new spirit in you; I will remove from you your heart of stone and give you a heart of flesh. And I will put my Spirit in you and move you to follow my decrees and be careful to keep my laws.

Ezekiel 36:26–27

As soon as Jesus was baptized, he went up out of the water. At that moment heaven was opened, and he saw the Spirit of God descending like a dove and lighting on him. And a voice from heaven said, "This is my Son, whom I love; with him I am well pleased."

Matthew 3:16–17

At that time Mary got ready and hurried to a town in the hill country of Judea, where she entered Zechariah's home and greeted Elizabeth. When Elizabeth heard Mary's greeting, the baby leaped in her womb, and Elizabeth was filled with the Holy Spirit.

Luke 1:39–41

The Spirit gives life; the flesh counts for nothing. The words I have spoken to you are spirit and they are life. Yet there are some of you who do not believe." For Jesus had known from the beginning which of them did not believe and who would betray him. He went on to say, "This is why I told you that no one can come to me unless the Father has enabled him."

John 6:63–65

The Spirit gives life; the flesh counts for nothing. The words I have spoken to you are spirit and they are life.

On the last and greatest day of the Feast, Jesus stood and said in a loud voice, "If anyone is thirsty, let him come to me and drink. Whoever believes in me, as the Scripture has said, streams of living water will flow from within him." By this he meant the Spirit, whom those who believed in him were later to receive. Up to that time the Spirit had not been given, since Jesus had not yet been glorified.

John 7:37–39

"If you love me, you will obey what I command. And I will ask the Father, and he will give you another Counselor to be with you forever—the Spirit of truth. The world cannot accept him, because it neither sees him nor knows him. But you know him, for he lives with you and will be in you.

John 14:15–17

But the Counselor, the Holy Spirit, whom the Father will send in my name, will teach you all things and will remind you of everything I have said to you. Peace I leave with you; my peace I give you. I do not give to you as the world gives. Do not let your hearts be troubled and do not be afraid.

John 14:26–27

But I tell you the truth: It is for your good that I am going away. Unless I go away, the Counselor will not come to you; but if I go, I will send him to you. When he comes, he will convict the world of guilt in regard to sin and righteousness and judgment:

John 16:7–8

But when he, the Spirit of truth, comes, he will guide you into all truth.

But when he, the Spirit of truth, comes, he will guide you into all truth. He will not speak on his own; he will speak only what he hears, and he will tell you what is yet to come. He will bring glory to me by taking from what is mine and making it known to you.

John 16:13–14

"We gave you strict orders not to teach in this name," he said. "Yet you have filled Jerusalem with your teaching and are determined to make us guilty of this man's blood." Peter and the other apostles replied: "We must obey God rather than men! The God of our fathers raised Jesus from the dead—whom you had killed by hanging him on a tree. God exalted him to his own right hand as Prince and Savior that he might give repentance and forgiveness of sins to Israel. We are witnesses of these things, and so is the Holy Spirit, whom God has given to those who obey him."

Acts 5:28–32

Therefore, since we have been justified through faith, we have peace with God through our Lord Jesus Christ, through whom we have gained access by faith into this grace in which we now stand. And we rejoice in the hope of the glory of God. Not only so, but we also rejoice in our sufferings, because we know that suffering produces perseverance; perseverance, character; and character, hope. And hope does not disappoint us, because God has poured out his love into our hearts by the Holy Spirit, whom he has given us.

Romans 5:1–5

Those who live according to the sinful nature have their minds set on what that nature desires; but those who live in accordance with the Spirit have their minds set on what the Spirit desires. The mind of sinful man is death, but the mind controlled by the Spirit is life and peace; the sinful mind is hostile to God. It does not submit to God's law, nor can it do so. Those controlled by the sinful nature cannot please God.

Romans 8:5–8

The mind of sinful man is death, but the mind controlled by the Spirit is life and peace;

You, however, are controlled not by the sinful nature but by the Spirit, if the Spirit of God lives in you. And if anyone does not have the Spirit of Christ, he does not belong to Christ. But if Christ is in you, your body is dead because of sin, yet your spirit is alive because of righteousness. And if the Spirit of him who raised Jesus from the dead is living in you, he who raised Christ from the dead will also give life to your mortal bodies through his Spirit, who lives in you.

Romans 8:9–11

In the same way, the Spirit helps us in our weakness. We do not know what we ought to pray for, but the Spirit himself intercedes for us with groans that words cannot express. And he who searches our hearts knows the mind of the Spirit, because the Spirit intercedes for the saints in accordance with God's will.

Romans 8:26–27

May the God of hope fill you with all joy and peace as you trust in him, so that you may overflow with hope by the power of the Holy Spirit.

Romans 15:13

May the God of hope fill you with all joy and peace as you trust in him, so that you may overflow with hope by the power of the Holy Spirit.

However, as it is written: "No eye has seen, no ear has heard, no mind has conceived what God has prepared for those who love him"—but God has revealed it to us by his Spirit. The Spirit searches all things, even the deep things of God. For who among men knows the thoughts of a man except the man's spirit within him? In the same way no one knows the thoughts of God except the Spirit of God.

1 Corinthians 2:9–11

We have not received the spirit of the world but the Spirit who is from God, that we may understand what God has freely given us. This is what we speak, not in words taught us by human wisdom but in words taught by the Spirit, expressing spiritual truths in spiritual words.

1 Corinthians 2:12–13

Do you not know that your bodies are members of Christ himself? Shall I then take the members of Christ and unite them with a prostitute? Never! Do you not know that he who unites himself with a prostitute is one with her in body? For it is said, "The two will become one flesh." But he who unites himself with the Lord is one with him in spirit.

1 Corinthians 6:15–17

Do you not know that your body is a temple of the Holy Spirit, who is in you, whom you have received from God? You are not your own;

1 Corinthians 6:19

He anointed us, set his seal of ownership on us, and put his Spirit in our hearts as a deposit, guaranteeing what is to come.

Therefore I tell you that no one who is speaking by the Spirit of God says, "Jesus be cursed," and no one can say, "Jesus is Lord," except by the Holy Spirit.

1 Corinthians 12:3

Now it is God who makes both us and you stand firm in Christ. He anointed us, set his seal of ownership on us, and put his Spirit in our hearts as a deposit, guaranteeing what is to come.

2 Corinthians 1:21–22

But whenever anyone turns to the Lord, the veil is taken away. Now the Lord is the Spirit, and where the Spirit of the Lord is, there is freedom. And we, who with unveiled faces all reflect the Lord's glory, are being transformed into his likeness with ever-increasing glory, which comes from the Lord, who is the Spirit.

2 Corinthians 3:16–18

But when the time had fully come, God sent his Son, born of a woman, born under law, to redeem those under law, that we might receive the full rights of sons. Because you are sons, God sent the Spirit of his Son into our hearts, the Spirit who calls out, Abba, Father. So you are no longer a slave, but a son; and since you are a son, God has made you also an heir.

Galatians 4:4–7

But the fruit of the Spirit is love, joy, peace, patience, kindness, goodness, faithfulness, gentleness and self-control.

But the fruit of the Spirit is love, joy, peace, patience, kindness, goodness, faithfulness, gentleness and self-control. Against such things there is no law. Those who belong to Christ Jesus have crucified the sinful nature with its passions and desires. Since we live by the Spirit, let us keep in step with the Spirit.

Galatians 5:22–25

And you also were included in Christ when you heard the word of truth, the gospel of your salvation. Having believed, you were marked in him with a seal, the promised Holy Spirit, who is a deposit guaranteeing our inheritance until the redemption of those who are God's possession—to the praise of his glory.

Ephesians 1:13–14

Consequently, you are no longer foreigners and aliens, but fellow citizens with God's people and members of God's household, built on the foundation of the apostles and prophets, with Christ Jesus himself as the chief cornerstone. In him the whole building is joined together and rises to become a holy temple in the Lord. And in him you too are being built together to become a dwelling in which God lives by his Spirit.

Ephesians 2:19–22

For this reason I kneel before the Father, from whom his whole family in heaven and on earth derives its name. I pray that out of his glorious riches he may strengthen you with power through his Spirit in your inner being, so that Christ may dwell in your hearts through faith. And I pray that you, being rooted and established in love, may have power, together with all the saints, to grasp how wide and long and high and deep is the love of Christ, and to know this love that surpasses knowledge—that you may be filled to the measure of all the fullness of God.

Ephesians 3:14–19

Do not get drunk on wine, which leads to debauchery. Instead, be filled with the Spirit.

Ephesians 5:17–18

For God did not give us a spirit of timidity, but a spirit of power, of love and of self-discipline.

2 Timothy 1:7

For God did not give us a spirit of timidity, but a spirit of power, of love and of self-discipline.

What you heard from me, keep as the pattern of sound teaching, with faith and love in Christ Jesus. Guard the good deposit that was entrusted to you—guard it with the help of the Holy Spirit who lives in us.

2 Timothy 1:13–14

At one time we too were foolish, disobedient, deceived and enslaved by all kinds of passions and pleasures. We lived in malice and envy, being hated and hating one another. But when the kindness and love of God our Savior appeared, he saved us, not because of righteous things we had done, but because of his mercy. He saved us through the washing of rebirth and renewal by the Holy Spirit, whom he poured out on us generously through Jesus Christ our Savior, so that, having been justified by his grace, we might become heirs having the hope of eternal life. This is a trustworthy saying. And I want you to stress these things, so that those who have trusted in God may be careful to devote themselves to doing what is good. These things are excellent and profitable for everyone.

Titus 3:3–8

He saved us through the washing of rebirth and renewal by the Holy Spirit, whom he poured out on us generously through Jesus Christ our Savior,

And this is his command: to believe in the name of his Son, Jesus Christ, and to love one another as he commanded us. Those who obey his commands live in him, and he in them. And this is how we know that he lives in us: We know it by the Spirit he gave us.

1 John 3:23–24

Chapter 8

God—The Trinity

As soon as Jesus was baptized, he went up out of the water. At that moment heaven was opened, and he saw the Spirit of God descending like a dove and lighting on him. And a voice from heaven said, "This is my Son, whom I love; with him I am well pleased."

Matthew 3:16–17

The *Trinity* is a term used to refer to God as being the union of three divine persons—God the Father, the Lord Jesus Christ, and the Holy Spirit. Although we are able to have some limited understanding of this idea, our human minds do not have the ability to fully comprehend this triune nature (being three-in-one) of God in all its dimensions.

Each of the Bible passages presented in this chapter references at least two of the three divine persons of the Trinity. It is clear from these verses that the Bible presents God as one God in essence, who consists of three distinct persons. May each of us trust the Word of God above the ideas of men as we seek to know and faithfully follow God the Father, the Lord Jesus Christ, and the Holy Spirit.

"Come near me and listen to this: "From the first announcement I have not spoken in secret; at the time it happens, I am there." And now the Sovereign LORD has sent me, with his Spirit. This is what the LORD says—your Redeemer, the Holy One of Israel: "I am the LORD your God, who teaches you what is best for you, who directs you in the way you should go.

Isaiah 48:16–17

As soon as Jesus was baptized, he went up out of the water. At that moment heaven was opened, and he saw the Spirit of God descending like a dove and lighting on him. And a voice from heaven said, "This is my Son, whom I love; with him I am well pleased."

Matthew 3:16–17

"All authority in heaven and on earth has been given to me. Therefore go and make disciples of all nations, baptizing them in the name of the Father and of the Son and of the Holy Spirit,

Then Jesus came to them and said, "All authority in heaven and on earth has been given to me. Therefore go and make disciples of all nations, baptizing them in the name of the Father and of the Son and of the Holy Spirit, and teaching them to obey everything I have commanded you. And surely I am with you always, to the very end of the age."

Matthew 28:18–20

For the one whom God has sent speaks the words of God, for God gives the Spirit without limit. The Father loves the Son and has placed everything in his hands. Whoever believes in the Son has eternal life, but whoever rejects the Son will not see life, for God's wrath remains on him."

John 3:34–36

Moreover, the Father judges no one, but has entrusted all judgment to the Son, that all may honor the Son just as they honor the Father. He who does not honor the Son does not honor the Father, who sent him.

John 5:22–23

The Spirit gives life; the flesh counts for nothing. The words I have spoken to you are spirit and they are life. Yet there are some of you who do not believe." For Jesus had known from the beginning which of them did not believe and who would betray him. He went on to say, "This is why I told you that no one can come to me unless the Father has enabled him."

John 6:63–65

I and the Father are one.

The reason my Father loves me is that I lay down my life— only to take it up again. No one takes it from me, but I lay it down of my own accord. I have authority to lay it down and authority to take it up again. This command I received from my Father."

John 10:17–18

Jesus answered, "I did tell you, but you do not believe. The miracles I do in my Father's name speak for me, but you do not believe because you are not my sheep. My sheep listen to my voice; I know them, and they follow me. I give them eternal life, and they shall never perish; no one can snatch them out of my hand. My Father, who has given them to me, is greater than all; no one can snatch them out of my Father's hand. I and the Father are one."

John 10:25–30

"Do not let your hearts be troubled. Trust in God; trust also in me. In my Father's house are many rooms; if it were not so, I would have told you. I am going there to prepare a place for you. And if I go and prepare a place for you, I will come back and take you to be with me that you also may be where I am.

John 14:1–3

"If you love me, you will obey what I command. And I will ask the Father, and he will give you another Counselor to be with you forever—the Spirit of truth. The world cannot accept him, because it neither sees him nor knows him. But you know him, for he lives with you and will be in you.

John 14:15–17

And I will ask the Father, and he will give you another Counselor to be with you forever —the Spirit of truth.

Jesus replied, "If anyone loves me, he will obey my teaching. My Father will love him, and we will come to him and make our home with him. He who does not love me will not obey my teaching. These words you hear are not my own; they belong to the Father who sent me.

John 14:23–24

But the Counselor, the Holy Spirit, whom the Father will send in my name, will teach you all things and will remind you of everything I have said to you. Peace I leave with you; my peace I give you. I do not give to you as the world gives. Do not let your hearts be troubled and do not be afraid.

John 14:26–27

but the world must learn that I love the Father and that I do exactly what my Father has commanded me. "Come now; let us leave.

John 14:31

"When the Counselor comes, whom I will send to you from the Father, the Spirit of truth who goes out from the Father, he will testify about me.

John 15:26

But when he, the Spirit of truth, comes, he will guide you into all truth. He will not speak on his own; he will speak only what he hears, and he will tell you what is yet to come. He will bring glory to me by taking from what is mine and making it known to you.

John 16:13–14

After Jesus said this, he looked toward heaven and prayed: "Father, the time has come. Glorify your Son, that your Son may glorify you. For you granted him authority over all people that he might give eternal life to all those you have given him. Now this is eternal life: that they may know you, the only true God, and Jesus Christ, whom you have sent. I have brought you glory on earth by completing the work you gave me to do. And now, Father, glorify me in your presence with the glory I had with you before the world began.

John 17:1–5

When the Counselor comes, whom I will send to you from the Father, the Spirit of truth who goes out from the Father, he will testify about me.

Therefore I tell you that no one who is speaking by the Spirit of God says, "Jesus be cursed," and no one can say, "Jesus is Lord," except by the Holy Spirit.

1 Corinthians 12:3

Now it is God who makes both us and you stand firm in Christ. He anointed us, set his seal of ownership on us, and put his Spirit in our hearts as a deposit, guaranteeing what is to come.

2 Corinthians 1:21–22

May the grace of the Lord Jesus Christ, and the love of God, and the fellowship of the Holy Spirit be with you all.

2 Corinthians 13:14

May the grace of the Lord Jesus Christ, and the love of God, and the fellowship of the Holy Spirit be with you all.

And you also were included in Christ when you heard the word of truth, the gospel of your salvation. Having believed, you were marked in him with a seal, the promised Holy Spirit, who is a deposit guaranteeing our inheritance until the redemption of those who are God's possession—to the praise of his glory.

Ephesians 1:13–14

For this reason, ever since I heard about your faith in the Lord Jesus and your love for all the saints, I have not stopped giving thanks for you, remembering you in my prayers. I keep asking that the God of our Lord Jesus Christ, the glorious Father, may give you the Spirit of wisdom and revelation, so that you may know him better.

Ephesians 1:15–17

For through him we both have access to the Father by one Spirit.

Ephesians 2:18

Consequently, you are no longer foreigners and aliens, but fellow citizens with God's people and members of God's household, built on the foundation of the apostles and prophets, with Christ Jesus himself as the chief cornerstone. In him the whole building is joined together and rises to become a holy temple in the Lord. And in him you too are being built together to become a dwelling in which God lives by his Spirit.

Ephesians 2:19–22

For this reason I kneel before the Father, from whom his whole family in heaven and on earth derives its name. I pray that out of his glorious riches he may strengthen you with power through his Spirit in your inner being, so that Christ may dwell in your hearts through faith. And I pray that you, being rooted and established in love, may have power, together with all the saints, to grasp how wide and long and high and deep is the love of Christ, and to know this love that surpasses knowledge—that you may be filled to the measure of all the fullness of God.

Ephesians 3:14–19

I pray that out of his glorious riches he may strengthen you with power through his Spirit in your inner being, so that Christ may dwell in your hearts through faith.

There is one body and one Spirit—just as you were called to one hope when you were called—one Lord, one faith, one baptism; one God and Father of all, who is over all and through all and in all.

Ephesians 4:4–6

To God's elect, strangers in the world, scattered throughout Pontus, Galatia, Cappadocia, Asia and Bithynia, who have been chosen according to the foreknowledge of God the Father, through the sanctifying work of the Spirit, for obedience to Jesus Christ and sprinkling by his blood: Grace and peace be yours in abundance.

1 Peter 1:1–2

For Christ died for sins once for all, the righteous for the unrighteous, to bring you to God. He was put to death in the body but made alive by the Spirit,

1 Peter 3:18

If anyone acknowledges that Jesus is the Son of God, God lives in him and he in God.

But you have an anointing from the Holy One, and all of you know the truth. I do not write to you because you do not know the truth, but because you do know it and because no lie comes from the truth. Who is the liar? It is the man who denies that Jesus is the Christ. Such a man is the antichrist—he denies the Father and the Son. No one who denies the Son has the Father; whoever acknowledges the Son has the Father also.

1 John 2:20–23

No one has ever seen God; but if we love one another, God lives in us and his love is made complete in us. We know that we live in him and he in us, because he has given us of his Spirit. And we have seen and testify that the Father has sent his Son to be the Savior of the world. If anyone acknowledges that Jesus is the Son of God, God lives in him and he in God.

1 John 4:12–15

This is the one who came by water and blood—Jesus Christ. He did not come by water only, but by water and blood. And it is the Spirit who testifies, because the Spirit is the truth. For there are three that testify: the Spirit, the water and the blood; and the three are in agreement. We accept man's testimony, but God's testimony is greater because it is the testimony of God, which he has given about his Son. Anyone who believes in the Son of God has this testimony in his heart. Anyone who does not believe God has made him out to be a liar, because he has not believed the testimony God has given about his Son. And this is the testimony: God has given us eternal life, and this life is in his Son. He who has the Son has life; he who does not have the Son of God does not have life. I write these things to you who believe in the name of the Son of God so that you may know that you have eternal life.

1 John 5:6–13

God has given us eternal life, and this life is in his Son. He who has the Son has life; he who does not have the Son of God does not have life.

Chapter 9

What Jesus Christ Says About Himself

Jesus said to her, "I am the resurrection and the life. He who believes in me will live, even though he dies; and whoever lives and believes in me will never die. Do you believe this?"

John 11:25–26

The purpose of this chapter is to present in one place a representative selection of statements from Jesus Christ about Himself. His words leave no doubt that He proclaims to be the Son of God—God in human form. Jesus Christ is both fully God and fully man. His words tell us that He came to earth to bring us salvation and enable us to walk in the light of God's truth rather than in the darkness of sin and deception. Sin is the breaking of God's laws, and the penalty for sin is spiritual death—eternal separation from God. Jesus Christ's words tell us that He came to earth to save us from the death penalty we deserve for sinning against the holy God of the Bible. Jesus Christ—the unblemished "Lamb of God"—is the only human being who has never sinned against God. He alone was qualified to be the perfect, sinless sacrifice needed to pay the full penalty for our past, present, and future sins. He did this by receiving the punishment that we deserve—God's wrath against sin. Jesus Christ, after going to the cross for us and accomplishing His mission on earth, was physically resurrected from the dead three days later. The Word of God tells us that Jesus Christ—the "King of Kings and Lord of Lords"—will return to earth to gather those who belong to Him so that they may live with Him for eternity. God always keeps His promises.

If you have any doubts as to whether Jesus Christ really is who He proclaims to be in the Bible, ask God to show you the truth about Him. Then as you read this chapter, I invite you to set aside your preconceptions while you ponder what Jesus Christ proclaims about Himself. May your understanding of Jesus Christ and your relationship with Him be totally consistent with what He reveals about Himself in the Bible.

"Do not think that I have come to abolish the Law or the Prophets; I have not come to abolish them but to fulfill them. I tell you the truth, until heaven and earth disappear, not the smallest letter, not the least stroke of a pen, will by any means disappear from the Law until everything is accomplished.

Matthew 5:17–18

"Come to me, all you who are weary and burdened, and I will give you rest. Take my yoke upon you and learn from me, for I am gentle and humble in heart, and you will find rest for your souls. For my yoke is easy and my burden is light."

Matthew 11:28–30

"All authority in heaven and on earth has been given to me.

Do you think I cannot call on my Father, and he will at once put at my disposal more than twelve legions of angels? But how then would the Scriptures be fulfilled that say it must happen in this way?"

Matthew 26:53–54

Then Jesus came to them and said, "All authority in heaven and on earth has been given to me. Therefore go and make disciples of all nations, baptizing them in the name of the Father and of the Son and of the Holy Spirit, and teaching them to obey everything I have commanded you. And surely I am with you always, to the very end of the age."

Matthew 28:18–20

He said to them, "This is what I told you while I was still with you: Everything must be fulfilled that is written about me in the Law of Moses, the Prophets and the Psalms." Then he opened their minds so they could understand the Scriptures. He told them, "This is what is written: The Christ will suffer and rise from the dead on the third day, and repentance and forgiveness of sins will be preached in his name to all nations, beginning at Jerusalem. You are witnesses of these things. I am going to send you what my Father has promised; but stay in the city until you have been clothed with power from on high."

Luke 24:44–48

By myself I can do nothing; I judge only as I hear, and my judgment is just, for I seek not to please myself but him who sent me.

John 5:30

For I have come down from heaven not to do my will but to do the will of him who sent me.

For I have come down from heaven not to do my will but to do the will of him who sent me. And this is the will of him who sent me, that I shall lose none of all that he has given me, but raise them up at the last day. For my Father's will is that everyone who looks to the Son and believes in him shall have eternal life, and I will raise him up at the last day."

John 6:38–40

I tell you the truth, he who believes has everlasting life. I am the bread of life.

John 6:47–48

133

I am the living bread that came down from heaven. If anyone eats of this bread, he will live forever. This bread is my flesh, which I will give for the life of the world." Then the Jews began to argue sharply among themselves, "How can this man give us his flesh to eat?" Jesus said to them, "I tell you the truth, unless you eat the flesh of the Son of Man and drink his blood, you have no life in you. Whoever eats my flesh and drinks my blood has eternal life, and I will raise him up at the last day. For my flesh is real food and my blood is real drink. Whoever eats my flesh and drinks my blood remains in me, and I in him.

John 6:51–56

"You are from below; I am from above. You are of this world; I am not of this world.

When Jesus spoke again to the people, he said, "I am the light of the world. Whoever follows me will never walk in darkness, but will have the light of life."

John 8:12

But he continued, "You are from below; I am from above. You are of this world; I am not of this world. I told you that you would die in your sins; if you do not believe that I am the one I claim to be, you will indeed die in your sins." "Who are you?" they asked. "Just what I have been claiming all along," Jesus replied.

John 8:23–25

Jesus said to them, "If God were your Father, you would love me, for I came from God and now am here. I have not come on my own; but he sent me.

John 8:42

"You are not yet fifty years old," the Jews said to him, "and you have seen Abraham!" "I tell you the truth," Jesus answered, "before Abraham was born, I am!" At this, they picked up stones to stone him, but Jesus hid himself, slipping away from the temple grounds.

John 8:57–59

I am the gate; whoever enters through me will be saved. He will come in and go out, and find pasture.

John 10:9

The reason my Father loves me is that I lay down my life—only to take it up again. No one takes it from me, but I lay it down of my own accord. I have authority to lay it down and authority to take it up again. This command I received from my Father."

John 10:17–18

"I tell you the truth," Jesus answered, "before Abraham was born, I am!"

Jesus said to her, "I am the resurrection and the life. He who believes in me will live, even though he dies; and whoever lives and believes in me will never die. Do you believe this?"

John 11:25–26

I have come into the world as a light, so that no one who believes in me should stay in darkness.

John 12:46

"As for the person who hears my words but does not keep them, I do not judge him. For I did not come to judge the world, but to save it. There is a judge for the one who rejects me and does not accept my words; that very word which I spoke will condemn him at the last day. For I did not speak of my own accord, but the Father who sent me commanded me what to say and how to say it. I know that his command leads to eternal life. So whatever I say is just what the Father has told me to say."

John 12:47–50

Jesus answered, "I am the way and the truth and the life. No one comes to the Father except through me.

"Do not let your hearts be troubled. Trust in God; trust also in me. In my Father's house are many rooms; if it were not so, I would have told you. I am going there to prepare a place for you. And if I go and prepare a place for you, I will come back and take you to be with me that you also may be where I am.

John 14:1–3

Jesus answered, "I am the way and the truth and the life. No one comes to the Father except through me.

John 14:6

"I am the true vine, and my Father is the gardener. He cuts off every branch in me that bears no fruit, while every branch that does bear fruit he prunes so that it will be even more fruitful. You are already clean because of the word I have spoken to you. Remain in me, and I will remain in you. No branch can bear fruit by itself; it must remain in the vine. Neither can you bear fruit unless you remain in me.

John 15:1–4

"I am the vine; you are the branches. If a man remains in me and I in him, he will bear much fruit; apart from me you can do nothing.

John 15:5

I came from the Father and entered the world; now I am leaving the world and going back to the Father."

John 16:28

Jesus said, "My kingdom is not of this world. If it were, my servants would fight to prevent my arrest by the Jews. But now my kingdom is from another place."

John 18:36

"You are a king, then!" said Pilate. Jesus answered, "You are right in saying I am a king. In fact, for this reason I was born, and for this I came into the world, to testify to the truth. Everyone on the side of truth listens to me."

John 18:37

"You are right in saying I am a king. In fact, for this reason I was born, and for this I came into the world, to testify to the truth.

"Then I asked, 'Who are you, Lord?' "'I am Jesus, whom you are persecuting,' the Lord replied. 'Now get up and stand on your feet. I have appeared to you to appoint you as a servant and as a witness of what you have seen of me and what I will show you. I will rescue you from your own people and from the Gentiles. I am sending you to them to open their eyes and turn them from darkness to light, and from the power of Satan to God, so that they may receive forgiveness of sins and a place among those who are sanctified by faith in me.'

Acts 26:15–18

When I saw him, I fell at his feet as though dead. Then he placed his right hand on me and said: "Do not be afraid. I am the First and the Last. I am the Living One; I was dead, and behold I am alive for ever and ever! And I hold the keys of death and Hades.

Revelation 1:17–18

I am coming soon. Hold on to what you have, so that no one will take your crown. Him who overcomes I will make a pillar in the temple of my God. Never again will he leave it. I will write on him the name of my God and the name of the city of my God, the new Jerusalem, which is coming down out of heaven from my God; and I will also write on him my new name.

Revelation 3:11–12

**Behold,
I am coming soon!
My reward is with me,
and I will give to
everyone according
to what he has done.**

Those whom I love I rebuke and discipline. So be earnest, and repent. Here I am! I stand at the door and knock. If anyone hears my voice and opens the door, I will come in and eat with him, and he with me.

Revelation 3:19–20

"Behold, I am coming soon! My reward is with me, and I will give to everyone according to what he has done. I am the Alpha and the Omega, the First and the Last, the Beginning and the End. "Blessed are those who wash their robes, that they may have the right to the tree of life and may go through the gates into the city. Outside are the dogs, those who practice magic arts, the sexually immoral, the murderers, the idolaters and everyone who loves and practices falsehood.

Revelation 22:12–15

138

Chapter 10

God Is Eternal

**Before the mountains were born or you brought forth
the earth and the world, from everlasting to everlasting
you are God.**

Psalm 90:2

What does it mean to be "eternal"? In relation to God, who is eternal, it has two aspects. First, it means that God is without beginning or end. Second, it means that God exists outside of time and is not bound by time the way we are. God existed before the beginning of the universe and before the beginning of time. He created both our physical universe and the time dimension we live in. Unlike human beings, God knows the past, the present, and the future.

Those who place their faith in and follow Jesus Christ are promised a personal, loving relationship with God for eternity. This eternal relationship is based on God's kind of love, not on the human kind of love that so often devastates relationships in our world. Your eternal relationship with God begins in this life when you become a spiritually reborn follower of Jesus Christ. This means that you truly believe in Jesus Christ as your sin-bearer, Savior, and Lord, and that you have repented of your sins. It means that you have willingly submitted your life to the Lordship of Jesus Christ. When you do this, the Holy Spirit comes to reside within you and you are spiritually born-again. When the life-support systems within a Christian's physical body cease to function, the Christian is ushered safely into God's presence in heaven. For Christians, what a wonderful blessing it is to have all one's sins forgiven through Jesus Christ, to be transformed by the Holy Spirit, to receive a glorified body, and to live forever with God in His eternal kingdom.

A Prayer of Moses, the man of God. Lord, you have been our dwelling place throughout all generations. Before the mountains were born or you brought forth the earth and the world, from everlasting to everlasting you are God.

Psalm 90:1–2

"The Lord brought me forth as the first of his works, before his deeds of old; I was appointed from eternity, from the beginning, before the world began.

Proverbs 8:22–23

For to us a child is born, to us a son is given, and the government will be on his shoulders. And he will be called Wonderful Counselor, Mighty God, Everlasting Father, Prince of Peace.

Isaiah 9:6

from everlasting to everlasting you are God.

"This is what the Lord says—Israel's King and Redeemer, the Lord Almighty: I am the first and I am the last; apart from me there is no God. Who then is like me? Let him proclaim it. Let him declare and lay out before me what has happened since I established my ancient people, and what is yet to come—yes, let him foretell what will come. Do not tremble, do not be afraid. Did I not proclaim this and foretell it long ago? You are my witnesses. Is there any God besides me? No, there is no other Rock; I know not one."

Isaiah 44:6–8

For this is what the high and lofty One says—he who lives forever, whose name is holy: "I live in a high and holy place, but also with him who is contrite and lowly in spirit, to revive the spirit of the lowly and to revive the heart of the contrite.

Isaiah 57:15

"You are not yet fifty years old," the Jews said to him, "and you have seen Abraham!" "I tell you the truth," Jesus answered, "before Abraham was born, I am!" At this, they picked up stones to stone him, but Jesus hid himself, slipping away from the temple grounds.

John 8:57–59

After Jesus said this, he looked toward heaven and prayed: "Father, the time has come. Glorify your Son, that your Son may glorify you. For you granted him authority over all people that he might give eternal life to all those you have given him. Now this is eternal life: that they may know you, the only true God, and Jesus Christ, whom you have sent. I have brought you glory on earth by completing the work you gave me to do. And now, Father, glorify me in your presence with the glory I had with you before the world began.

John 17:1–5

And now, Father, glorify me in your presence with the glory I had with you before the world began.

So do not be ashamed to testify about our Lord, or ashamed of me his prisoner. But join with me in suffering for the gospel, by the power of God, who has saved us and called us to a holy life—not because of anything we have done but because of his own purpose and grace. This grace was given us in Christ Jesus before the beginning of time, but it has now been revealed through the appearing of our Savior, Christ Jesus, who has destroyed death and has brought life and immortality to light through the gospel.

2 Timothy 1:8–10

How much more, then, will the blood of Christ, who through the eternal Spirit offered himself unblemished to God, cleanse our consciences from acts that lead to death, so that we may serve the living God!

Hebrews 9:14

This grace was given us in Christ Jesus before the beginning of time,

Since you call on a Father who judges each man's work impartially, live your lives as strangers here in reverent fear. For you know that it was not with perishable things such as silver or gold that you were redeemed from the empty way of life handed down to you from your forefathers, but with the precious blood of Christ, a lamb without blemish or defect. He was chosen before the creation of the world, but was revealed in these last times for your sake. Through him you believe in God, who raised him from the dead and glorified him, and so your faith and hope are in God.

1 Peter 1:17–21

For you have been born again, not of perishable seed, but
of imperishable, through the living and enduring word of
God. For, "All men are like grass, and all their glory is like
the flowers of the field; the grass withers and the flowers fall,
but the word of the Lord stands forever." And this is the
word that was preached to you.

1 Peter 1:23–25

John, To the seven churches in the province of Asia: Grace
and peace to you from him who is, and who was, and who
is to come, and from the seven spirits before his throne, and
from Jesus Christ, who is the faithful witness, the firstborn
from the dead, and the ruler of the kings of the earth. To
him who loves us and has freed us from our sins by his
blood, and has made us to be a kingdom and priests to serve
his God and Father—to him be glory and power for ever
and ever! Amen. Look, he is coming with the clouds, and
every eye will see him, even those who pierced him; and
all the peoples of the earth will mourn because of him. So
shall it be! Amen. "I am the Alpha and the Omega," says
the Lord God, "who is, and who was, and who is to come,
the Almighty."

Revelation 1:4–8

**"I am the Alpha
and the Omega,"
says the Lord God, "
who is, and who was,
and who is to come,
the Almighty."**

Chapter 11

God Knows the Future

Remember the former things, those of long ago; I am God, and there is no other; I am God, and there is none like me. I make known the end from the beginning, from ancient times, what is still to come. I say: My purpose will stand, and I will do all that I please. From the east I summon a bird of prey; from a far-off land, a man to fulfill my purpose. What I have said, that will I bring about; what I have planned, that will I do.

Isaiah 46:9–11

The eternal God of the Bible is the creator of the universe, the earth, the laws of nature, and all of life. This includes everything that is visible and invisible. He also rules over the time dimension, and He is not bound by time as is His creation. God alone accurately knows the past, present, and future.

God has included in the Bible certain future events which He wants people to be aware of and take seriously. He does this for at least three reasons. One reason is to authenticate that He is in fact the author of the Bible by precisely fulfilling Bible prophecies often far into the future. Only God is able to accomplish this. A second reason is to inform people of the certainty of heaven and hell, and to alert them to the eternal consequences of either following or rejecting Jesus Christ. A third reason is to warn and prepare His people regarding the future dangers they will face. God, who alone knows the future with certainty, is able to guide our lives into the future as no one else can. For these reasons, we would be wise to trust God and His Word—the Bible—above our own thinking and above the wisdom of this world. To what extent will you trust God and the Bible to guide you as you choose your steps into the future?

"I am the LORD; that is my name! I will not give my glory to another or my praise to idols. See, the former things have taken place, and new things I declare; before they spring into being I announce them to you."

Isaiah 42:8–9

"This is what the Lord says—Israel's King and Redeemer, the Lord Almighty: I am the first and I am the last; apart from me there is no God. Who then is like me? Let him proclaim it. Let him declare and lay out before me what has happened since I established my ancient people, and what is yet to come—yes, let him foretell what will come. Do not tremble, do not be afraid. Did I not proclaim this and foretell it long ago? You are my witnesses. Is there any God besides me? No, there is no other Rock; I know not one."

Isaiah 44:6–8

See, the former things have taken place, and new things I declare; before they spring into being I announce them to you."

"This is what the LORD says—your Redeemer, who formed you in the womb: I am the LORD, who has made all things, who alone stretched out the heavens, who spread out the earth by myself, who foils the signs of false prophets and makes fools of diviners, who overthrows the learning of the wise and turns it into nonsense, who carries out the words of his servants and fulfills the predictions of his messengers,

Isaiah 44:24–26

"Gather together and come; assemble, you fugitives from the nations. Ignorant are those who carry about idols of wood, who pray to gods that cannot save. Declare what is to be, present it—let them take counsel together. Who foretold this long ago, who declared it from the distant past? Was it not I, the LORD? And there is no God apart from me, a righteous God and a Savior; there is none but me. "Turn to me and be saved, all you ends of the earth; for I am God, and there is no other.

Isaiah 45:20–22

Remember the former things, those of long ago; I am God, and there is no other; I am God, and there is none like me. I make known the end from the beginning, from ancient times, what is still to come. I say: My purpose will stand, and I will do all that I please. From the east I summon a bird of prey; from a far-off land, a man to fulfill my purpose. What I have said, that will I bring about; what I have planned, that will I do.

Isaiah 46:9–11

I make known the end from the beginning, from ancient times, what is still to come.

I foretold the former things long ago, my mouth announced them and I made them known; then suddenly I acted, and they came to pass. For I knew how stubborn you were; the sinews of your neck were iron, your forehead was bronze. Therefore I told you these things long ago; before they happened I announced them to you so that you could not say, 'My idols did them; my wooden image and metal god ordained them.' You have heard these things; look at them all. Will you not admit them? "From now on I will tell you of new things, of hidden things unknown to you.

Isaiah 48:3–6

At that time if anyone says to you, Look, here is the Christ! or, There he is! do not believe it. For false Christs and false prophets will appear and perform great signs and miracles to deceive even the elect if that were possible. See, I have told you ahead of time.

Matthew 24:23–25

Do you think I cannot call on my Father, and he will at once put at my disposal more than twelve legions of angels? But how then would the Scriptures be fulfilled that say it must happen in this way?"

Matthew 26:53–54

"How foolish you are, and how slow of heart to believe all that the prophets have spoken!

At that time if anyone says to you, Look, here is the Christ! or, Look, there he is! do not believe it. For false Christs and false prophets will appear and perform signs and miracles to deceive the elect if that were possible. So be on your guard; I have told you everything ahead of time.

Mark 13:21–23

He said to them, "How foolish you are, and how slow of heart to believe all that the prophets have spoken! Did not the Christ have to suffer these things and then enter his glory?" And beginning with Moses and all the Prophets, he explained to them what was said in all the Scriptures concerning himself.

Luke 24:25–27

He said to them, "This is what I told you while I was still with you: Everything must be fulfilled that is written about me in the Law of Moses, the Prophets and the Psalms." Then he opened their minds so they could understand the Scriptures. He told them, "This is what is written: The Christ will suffer and rise from the dead on the third day, and repentance and forgiveness of sins will be preached in his name to all nations, beginning at Jerusalem. You are witnesses of these things. I am going to send you what my Father has promised; but stay in the city until you have been clothed with power from on high."

Luke 24:44–48

"I am telling you now before it happens, so that when it does happen you will believe that I am He. I tell you the truth, whoever accepts anyone I send accepts me; and whoever accepts me accepts the one who sent me." After he had said this, Jesus was troubled in spirit and testified, "I tell you the truth, one of you is going to betray me."

John 13:19–21

I am telling you now before it happens, so that when it does happen you will believe that I am He.

But when he, the Spirit of truth, comes, he will guide you into all truth. He will not speak on his own; he will speak only what he hears, and he will tell you what is yet to come. He will bring glory to me by taking from what is mine and making it known to you.

John 16:13–14

The Spirit clearly says that in later times some will abandon the faith and follow deceiving spirits and things taught by demons. Such teachings come through hypocritical liars, whose consciences have been seared as with a hot iron.

1 Timothy 4:1–2

Chapter 12

God's Awareness of Your Life

**The heart is deceitful above all things and beyond cure.
Who can understand it? "I the LORD search the heart
and examine the mind, to reward a man according to his
conduct, according to what his deeds deserve."**
Jeremiah 17:9–10

God is omniscient—He has total knowledge and understanding of everything. God is omnipresent—He sees all and is everywhere at once. God is omnipotent—He is almighty and has the power to do whatever He chooses. God created the universe, the physical laws of nature that govern it, and everything within it. He is not confined to our three physical dimensions and our time dimension as we are. He is also not subject to the laws of nature as we are. He cares about and is closely watching the life of every human being. In addition, the Holy Spirit resides within every spiritually reborn follower of Jesus Christ.

As you read the verses in this chapter, know that God is fully aware of everything about you, both physically and spiritually. God knows your thoughts and intents, your concerns and fears, how you view Him, and how you view and treat other people. God knows everything about your spiritual and physical health. God knows how and when your body will die.

God always considers His *big picture* when He decides how He will become involved in your life. God's big picture includes the present world around you, His eternal kingdom, how you choose to live your life, the other people in your sphere of influence, the spiritual realm and its beings, the spiritual battle between good and evil, His overall plan for mankind, the personal relationship that He desires to have with you, the condition of your spiritual heart toward Him, and more. God, who alone is able to see the true big picture, desires what is best for you—eternal life in a right relationship with Him. God, who is fully aware of everything about you, allows you the freedom to choose whether or not you will trust Him with your life, both now and for eternity.

"Do not keep talking so proudly or let your mouth speak such arrogance, for the LORD is a God who knows, and by him deeds are weighed.

1 Samuel 2:3

And you, my son Solomon, acknowledge the God of your father, and serve him with wholehearted devotion and with a willing mind, for the LORD searches every heart and understands every motive behind the thoughts. If you seek him, he will be found by you; but if you forsake him, he will reject you forever.

1 Chronicles 28:9

for the LORD searches every heart and understands every motive behind the thoughts.

For the eyes of the Lord range throughout the earth to strengthen those whose hearts are fully committed to him.

2 Chronicles 16:9a

Does he not see my ways and count my every step? "If I have walked in falsehood or my foot has hurried after deceit—let God weigh me in honest scales and he will know that I am blameless—

Job 31:4–6

For the LORD watches over the way of the righteous, but the way of the wicked will perish.

Psalm 1:6

The fool says in his heart, "There is no God." They are corrupt, their deeds are vile; there is no one who does good. The LORD looks down from heaven on the sons of men to see if there are any who understand, any who seek God.

Psalm 14:1–2

May the words of my mouth and the meditation of my heart be pleasing in your sight, O LORD, my Rock and my Redeemer.

Psalm 19:14

From heaven the LORD looks down and sees all mankind; from his dwelling place he watches all who live on earth— he who forms the hearts of all, who considers everything they do.

Psalm 33:13–15

The eyes of the LORD are on the righteous and his ears are attentive to their cry; the face of the LORD is against those who do evil, to cut off the memory of them from the earth.

Psalm 34:15–16

From heaven the LORD looks down and sees all mankind;

. . .

he who forms the hearts of all, who considers everything they do.

Take heed, you senseless ones among the people; you fools, when will you become wise? Does he who implanted the ear not hear? Does he who formed the eye not see? Does he who disciplines nations not punish? Does he who teaches man lack knowledge? The LORD knows the thoughts of man; he knows that they are futile.

Psalm 94:8–11

I wait for your salvation, O LORD, and I follow your commands. I obey your statutes, for I love them greatly. I obey your precepts and your statutes, for all my ways are known to you.

Psalm 119:166–168

O LORD, you have searched me and you know me. You know when I sit and when I rise; you perceive my thoughts from afar. You discern my going out and my lying down; you are familiar with all my ways. Before a word is on my tongue you know it completely, O LORD.

Psalm 139:1–4

Search me, O God, and know my heart; test me and know my anxious thoughts. See if there is any offensive way in me, and lead me in the way everlasting.

Psalm 139:23–24

O LORD, you have searched me and you know me.

. . .

you perceive my thoughts from afar.

Great is our Lord and mighty in power; his understanding has no limit.

Psalm 147:5

For a man's ways are in full view of the LORD, and he examines all his paths. The evil deeds of a wicked man ensnare him; the cords of his sin hold him fast. He will die for lack of discipline, led astray by his own great folly.

Proverbs 5:21–23

The eyes of the LORD are everywhere, keeping watch on the wicked and the good.

Proverbs 15:3

The LORD detests the thoughts of the wicked, but those of the pure are pleasing to him.

Proverbs 15:26

The LORD detests all the proud of heart. Be sure of this: They will not go unpunished.

Proverbs 16:5

In his heart a man plans his course, but the LORD determines his steps.

Proverbs 16:9

The crucible for silver and the furnace for gold, but the LORD tests the heart.

Proverbs 17:3

The lamp of the LORD searches the spirit of a man; it searches out his inmost being.

Proverbs 20:27

The lamp of the LORD searches the spirit of a man; it searches out his inmost being.

The king's heart is in the hand of the Lord; he directs it like a watercourse wherever he pleases.

Proverbs 21:1

All a man's ways seem right to him, but the LORD weighs the heart.

Proverbs 21:2

Now all has been heard; here is the conclusion of the matter: Fear God and keep his commandments, for this is the whole duty of man. For God will bring every deed into judgment, including every hidden thing, whether it is good or evil.

Ecclesiastes 12:13–14

My eyes are on all their ways; they are not hidden from me,
nor is their sin concealed from my eyes.

Jeremiah 16:17

The heart is deceitful above all things and beyond cure.
Who can understand it? "I the LORD search the heart
and examine the mind, to reward a man according to his
conduct, according to what his deeds deserve."

Jeremiah 17:9–10

Can anyone hide in secret places so that I cannot see him?"
declares the LORD. "Do not I fill heaven and earth?"
declares the LORD.

Jeremiah 23:24

**"I the LORD
search the heart
and examine the mind,**

. . . O great and powerful God, whose name is the LORD
Almighty, great are your purposes and mighty are your
deeds. Your eyes are open to all the ways of men; you
reward everyone according to his conduct and as his
deeds deserve.

Jeremiah 32:18b–19

but they do not realize that I remember all their evil deeds.
Their sins engulf them; they are always before me.

Hosea 7:2

Knowing their thoughts, Jesus said, "Why do you entertain
evil thoughts in your hearts?

Matthew 9:4

Jesus knew their thoughts and said to them, "Every kingdom divided against itself will be ruined, and every city or household divided against itself will not stand.
Matthew 12:25

But I tell you that men will have to give account on the day of judgment for every careless word they have spoken. For by your words you will be acquitted, and by your words you will be condemned."
Matthew 12:36–37

He said to them, "You are the ones who justify yourselves in the eyes of men, but God knows your hearts. What is highly valued among men is detestable in God's sight.
Luke 16:15

He said to them, "You are the ones who justify yourselves in the eyes of men, but God knows your hearts.

Now while he was in Jerusalem at the Passover Feast, many people saw the miraculous signs he was doing and believed in his name. But Jesus would not entrust himself to them, for he knew all men. He did not need man's testimony about man, for he knew what was in a man.
John 2:24–25

The Spirit gives life; the flesh counts for nothing. The words I have spoken to you are spirit and they are life. Yet there are some of you who do not believe." For Jesus had known from the beginning which of them did not believe and who would betray him. He went on to say, "This is why I told you that no one can come to me unless the Father has enabled him."
John 6:63–65

So then, men ought to regard us as servants of Christ and as those entrusted with the secret things of God. Now it is required that those who have been given a trust must prove faithful. I care very little if I am judged by you or by any human court; indeed, I do not even judge myself. My conscience is clear, but that does not make me innocent. It is the Lord who judges me. Therefore judge nothing before the appointed time; wait till the Lord comes. He will bring to light what is hidden in darkness and will expose the motives of men's hearts. At that time each will receive his praise from God.

1 Corinthians 4:1–5

Nothing in all creation is hidden from God's sight. Everything is uncovered and laid bare before the eyes of him to whom we must give account.

For the word of God is living and active. Sharper than any double-edged sword, it penetrates even to dividing soul and spirit, joints and marrow; it judges the thoughts and attitudes of the heart.

Hebrews 4:12

Nothing in all creation is hidden from God's sight. Everything is uncovered and laid bare before the eyes of him to whom we must give account.

Hebrews 4:13

Dear children, let us not love with words or tongue but with actions and in truth. This then is how we know that we belong to the truth, and how we set our hearts at rest in his presence whenever our hearts condemn us. For God is greater than our hearts, and he knows everything.

1 John 3:18–20

Chapter 13

God's Character

Righteous are you, O LORD, and your laws are right.
The statutes you have laid down are righteous; they are
fully trustworthy.

Psalm 119:137–138

This chapter looks at God's personal character traits, particularly those that relate to His values and moral standards. God's character traits reflect His heart. They are foundational to who He is and to the kind of relationship that He desires to have with each one of us. God calls us to love Him, obey Him, and adopt His values and moral standards. God—and this includes His character—is the same yesterday, today, and for all eternity.

In this life we are unable to fully comprehend and understand everything about God. However, God has clearly revealed in the Bible what He wants us to know about His character. If we are sincere about desiring to love, obey, and please God, then it is important that our understanding of His character be accurate. It is important to God that we truly know Him and not be ignorant or deceived regarding the true nature of who He is and what He stands for. If we say that we know and love God, but in reality have a wrong understanding of His character, then our relationship with Him will suffer. May this chapter be helpful to you as you seek to grow in your understanding of God's character and in your relationship with Him.

It is because of God's character and his unchanging nature that we can count on him to be trustworthy in fulfilling all of His promises. In the midst of this fallen, deceptive, and troubled world, knowing that we can trust God's character is a great comfort for Christians. For more information on God's promises, please see Chapter 25 of this book.

Then the LORD came down in the cloud and stood there with him and proclaimed his name, the LORD. And he passed in front of Moses, proclaiming, "The LORD, the LORD, the compassionate and gracious God, slow to anger, abounding in love and faithfulness,

Exodus 34:5–6

For the LORD your God is God of gods and Lord of lords, the great God, mighty and awesome, who shows no partiality and accepts no bribes.

Deuteronomy 10:17

He is the Rock, his works are perfect, and all his ways are just. A faithful God who does no wrong, upright and just is he.

He is the Rock, his works are perfect, and all his ways are just. A faithful God who does no wrong, upright and just is he.

Deuteronomy 32:4

I know, my God, that you test the heart and are pleased with integrity. . . .

1 Chronicles 29:17a

You are not a God who takes pleasure in evil; with you the wicked cannot dwell. The arrogant cannot stand in your presence; you hate all who do wrong. You destroy those who tell lies; bloodthirsty and deceitful men the LORD abhors.

Psalm 5:4–6

For the LORD is righteous, he loves justice; upright men will see his face.

Psalm 11:7

160

And the words of the LORD are flawless, like silver refined in a furnace of clay, purified seven times.

Psalm 12:6

As for God, his way is perfect; the word of the LORD is flawless. He is a shield for all who take refuge in him.

Psalm 18:30

The law of the LORD is perfect, reviving the soul. The statutes of the LORD are trustworthy, making wise the simple. The precepts of the LORD are right, giving joy to the heart. The commands of the LORD are radiant, giving light to the eyes. The fear of the LORD is pure, enduring forever. The ordinances of the LORD are sure and altogether righteous. They are more precious than gold, than much pure gold; they are sweeter than honey, than honey from the comb. By them is your servant warned; in keeping them there is great reward.

Psalm 19:7–11

As for God, his way is perfect; the word of the LORD is flawless.

All the ways of the LORD are loving and faithful for those who keep the demands of his covenant.

Psalm 25:10

For the word of the Lord is right and true; he is faithful in all he does. The Lord loves righteousness and justice; the earth is full of his unfailing love.

Psalm 33:4–5

Your love, O LORD, reaches to the heavens, your faithfulness to the skies. Your righteousness is like the mighty mountains, your justice like the great deep. O LORD, you preserve both man and beast. How priceless is your unfailing love! Both high and low among men find refuge in the shadow of your wings.

Psalm 36:5–7

Surely you desire truth in the inner parts; you teach me wisdom in the inmost place.

Psalm 51:6

For the LORD is good and his love endures forever; his faithfulness continues through all generations.

For the LORD is good and his love endures forever; his faithfulness continues through all generations.

Psalm 100:5

The LORD is compassionate and gracious, slow to anger, abounding in love. He will not always accuse, nor will he harbor his anger forever; he does not treat us as our sins deserve or repay us according to our iniquities. For as high as the heavens are above the earth, so great is his love for those who fear him;

Psalm 103:8–11

For great is your love, higher than the heavens; your faithfulness reaches to the skies. Be exalted, O God, above the heavens, and let your glory be over all the earth.

Psalm 108:4–5

Righteous are you, O LORD, and your laws are right.
The statutes you have laid down are righteous; they are
fully trustworthy.

Psalm 119:137–138

Your righteousness is everlasting and your law is true.

Psalm 119:142

The LORD is righteous in all his ways and loving toward all
he has made.

Psalm 145:17

"To you, O men, I call out; I raise my voice to all mankind.
You who are simple, gain prudence; you who are foolish,
gain understanding. Listen, for I have worthy things to
say; I open my lips to speak what is right. My mouth speaks
what is true, for my lips detest wickedness. All the words
of my mouth are just; none of them is crooked or perverse.
To the discerning all of them are right; they are faultless to
those who have knowledge. Choose my instruction instead
of silver, knowledge rather than choice gold, for wisdom
is more precious than rubies, and nothing you desire can
compare with her.

Proverbs 8:4–11

Counsel and sound judgment are mine; I have
understanding and power.

Proverbs 8:14

The LORD abhors dishonest scales, but accurate weights
are his delight.

Proverbs 11:1

**The LORD
is righteous
in all his ways
and loving toward
all he has made.**

Be sure of this: The wicked will not go unpunished, but those who are righteous will go free.

Proverbs 11:21

The LORD detests the way of the wicked but he loves those who pursue righteousness.

Proverbs 15:9

So this is what the Sovereign LORD says: "See, I lay a stone in Zion, a tested stone, a precious cornerstone for a sure foundation; the one who trusts will never be dismayed. I will make justice the measuring line and righteousness the plumb line; hail will sweep away your refuge, the lie, and water will overflow your hiding place.

Isaiah 28:16–17

The LORD detests the way of the wicked but he loves those who pursue righteousness.

The LORD is exalted, for he dwells on high; he will fill Zion with justice and righteousness. He will be the sure foundation for your times, a rich store of salvation and wisdom and knowledge; the fear of the LORD is the key to this treasure.

Isaiah 33:5–6

For this is what the LORD says—he who created the heavens, he is God; he who fashioned and made the earth, he founded it; he did not create it to be empty, but formed it to be inhabited—he says: "I am the LORD, and there is no other. I have not spoken in secret, from somewhere in a land of darkness; I have not said to Jacob's descendants, 'Seek me in vain.' I, the LORD, speak the truth; I declare what is right.

Isaiah 45:18–19

This is what the LORD says: "Let not the wise man boast of his wisdom or the strong man boast of his strength or the rich man boast of his riches, but let him who boasts boast about this: that he understands and knows me, that I am the LORD, who exercises kindness, justice and righteousness on earth, for in these I delight," declares the LORD.

Jeremiah 9:23–24

Who is wise? He will realize these things. Who is discerning? He will understand them. The ways of the LORD are right; the righteous walk in them, but the rebellious stumble in them.

Hosea 14:9

Your eyes are too pure to look on evil; you cannot tolerate wrong. Why then do you tolerate the treacherous? Why are you silent while the wicked swallow up those more righteous than themselves?

Habakkuk 1:13

Your eyes are too pure to look on evil; you cannot tolerate wrong.

These are the things you are to do: Speak the truth to each other, and render true and sound judgment in your courts; do not plot evil against your neighbor, and do not love to swear falsely. I hate all this," declares the LORD.

Zechariah 8:16–17

"I the LORD do not change. . . .

Malachi 3:6a

"You have heard that it was said, `Eye for eye, and tooth for tooth.' But I tell you, Do not resist an evil person. If someone strikes you on the right cheek, turn to him the other also. And if someone wants to sue you and take your tunic, let him have your cloak as well. If someone forces you to go one mile, go with him two miles. Give to the one who asks you, and do not turn away from the one who wants to borrow from you.

Matthew 5:38–42

But the fruit of the spirit is love, joy, peace, patience, kindness, goodness, faithfulness, gentleness and self-control.

Love is patient, love is kind. It does not envy, it does not boast, it is not proud. It is not rude, it is not self-seeking, it is not easily angered, it keeps no record of wrongs. Love does not delight in evil but rejoices with the truth. It always protects, always trusts, always hopes, always perseveres.

1 Corinthians 13:4–7

But the fruit of the Spirit is love, joy, peace, patience, kindness, goodness, faithfulness, gentleness and self-control. Against such things there is no law. Those who belong to Christ Jesus have crucified the sinful nature with its passions and desires. Since we live by the Spirit, let us keep in step with the Spirit.

Galatians 5:22–25

Get rid of all bitterness, rage and anger, brawling and slander, along with every form of malice. Be kind and compassionate to one another, forgiving each other, just as in Christ God forgave you.

Ephesians 4:31–32

Finally, brothers, whatever is true, whatever is noble, whatever is right, whatever is pure, whatever is lovely, whatever is admirable—if anything is excellent or praiseworthy—think about such things. Whatever you have learned or received or heard from me, or seen in me—put it into practice. And the God of peace will be with you.

Philippians 4:8–9

Therefore, as God's chosen people, holy and dearly loved, clothe yourselves with compassion, kindness, humility, gentleness and patience. Bear with each other and forgive whatever grievances you may have against one another. Forgive as the Lord forgave you. And over all these virtues put on love, which binds them all together in perfect unity.

Colossians 3:12–14

Paul, a servant of God and an apostle of Jesus Christ for the faith of God's elect and the knowledge of the truth that leads to godliness—a faith and knowledge resting on the hope of eternal life, which God, who does not lie, promised before the beginning of time,

Titus 1:1–2

Because God wanted to make the unchanging nature of his purpose very clear to the heirs of what was promised, he confirmed it with an oath. God did this so that, by two unchangeable things in which it is impossible for God to lie, we who have fled to take hold of the hope offered to us may be greatly encouraged. We have this hope as an anchor for the soul, firm and secure. It enters the inner sanctuary behind the curtain, where Jesus, who went before us, has entered on our behalf. He has become a high priest forever, in the order of Melchizedek.

Hebrews 6:17–20

Finally, brothers, whatever is true, whatever is noble, whatever is right, whatever is pure, whatever is lovely, whatever is admirable— if anything is excellent or praiseworthy— think about such things.

Jesus Christ is the same yesterday and today and forever.
Hebrews 13:8

To this you were called, because Christ suffered for you, leaving you an example, that you should follow in his steps. "He committed no sin, and no deceit was found in his mouth."
1 Peter 2:21–22

Jesus Christ is the same yesterday and today and forever.

His divine power has given us everything we need for life and godliness through our knowledge of him who called us by his own glory and goodness. Through these he has given us his very great and precious promises, so that through them you may participate in the divine nature and escape the corruption in the world caused by evil desires.
2 Peter 1:3–4

This is the message we have heard from him and declare to you: God is light; in him there is no darkness at all. If we claim to have fellowship with him yet walk in the darkness, we lie and do not live by the truth. But if we walk in the light, as he is in the light, we have fellowship with one another, and the blood of Jesus, his Son, purifies us from all sin.
1 John 1:5–7

Do not love the world or anything in the world. If anyone loves the world, the love of the Father is not in him. For everything in the world—the cravings of sinful man, the lust of his eyes and the boasting of what he has and does—comes not from the Father but from the world. The world and its desires pass away, but the man who does the will of God lives forever.

1 John 2:15–17

For everything in the world— the cravings of sinful man, the lust of his eyes and the boasting of what he has and does— comes not from the Father but from the world.

Chapter 14

God's Claim to Be the One True God

For this is what the LORD says—he who created the heavens, he is God; he who fashioned and made the earth, he founded it; he did not create it to be empty, but formed it to be inhabited—he says: "I am the LORD, and there is no other.

Isaiah 45:18

The Bible clearly proclaims that the God of the Bible is the one true God. God tells us in the Bible that He alone is the Creator God and rules over everything—the physical universe, the spiritual realm, and every living thing.

All through history people around the world have believed in a wide variety of higher powers apart from the true God of the Bible. Today, some people believe in a single god. Others believe in a collection of gods. There are those who believe that god is an impersonal force. Many others believe that everyone and everything is god. Then there are atheists who believe that God does not exist. These various belief systems reflect fundamentally different and incompatible realities, and more than one of these realities cannot be true. There can be only one reality regarding the existence of the Creator God and the origin of the universe, the earth, life, and human beings.

God has designed and equipped us to discover and test for truth so that we may live our lives in touch with reality. Living out of touch with either physical or spiritual reality eventually results in our harming ourselves as well as others. The God of the Bible has provided us with ample evidence that He is the Creator and that we are His created beings. God wants us to know the truth about Himself, ourselves, and the eternal relationship that He desires to have with each one of us. His Word is the only foundation for knowing the absolute truth about these things. He holds you accountable to earnestly seek Him with all of your heart. God promises in Jeremiah 29:13 *"You will seek me and find me when you seek me with all your heart."*

For the LORD your God is God of gods and Lord of lords, the great God, mighty and awesome, who shows no partiality and accepts no bribes.

Deuteronomy 10:17

You may say to yourselves, "How can we know when a message has not been spoken by the LORD?" If what a prophet proclaims in the name of the LORD does not take place or come true, that is a message the LORD has not spoken. That prophet has spoken presumptuously. Do not be afraid of him.

Deuteronomy 18:21–22

For the Lord is the great God, the great King above all gods.

For the Lord is the great God, the great King above all gods. In his hand are the depths of the earth, and the mountain peaks belong to him. The sea is his, for he made it, and his hands formed the dry land.

Psalm 95:3–5

For great is the Lord and most worthy of praise; he is to be feared above all gods. For all the gods of the nations are idols, but the Lord made the heavens. Splendor and majesty are before him; strength and glory are in his sanctuary.

Psalm 96:4–6

"I am the LORD; that is my name! I will not give my glory to another or my praise to idols. See, the former things have taken place, and new things I declare; before they spring into being I announce them to you."

Isaiah 42:8–9

"You are my witnesses," declares the LORD, "and my servant whom I have chosen, so that you may know and believe me and understand that I am he. Before me no god was formed, nor will there be one after me. I, even I, am the LORD, and apart from me there is no savior. I have revealed and saved and proclaimed—I, and not some foreign god among you. You are my witnesses," declares the LORD, "that I am God. Yes, and from ancient days I am he. No one can deliver out of my hand. When I act, who can reverse it?"

Isaiah 43:10–13

"This is what the LORD says—Israel's King and Redeemer, the LORD Almighty: I am the first and I am the last; apart from me there is no God.

Isaiah 44:6

This is what the LORD says—Israel's King and Redeemer, the LORD Almighty: I am the first and I am the last; apart from me there is no God.

For this is what the LORD says—he who created the heavens, he is God; he who fashioned and made the earth, he founded it; he did not create it to be empty, but formed it to be inhabited—he says: "I am the LORD, and there is no other.

Isaiah 45:18

"Gather together and come; assemble, you fugitives from the nations. Ignorant are those who carry about idols of wood, who pray to gods that cannot save. Declare what is to be, present it—let them take counsel together. Who foretold this long ago, who declared it from the distant past? Was it not I, the LORD? And there is no God apart from me, a righteous God and a Savior; there is none but me. "Turn to me and be saved, all you ends of the earth; for I am God, and there is no other.

Isaiah 45:20–22

Remember the former things, those of long ago; I am God, and there is no other; I am God, and there is none like me. I make known the end from the beginning, from ancient times, what is still to come. I say: My purpose will stand, and I will do all that I please. From the east I summon a bird of prey; from a far-off land, a man to fulfill my purpose. What I have said, that will I bring about; what I have planned, that will I do.

Isaiah 46:9–11

"This is what the LORD says, he who made the earth, the LORD who formed it and established it—the LORD is his name: 'Call to me and I will answer you and tell you great and unsearchable things you do not know.'

Jeremiah 33:2–3

Now this is eternal life: that they may know you, the only true God, and Jesus Christ, whom you have sent.

"The most important one," answered Jesus, "is this: 'Hear, O Israel, the Lord our God, the Lord is one. Love the Lord your God with all your heart and with all your soul and with all your mind and with all your strength.' The second is this: 'Love your neighbor as yourself.' There is no commandment greater than these."

Mark 12:29–31

After Jesus said this, he looked toward heaven and prayed: "Father, the time has come. Glorify your Son, that your Son may glorify you. For you granted him authority over all people that he might give eternal life to all those you have given him. Now this is eternal life: that they may know you, the only true God, and Jesus Christ, whom you have sent.

John 17:1–3

yet for us there is but one God, the Father, from whom all things came and for whom we live; and there is but one Lord, Jesus Christ, through whom all things came and through whom we live.

1 Corinthians 8:6

This is good, and pleases God our Savior, who wants all men to be saved and to come to a knowledge of the truth. For there is one God and one mediator between God and men, the man Christ Jesus, who gave himself as a ransom for all men—the testimony given in its proper time.

1 Timothy 2:3–6

We know that we are children of God, and that the whole world is under the control of the evil one. We know also that the Son of God has come and has given us understanding, so that we may know him who is true. And we are in him who is true—even in his Son Jesus Christ. He is the true God and eternal life.

1 John 5:19–20

And we are in him who is true—even in his Son Jesus Christ. He is the true God and eternal life.

When I saw him, I fell at his feet as though dead. Then he placed his right hand on me and said: "Do not be afraid. I am the First and the Last. I am the Living One; I was dead, and behold I am alive for ever and ever! And I hold the keys of death and Hades.

Revelation 1:17–18

"Behold, I am coming soon! My reward is with me, and I will give to everyone according to what he has done. I am the Alpha and the Omega, the First and the Last, the Beginning and the End. "Blessed are those who wash their robes, that they may have the right to the tree of life and may go through the gates into the city. Outside are the dogs, those who practice magic arts, the sexually immoral, the murderers, the idolaters and everyone who loves and practices falsehood.

Revelation 22:12–15

**I am
the Alpha
and the Omega,
the First and the Last,
the Beginning and the End.**

Chapter 15

God's Desire for a Relationship with You

"For God so loved the world that he gave his one and only Son, that whoever believes in him shall not perish but have eternal life. For God did not send his Son into the world to condemn the world, but to save the world through him.
John 3:16–17

God tells us in the Bible that He created us in His image. God desires a personal relationship with each one of us for eternity. However, God is too holy and righteous to enter into an eternal relationship with selfish, prideful human beings who have sinned against Him. This describes every human being—with the exception of Jesus Christ—ever since Adam and Eve sinned against God. Sin is the breaking of God's laws, and the penalty for sinning against God is physical and spiritual death—separation from God—for eternity. God's justice demands that the penalty for sin must be paid.

Out of love, God sent His Son, Jesus Christ, to earth to pay the just and deserved penalty for our sins. When Jesus Christ—the sinless Lamb of God—went to the cross for us, He received the punishment that we deserve—the wrath of God against sin. On the cross, Jesus paid the full penalty for our past, present, and future sins. Only Jesus Christ is able to offer human beings total forgiveness for sinning against God. To accept this offer means that you acknowledge that you have sinned against God, that you repent of your sins, and that you believe in and follow Jesus Christ as your sin-bearer, Savior, and Lord.

Those people who are unwilling to seek and follow the God of the Bible will reject this offer. The result will be their paying the penalty for their own sins through eternal separation from God in a place called hell. All who choose to believe in and follow Jesus Christ as their Lord and Savior will be spiritually reborn. God then views them as having the righteousness of Jesus Christ and gives them eternal life. This is what God desires for you. God will not take away your free will and force you to follow Him. You are free to either choose or reject the relationship that the Lord Jesus Christ offers you. Keep in mind that this relationship is defined by God in the Bible, not by human beings.

"How long will you simple ones love your simple ways?
How long will mockers delight in mockery and fools hate
knowledge? If you had responded to my rebuke, I would
have poured out my heart to you and made my thoughts
known to you.

Proverbs 1:22–23

Has not my hand made all these things, and so they came
into being?" declares the LORD. "This is the one I esteem:
he who is humble and contrite in spirit, and trembles
at my word.

Isaiah 66:2

**For God
did not send his
Son into the world
to condemn the world,
but to save the world
through him.**

"Come to me, all you who are weary and burdened, and
I will give you rest. Take my yoke upon you and learn
from me, for I am gentle and humble in heart, and you
will find rest for your souls. For my yoke is easy and my
burden is light."

Matthew 11:28–30

"For God so loved the world that he gave his one and only
Son, that whoever believes in him shall not perish but have
eternal life. For God did not send his Son into the world to
condemn the world, but to save the world through him.

John 3:16–17

My sheep listen to my voice; I know them, and they follow
me. I give them eternal life, and they shall never perish; no
one can snatch them out of my hand. My Father, who has
given them to me, is greater than all; no one can snatch
them out of my Father's hand. I and the Father are one."

John 10:27–30

Jesus said to her, "I am the resurrection and the life. He who believes in me will live, even though he dies; and whoever lives and believes in me will never die. Do you believe this?"

John 11:25–26

"Do not let your hearts be troubled. Trust in God; trust also in me. In my Father's house are many rooms; if it were not so, I would have told you. I am going there to prepare a place for you. And if I go and prepare a place for you, I will come back and take you to be with me that you also may be where I am.

John 14:1–3

"As the Father has loved me, so have I loved you. Now remain in my love. If you obey my commands, you will remain in my love, just as I have obeyed my Father's commands and remain in his love. I have told you this so that my joy may be in you and that your joy may be complete.

John 15:9–11

But God demonstrates his own love for us in this: While we were still sinners, Christ died for us.

But God demonstrates his own love for us in this: While we were still sinners, Christ died for us.

Romans 5:8

However, as it is written: "No eye has seen, no ear has heard, no mind has conceived what God has prepared for those who love him"—

1 Corinthians 2:9

For you know that we dealt with each of you as a father deals with his own children, encouraging, comforting and urging you to live lives worthy of God, who calls you into his kingdom and glory.

1 Thessalonians 2:11–12

But since we belong to the day, let us be self-controlled, putting on faith and love as a breastplate, and the hope of salvation as a helmet. For God did not appoint us to suffer wrath but to receive salvation through our Lord Jesus Christ.

1 Thessalonians 5:8–9

This is good, and pleases God our Savior, who wants all men to be saved and to come to a knowledge of the truth.

But we ought always to thank God for you, brothers loved by the Lord, because from the beginning God chose you to be saved through the sanctifying work of the Spirit and through belief in the truth. He called you to this through our gospel, that you might share in the glory of our Lord Jesus Christ.

2 Thessalonians 2:13–14

This is good, and pleases God our Savior, who wants all men to be saved and to come to a knowledge of the truth. For there is one God and one mediator between God and men, the man Christ Jesus, who gave himself as a ransom for all men—the testimony given in its proper time.

1 Timothy 2:3–6

So do not be ashamed to testify about our Lord, or ashamed of me his prisoner. But join with me in suffering for the gospel, by the power of God, who has saved us and called us to a holy life—not because of anything we have done but because of his own purpose and grace. This grace was given us in Christ Jesus before the beginning of time,

2 Timothy 1:8–9

This is the message we have heard from him and declare to you: God is light; in him there is no darkness at all. If we claim to have fellowship with him yet walk in the darkness, we lie and do not live by the truth. But if we walk in the light, as he is in the light, we have fellowship with one another, and the blood of Jesus, his Son, purifies us from all sin.

1 John 1:5–7

But if we walk in the light, as he is in the light, we have fellowship with one another, and the blood of Jesus, his Son, purifies us from all sin.

My dear children, I write this to you so that you will not sin. But if anybody does sin, we have one who speaks to the Father in our defense—Jesus Christ, the Righteous One. He is the atoning sacrifice for our sins, and not only for ours but also for the sins of the whole world.

1 John 2:1–2

We know that we have come to know him if we obey his commands. The man who says, "I know him," but does not do what he commands is a liar, and the truth is not in him. But if anyone obeys his word, God's love is truly made complete in him. This is how we know we are in him: Whoever claims to live in him must walk as Jesus did.

1 John 2:3–6

How great is the love the Father has lavished on us, that we should be called children of God! And that is what we are! The reason the world does not know us is that it did not know him.

1 John 3:1

This is how God showed his love among us: He sent his one and only Son into the world that we might live through him. This is love: not that we loved God, but that he loved us and sent his Son as an atoning sacrifice for our sins. Dear friends, since God so loved us, we also ought to love one another. No one has ever seen God; but if we love one another, God lives in us and his love is made complete in us.

1 John 4:9–12

**This is love:
not that we loved God,
but that he loved us
and sent his Son
as an atoning sacrifice
for our sins.**

Chapter 16

God's Forgiveness

Therefore, there is now no condemnation for those who are in Christ Jesus, because through Christ Jesus the law of the Spirit of life set me free from the law of sin and death.
Romans 8:1–2

The attributes of God include perfect love, mercy, grace, and forgiveness. However, God's attributes also include perfect righteousness, justice, and judgment. God is holy and will not compromise any of his attributes. Even though God loves human beings whom He created, He cannot overlook their sinning against Him. God does not weigh the good and the bad in a person's life and then forgive those people who, in their minds, have lived mostly good lives. God will not compromise His justice, and His justice demands that the penalty for sin must be paid. Every sin is a sin against God. Romans 6:23 clearly reveals the penalty for sinning against God: "*For the wages of sin is death, but the gift of God is eternal life in Christ Jesus our Lord.*"

Out of love, mercy, and grace toward us, God sent His Son, Jesus Christ, to earth to pay the penalty for our sins so that we could be forgiven. Jesus Christ, who was without sin, took upon Himself the punishment that we deserve—the full wrath of God against sin. God's forgiveness comes through Jesus Christ alone. Jesus Christ proclaims this in John 14:6: "*Jesus answered, 'I am the way and the truth and the life. No one comes to the Father except through me.'*" In order for you to be forgiven for your sins you must acknowledge that you have sinned against God. You must repent of—turn away from—your sins. You must believe in and follow Jesus Christ as your sin-bearer, your Savior, and your Lord. Then, when you ask God for forgiveness, He will forgive you for all of your past, present, and future sins. God withholds His forgiveness from those people who refuse to place their faith in Jesus Christ as their personal Savior and Lord, who refuse to submit their lives to Him, and who refuse to repent of their sins. These lost people have rejected the Lord Jesus Christ, the only way to receive God's forgiveness and eternal life with Him.

See, I set before you today life and prosperity, death and destruction. For I command you today to love the Lord your God, to walk in his ways, and to keep his commands, decrees and laws; then you will live and increase, and the Lord your God will bless you in the land you are entering to possess. But if your heart turns away and you are not obedient, and if you are drawn away to bow down to other gods and worship them, I declare to you this day that you will certainly be destroyed. You will not live long in the land you are crossing the Jordan to enter and possess.

Deuteronomy 30:15–18

**if . . . then
will I hear from heaven
and will forgive their sin
and will heal their land.**

if my people, who are called by my name, will humble themselves and pray and seek my face and turn from their wicked ways, then will I hear from heaven and will forgive their sin and will heal their land.

2 Chronicles 7:14

Who can discern his errors? Forgive my hidden faults. Keep your servant also from willful sins; may they not rule over me. Then will I be blameless, innocent of great transgression. May the words of my mouth and the meditation of my heart be pleasing in your sight, O LORD, my Rock and my Redeemer.

Psalm 19:12–14

Praise the LORD, O my soul; all my inmost being, praise his holy name. Praise the LORD, O my soul, and forget not all his benefits—who forgives all your sins and heals all your diseases, who redeems your life from the pit and crowns you with love and compassion, who satisfies your desires with good things so that your youth is renewed like the eagle's.

Psalm 103:1–5

The LORD is compassionate and gracious, slow to anger, abounding in love. He will not always accuse, nor will he harbor his anger forever; he does not treat us as our sins deserve or repay us according to our iniquities. For as high as the heavens are above the earth, so great is his love for those who fear him; as far as the east is from the west, so far has he removed our transgressions from us. As a father has compassion on his children, so the LORD has compassion on those who fear him;

Psalm 103:8–13

He who conceals his sins does not prosper, but whoever confesses and renounces them finds mercy.

Proverbs 28:13

He who conceals his sins does not prosper, but whoever confesses and renounces them finds mercy.

'Even now,' declares the LORD, 'return to me with all your heart, with fasting and weeping and mourning.' Rend your heart and not your garments. Return to the LORD your God, for he is gracious and compassionate, slow to anger and abounding in love, and he relents from sending calamity.

Joel 2:12–13

"This, then, is how you should pray: "'Our Father in heaven, hallowed be your name, your kingdom come, your will be done on earth as it is in heaven. Give us today our daily bread. Forgive us our debts, as we also have forgiven our debtors. And lead us not into temptation, but deliver us from the evil one.

Matthew 6:9–13

For if you forgive men when they sin against you, your heavenly Father will also forgive you. But if you do not forgive men their sins, your Father will not forgive your sins.

Matthew 6:14–15

And so I tell you, every sin and blasphemy will be forgiven men, but the blasphemy against the Spirit will not be forgiven. Anyone who speaks a word against the Son of Man will be forgiven, but anyone who speaks against the Holy Spirit will not be forgiven, either in this age or in the age to come.

Matthew 12:31–32

For if you forgive men when they sin against you, your heavenly Father will also forgive you.

I tell you the truth, all the sins and blasphemies of men will be forgiven them. But whoever blasphemes against the Holy Spirit will never be forgiven; he is guilty of an eternal sin."

Mark 3:28–29

And when you stand praying, if you hold anything against anyone, forgive him, so that your Father in heaven may forgive you your sins."

Mark 11:25

But love your enemies, do good to them, and lend to them without expecting to get anything back. Then your reward will be great, and you will be sons of the Most High, because he is kind to the ungrateful and wicked. Be merciful, just as your Father is merciful.

Luke 6:35–36

And everyone who speaks a word against the Son of Man will be forgiven, but anyone who blasphemes against the Holy Spirit will not be forgiven.

Luke 12:10

He said to them, "This is what I told you while I was still with you: Everything must be fulfilled that is written about me in the Law of Moses, the Prophets and the Psalms." Then he opened their minds so they could understand the Scriptures. He told them, "This is what is written: The Christ will suffer and rise from the dead on the third day, and repentance and forgiveness of sins will be preached in his name to all nations, beginning at Jerusalem. You are witnesses of these things. I am going to send you what my Father has promised; but stay in the city until you have been clothed with power from on high."

Luke 24:44–48

He then brought them out and asked, "Sirs, what must I do to be saved?" They replied, "Believe in the Lord Jesus, and you will be saved—you and your household."

Acts 16:30–31

Therefore, there is now no condemnation for those who are in Christ Jesus, because through Christ Jesus the law of the Spirit of life set me free from the law of sin and death.

Romans 8:1–2

Therefore, there is now no condemnation for those who are in Christ Jesus,

In him we have redemption through his blood, the forgiveness of sins, in accordance with the riches of God's grace that he lavished on us with all wisdom and understanding. And he made known to us the mystery of his will according to his good pleasure, which he purposed in Christ,

Ephesians 1:7–9

Get rid of all bitterness, rage and anger, brawling and slander, along with every form of malice. Be kind and compassionate to one another, forgiving each other, just as in Christ God forgave you.

Ephesians 4:31–32

Be kind and compassionate to one another, forgiving each other, just as in Christ God forgave you.

For he has rescued us from the dominion of darkness and brought us into the kingdom of the Son he loves, in whom we have redemption, the forgiveness of sins.

Colossians 1:13–14

When you were dead in your sins and in the uncircumcision of your sinful nature, God made you alive with Christ. He forgave us all our sins, having canceled the written code, with its regulations, that was against us and that stood opposed to us; he took it away, nailing it to the cross.

Colossians 2:13–14

Therefore, as God's chosen people, holy and dearly loved, clothe yourselves with compassion, kindness, humility, gentleness and patience. Bear with each other and forgive whatever grievances you may have against one another. Forgive as the Lord forgave you. And over all these virtues put on love, which binds them all together in perfect unity.

Colossians 3:12–14

Here is a trustworthy saying that deserves full acceptance:
Christ Jesus came into the world to save sinners—of whom
I am the worst. But for that very reason I was shown mercy
so that in me, the worst of sinners, Christ Jesus might
display his unlimited patience as an example for those who
would believe on him and receive eternal life.

1 Timothy 1:15–16

It is impossible for those who have once been enlightened,
who have tasted the heavenly gift, who have shared in the
Holy Spirit, who have tasted the goodness of the word of
God and the powers of the coming age, if they fall away, to
be brought back to repentance, because to their loss they
are crucifying the Son of God all over again and subjecting
him to public disgrace.

Hebrews 6:4–6

**If we confess
our sins,
he is faithful and just
and will forgive us
our sins
and purify us from
all unrighteousness.**

This is the message we have heard from him and declare
to you: God is light; in him there is no darkness at all.
If we claim to have fellowship with him yet walk in the
darkness, we lie and do not live by the truth. But if we walk
in the light, as he is in the light, we have fellowship with
one another, and the blood of Jesus, his Son, purifies us
from all sin.

1 John 1:5–7

If we claim to be without sin, we deceive ourselves and
the truth is not in us. If we confess our sins, he is faithful
and just and will forgive us our sins and purify us from all
unrighteousness. If we claim we have not sinned, we make
him out to be a liar and his word has no place in our lives.

1 John 1:8–10

My dear children, I write this to you so that you will not sin. But if anybody does sin, we have one who speaks to the Father in our defense—Jesus Christ, the Righteous One. He is the atoning sacrifice for our sins, and not only for ours but also for the sins of the whole world.

1 John 2:1–2

This is how God showed his love among us: He sent his one and only Son into the world that we might live through him. This is love: not that we loved God, but that he loved us and sent his Son as an atoning sacrifice for our sins. Dear friends, since God so loved us, we also ought to love one another. No one has ever seen God; but if we love one another, God lives in us and his love is made complete in us.

1 John 4:9–12

**This is love:
not that we loved God,
but that he loved us
and sent his Son
as an atoning sacrifice
for our sins.**

Chapter 17

God's Grace

**May the grace of the Lord Jesus Christ, and the love of God,
and the fellowship of the Holy Spirit be with you all.**
2 Corinthians 13:14

In order to understand and appreciate God's grace, it is helpful to understand how it differs from His mercy and justice. These three attributes of God—justice, mercy, and grace—help us to understand how God chooses to respond to sin. If we are to really understand who God is and how He loves us, we must understand these concepts:

- Sin—The breaking of God's laws. Every sin is a sin against the holy God of the Bible. In God's eyes all sin is evil and deserves punishment and eternal separation from Him.

- Justice—Carrying out fair and right punishment against those who break the law.

- Mercy—Treating a lawbreaker better than he or she deserves.

- **Grace**—Giving someone something good that he or she does not deserve.

In your life, have you ever enjoyed good health, a breath of fresh air, nourishing food, a thirst-quenching drink of water, a loving family, trusted friends, the ability to appreciate the beauty of nature, or the satisfaction of helping someone in need? These and other blessings are the result of God's grace, which is a reflection of His love. It is also through God's love and grace that He sent His Son, Jesus Christ, into the world to pay the just penalty for our sins. God did this for us so that we may live with Him in heaven for eternity. The Apostle Paul tells us in Ephesians 2:4–5: "*But because of his great love for us, God, who is rich in mercy, made us alive with Christ even when we were dead in transgressions—it is by grace you have been saved.*"

Then the LORD came down in the cloud and stood there with him and proclaimed his name, the LORD. And he passed in front of Moses, proclaiming, "The LORD, the LORD, the compassionate and gracious God, slow to anger, abounding in love and faithfulness,

Exodus 34:5–6

Praise the LORD, O my soul; all my inmost being, praise his holy name. Praise the LORD, O my soul, and forget not all his benefits—who forgives all your sins and heals all your diseases, who redeems your life from the pit and crowns you with love and compassion, who satisfies your desires with good things so that your youth is renewed like the eagle's.

Psalm 103:1–5

The LORD is compassionate and gracious, slow to anger, abounding in love.

The LORD is compassionate and gracious, slow to anger, abounding in love. He will not always accuse, nor will he harbor his anger forever; he does not treat us as our sins deserve or repay us according to our iniquities. For as high as the heavens are above the earth, so great is his love for those who fear him;

Psalm 103:8–11

He mocks proud mockers but gives grace to the humble.

Proverbs 3:34

A good man obtains favor from the LORD, but the LORD condemns a crafty man.

Proverbs 12:2

'Even now,' declares the LORD, 'return to me with all
your heart, with fasting and weeping and mourning.' Rend
your heart and not your garments. Return to the LORD
your God, for he is gracious and compassionate, slow
to anger and abounding in love, and he relents from
sending calamity.

Joel 2:12–13

The Word became flesh and made his dwelling among us.
We have seen his glory, the glory of the One and Only, who
came from the Father, full of grace and truth. John testifies
concerning him. He cries out, saying, "This was he of whom
I said, 'He who comes after me has surpassed me because he
was before me.'" From the fullness of his grace we have all
received one blessing after another. For the law was given
through Moses; grace and truth came through Jesus Christ.

John 1:14–17

I am the gate; whoever enters through me will be saved. He
will come in and go out, and find pasture.

John 10:9

**The Word became flesh
and made his dwelling
among us.
We have seen his glory,
the glory of
the One and Only,
who came
from the Father,
full of grace and truth.**

But now a righteousness from God, apart from law, has been made known, to which the Law and the Prophets testify. This righteousness from God comes through faith in Jesus Christ to all who believe. There is no difference, for all have sinned and fall short of the glory of God, and are justified freely by his grace through the redemption that came by Christ Jesus. God presented him as a sacrifice of atonement, through faith in his blood. He did this to demonstrate his justice, because in his forbearance he had left the sins committed beforehand unpunished—he did it to demonstrate his justice at the present time, so as to be just and the one who justifies those who have faith in Jesus.

Romans 3:21–26

But he said to me, "My grace is sufficient for you, for my power is made perfect in weakness."

Therefore, since we have been justified through faith, we have peace with God through our Lord Jesus Christ, through whom we have gained access by faith into this grace in which we now stand. And we rejoice in the hope of the glory of God. Not only so, but we also rejoice in our sufferings, because we know that suffering produces perseverance; perseverance, character; and character, hope. And hope does not disappoint us, because God has poured out his love into our hearts by the Holy Spirit, whom he has given us.

Romans 5:1–5

But he said to me, "My grace is sufficient for you, for my power is made perfect in weakness." Therefore I will boast all the more gladly about my weaknesses, so that Christ's power may rest on me. That is why, for Christ's sake, I delight in weaknesses, in insults, in hardships, in persecutions, in difficulties. For when I am weak, then I am strong.

2 Corinthians 12:9–10

May the grace of the Lord Jesus Christ, and the love of God, and the fellowship of the Holy Spirit be with you all.

2 Corinthians 13:14

I have been crucified with Christ and I no longer live, but Christ lives in me. The life I live in the body, I live by faith in the Son of God, who loved me and gave himself for me. I do not set aside the grace of God, for if righteousness could be gained through the law, Christ died for nothing!"

Galatians 2:20–21

In him we have redemption through his blood, the forgiveness of sins, in accordance with the riches of God's grace that he lavished on us with all wisdom and understanding. And he made known to us the mystery of his will according to his good pleasure, which he purposed in Christ,

Ephesians 1:7–9

For it is by grace you have been saved, through faith

For it is by grace you have been saved, through faith—and this not from yourselves, it is the gift of God—not by works, so that no one can boast. For we are God's workmanship, created in Christ Jesus to do good works, which God prepared in advance for us to do.

Ephesians 2:8–10

So do not be ashamed to testify about our Lord, or ashamed of me his prisoner. But join with me in suffering for the gospel, by the power of God, who has saved us and called us to a holy life—not because of anything we have done but because of his own purpose and grace. This grace was given us in Christ Jesus before the beginning of time,

2 Timothy 1:8–9

For the grace of God that brings salvation has appeared to all men. It teaches us to say "No" to ungodliness and worldly passions, and to live self-controlled, upright and godly lives in this present age, while we wait for the blessed hope—the glorious appearing of our great God and Savior, Jesus Christ, who gave himself for us to redeem us from all wickedness and to purify for himself a people that are his very own, eager to do what is good. These, then, are the things you should teach. Encourage and rebuke with all authority. Do not let anyone despise you.

Titus 2:11–15

For the grace of God that brings salvation has appeared to all men.

At one time we too were foolish, disobedient, deceived and enslaved by all kinds of passions and pleasures. We lived in malice and envy, being hated and hating one another. But when the kindness and love of God our Savior appeared, he saved us, not because of righteous things we had done, but because of his mercy. He saved us through the washing of rebirth and renewal by the Holy Spirit, whom he poured out on us generously through Jesus Christ our Savior, so that, having been justified by his grace, we might become heirs having the hope of eternal life. This is a trustworthy saying. And I want you to stress these things, so that those who have trusted in God may be careful to devote themselves to doing what is good. These things are excellent and profitable for everyone.

Titus 3:3–8

Make every effort to live in peace with all men and to be holy; without holiness no one will see the Lord. See to it that no one misses the grace of God and that no bitter root grows up to cause trouble and defile many.

Hebrews 12:14–15

Don't be deceived, my dear brothers. Every good and perfect gift is from above, coming down from the Father of the heavenly lights, who does not change like shifting shadows. He chose to give us birth through the word of truth, that we might be a kind of firstfruits of all he created.

James 1:16–18

But he gives us more grace. That is why Scripture says: "God opposes the proud but gives grace to the humble."

James 4:6

Therefore, prepare your minds for action; be self-controlled; set your hope fully on the grace to be given you when Jesus Christ is revealed. As obedient children, do not conform to the evil desires you had when you lived in ignorance. But just as he who called you is holy, so be holy in all you do; for it is written: "Be holy, because I am holy."

1 Peter 1:13–16

"God opposes the proud but gives grace to the humble."

Each one should use whatever gift he has received to serve others, faithfully administering God's grace in its various forms.

1 Peter 4:10

Young men, in the same way be submissive to those who are older. All of you, clothe yourselves with humility toward one another, because, "God opposes the proud but gives grace to the humble." Humble yourselves, therefore, under God's mighty hand, that he may lift you up in due time. Cast all your anxiety on him because he cares for you.

1 Peter 5:5–7

Grace and peace be yours in abundance through the knowledge of God and of Jesus our Lord. His divine power has given us everything we need for life and godliness through our knowledge of him who called us by his own glory and goodness. Through these he has given us his very great and precious promises, so that through them you may participate in the divine nature and escape the corruption in the world caused by evil desires.

2 Peter 1:2–4

But grow in the grace and knowledge of our Lord and Savior Jesus Christ. To him be glory both now and forever! Amen.

Therefore, dear friends, since you already know this, be on your guard so that you may not be carried away by the error of lawless men and fall from your secure position. But grow in the grace and knowledge of our Lord and Savior Jesus Christ. To him be glory both now and forever! Amen.

2 Peter 3:17–18

The grace of the Lord Jesus be with God's people. Amen.

Revelation 22:21

Chapter 18

God's Holiness

**This is the message we have heard from him and declare
to you: God is light; in him there is no darkness at all.**

1 John 1:5

The Bible proclaims that God is holy. What does holy mean? A good definition is found in Noah Webster's 1828 First Edition of the American Dictionary of the English Language[1]: "*1. Properly, whole, entire or perfect, in a moral sense. Hence, pure in heart, temper or dispositions; free from sin and sinful affections. Applied to the Supreme Being, holy signifies perfectly pure, immaculate and complete in moral character.*" The word *holy* also implies to be set apart from anything morally impure, sinful, or evil (by God's standards). God's holiness is why sinful human beings—and this means all of us—are doomed if we are not justified by Jesus Christ. Romans 3:23 tells us that "*all have sinned and fall short of the glory of God.*" The penalty for sinning against God is death—eternal separation from God in a place called hell. Romans 6:23 confirms this, but also gives us hope through Jesus Christ: "*For the wages of sin is death, but the gift of God is eternal life in Christ Jesus our Lord.*"

God, in His mercy and grace, sent His holy and sinless Son, Jesus Christ, to earth to pay the just penalty for our sins so that we may be forgiven. This is why Jesus Christ is central to an eternal relationship with God. John the Baptist said of Jesus Christ in John 1:29, "*Look, the Lamb of God, who takes away the sin of the world!*" Jesus said of Himself in John 14:6: "*I am the way and the truth and the life. No one comes to the Father except through me.*" Understanding God's holiness and our need for a Savior is essential to keep from being deceived by those who falsely claim that there are many paths to eternal life with God. If you are already a Christian, your understanding of God's holiness is essential to your being a consistent, God-honoring follower of Jesus Christ. Whether you are a non-Christian who is investigating biblical Christianity or are already a Christian, I encourage you to ponder the implications of God's holiness for your life now and for eternity.

The LORD said to Moses, "Speak to the entire assembly of Israel and say to them: 'Be holy because I, the LORD your God, am holy.

Leviticus 19:1–2

He is the Rock, his works are perfect, and all his ways are just. A faithful God who does no wrong, upright and just is he.

Deuteronomy 32:4

There is no one holy like the Lord; there is no one besides you; there is no Rock like our God.

1 Samuel 2:2

There is no one holy like the Lord; there is no one besides you; there is no Rock like our God.

The law of the LORD is perfect, reviving the soul. The statutes of the LORD are trustworthy, making wise the simple. The precepts of the LORD are right, giving joy to the heart. The commands of the LORD are radiant, giving light to the eyes. The fear of the LORD is pure, enduring forever. The ordinances of the LORD are sure and altogether righteous.

Psalm 19:7–9

Exalt the Lord our God and worship at his holy mountain, for the Lord our God is holy.

Psalm 99:9

"The fear of the LORD is the beginning of wisdom, and knowledge of the Holy One is understanding.

Proverbs 9:10

"Every word of God is flawless; he is a shield to those who take refuge in him. Do not add to his words, or he will rebuke you and prove you a liar.

Proverbs 30:5–6

But the Lord Almighty will be exalted by his justice, and the holy God will show himself holy by his righteousness.

Isaiah 5:16

In the year that King Uzziah died, I saw the Lord seated on a throne, high and exalted, and the train of his robe filled the temple. Above him were seraphs, each with six wings: With two wings they covered their faces, with two they covered their feet, and with two they were flying. And they were calling to one another: Holy, holy, holy is the Lord Almighty; the whole earth is full of his glory.

Isaiah 6:1–3

And they were calling to one another: Holy, holy, holy is the Lord Almighty; the whole earth is full of his glory.

"For my thoughts are not your thoughts, neither are your ways my ways," declares the LORD. "As the heavens are higher than the earth, so are my ways higher than your ways and my thoughts than your thoughts.

Isaiah 55:8–9

For this is what the high and lofty One says—he who lives forever, whose name is holy: "I live in a high and holy place, but also with him who is contrite and lowly in spirit, to revive the spirit of the lowly and to revive the heart of the contrite.

Isaiah 57:15

They are to teach my people the difference between the holy and the common and show them how to distinguish between the unclean and the clean. "'In any dispute, the priests are to serve as judges and decide it according to my ordinances. They are to keep my laws and my decrees for all my appointed feasts, and they are to keep my Sabbaths holy.

Ezekiel 44:23–24

Your eyes are too pure to look on evil; you cannot tolerate wrong. Why then do you tolerate the treacherous? Why are you silent while the wicked swallow up those more righteous than themselves?

Habakkuk 1:13

Your eyes are too pure to look on evil; you cannot tolerate wrong.

Therefore, I urge you, brothers, in view of God's mercy, to offer your bodies as living sacrifices, holy and pleasing to God—this is your spiritual act of worship. Do not conform any longer to the pattern of this world, but be transformed by the renewing of your mind. Then you will be able to test and approve what God's will is—his good, pleasing and perfect will.

Romans 12:1-2

Praise be to the God and Father of our Lord Jesus Christ, who has blessed us in the heavenly realms with every spiritual blessing in Christ. For he chose us in him before the creation of the world to be holy and blameless in his sight. In love

Ephesians 1:3–4

Finally, brothers, whatever is true, whatever is noble, whatever is right, whatever is pure, whatever is lovely, whatever is admirable—if anything is excellent or praiseworthy—think about such things. Whatever you have learned or received or heard from me, or seen in me—put it into practice. And the God of peace will be with you.

Philippians 4:8–9

Make every effort to live in peace with all men and to be holy; without holiness no one will see the Lord. See to it that no one misses the grace of God and that no bitter root grows up to cause trouble and defile many.

Hebrews 12:14–15

Therefore, prepare your minds for action; be self-controlled; set your hope fully on the grace to be given you when Jesus Christ is revealed. As obedient children, do not conform to the evil desires you had when you lived in ignorance. But just as he who called you is holy, so be holy in all you do; for it is written: "Be holy, because I am holy."

1 Peter 1:13–16

But just as he who called you is holy, so be holy in all you do; for it is written: "Be holy, because I am holy."

This is the message we have heard from him and declare to you: God is light; in him there is no darkness at all. If we claim to have fellowship with him yet walk in the darkness, we lie and do not live by the truth. But if we walk in the light, as he is in the light, we have fellowship with one another, and the blood of Jesus, his Son, purifies us from all sin.

1 John 1:5–7

Chapter 19

God's Judgment, Wrath, and Punishment

Whoever believes in the Son has eternal life, but whoever rejects the Son will not see life, for God's wrath remains on him."

John 3:36

God's judgment, wrath, and punishment are His righteous and just responses to sin. God, through the Bible, has put in place and communicated to mankind His truth and His moral laws. Failing to follow God's laws is sin, and every sin is a sin against Him. We are told in the Bible that every human being, with the exception of Jesus Christ, has sinned. The Bible also teaches that the penalty for sinning against God must be paid. God's holy character demands this. The following verses speak to these truths:

Your eyes are too pure to look on evil; you cannot tolerate wrong. *Habakkuk 1:13a*

Everyone who sins breaks the law; in fact, sin is lawlessness. *1 John 3:4*

for all have sinned and fall short of the glory of God, *Romans 3:23*

For the wages of sin is death, but the gift of God is eternal life in Christ Jesus our Lord. *Romans 6:23*

The penalty for sinning against the holy God of the Bible must be paid in one of two ways. One way is to receive God's judgment, wrath, and punishment and to be eternally separated from Him in a place called hell. The other way is for Jesus Christ to pay the full penalty for your past, present, and future sins for you. This requires that you acknowledge that you have sinned against God, that you repent of your sins, and that you believe in and follow Jesus Christ as your Savior and Lord. If you have done this, you must still face the consequences of your actions here on earth. However, when you die you will not have to face God's eternal punishment for sinning against Him. This is because Jesus Christ has taken all of your sins upon Himself, paid the full penalty for you, and declares you righteous before God.

"'But if you will not listen to me and carry out all these commands, and if you reject my decrees and abhor my laws and fail to carry out all my commands and so violate my covenant, then I will do this to you: I will bring upon you sudden terror, wasting diseases and fever that will destroy your sight and drain away your life. You will plant seed in vain, because your enemies will eat it. I will set my face against you so that you will be defeated by your enemies; those who hate you will rule over you, and you will flee even when no one is pursuing you. If after all this you will not listen to me, I will punish you for your sins seven times over. I will break down your stubborn pride and make the sky above you like iron and the ground beneath you like bronze. Your strength will be spent in vain, because your soil will not yield its crops, nor will the trees of the land yield their fruit.

Leviticus 26:14–20

You are not a God who takes pleasure in evil; with you the wicked cannot dwell.

"Go and inquire of the LORD for me and for the people and for all Judah about what is written in this book that has been found. Great is the LORD's anger that burns against us because our fathers have not obeyed the words of this book; they have not acted in accordance with all that is written there concerning us."

2 Kings 22:13

You are not a God who takes pleasure in evil; with you the wicked cannot dwell. The arrogant cannot stand in your presence; you hate all who do wrong. You destroy those who tell lies; bloodthirsty and deceitful men the LORD abhors.

Psalm 5:4–6

My shield is God Most High, who saves the upright in heart. God is a righteous judge, a God who expresses his wrath every day.

Psalm 7:10–11

The eyes of the LORD are on the righteous and his ears are attentive to their cry; the face of the LORD is against those who do evil, to cut off the memory of them from the earth.

Psalm 34:15–16

Take heed, you senseless ones among the people; you fools, when will you become wise? Does he who implanted the ear not hear? Does he who formed the eye not see? Does he who disciplines nations not punish? Does he who teaches man lack knowledge? The LORD knows the thoughts of man; he knows that they are futile.

Psalm 94:8–11

God is a righteous judge, a God who expresses his wrath every day.

You reject all who stray from your decrees, for their deceitfulness is in vain. All the wicked of the earth you discard like dross; therefore I love your statutes. My flesh trembles in fear of you; I stand in awe of your laws.

Psalm 119:118–120

But since you rejected me when I called and no one gave heed when I stretched out my hand, since you ignored all my advice and would not accept my rebuke, I in turn will laugh at your disaster; I will mock when calamity overtakes you—when calamity overtakes you like a storm, when disaster sweeps over you like a whirlwind, when distress and trouble overwhelm you.

Proverbs 1:24–27

"Then they will call to me but I will not answer; they will look for me but will not find me. Since they hated knowledge and did not choose to fear the LORD, since they would not accept my advice and spurned my rebuke, they will eat the fruit of their ways and be filled with the fruit of their schemes. For the waywardness of the simple will kill them, and the complacency of fools will destroy them; but whoever listens to me will live in safety and be at ease, without fear of harm."

Proverbs 1:28–33

The LORD detests the way of the wicked but he loves those who pursue righteousness.

Proverbs 15:9

The LORD detests all the proud of heart. Be sure of this: They will not go unpunished.

Stern discipline awaits him who leaves the path; he who hates correction will die.

Proverbs 15:10

The LORD detests all the proud of heart. Be sure of this: They will not go unpunished.

Proverbs 16:5

A false witness will not go unpunished, and he who pours out lies will not go free.

Proverbs 19:5

A man who remains stiff-necked after many rebukes will suddenly be destroyed—without remedy.

Proverbs 29:1

So this is what the Sovereign LORD says: "See, I lay a stone in Zion, a tested stone, a precious cornerstone for a sure foundation; the one who trusts will never be dismayed. I will make justice the measuring line and righteousness the plumb line; hail will sweep away your refuge, the lie, and water will overflow your hiding place.

Isaiah 28:16–17

I will lead the blind by ways they have not known, along unfamiliar paths I will guide them; I will turn the darkness into light before them and make the rough places smooth. These are the things I will do; I will not forsake them. But those who trust in idols, who say to images, 'You are our gods,' will be turned back in utter shame.

Isaiah 42:16–17

I will make justice the measuring line and righteousness the plumb line;

"Come near me and listen to this: "From the first announcement I have not spoken in secret; at the time it happens, I am there." And now the Sovereign Lord has sent me, with his Spirit. This is what the Lord says—your Redeemer, the Holy One of Israel: "I am the Lord your God, who teaches you what is best for you, who directs you in the way you should go. If only you had paid attention to my commands, your peace would have been like a river, your righteousness like the waves of the sea.

Isaiah 48:16–18

Surely the arm of the LORD is not too short to save, nor his ear too dull to hear. But your iniquities have separated you from your God; your sins have hidden his face from you, so that he will not hear.

Isaiah 59:1–2

This is what the LORD says: "Stand at the crossroads and look; ask for the ancient paths, ask where the good way is, and walk in it, and you will find rest for your souls. But you said, 'We will not walk in it.' I appointed watchmen over you and said, 'Listen to the sound of the trumpet!' But you said, 'We will not listen.' Therefore hear, O nations; observe, O witnesses, what will happen to them. Hear, O earth: I am bringing disaster on this people, the fruit of their schemes, because they have not listened to my words and have rejected my law.

Jeremiah 6:16–19

'This is the nation that has not obeyed the LORD its God or responded to correction.

Therefore say to them, 'This is the nation that has not obeyed the LORD its God or responded to correction. Truth has perished; it has vanished from their lips. Cut off your hair and throw it away; take up a lament on the barren heights, for the LORD has rejected and abandoned this generation that is under his wrath.

Jeremiah 7:28–29

The heart is deceitful above all things and beyond cure. Who can understand it? "I the LORD search the heart and examine the mind, to reward a man according to his conduct, according to what his deeds deserve."

Jeremiah 17:9–10

my people are destroyed from lack of knowledge. "Because you have rejected knowledge, I also reject you as my priests; because you have ignored the law of your God, I also will ignore your children.

Hosea 4–6

When I fed them, they were satisfied; when they were satisfied, they became proud; then they forgot me. So I will come upon them like a lion, like a leopard I will lurk by the path. Like a bear robbed of her cubs, I will attack them and rip them open. Like a lion I will devour them; a wild animal will tear them apart.

Hosea 13:6–8

"But they refused to pay attention; stubbornly they turned their backs and stopped up their ears. They made their hearts as hard as flint and would not listen to the law or to the words that the LORD Almighty had sent by his Spirit through the earlier prophets. So the LORD Almighty was very angry. "'When I called, they did not listen; so when they called, I would not listen,' says the LORD Almighty.

Zechariah 7:11–13

'When I called, they did not listen; so when they called, I would not listen,' says the LORD Almighty.

And so I tell you, every sin and blasphemy will be forgiven men, but the blasphemy against the Spirit will not be forgiven. Anyone who speaks a word against the Son of Man will be forgiven, but anyone who speaks against the Holy Spirit will not be forgiven, either in this age or in the age to come.

Matthew 12:31–32

But I tell you that men will have to give account on the day of judgment for every careless word they have spoken. For by your words you will be acquitted, and by your words you will be condemned."

Matthew 12:36–37

The Son of Man will go just as it is written about him. But woe to that man who betrays the Son of Man! It would be better for him if he had not been born."

Mark 14:21

And everyone who speaks a word against the Son of Man will be forgiven, but anyone who blasphemes against the Holy Spirit will not be forgiven.

Luke 12:10

Whoever believes in the Son has eternal life, but whoever rejects the Son will not see life, for God's wrath remains on him."

For the one whom God has sent speaks the words of God, for God gives the Spirit without limit. The Father loves the Son and has placed everything in his hands. Whoever believes in the Son has eternal life, but whoever rejects the Son will not see life, for God's wrath remains on him."

John 3:34–36

"Therefore since we are God's offspring, we should not think that the divine being is like gold or silver or stone—an image made by man's design and skill. In the past God overlooked such ignorance, but now he commands all people everywhere to repent. For he has set a day when he will judge the world with justice by the man he has appointed. He has given proof of this to all men by raising him from the dead."

Acts 17:29–31

The wrath of God is being revealed from heaven against all the godlessness and wickedness of men who suppress the truth by their wickedness, since what may be known about God is plain to them, because God has made it plain to them. For since the creation of the world God's invisible qualities—his eternal power and divine nature—have been clearly seen, being understood from what has been made, so that men are without excuse.

Romans 1:18–20

For although they knew God, they neither glorified him as God nor gave thanks to him, but their thinking became futile and their foolish hearts were darkened. Although they claimed to be wise, they became fools and exchanged the glory of the immortal God for images made to look like mortal man and birds and animals and reptiles.

Romans 1:21–23

The wrath of God is being revealed from heaven against all the godlessness and wickedness of men who suppress the truth by their wickedness,

They exchanged the truth of God for a lie, and worshiped and served created things rather than the Creator—who is forever praised. Amen. Because of this, God gave them over to shameful lusts. Even their women exchanged natural relations for unnatural ones. In the same way the men also abandoned natural relations with women and were inflamed with lust for one another. Men committed indecent acts with other men, and received in themselves the due penalty for their perversion.

Romans 1:25–27

Furthermore, since they did not think it worthwhile to retain the knowledge of God, he gave them over to a depraved mind, to do what ought not to be done. They have become filled with every kind of wickedness, evil, greed and depravity. They are full of envy, murder, strife, deceit and malice. They are gossips, slanderers, God-haters, insolent, arrogant and boastful; they invent ways of doing evil; they disobey their parents; they are senseless, faithless, heartless, ruthless. Although they know God's righteous decree that those who do such things deserve death, they not only continue to do these very things but also approve of those who practice them.

Romans 1:28–32

But for those who are self-seeking and who reject the truth and follow evil, there will be wrath and anger.

But because of your stubbornness and your unrepentant heart, you are storing up wrath against yourself for the day of God's wrath, when his righteous judgment will be revealed. God "will give to each person according to what he has done." To those who by persistence in doing good seek glory, honor and immortality, he will give eternal life. But for those who are self-seeking and who reject the truth and follow evil, there will be wrath and anger.

Romans 2:5–8

For the wages of sin is death, but the gift of God is eternal life in Christ Jesus our Lord.

Romans 6:23

Do not repay anyone evil for evil. Be careful to do what is right in the eyes of everybody. If it is possible, as far as it depends on you, live at peace with everyone. Do not take revenge, my friends, but leave room for God's wrath, for it is written: "It is mine to avenge; I will repay," says the Lord.

Romans 12:17–19

Do you not know that the wicked will not inherit the kingdom of God? Do not be deceived: Neither the sexually immoral nor idolaters nor adulterers nor male prostitutes nor homosexual offenders nor thieves nor the greedy nor drunkards nor slanderers nor swindlers will inherit the kingdom of God. And that is what some of you were. But you were washed, you were sanctified, you were justified in the name of the Lord Jesus Christ and by the Spirit of our God.

1 Corinthians 6:9–11

Do not be deceived: God cannot be mocked. A man reaps what he sows. The one who sows to please his sinful nature, from that nature will reap destruction; the one who sows to please the Spirit, from the Spirit will reap eternal life. Let us not become weary in doing good, for at the proper time we will reap a harvest if we do not give up. Therefore, as we have opportunity, let us do good to all people, especially to those who belong to the family of believers.

Galatians 6:7–10

Do not be deceived: God cannot be mocked. A man reaps what he sows.

But among you there must not be even a hint of sexual immorality, or of any kind of impurity, or of greed, because these are improper for God's holy people. Nor should there be obscenity, foolish talk or coarse joking, which are out of place, but rather thanksgiving. For of this you can be sure: No immoral, impure or greedy person—such a man is an idolater—has any inheritance in the kingdom of Christ and of God. Let no one deceive you with empty words, for because of such things God's wrath comes on those who are disobedient. Therefore do not be partners with them.

Ephesians 5:3–7

For you were once darkness, but now you are light in the Lord. Live as children of light (for the fruit of the light consists in all goodness, righteousness and truth) and find out what pleases the Lord. Have nothing to do with the fruitless deeds of darkness, but rather expose them. For it is shameful even to mention what the disobedient do in secret.

Ephesians 5:8–12

For, as I have often told you before and now say again even with tears, many live as enemies of the cross of Christ. Their destiny is destruction, their god is their stomach, and their glory is in their shame. Their mind is on earthly things.

Philippians 3:18–19

Because of these, the wrath of God is coming.

Put to death, therefore, whatever belongs to your earthly nature: sexual immorality, impurity, lust, evil desires and greed, which is idolatry. Because of these, the wrath of God is coming. You used to walk in these ways, in the life you once lived. But now you must rid yourselves of all such things as these: anger, rage, malice, slander, and filthy language from your lips. Do not lie to each other, since you have taken off your old self with its practices and have put on the new self, which is being renewed in knowledge in the image of its Creator.

Colossians 3:5–10

We ought always to thank God for you, brothers, and rightly so, because your faith is growing more and more, and the love every one of you has for each other is increasing. Therefore, among God's churches we boast about your perseverance and faith in all the persecutions and trials you are enduring. All this is evidence that God's judgment is right, and as a result you will be counted worthy of the kingdom of God, for which you are suffering. God is just: He will pay back trouble to those who trouble you and give relief to you who are troubled, and to us as well. This will happen when the Lord Jesus is revealed from heaven in blazing fire with his powerful angels. He will punish those who do not know God and do not obey the gospel of our Lord Jesus. They will be punished with everlasting destruction and shut out from the presence of the Lord and from the majesty of his power on the day he comes to be glorified in his holy people and to be marveled at among all those who have believed. This includes you, because you believed our testimony to you.

2 Thessalonians 1:3–10

He will punish those who do not know God and do not obey the gospel of our Lord Jesus.

The coming of the lawless one will be in accordance with the work of Satan displayed in all kinds of counterfeit miracles, signs and wonders, and in every sort of evil that deceives those who are perishing. They perish because they refused to love the truth and so be saved. For this reason God sends them a powerful delusion so that they will believe the lie and so that all will be condemned who have not believed the truth but have delighted in wickedness.

2 Thessalonians 2:9–12

If we deliberately keep on sinning after we have received the knowledge of the truth, no sacrifice for sins is left, but only a fearful expectation of judgment and of raging fire that will consume the enemies of God.

Hebrews 10:26–27

How much more severely do you think a man deserves to be punished who has trampled the Son of God under foot, who has treated as an unholy thing the blood of the covenant that sanctified him, and who has insulted the Spirit of grace?

Hebrews 10:29

But there were also false prophets among the people, just as there will be false teachers among you. They will secretly introduce destructive heresies, even denying the sovereign Lord who bought them—bringing swift destruction on themselves. Many will follow their shameful ways and will bring the way of truth into disrepute. In their greed these teachers will exploit you with stories they have made up. Their condemnation has long been hanging over them, and their destruction has not been sleeping.

2 Peter 2:1–3

If they have escaped the corruption of the world by knowing our Lord and Savior Jesus Christ and are again entangled in it and overcome, they are worse off at the end than they were at the beginning. It would have been better for them not to have known the way of righteousness, than to have known it and then to turn their backs on the sacred command that was passed on to them.

2 Peter 2:20–21

If we deliberately keep on sinning after we have received the knowledge of the truth,

no sacrifice for sins is left, but only a fearful expectation of judgment and of raging fire that will consume the enemies of God.

First of all, you must understand that in the last days scoffers will come, scoffing and following their own evil desires. They will say, "Where is this 'coming' he promised? Ever since our fathers died, everything goes on as it has since the beginning of creation." But they deliberately forget that long ago by God's word the heavens existed and the earth was formed out of water and by water. By these waters also the world of that time was deluged and destroyed. By the same word the present heavens and earth are reserved for fire, being kept for the day of judgment and destruction of ungodly men.

2 Peter 3:3–7

Since everything will be destroyed in this way, what kind of people ought you to be? You ought to live holy and godly lives as you look forward to the day of God and speed its coming. That day will bring about the destruction of the heavens by fire, and the elements will melt in the heat. But in keeping with his promise we are looking forward to a new heaven and a new earth, the home of righteousness. So then, dear friends, since you are looking forward to this, make every effort to be found spotless, blameless and at peace with him.

2 Peter 3:11–14

By the same word the present heavens and earth are reserved for fire, being kept for the day of judgment and destruction of ungodly men.

Bear in mind that our Lord's patience means salvation, just as our dear brother Paul also wrote you with the wisdom that God gave him. He writes the same way in all his letters, speaking in them of these matters. His letters contain some things that are hard to understand, which ignorant and unstable people distort, as they do the other Scriptures, to their own destruction.

2 Peter 3:15–16

Then I saw another angel flying in midair, and he had the eternal gospel to proclaim to those who live on the earth—to every nation, tribe, language and people. He said in a loud voice, "Fear God and give him glory, because the hour of his judgment has come. Worship him who made the heavens, the earth, the sea and the springs of water."

Revelation 14:6–7

"Behold, I am coming soon! My reward is with me, and I will give to everyone according to what he has done. I am the Alpha and the Omega, the First and the Last, the Beginning and the End. "Blessed are those who wash their robes, that they may have the right to the tree of life and may go through the gates into the city. Outside are the dogs, those who practice magic arts, the sexually immoral, the murderers, the idolaters and everyone who loves and practices falsehood.

Revelation 22:12–15

"Behold, I am coming soon! My reward is with me, and I will give to everyone according to what he has done.

Chapter 20

God's Justice

He is the Rock, his works are perfect, and all his ways are just. A faithful God who does no wrong, upright and just is he.

Deuteronomy 32:4

What is God's justice, and how does it relate to His mercy and grace? If we are to accurately understand who God really is and how He loves us, we must understand these concepts:

- Sin—The breaking of God's laws. Every sin is a sin against the holy God of the Bible. In God's eyes all sin is evil and deserves punishment and eternal separation from Him.

- **Justice**—Carrying out fair and right punishment against those who break the law.

- Mercy—Treating a lawbreaker better than he or she deserves.

- Grace—Giving someone something good that he or she does not deserve.

The Bible tells us that "*all have sinned*" (Romans 3:23) and that the "*wages of sin is death*" (Romans 6:23). We must never forget that God is a God of justice and that the just penalty for sin must be paid. Thankfully, our loving God, in His grace and mercy, sent Jesus Christ to earth to pay the penalty for our sins. God, through the Bible, calls human beings to repent of their sins and put their faith in Jesus Christ as their Savior and Lord. Jesus tells us in John 14:6 that God's forgiveness for our sins and eternal life in heaven come only through Him: "*Jesus answered, 'I am the way and the truth and the life. No one comes to the Father except through me.'*"

For those who choose to follow the Lord Jesus Christ and repent of their sins, the just penalty for their sins has been paid in full by Him. For those unwilling to repent and trust in Him, they themselves will pay the just penalty for their sins through eternal separation from God in a place called hell. God's perfect justice prevails—one way or the other.

"'But if you will not listen to me and carry out all these commands, and if you reject my decrees and abhor my laws and fail to carry out all my commands and so violate my covenant, then I will do this to you: I will bring upon you sudden terror, wasting diseases and fever that will destroy your sight and drain away your life. You will plant seed in vain, because your enemies will eat it. I will set my face against you so that you will be defeated by your enemies; those who hate you will rule over you, and you will flee even when no one is pursuing you. If after all this you will not listen to me, I will punish you for your sins seven times over. I will break down your stubborn pride and make the sky above you like iron and the ground beneath you like bronze. Your strength will be spent in vain, because your soil will not yield its crops, nor will the trees of the land yield their fruit.

Leviticus 26:14–20

For the LORD your God is God of gods and Lord of lords, the great God, mighty and awesome, who shows no partiality and accepts no bribes.

For the LORD your God is God of gods and Lord of lords, the great God, mighty and awesome, who shows no partiality and accepts no bribes.

Deuteronomy 10:17

Now what I am commanding you today is not too difficult for you or beyond your reach. It is not up in heaven, so that you have to ask, "Who will ascend into heaven to get it and proclaim it to us so we may obey it?" Nor is it beyond the sea, so that you have to ask, "Who will cross the sea to get it and proclaim it to us so we may obey it?" No, the word is very near you; it is in your mouth and in your heart so you may obey it.

Deuteronomy 30:11–14

See, I set before you today life and prosperity, death and destruction. For I command you today to love the Lord your God, to walk in his ways, and to keep his commands, decrees and laws; then you will live and increase, and the Lord your God will bless you in the land you are entering to possess. But if your heart turns away and you are not obedient, and if you are drawn away to bow down to other gods and worship them, I declare to you this day that you will certainly be destroyed. You will not live long in the land you are crossing the Jordan to enter and possess.

Deuteronomy 30:15–18

This day I call heaven and earth as witnesses against you that I have set before you life and death, blessings and curses. Now choose life, so that you and your children may live and that you may love the Lord your God, listen to his voice, and hold fast to him. For the Lord is your life, and he will give you many years in the land he swore to give to your fathers, Abraham, Isaac and Jacob.

Deuteronomy 30:19–20

He is the Rock, his works are perfect, and all his ways are just. A faithful God who does no wrong, upright and just is he.

He is the Rock, his works are perfect, and all his ways are just. A faithful God who does no wrong, upright and just is he.

Deuteronomy 32:4

My shield is God Most High, who saves the upright in heart. God is a righteous judge, a God who expresses his wrath every day.

Psalm 7:10–11

The LORD reigns forever; he has established his throne for judgment. He will judge the world in righteousness; he will govern the peoples with justice.

Psalm 9:7–8

For the LORD is righteous, he loves justice; upright men will see his face.

Psalm 11:7

For the LORD is righteous, he loves justice; upright men will see his face.

The law of the LORD is perfect, reviving the soul. The statutes of the LORD are trustworthy, making wise the simple. The precepts of the LORD are right, giving joy to the heart. The commands of the LORD are radiant, giving light to the eyes. The fear of the LORD is pure, enduring forever. The ordinances of the LORD are sure and altogether righteous. They are more precious than gold, than much pure gold; they are sweeter than honey, than honey from the comb. By them is your servant warned; in keeping them there is great reward.

Psalm 19:7–11

For the word of the Lord is right and true; he is faithful in all he does. The Lord loves righteousness and justice; the earth is full of his unfailing love.

Psalm 33:4–5

Your love, O LORD, reaches to the heavens, your faithfulness to the skies. Your righteousness is like the mighty mountains, your justice like the great deep. O LORD, you preserve both man and beast. How priceless is your unfailing love! Both high and low among men find refuge in the shadow of your wings.

Psalm 36:5–7

Commit your way to the LORD; trust in him and he will do this: He will make your righteousness shine like the dawn, the justice of your cause like the noonday sun.

Psalm 37:5–6

Turn from evil and do good; then you will dwell in the land forever. For the Lord loves the just and will not forsake his faithful ones. They will be protected forever, but the offspring of the wicked will be cut off; the righteous will inherit the land and dwell in it forever. The mouth of the righteous man utters wisdom, and his tongue speaks what is just. The law of his God is in his heart; his feet do not slip.

Psalm 37:27–31

Righteous are you, O LORD, and your laws are right. The statutes you have laid down are righteous; they are fully trustworthy.

Psalm 119:137–138

The LORD abhors dishonest scales, but accurate weights are his delight.

Proverbs 11:1

A false witness will not go unpunished, and he who pours out lies will not go free.

Proverbs 19:5

To do what is right and just is more acceptable to the LORD than sacrifice.

Proverbs 21:3

Turn from evil and do good; then you will dwell in the land forever. For the Lord loves the just and will not forsake his faithful ones.

Evil men do not understand justice, but those who seek the LORD understand it fully.

Proverbs 28:5

Woe to those who call evil good and good evil, who put darkness for light and light for darkness, who put bitter for sweet and sweet for bitter. Woe to those who are wise in their own eyes and clever in their own sight.

Isaiah 50:20–21

> **Evil men do not understand justice, but those who seek the LORD understand it fully.**

So this is what the Sovereign LORD says: "See, I lay a stone in Zion, a tested stone, a precious cornerstone for a sure foundation; the one who trusts will never be dismayed. I will make justice the measuring line and righteousness the plumb line; hail will sweep away your refuge, the lie, and water will overflow your hiding place.

Isaiah 28:16–17

Yet the LORD longs to be gracious to you; he rises to show you compassion. For the LORD is a God of justice. Blessed are all who wait for him!

Isaiah 30:18

The LORD is exalted, for he dwells on high; he will fill Zion with justice and righteousness. He will be the sure foundation for your times, a rich store of salvation and wisdom and knowledge; the fear of the LORD is the key to this treasure.

Isaiah 33:5–6

For the LORD is our judge, the LORD is our lawgiver, the LORD is our king; it is he who will save us.

Isaiah 33:22

I have not spoken in secret, from somewhere in a land of darkness; I have not said to Jacob's descendants, 'Seek me in vain.' I, the LORD, speak the truth; I declare what is right.

Isaiah 45:19

"Come near me and listen to this: "From the first announcement I have not spoken in secret; at the time it happens, I am there." And now the Sovereign Lord has sent me, with his Spirit. This is what the Lord says—your Redeemer, the Holy One of Israel: "I am the Lord your God, who teaches you what is best for you, who directs you in the way you should go. If only you had paid attention to my commands, your peace would have been like a river, your righteousness like the waves of the sea.

Isaiah 48:16–18

So justice is driven back, and righteousness stands at a distance; truth has stumbled in the streets, honesty cannot enter.

So justice is driven back, and righteousness stands at a distance; truth has stumbled in the streets, honesty cannot enter. Truth is nowhere to be found, and whoever shuns evil becomes a prey. The LORD looked and was displeased that there was no justice.

Isaiah 59:14–15

This is what the LORD says: "Let not the wise man boast of his wisdom or the strong man boast of his strength or the rich man boast of his riches, but let him who boasts boast about this: that he understands and knows me, that I am the LORD, who exercises kindness, justice and righteousness on earth, for in these I delight," declares the LORD.

Jeremiah 9:23–24

And if at another time I announce that a nation or kingdom is to be built up and planted, and if it does evil in my sight and does not obey me, then I will reconsider the good I had intended to do for it.

Jeremiah 18:9–10

that I am the LORD, who exercises kindness, justice and righteousness on earth, for in these I delight," declares the LORD.

Now I, Nebuchadnezzar, praise and exalt and glorify the King of heaven, because everything he does is right and all his ways are just. And those who walk in pride he is able to humble.

Daniel 4:37

"But they refused to pay attention; stubbornly they turned their backs and stopped up their ears. They made their hearts as hard as flint and would not listen to the law or to the words that the LORD Almighty had sent by his Spirit through the earlier prophets. So the LORD Almighty was very angry. "'When I called, they did not listen; so when they called, I would not listen,' says the LORD Almighty.

Zechariah 7:11–13

"Woe to the world because of the things that cause people to sin! Such things must come, but woe to the man through whom they come!

Matthew 18:7

The Son of Man will go just as it is written about him. But woe to that man who betrays the Son of Man! It would be better for him if he had not been born."

Mark 14:21

Moreover, the Father judges no one, but has entrusted all judgment to the Son, that all may honor the Son just as they honor the Father. He who does not honor the Son does not honor the Father, who sent him.

John 5:22–23

"Therefore since we are God's offspring, we should not think that the divine being is like gold or silver or stone—an image made by man's design and skill. In the past God overlooked such ignorance, but now he commands all people everywhere to repent. For he has set a day when he will judge the world with justice by the man he has appointed. He has given proof of this to all men by raising him from the dead."

Acts 17:29–31

For he has set a day when he will judge the world with justice by the man he has appointed. He has given proof of this to all men by raising him from the dead."

But because of your stubbornness and your unrepentant heart, you are storing up wrath against yourself for the day of God's wrath, when his righteous judgment will be revealed. God "will give to each person according to what he has done." To those who by persistence in doing good seek glory, honor and immortality, he will give eternal life. But for those who are self-seeking and who reject the truth and follow evil, there will be wrath and anger.

Romans 2:5–8

For the wages of sin is death, but the gift of God is eternal life in Christ Jesus our Lord.

Romans 6:23

For the wages of sin is death, but the gift of God is eternal life in Christ Jesus our Lord.

Do not repay anyone evil for evil. Be careful to do what is right in the eyes of everybody. If it is possible, as far as it depends on you, live at peace with everyone. Do not take revenge, my friends, but leave room for God's wrath, for it is written: "It is mine to avenge; I will repay," says the Lord.

Romans 12:17–19

When you were dead in your sins and in the uncircumcision of your sinful nature, God made you alive with Christ. He forgave us all our sins, having canceled the written code, with its regulations, that was against us and that stood opposed to us; he took it away, nailing it to the cross.

Colossians 2:13-14

How much more severely do you think a man deserves
to be punished who has trampled the Son of God under
foot, who has treated as an unholy thing the blood of the
covenant that sanctified him, and who has insulted the
Spirit of grace?

Hebrews 10:29

For Christ died for sins once for all, the righteous for the
unrighteous, to bring you to God. He was put to death in
the body but made alive by the Spirit,

1 Peter 3:18

I saw heaven standing open and there before me was a white
horse, whose rider is called Faithful and True. With justice
he judges and makes war. His eyes are like blazing fire, and
on his head are many crowns. He has a name written on
him that no one knows but he himself. He is dressed in a
robe dipped in blood, and his name is the Word of God.
The armies of heaven were following him, riding on white
horses and dressed in fine linen, white and clean. Out of his
mouth comes a sharp sword with which to strike down the
nations. "He will rule them with an iron scepter." He treads
the winepress of the fury of the wrath of God Almighty.
On his robe and on his thigh he has this name written:
KING OF KINGS AND LORD OF LORDS.

Revelation 19:11–16

**For Christ died
for sins once for all,
the righteous
for the unrighteous,
to bring you to God.**

I warn everyone who hears the words of the prophecy of
this book: If anyone adds anything to them, God will add
to him the plagues described in this book. And if anyone
takes words away from this book of prophecy, God will
take away from him his share in the tree of life and in the
holy city, which are described in this book.

Revelation 22:18–19

Chapter 21

God's Love

But God demonstrates his own love for us in this: While we were still sinners, Christ died for us.

Romans 5:8

God is love. God created us in His image so that He could love us and so that we could love Him in return. God's love is reflected throughout the Bible by His desire for, and pursuit of, a loving relationship with each person for eternity. God's divine love is a love that perseveres in pursuing us even while we are sinning against Him. Sin is the breaking of God's laws, and every sin is a sin against the holy God of the Bible. God's love is reflected in the patience, mercy, and grace that He shows each one of us.

God is indeed a God of love. However, God's nature and character are not limited to one trait like love. God has many additional traits, such as patience, kindness, mercy, and grace. But His traits also include righteousness and justice. God perfectly demonstrates all of His traits as he deals with human beings. We should never presume that because God is a God of love that He will allow a person's sins to go unpunished forever. God's justice requires that the penalty for sin, any sin, must always be paid. Romans 6:23 tells us, *"For the wages of sin is death, but the gift of God is eternal life in Christ Jesus our Lord."*

It is because of God's great love for us that He sent His sinless Son, Jesus Christ, into the world to pay the full penalty for our past, present, and future sins. Out of love for us, the Lord Jesus Christ took upon Himself the punishment that we deserve—God's wrath against sin. However, Jesus Christ's sacrifice on the cross only covers the sins of those who acknowledge that they have sinned against God, repent of their sins, ask God for His forgiveness, and believe in and follow Jesus Christ as their sin-bearer, Savior, and Lord. Those who truly follow this path will fully experience God's love and will live with Jesus Christ in heaven for eternity.

Then the LORD came down in the cloud and stood there with him and proclaimed his name, the LORD. And he passed in front of Moses, proclaiming, "The LORD, the LORD, the compassionate and gracious God, slow to anger, abounding in love and faithfulness,

Exodus 34:5–6

All the ways of the LORD are loving and faithful for those who keep the demands of his covenant.

Psalm 25:10

Many are the woes of the wicked, but the LORD's unfailing love surrounds the man who trusts in him.

Psalm 32:10

All the ways of the LORD are loving and faithful for those who keep the demands of his covenant.

Your love, O LORD, reaches to the heavens, your faithfulness to the skies. Your righteousness is like the mighty mountains, your justice like the great deep. O LORD, you preserve both man and beast. How priceless is your unfailing love! Both high and low among men find refuge in the shadow of your wings.

Psalm 36:5–7

Teach me your way, O LORD, and I will walk in your truth; give me an undivided heart, that I may fear your name. I will praise you, O Lord my God, with all my heart; I will glorify your name forever. For great is your love toward me; you have delivered me from the depths of the grave.

Psalm 86:11–13

For the LORD is good and his love endures forever; his faithfulness continues through all generations.

Psalm 100:5

Praise the LORD, O my soul; all my inmost being, praise his holy name. Praise the LORD, O my soul, and forget not all his benefits—who forgives all your sins and heals all your diseases, who redeems your life from the pit and crowns you with love and compassion, who satisfies your desires with good things so that your youth is renewed like the eagle's.

Psalm 103:1–5

The LORD is compassionate and gracious, slow to anger, abounding in love. He will not always accuse, nor will he harbor his anger forever; he does not treat us as our sins deserve or repay us according to our iniquities. For as high as the heavens are above the earth, so great is his love for those who fear him;

Psalm 103:8–11

For as high as the heavens are above the earth, so great is his love for those who fear him;

As a father has compassion on his children, so the LORD has compassion on those who fear him;

Psalm 103:13

For great is your love, higher than the heavens; your faithfulness reaches to the skies. Be exalted, O God, above the heavens, and let your glory be over all the earth.

Psalm 108:4–5

The LORD is righteous in all his ways and loving toward all he has made.

Psalm 145:17

My son, do not despise the LORD's discipline and do not resent his rebuke, because the LORD disciplines those he loves, as a father the son he delights in.

Proverbs 3:11–12

I love those who love me, and those who seek me find me.

Proverbs 8:17

**My son,
do not despise
the LORD's discipline
and do not resent
his rebuke,
because the LORD
disciplines those he loves,
as a father the son
he delights in.**

The LORD detests the way of the wicked but he loves those who pursue righteousness.

Proverbs 15:9

Through love and faithfulness sin is atoned for; through the fear of the LORD a man avoids evil.

Proverbs 16:6

Yet the LORD longs to be gracious to you; he rises to show you compassion. For the LORD is a God of justice. Blessed are all who wait for him!

Isaiah 30:18

"For God so loved the world that he gave his one and only Son, that whoever believes in him shall not perish but have eternal life. For God did not send his Son into the world to condemn the world, but to save the world through him. Whoever believes in him is not condemned, but whoever does not believe stands condemned already because he has not believed in the name of God's one and only Son.

John 3:16–18

"As the Father has loved me, so have I loved you. Now remain in my love. If you obey my commands, you will remain in my love, just as I have obeyed my Father's commands and remain in his love. I have told you this so that my joy may be in you and that your joy may be complete.

John 15:9–11

Not only so, but we also rejoice in our sufferings, because we know that suffering produces perseverance; perseverance, character; and character, hope. And hope does not disappoint us, because God has poured out his love into our hearts by the Holy Spirit, whom he has given us.

Romans 5:3–5

But God demonstrates his own love for us in this: While we were still sinners, Christ died for us.

Romans 5:8

For the wages of sin is death, but the gift of God is eternal life in Christ Jesus our Lord.

Romans 6:23

For God so loved the world that he gave his one and only Son, that whoever believes in him shall not perish but have eternal life.

Who shall separate us from the love of Christ? Shall trouble or hardship or persecution or famine or nakedness or danger or sword? As it is written: "For your sake we face death all day long; we are considered as sheep to be slaughtered." No, in all these things we are more than conquerors through him who loved us. For I am convinced that neither death nor life, neither angels nor demons, neither the present nor the future, nor any powers, neither height nor depth, nor anything else in all creation, will be able to separate us from the love of God that is in Christ Jesus our Lord.

Romans 8:35–39

**"No eye has seen,
no ear has heard,
no mind has conceived
what God has prepared
for those who love him"**

However, as it is written: "No eye has seen, no ear has heard, no mind has conceived what God has prepared for those who love him"—

1 Corinthians 2:9

May the grace of the Lord Jesus Christ, and the love of God, and the fellowship of the Holy Spirit be with you all.

2 Corinthians 13:14

But because of his great love for us, God, who is rich in mercy, made us alive with Christ even when we were dead in transgressions—it is by grace you have been saved.

Ephesians 2:4–5

For it is by grace you have been saved, through faith—and this not from yourselves, it is the gift of God—not by works, so that no one can boast. For we are God's workmanship, created in Christ Jesus to do good works, which God prepared in advance for us to do.

Ephesians 2:8–10

For this reason I kneel before the Father, from whom his whole family in heaven and on earth derives its name. I pray that out of his glorious riches he may strengthen you with power through his Spirit in your inner being, so that Christ may dwell in your hearts through faith. And I pray that you, being rooted and established in love, may have power, together with all the saints, to grasp how wide and long and high and deep is the love of Christ, and to know this love that surpasses knowledge—that you may be filled to the measure of all the fullness of God.

Ephesians 3:14–19

But we ought always to thank God for you, brothers loved by the Lord, because from the beginning God chose you to be saved through the sanctifying work of the Spirit and through belief in the truth. He called you to this through our gospel, that you might share in the glory of our Lord Jesus Christ.

2 Thessalonians 2:13–14

Here is a trustworthy saying that deserves full acceptance: Christ Jesus came into the world to save sinners—of whom I am the worst. But for that very reason I was shown mercy so that in me, the worst of sinners, Christ Jesus might display his unlimited patience as an example for those who would believe on him and receive eternal life.

1 Timothy 1:15–16

This is good, and pleases God our Savior, who wants all men to be saved and to come to a knowledge of the truth. For there is one God and one mediator between God and men, the man Christ Jesus, who gave himself as a ransom for all men—the testimony given in its proper time.

1 Timothy 2:3–6

And I pray that you, being rooted and established in love, may have power, together with all the saints, to grasp how wide and long and high and deep is the love of Christ, and to know this love that surpasses knowledge

So do not be ashamed to testify about our Lord, or ashamed of me his prisoner. But join with me in suffering for the gospel, by the power of God, who has saved us and called us to a holy life—not because of anything we have done but because of his own purpose and grace. This grace was given us in Christ Jesus before the beginning of time,

2 Timothy 1:8–9

At one time we too were foolish, disobedient, deceived and enslaved by all kinds of passions and pleasures. We lived in malice and envy, being hated and hating one another. But when the kindness and love of God our Savior appeared, he saved us, not because of righteous things we had done, but because of his mercy. He saved us through the washing of rebirth and renewal by the Holy Spirit, whom he poured out on us generously through Jesus Christ our Savior, so that, having been justified by his grace, we might become heirs having the hope of eternal life. This is a trustworthy saying. And I want you to stress these things, so that those who have trusted in God may be careful to devote themselves to doing what is good. These things are excellent and profitable for everyone.

Titus 3:3–8

But when the kindness and love of God our Savior appeared, he saved us, not because of righteous things we had done, but because of his mercy.

The Lord is not slow in keeping his promise, as some understand slowness. He is patient with you, not wanting anyone to perish, but everyone to come to repentance.

2 Peter 3:9

How great is the love the Father has lavished on us, that we should be called children of God! And that is what we are! The reason the world does not know us is that it did not know him.

1 John 3:1

This is how God showed his love among us: He sent his one and only Son into the world that we might live through him. This is love: not that we loved God, but that he loved us and sent his Son as an atoning sacrifice for our sins. Dear friends, since God so loved us, we also ought to love one another.

1 John 4:9–11

And so we know and rely on the love God has for us. God is love. Whoever lives in love lives in God, and God in him.

1 John 4:16

**This is love:
not that we loved God,
but that he loved us
and sent his Son
as an atoning sacrifice
for our sins.**

241

Chapter 22

God's Mercy

**Therefore, I urge you, brothers, in view of God's mercy,
to offer your bodies as living sacrifices, holy and pleasing
to God—this is your spiritual act of worship.**

Romans 12:1

In order to understand and appreciate God's mercy it is helpful to understand how it differs from His grace and justice. These three attributes of God—justice, mercy, and grace—help us to understand how God chooses to respond to sin. If we are to accurately understand who God really is and how He loves us, we must understand these concepts:

- Sin—The breaking of God's laws. Every sin is a sin against the holy God of the Bible. In God's eyes all sin is evil and deserves punishment and eternal separation from Him.

- Justice—Carrying out fair and right punishment against those who break the law.

- **Mercy**—Treating a lawbreaker better than he or she deserves.

- Grace—Giving someone something good that he or she does not deserve.

The Bible tells us that "*all have sinned*" (Romans 3:23) and that the "*wages of sin is death*" (Romans 6:23). The just punishment for sinning against God is receiving God's wrath against sin and being separated from Him for eternity in a place called hell. However, God, through His grace, sent Jesus Christ into this world to pay the full penalty for our sins so that we may be forgiven. God desires that all people would seek Him, repent of their sins, and place their faith in Jesus Christ as their sin-bearer, Savior, and Lord. Jeremiah 29:13 tells us, "*You will seek me and find me when you seek me with all your heart.*" It is God's mercy that delays for a time His final judgment for our sins, thereby giving us precious time to truly seek Him and find Him. It is because of God's mercy that we are able to enjoy for a time many of His blessings each day. May we never take God's mercy for granted.

Then the LORD came down in the cloud and stood there with him and proclaimed his name, the LORD. And he passed in front of Moses, proclaiming, "The LORD, the LORD, the compassionate and gracious God, slow to anger, abounding in love and faithfulness,

Exodus 34:5–6

For the LORD is good and his love endures forever; his faithfulness continues through all generations.

Psalm 100:5

he does not treat us as our sins deserve or repay us according to our iniquities.

For as high as the heavens are above the earth, so great is his love for those who fear him;

The LORD is compassionate and gracious, slow to anger, abounding in love. He will not always accuse, nor will he harbor his anger forever; he does not treat us as our sins deserve or repay us according to our iniquities. For as high as the heavens are above the earth, so great is his love for those who fear him; as far as the east is from the west, so far has he removed our transgressions from us. As a father has compassion on his children, so the LORD has compassion on those who fear him;

Psalm 103:8–13

For great is your love, higher than the heavens; your faithfulness reaches to the skies. Be exalted, O God, above the heavens, and let your glory be over all the earth.

Psalm 108:4–5

He who conceals his sins does not prosper, but whoever confesses and renounces them finds mercy.

Proverbs 28:13

Yet the LORD longs to be gracious to you; he rises to show you compassion. For the LORD is a God of justice. Blessed are all who wait for him!

Isaiah 30:18

Seek the LORD while he may be found; call on him while he is near. Let the wicked forsake his way and the evil man his thoughts. Let him turn to the LORD, and he will have mercy on him, and to our God, for he will freely pardon.

Isaiah 55:6–7

'Even now,' declares the LORD, 'return to me with all your heart, with fasting and weeping and mourning.' Rend your heart and not your garments. Return to the LORD your God, for he is gracious and compassionate, slow to anger and abounding in love, and he relents from sending calamity.

Joel 2:12–13

Blessed are the merciful, for they will be shown mercy.

Now when he saw the crowds, he went up on a mountainside and sat down. His disciples came to him, and he began to teach them, saying: "Blessed are the poor in spirit, for theirs is the kingdom of heaven. Blessed are those who mourn, for they will be comforted. Blessed are the meek, for they will inherit the earth. Blessed are those who hunger and thirst for righteousness, for they will be filled. Blessed are the merciful, for they will be shown mercy.

Matthew 5:1–7

But love your enemies, do good to them, and lend to them without expecting to get anything back. Then your reward will be great, and you will be sons of the Most High, because he is kind to the ungrateful and wicked. Be merciful, just as your Father is merciful.

Luke 6:35–36

Therefore, I urge you, brothers, in view of God's mercy, to offer your bodies as living sacrifices, holy and pleasing to God—this is your spiritual act of worship.

Romans 12:1

But because of his great love for us, God, who is rich in mercy, made us alive with Christ even when we were dead in transgressions

Praise be to the God and Father of our Lord Jesus Christ, the Father of compassion and the God of all comfort, who comforts us in all our troubles, so that we can comfort those in any trouble with the comfort we ourselves have received from God.

2 Corinthians 1:3–4

As for you, you were dead in your transgressions and sins, in which you used to live when you followed the ways of this world and of the ruler of the kingdom of the air, the spirit who is now at work in those who are disobedient. All of us also lived among them at one time, gratifying the cravings of our sinful nature and following its desires and thoughts. Like the rest, we were by nature objects of wrath. But because of his great love for us, God, who is rich in mercy, made us alive with Christ even when we were dead in transgressions—it is by grace you have been saved.

Ephesians 2:1–5

Here is a trustworthy saying that deserves full acceptance:
Christ Jesus came into the world to save sinners—of whom
I am the worst. But for that very reason I was shown mercy
so that in me, the worst of sinners, Christ Jesus might
display his unlimited patience as an example for those who
would believe on him and receive eternal life.

1 Timothy 1:15–16

At one time we too were foolish, disobedient, deceived and
enslaved by all kinds of passions and pleasures. We lived in
malice and envy, being hated and hating one another. But
when the kindness and love of God our Savior appeared, he
saved us, not because of righteous things we had done, but
because of his mercy. He saved us through the washing of
rebirth and renewal by the Holy Spirit, whom he poured
out on us generously through Jesus Christ our Savior, so
that, having been justified by his grace, we might become
heirs having the hope of eternal life. This is a trustworthy
saying. And I want you to stress these things, so that
those who have trusted in God may be careful to devote
themselves to doing what is good. These things are excellent
and profitable for everyone.

Titus 3:3–8

**But when the
kindness and love
of God our Savior
appeared,
he saved us,
not because
of righteous things
we had done,
but because of
his mercy.**

Praise be to the God and Father of our Lord Jesus Christ!
In his great mercy he has given us new birth into a living
hope through the resurrection of Jesus Christ from the
dead, and into an inheritance that can never perish, spoil or
fade—kept in heaven for you,

1 Peter 1:3–4

Chapter 23

God's Patience

The Lord is not slow in keeping his promise, as some understand slowness. He is patient with you, not wanting anyone to perish, but everyone to come to repentance.

2 Peter 3:9

What does the Bible teach us about God's kind of patience? The following are some things I have learned about patience from studying the Bible:

- God is love, and God's kind of love includes patience.

- Throughout the Bible God demonstrates His patience with sinful people.

- God calls us to love others. He tells us that being patient with another person is part of what it means to love that person.

- Being patient with another person means that we must put aside being selfish and prideful. It means sometimes delaying or giving up something we want very much.

- Patience is one of the fruits of the Holy Spirit (Galatians 5:22-23). Patience should be a trait that others recognize in every Christian.

The Bible says that one of the reasons that God is patient with people is to give them additional time to choose to repent of their sins and place their faith in Jesus Christ as their sin-bearer, Savior, and Lord. However, there comes a point in time when God's patience ends with individuals who continue to reject the Holy Spirit's prompting. This can happen either at or before physical death from continually hardening one's heart toward God. When this happens, a person's window of opportunity to come into an eternal relationship with God is permanently closed. May we never take God's patience for granted. May we also be understanding and patient with one another as we strive to live out God's command in Mark 12:31: *"Love your neighbor as yourself."*

Then the LORD came down in the cloud and stood there with him and proclaimed his name, the LORD. And he passed in front of Moses, proclaiming, "The LORD, the LORD, the compassionate and gracious God, slow to anger, abounding in love and faithfulness,

Exodus 34:5–6

"The LORD, the LORD, the compassionate and gracious God, slow to anger, abounding in love and faithfulness,

The LORD is compassionate and gracious, slow to anger, abounding in love. He will not always accuse, nor will he harbor his anger forever; he does not treat us as our sins deserve or repay us according to our iniquities. For as high as the heavens are above the earth, so great is his love for those who fear him; as far as the east is from the west, so far has he removed our transgressions from us. As a father has compassion on his children, so the LORD has compassion on those who fear him;

Psalm 103:8–13

Then Isaiah said, "Hear now, you house of David! Is it not enough to try the patience of men? Will you try the patience of my God also? Therefore the Lord himself will give you a sign: The virgin will be with child and will give birth to a son, and will call him Immanuel.

Isaiah 7:13–14

Seek the LORD while he may be found; call on him while he is near. Let the wicked forsake his way and the evil man his thoughts. Let him turn to the LORD, and he will have mercy on him, and to our God, for he will freely pardon.

Isaiah 55:6–7

'Even now,' declares the LORD, 'return to me with all
your heart, with fasting and weeping and mourning.'
Rend your heart and not your garments. Return to the
LORD your God, for he is gracious and compassionate,
slow to anger and abounding in love, and he relents from
sending calamity.

Joel 2:12–13

May the God who gives endurance and encouragement give
you a spirit of unity among yourselves as you follow Christ
Jesus, so that with one heart and mouth you may glorify
the God and Father of our Lord Jesus Christ. Accept one
another, then, just as Christ accepted you, in order to bring
praise to God.

Romans 15:5–7

**But the
fruit of the Spirit
is love, joy, peace,
patience, kindness,
goodness, faithfulness,
gentleness and
self-control.**

Love is patient, love is kind. It does not envy, it does not
boast, it is not proud. It is not rude, it is not self-seeking,
it is not easily angered, it keeps no record of wrongs. Love
does not delight in evil but rejoices with the truth. It always
protects, always trusts, always hopes, always perseveres.

1 Corinthians 13:4–7

But the fruit of the Spirit is love, joy, peace, patience,
kindness, goodness, faithfulness, gentleness and self-control.
Against such things there is no law. Those who belong
to Christ Jesus have crucified the sinful nature with its
passions and desires. Since we live by the Spirit, let us keep
in step with the Spirit.

Galatians 5:22–25

Here is a trustworthy saying that deserves full acceptance: Christ Jesus came into the world to save sinners—of whom I am the worst. But for that very reason I was shown mercy so that in me, the worst of sinners, Christ Jesus might display his unlimited patience as an example for those who would believe on him and receive eternal life.

1 Timothy 1:15–16

The Lord is not slow in keeping his promise, as some understand slowness. He is patient with you, not wanting anyone to perish, but everyone to come to repentance.

2 Peter 3:9

He is patient with you, not wanting anyone to perish, but everyone to come to repentance.

Bear in mind that our Lord's patience means salvation, just as our dear brother Paul also wrote you with the wisdom that God gave him. He writes the same way in all his letters, speaking in them of these matters. His letters contain some things that are hard to understand, which ignorant and unstable people distort, as they do the other Scriptures, to their own destruction.

2 Peter 3:15–16

Chapter 24

God's Power Over the Universe

In the beginning God created the heavens and the earth.
Genesis 1:1

God is the creator and sustainer of all creation: the physical universe, the earth, and everything that is visible and invisible. This includes all life on earth as well as the living beings that inhabit the spiritual realm—the angels that serve God and the fallen angels that oppose Him. God is in control of the laws of nature that govern our physical universe. These include the laws of physics, chemistry, and biology. He is the source of the order and beauty that we see everywhere in the natural world. He literally holds the universe together at all levels—from galaxy clusters and beyond, to living cells, down to the smallest subatomic particles and energy. Apart from God's sustaining power and imposed order, our physical universe and all of life would cease to exist as we know it. We should be eternally grateful that the all-powerful Creator of the universe is not only a God of righteousness and justice, but is also a God of love, mercy, and grace.

God, who is holy, loving, and all-powerful, invites us into a personal relationship with Him for eternity. He allows us to choose how we will live our lives and how we will respond to His invitation to know Jesus Christ as our Savior and Lord. As powerful as God is, He will not force us to believe in and follow Jesus Christ. The Lord Jesus Christ tells us in John 3:16–18: *"For God so loved the world that he gave his one and only Son, that whoever believes in him shall not perish but have eternal life. For God did not send his Son into the world to condemn the world, but to save the world through him. Whoever believes in him is not condemned, but whoever does not believe stands condemned already because he has not believed in the name of God's one and only Son."* The all-powerful Creator of the universe allows you to choose what role, if any, you will allow the Lord Jesus Christ to have in your life.

In the beginning God created the heavens and the earth.

Genesis 1:1

Then God said, "Let the land produce vegetation: seed-bearing plants and trees on the land that bear fruit with seed in it, according to their various kinds." And it was so.

Genesis 1:11

Yours, O Lord, is the greatness and the power and the glory and the majesty and the splendor, for everything in heaven and earth is yours. Yours, O Lord, is the kingdom; you are exalted as head over all. Wealth and honor come from you; you are the ruler of all things. In your hands are strength and power to exalt and give strength to all. Now, our God, we give you thanks, and praise your glorious name.

1 Chronicles 29:11–13

He performs wonders that cannot be fathomed, miracles that cannot be counted.

For the eyes of the Lord range throughout the earth to strengthen those whose hearts are fully committed to him.

2 Chronicles 16:9a

He alone stretches out the heavens and treads on the waves of the sea. He is the Maker of the Bear and Orion, the Pleiades and the constellations of the south. He performs wonders that cannot be fathomed, miracles that cannot be counted.

Job 9:8–10

"But ask the animals, and they will teach you, or the birds of the air, and they will tell you; or speak to the earth, and it will teach you, or let the fish of the sea inform you. Which of all these does not know that the hand of the LORD has done this? In his hand is the life of every creature and the breath of all mankind.

Job 12:7–10

"To God belong wisdom and power; counsel and understanding are his.

Job 12:13

He spreads out the northern skies over empty space; he suspends the earth over nothing. He wraps up the waters in his clouds, yet the clouds do not burst under their weight. He covers the face of the full moon, spreading his clouds over it. He marks out the horizon on the face of the waters for a boundary between light and darkness.

Job 26:7–10

In his hand is the life of every creature and the breath of all mankind.

Then Job replied to the LORD: "I know that you can do all things; no plan of yours can be thwarted.

Job 42:1–2

The earth is the LORD's, and everything in it, the world, and all who live in it; for he founded it upon the seas and established it upon the waters.

Psalm 24:1–2

By the word of the Lord were the heavens made, their starry host by the breath of his mouth. He gathers the waters of the sea into jars; he puts the deep into storehouses. Let all the earth fear the Lord; let all the people of the world revere him. For he spoke, and it came to be; he commanded, and it stood firm.

Psalm 33:6–9

Blessed is the nation whose God is the LORD, the people he chose for his inheritance. From heaven the LORD looks down and sees all mankind; from his dwelling place he watches all who live on earth—he who forms the hearts of all, who considers everything they do. No king is saved by the size of his army; no warrior escapes by his great strength.

Psalm 33:12–16

By the word of the Lord were the heavens made, their starry host by the breath of his mouth.

Take heed, you senseless ones among the people; you fools, when will you become wise? Does he who implanted the ear not hear? Does he who formed the eye not see? Does he who disciplines nations not punish? Does he who teaches man lack knowledge? The LORD knows the thoughts of man; he knows that they are futile.

Psalm 94:8–11

For the Lord is the great God, the great King above all gods. In his hand are the depths of the earth, and the mountain peaks belong to him. The sea is his, for he made it, and his hands formed the dry land.

Psalm 95:3–5

For great is the Lord and most worthy of praise; he is to be feared above all gods. For all the gods of the nations are idols, but the Lord made the heavens. Splendor and majesty are before him; strength and glory are in his sanctuary.

Psalm 96:4–6

Praise the LORD, O my soul. O LORD my God, you are very great; you are clothed with splendor and majesty. He wraps himself in light as with a garment; he stretches out the heavens like a tent

Psalm 104:1–2

Our God is in heaven; he does whatever pleases him.

Psalm 115:3

Our God is in heaven; he does whatever pleases him.

I know that the LORD is great, that our Lord is greater than all gods. The LORD does whatever pleases him, in the heavens and on the earth, in the seas and all their depths. He makes clouds rise from the ends of the earth; he sends lightning with the rain and brings out the wind from his storehouses.

Psalm 135:5–7

O LORD, you have searched me and you know me. You know when I sit and when I rise; you perceive my thoughts from afar. You discern my going out and my lying down; you are familiar with all my ways. Before a word is on my tongue you know it completely, O LORD.

Psalm 139:1–4

He determines the number of the stars and calls them each by name. Great is our Lord and mighty in power; his understanding has no limit.

Psalm 147:4–5

Praise the LORD. Praise the LORD from the heavens, praise him in the heights above. Praise him, all his angels, praise him, all his heavenly hosts. Praise him, sun and moon, praise him, all you shining stars. Praise him, you highest heavens and you waters above the skies. Let them praise the name of the LORD, for he commanded and they were created.

Psalm 148:1–5

He determines the number of the stars and calls them each by name. Great is our Lord and mighty in power; his understanding has no limit.

By wisdom the LORD laid the earth's foundations, by understanding he set the heavens in place; by his knowledge the deeps were divided, and the clouds let drop the dew.

Proverbs 3:19–20

In his heart a man plans his course, but the LORD determines his steps.

Proverbs 16:9

Many are the plans in a man's heart, but it is the LORD's purpose that prevails.

Proverbs 19:21

A man's steps are directed by the LORD. How then can anyone understand his own way?

Proverbs 20:24

The king's heart is in the hand of the Lord; he directs it like a watercourse wherever he pleases.

Proverbs 21:1

There is no wisdom, no insight, no plan that can succeed against the LORD.

Proverbs 21:30

Then Isaiah said, "Hear now, you house of David! Is it not enough to try the patience of men? Will you try the patience of my God also? Therefore the Lord himself will give you a sign: The virgin will be with child and will give birth to a son, and will call him Immanuel.

Isaiah 7:13–14

There is no wisdom, no insight, no plan that can succeed against the LORD.

Lift your eyes and look to the heavens: Who created all these? He who brings out the starry host one by one, and calls them each by name. Because of his great power and mighty strength, not one of them is missing.

Isaiah 40:26

Do you not know? Have you not heard? The LORD is the everlasting God, the Creator of the ends of the earth. He will not grow tired or weary, and his understanding no one can fathom.

Isaiah 40:28

"I am the LORD; that is my name! I will not give my glory to another or my praise to idols. See, the former things have taken place, and new things I declare; before they spring into being I announce them to you."

Isaiah 42:8–9

"This is what the LORD says—your Redeemer, who formed you in the womb: I am the LORD, who has made all things, who alone stretched out the heavens, who spread out the earth by myself, who foils the signs of false prophets and makes fools of diviners, who overthrows the learning of the wise and turns it into nonsense, who carries out the words of his servants and fulfills the predictions of his messengers,

Isaiah 44:24–26

It is I who made the earth and created mankind upon it. My own hands stretched out the heavens; I marshaled their starry hosts.

Isaiah 45:12

It is I who made the earth and created mankind upon it. My own hands stretched out the heavens;

Remember the former things, those of long ago; I am God, and there is no other; I am God, and there is none like me. I make known the end from the beginning, from ancient times, what is still to come. I say: My purpose will stand, and I will do all that I please. From the east I summon a bird of prey; from a far-off land, a man to fulfill my purpose. What I have said, that will I bring about; what I have planned, that will I do.

Isaiah 46:9–11

But the Lord is the true God; he is the living God, the eternal King. When he is angry, the earth trembles; the nations cannot endure his wrath. "Tell them this: 'These gods, who did not make the heavens and the earth, will perish from the earth and from under the heavens.'" But God made the earth by his power; he founded the world by his wisdom and stretched out the heavens by his understanding.

Jeremiah 10:10–12

Can anyone hide in secret places so that I cannot see him?"
declares the LORD. "Do not I fill heaven and earth?"
declares the LORD.

Jeremiah 23:24

This is what the Lord says, he who appoints the sun to
shine by day, who decrees the moon and stars to shine by
night, who stirs up the sea so that its waves roar—the Lord
Almighty is his name: "Only if these decrees vanish from
my sight," declares the Lord, "will the descendants of Israel
ever cease to be a nation before me." This is what the Lord
says: "Only if the heavens above can be measured and the
foundations of the earth below be searched out will I reject
all the descendants of Israel because of all they have done,"
declares the Lord.

Jeremiah 31:35–37

**Ah,
Sovereign LORD,
you have made the
heavens and the earth
by your great power
and outstretched arm.
Nothing is too hard
for you.**

"Ah, Sovereign LORD, you have made the heavens and the
earth by your great power and outstretched arm. Nothing is
too hard for you.

Jeremiah 32:17

"This is what the LORD says, he who made the earth, the
LORD who formed it and established it—the LORD is his
name: 'Call to me and I will answer you and tell you great
and unsearchable things you do not know.'

Jeremiah 33:2–3

"He made the earth by his power; he founded the world by his wisdom and stretched out the heavens by his understanding. When he thunders, the waters in the heavens roar; he makes clouds rise from the ends of the earth. He sends lightning with the rain and brings out the wind from his storehouses.

Jeremiah 51:15–16

If we are thrown into the blazing furnace, the God we serve is able to save us from it, and he will rescue us from your hand, O king. But even if he does not, we want you to know, O king, that we will not serve your gods or worship the image of gold you have set up."

Daniel 3:17–18

**The LORD,
who stretches
out the heavens,
who lays
the foundation
of the earth,
and who forms
the spirit of man
within him,**

He who forms the mountains, creates the wind, and reveals his thoughts to man, he who turns dawn to darkness, and treads the high places of the earth—the LORD God Almighty is his name.

Amos 4:13

This is the word of the LORD concerning Israel. The LORD, who stretches out the heavens, who lays the foundation of the earth, and who forms the spirit of man within him, declares: "I am going to make Jerusalem a cup that sends all the surrounding peoples reeling. Judah will be besieged as well as Jerusalem. On that day, when all the nations of the earth are gathered against her, I will make Jerusalem an immovable rock for all the nations. All who try to move it will injure themselves.

Zechariah 12:1–3

Do not be afraid of those who kill the body but cannot kill the soul. Rather, be afraid of the One who can destroy both soul and body in hell.

Matthew 10:28

Jesus looked at them and said, "With man this is impossible, but not with God; all things are possible with God."

Mark 10:27

"I tell you, my friends, do not be afraid of those who kill the body and after that can do no more. But I will show you whom you should fear: Fear him who, after the killing of the body, has power to throw you into hell. Yes, I tell you, fear him.

Luke 12:4–5

Jesus replied, "What is impossible with men is possible with God."

Luke 18:27

Jesus looked at them and said, "With man this is impossible, but not with God; all things are possible with God."

He said to them, "This is what I told you while I was still with you: Everything must be fulfilled that is written about me in the Law of Moses, the Prophets and the Psalms." Then he opened their minds so they could understand the Scriptures. He told them, "This is what is written: The Christ will suffer and rise from the dead on the third day, and repentance and forgiveness of sins will be preached in his name to all nations, beginning at Jerusalem. You are witnesses of these things. I am going to send you what my Father has promised; but stay in the city until you have been clothed with power from on high."

Luke 24:44–48

In the beginning was the Word, and the Word was with God, and the Word was God. He was with God in the beginning. Through him all things were made; without him nothing was made that has been made.

John 1:1–3

For the one whom God has sent speaks the words of God, for God gives the Spirit without limit. The Father loves the Son and has placed everything in his hands. Whoever believes in the Son has eternal life, but whoever rejects the Son will not see life, for God's wrath remains on him."

John 3:34–36

Through him all things were made; without him nothing was made that has been made.

After Jesus said this, he looked toward heaven and prayed: "Father, the time has come. Glorify your Son, that your Son may glorify you. For you granted him authority over all people that he might give eternal life to all those you have given him. Now this is eternal life: that they may know you, the only true God, and Jesus Christ, whom you have sent.

John 17:1–3

"The God who made the world and everything in it is the Lord of heaven and earth and does not live in temples built by hands. And he is not served by human hands, as if he needed anything, because he himself gives all men life and breath and everything else. From one man he made every nation of men, that they should inhabit the whole earth; and he determined the times set for them and the exact places where they should live. God did this so that men would seek him and perhaps reach out for him and find him, though he is not far from each one of us. 'For in him we live and move and have our being.' As some of your own poets have said, 'We are his offspring.'

Acts 17:24–28

For since the creation of the world God's invisible qualities—his eternal power and divine nature—have been clearly seen, being understood from what has been made, so that men are without excuse.

Romans 1:20

Oh, the depth of the riches of the wisdom and knowledge of God! How unsearchable his judgments, and his paths beyond tracing out!

Romans 11:33

For it is by grace you have been saved, through faith—and this not from yourselves, it is the gift of God—not by works, so that no one can boast. For we are God's workmanship, created in Christ Jesus to do good works, which God prepared in advance for us to do.

Ephesians 2:8–10

For by him all things were created: things in heaven and on earth, visible and invisible,

But our citizenship is in heaven. And we eagerly await a Savior from there, the Lord Jesus Christ, who, by the power that enables him to bring everything under his control, will transform our lowly bodies so that they will be like his glorious body.

Philippians 3:20–21

He is the image of the invisible God, the firstborn over all creation. For by him all things were created: things in heaven and on earth, visible and invisible, whether thrones or powers or rulers or authorities; all things were created by him and for him. He is before all things, and in him all things hold together.

Colossians 1:15–17

In the past God spoke to our forefathers through the prophets at many times and in various ways, but in these last days he has spoken to us by his Son, whom he appointed heir of all things, and through whom he made the universe. The Son is the radiance of God's glory and the exact representation of his being, sustaining all things by his powerful word. After he had provided purification for sins, he sat down at the right hand of the Majesty in heaven.

Hebrews 1:1–3

Nothing in all creation is hidden from God's sight. Everything is uncovered and laid bare before the eyes of him to whom we must give account.

Hebrews 4:13

By faith we understand that the universe was formed at God's command, so that what is seen was not made out of what was visible.

By faith we understand that the universe was formed at God's command, so that what is seen was not made out of what was visible.

Hebrews 11:3

First of all, you must understand that in the last days scoffers will come, scoffing and following their own evil desires. They will say, "Where is this 'coming' he promised? Ever since our fathers died, everything goes on as it has since the beginning of creation." But they deliberately forget that long ago by God's word the heavens existed and the earth was formed out of water and by water. By these waters also the world of that time was deluged and destroyed. By the same word the present heavens and earth are reserved for fire, being kept for the day of judgment and destruction of ungodly men.

2 Peter 3:3–7

Chapter 25

God's Promises

You will seek me and find me when you seek me with all your heart.

Jeremiah 29:13

God has given us His promises in the Bible. There are at least four challenges that we face regarding our understanding of a specific promise from God:

The first challenge is to accurately understand what it is that God is promising. For example, some of God's promises speak to things of this physical world, some speak to spiritual things, and some speak to both.

The second challenge is to know to whom God is making the promise. Was the promise offered only to a certain group of people? Was the promise made only for people living at a specific time and place in history? Does the promise have application for us in the present?

The third challenge is to understand when and where the promise is to be fulfilled. We must realize that God does not limit His perspective to just our present life on earth. Some of God's promises are meant to be fulfilled in this life, and some are meant to be fulfilled after our current physical bodies die.

The fourth challenge is to know whether or not there is something that we must do in order to receive what God has promised. Although some of God's promises require nothing of us, many of His promises are conditional upon something that we must do. Some of God's conditional promises depend upon one's behavior. Other promises depend upon the condition of one's spiritual heart and attitude toward God. We must realize that God is not obligated to fulfill a conditional promise just because we think we have satisfied the requirements. It is God who decides whether or not the requirements have been met. It is our responsibility to study the Bible in order to understand God's promises and what is required of us, if anything, to participate in them.

The value of a promise is only as good as the character of the one making the promise. Among God's unchanging character traits are holiness, truthfulness, trustworthiness, righteousness, and faithfulness. God's promises always reflect His character.

Know therefore that the Lord your God is God; he is the faithful God, keeping his covenant of love to a thousand generations of those who love him and keep his commands.

Deuteronomy 7:9

See, I am setting before you today a blessing and a curse—the blessing if you obey the commands of the LORD your God that I am giving you today; the curse if you disobey the commands of the LORD your God and turn from the way that I command you today by following other gods, which you have not known.

Deuteronomy 11:26–28

**Know therefore
that the Lord your God
is God;
he is the faithful God,
keeping
his covenant of love
to a thousand
generations
of those
who love him
and keep his commands.**

Be strong and courageous. Do not be afraid or terrified because of them, for the LORD your God goes with you; he will never leave you nor forsake you."

Deuteronomy 31:6

Do not let this Book of the Law depart from your mouth; meditate on it day and night, so that you may be careful to do everything written in it. Then you will be prosperous and successful. Have I not commanded you? Be strong and courageous. Do not be terrified; do not be discouraged, for the LORD your God will be with you wherever you go."

Joshua 1:8–9

if my people, who are called by my name, will humble themselves and pray and seek my face and turn from their wicked ways, then will I hear from heaven and will forgive their sin and will heal their land.

2 Chronicles 7:14

Who, then, is the man that fears the LORD? He will instruct him in the way chosen for him. He will spend his days in prosperity, and his descendants will inherit the land. The LORD confides in those who fear him; he makes his covenant known to them.

Psalm 25:12–14

Evil will slay the wicked; the foes of the righteous will be condemned. The LORD redeems his servants; no one will be condemned who takes refuge in him.

Psalm 34:21–22

Commit your way to the LORD; trust in him and he will do this: He will make your righteousness shine like the dawn, the justice of your cause like the noonday sun.

Psalm 37:5–6

The LORD confides in those who fear him; he makes his covenant known to them.

"Then they will call to me but I will not answer; they will look for me but will not find me. Since they hated knowledge and did not choose to fear the LORD, since they would not accept my advice and spurned my rebuke, they will eat the fruit of their ways and be filled with the fruit of their schemes. For the waywardness of the simple will kill them, and the complacency of fools will destroy them; but whoever listens to me will live in safety and be at ease, without fear of harm."

Proverbs 1:28–33

My son, if you accept my words and store up my commands within you, turning your ear to wisdom and applying your heart to understanding, and if you call out for insight and cry aloud for understanding, and if you look for it as for silver and search for it as for hidden treasure, then you will understand the fear of the LORD and find the knowledge of God.

Proverbs 2:1–5

Trust in the LORD with all your heart and lean not on your own understanding; in all your ways acknowledge him, and he will make your paths straight.

For the LORD gives wisdom, and from his mouth come knowledge and understanding. He holds victory in store for the upright, he is a shield to those whose walk is blameless, for he guards the course of the just and protects the way of his faithful ones. Then you will understand what is right and just and fair—every good path. For wisdom will enter your heart, and knowledge will be pleasant to your soul. Discretion will protect you, and understanding will guard you.

Proverbs 2:6–11

Trust in the LORD with all your heart and lean not on your own understanding; in all your ways acknowledge him, and he will make your paths straight.

Proverbs 3:5–6

Honor the LORD with your wealth, with the firstfruits of all your crops; then your barns will be filled to overflowing, and your vats will brim over with new wine.

Proverbs 3:9–10

My son, preserve sound judgment and discernment, do
not let them out of your sight; they will be life for you, an
ornament to grace your neck. Then you will go on your
way in safety, and your foot will not stumble; when you lie
down, you will not be afraid; when you lie down, your sleep
will be sweet. Have no fear of sudden disaster or of the
ruin that overtakes the wicked, for the LORD will be your
confidence and will keep your foot from being snared.

Proverbs 3:21–26

Commit to the LORD whatever you do, and your plans
will succeed.

Proverbs 16:3

You will keep in perfect peace him whose mind is steadfast,
because he trusts in you. Trust in the LORD forever, for
the LORD, the LORD, is the Rock eternal.

Isaiah 26:3–4

**Commit
to the LORD
whatever you do,
and your plans
will succeed.**

but those who hope in the LORD will renew their strength.
They will soar on wings like eagles; they will run and not
grow weary, they will walk and not be faint.

Isaiah 40:31

So do not fear, for I am with you; do not be dismayed, for
I am your God. I will strengthen you and help you; I will
uphold you with my righteous right hand.

Isaiah 41:10

For this is what the high and lofty One says—he who lives forever, whose name is holy: "I live in a high and holy place, but also with him who is contrite and lowly in spirit, to revive the spirit of the lowly and to revive the heart of the contrite.

Isaiah 57:15

This is what the LORD says: "Stand at the crossroads and look; ask for the ancient paths, ask where the good way is, and walk in it, and you will find rest for your souls. But you said, 'We will not walk in it.'

Jeremiah 6:16

You will seek me and find me when you seek me with all your heart.

You will seek me and find me when you seek me with all your heart.

Jeremiah 29:13

This is what the Lord says, he who appoints the sun to shine by day, who decrees the moon and stars to shine by night, who stirs up the sea so that its waves roar—the Lord Almighty is his name: "Only if these decrees vanish from my sight," declares the Lord, "will the descendants of Israel ever cease to be a nation before me." This is what the Lord says: "Only if the heavens above can be measured and the foundations of the earth below be searched out will I reject all the descendants of Israel because of all they have done," declares the Lord.

Jeremiah 31:35–37

"This is what the LORD says, he who made the earth, the LORD who formed it and established it—the LORD is his name: 'Call to me and I will answer you and tell you great and unsearchable things you do not know.'

Jeremiah 33:2–3

But seek first his kingdom and his righteousness, and all these things will be given to you as well. Therefore do not worry about tomorrow, for tomorrow will worry about itself. Each day has enough trouble of its own.

Matthew 6:33–34

"Ask and it will be given to you; seek and you will find; knock and the door will be opened to you. For everyone who asks receives; he who seeks finds; and to him who knocks, the door will be opened.

Matthew 7:7–8

'Call to me and I will answer you and tell you great and unsearchable things you do not know.'

All men will hate you because of me, but he who stands firm to the end will be saved.

Matthew 10:22

"Whoever acknowledges me before men, I will also acknowledge him before my Father in heaven. But whoever disowns me before men, I will disown him before my Father in heaven.

Matthew 10:32–33

Then Jesus came to them and said, "All authority in heaven and on earth has been given to me. Therefore go and make disciples of all nations, baptizing them in the name of the Father and of the Son and of the Holy Spirit, and teaching them to obey everything I have commanded you. And surely I am with you always, to the very end of the age."

Matthew 28:18–20

Peter said to him, "We have left all we had to follow you!"
"I tell you the truth," Jesus said to them, "no one who has left home or wife or brothers or parents or children for the sake of the kingdom of God will fail to receive many times as much in this age and, in the age to come, eternal life."

Luke 18:28–30

For God so loved the world that he gave his one and only Son, that whoever believes in him shall not perish but have eternal life.

"For God so loved the world that he gave his one and only Son, that whoever believes in him shall not perish but have eternal life. For God did not send his Son into the world to condemn the world, but to save the world through him.

John 3:16–17

For the one whom God has sent speaks the words of God, for God gives the Spirit without limit. The Father loves the Son and has placed everything in his hands. Whoever believes in the Son has eternal life, but whoever rejects the Son will not see life, for God's wrath remains on him."

John 3:34–36

"I tell you the truth, whoever hears my word and believes him who sent me has eternal life and will not be condemned; he has crossed over from death to life.

John 5:24

I tell you the truth, he who believes has everlasting life. I am the bread of life.

John 6:47–48

When Jesus spoke again to the people, he said, "I am the light of the world. Whoever follows me will never walk in darkness, but will have the light of life."

John 8:12

I am the gate; whoever enters through me will be saved. He will come in and go out, and find pasture.

John 10:9

Jesus said to her, "I am the resurrection and the life. He who believes in me will live, even though he dies; and whoever lives and believes in me will never die. Do you believe this?"

John 11:25–26

"Do not let your hearts be troubled. Trust in God; trust also in me. In my Father's house are many rooms; if it were not so, I would have told you. I am going there to prepare a place for you. And if I go and prepare a place for you, I will come back and take you to be with me that you also may be where I am.

John 14:1–3

Whoever has my commands and obeys them, he is the one who loves me. He who loves me will be loved by my Father, and I too will love him and show myself to him."

John 14:21

When Jesus spoke again to the people, he said, "I am the light of the world. Whoever follows me will never walk in darkness, but will have the light of life."

Jesus replied, "If anyone loves me, he will obey my teaching. My Father will love him, and we will come to him and make our home with him. He who does not love me will not obey my teaching. These words you hear are not my own; they belong to the Father who sent me.

John 14:23–24

"I am the vine; you are the branches. If a man remains in me and I in him, he will bear much fruit; apart from me you can do nothing. If anyone does not remain in me, he is like a branch that is thrown away and withers; such branches are picked up, thrown into the fire and burned. If you remain in me and my words remain in you, ask whatever you wish, and it will be given you. This is to my Father's glory, that you bear much fruit, showing yourselves to be my disciples.

John 15:5–8

If you obey my commands, you will remain in my love, just as I have obeyed my Father's commands and remain in his love.

"As the Father has loved me, so have I loved you. Now remain in my love. If you obey my commands, you will remain in my love, just as I have obeyed my Father's commands and remain in his love. I have told you this so that my joy may be in you and that your joy may be complete.

John 15:9–11

"I have told you these things, so that in me you may have peace. In this world you will have trouble. But take heart! I have overcome the world."

John 16:33

That if you confess with your mouth, "Jesus is Lord," and believe in your heart that God raised him from the dead, you will be saved. For it is with your heart that you believe and are justified, and it is with your mouth that you confess and are saved. As the Scripture says, "Anyone who trusts in him will never be put to shame."

Romans 10:9–11

For there is no difference between Jew and Gentile—the same Lord is Lord of all and richly blesses all who call on him, for, "Everyone who calls on the name of the Lord will be saved.

Romans 10:12–13

So, if you think you are standing firm, be careful that you don't fall! No temptation has seized you except what is common to man. And God is faithful; he will not let you be tempted beyond what you can bear. But when you are tempted, he will also provide a way out so that you can stand up under it.

1 Corinthians 10:12–13

That if you confess with your mouth, "Jesus is Lord," and believe in your heart that God raised him from the dead, you will be saved.

Remember this: Whoever sows sparingly will also reap sparingly, and whoever sows generously will also reap generously.

2 Corinthians 9:6

Do not be deceived: God cannot be mocked. A man reaps what he sows. The one who sows to please his sinful nature, from that nature will reap destruction; the one who sows to please the Spirit, from the Spirit will reap eternal life. Let us not become weary in doing good, for at the proper time we will reap a harvest if we do not give up. Therefore, as we have opportunity, let us do good to all people, especially to those who belong to the family of believers.

Galatians 6:7–10

Do not be deceived: God cannot be mocked. A man reaps what he sows.

Do not be anxious about anything, but in everything, by prayer and petition, with thanksgiving, present your requests to God. And the peace of God, which transcends all understanding, will guard your hearts and your minds in Christ Jesus.

Philippians 4:6–7

Finally, brothers, whatever is true, whatever is noble, whatever is right, whatever is pure, whatever is lovely, whatever is admirable—if anything is excellent or praiseworthy—think about such things. Whatever you have learned or received or heard from me, or seen in me—put it into practice. And the God of peace will be with you.

Philippians 4:8–9

For the Lord himself will come down from heaven, with a loud command, with the voice of the archangel and with the trumpet call of God, and the dead in Christ will rise first. After that, we who are still alive and are left will be caught up together with them in the clouds to meet the Lord in the air. And so we will be with the Lord forever. Therefore encourage each other with these words.

1 Thessalonians 4:16–18

For God did not give us a spirit of timidity, but a spirit of power, of love and of self-discipline.

2 Timothy 1:7

But when this priest had offered for all time one sacrifice for sins, he sat down at the right hand of God. Since that time he waits for his enemies to be made his footstool, because by one sacrifice he has made perfect forever those who are being made holy. The Holy Spirit also testifies to us about this. First he says: "This is the covenant I will make with them after that time, says the Lord. I will put my laws in their hearts, and I will write them on their minds." Then he adds: "Their sins and lawless acts I will remember no more." And where these have been forgiven, there is no longer any sacrifice for sin.

Hebrews 10:12–18

Blessed is the man who perseveres under trial, because when he has stood the test, he will receive the crown of life that God has promised to those who love him.

Keep your lives free from the love of money and be content with what you have, because God has said, "Never will I leave you; never will I forsake you."

Hebrews 13:5

Blessed is the man who perseveres under trial, because when he has stood the test, he will receive the crown of life that God has promised to those who love him.

James 1:12

But he gives us more grace. That is why Scripture says: "God opposes the proud but gives grace to the humble." Submit yourselves, then, to God. Resist the devil, and he will flee from you. Come near to God and he will come near to you. Wash your hands, you sinners, and purify your hearts, you double-minded. Grieve, mourn and wail. Change your laughter to mourning and your joy to gloom. Humble yourselves before the Lord, and he will lift you up.

James 4:6–10

Humble yourselves before the Lord, and he will lift you up.

Grace and peace be yours in abundance through the knowledge of God and of Jesus our Lord. His divine power has given us everything we need for life and godliness through our knowledge of him who called us by his own glory and goodness. Through these he has given us his very great and precious promises, so that through them you may participate in the divine nature and escape the corruption in the world caused by evil desires.

2 Peter 1:2–4

For this very reason, make every effort to add to your faith goodness; and to goodness, knowledge; and to knowledge, self-control; and to self-control, perseverance; and to perseverance, godliness; and to godliness, brotherly kindness; and to brotherly kindness, love. For if you possess these qualities in increasing measure, they will keep you from being ineffective and unproductive in your knowledge of our Lord Jesus Christ. But if anyone does not have them, he is nearsighted and blind, and has forgotten that he has been cleansed from his past sins. Therefore, my brothers, be all the more eager to make your calling and election sure. For if you do these things, you will never fall, and you will receive a rich welcome into the eternal kingdom of our Lord and Savior Jesus Christ.

2 Peter 1:5–11

Do not love the world or anything in the world. If anyone loves the world, the love of the Father is not in him. For everything in the world—the cravings of sinful man, the lust of his eyes and the boasting of what he has and does—comes not from the Father but from the world. The world and its desires pass away, but the man who does the will of God lives forever.

1 John 2:15–17

This is the confidence we have in approaching God: that if we ask anything according to his will, he hears us. And if we know that he hears us—whatever we ask—we know that we have what we asked of him.

1 John 5:14–15

The world and its desires pass away, but the man who does the will of God lives forever.

I am coming soon. Hold on to what you have, so that no one will take your crown. Him who overcomes I will make a pillar in the temple of my God. Never again will he leave it. I will write on him the name of my God and the name of the city of my God, the new Jerusalem, which is coming down out of heaven from my God; and I will also write on him my new name.

Revelation 3:11–12

Those whom I love I rebuke and discipline. So be earnest, and repent. Here I am! I stand at the door and knock. If anyone hears my voice and opens the door, I will come in and eat with him, and he with me.

Revelation 3:19–20

Chapter 26

God's Protection

**"As for God, his way is perfect; the word of the LORD
is flawless. He is a shield for all who take refuge in him.**
2 Samuel 22:31

Before Adam and Eve disobeyed God in the Garden of Eden they had God's full protection from any possible physical or spiritual danger—with one exception. To continue enjoying God's full blessings and protection forever, they simply had to trust and obey God. Adam and Eve instead chose to disobey God's command. Their sinning against God resulted in their passing on their sinful nature to all of their natural descendants. Another consequence of Adam and Eve sinning against God was that God changed the whole nature and order of His creation. They found themselves no longer in a perfect world, but in a fallen, sinful world full of physical and spiritual dangers, suffering, and death. This continues to describe our world today. Our fallen world reflects the sinful heart of man.

Becoming a spiritually reborn follower of Jesus Christ does not mean that we are free from the dangers and suffering of living in this world. Jesus tells us in John 16:33: "*I have told you these things, so that in me you may have peace. In this world you will have trouble. But take heart! I have overcome the world.*" However, there is great spiritual protection for those who have placed their faith in Jesus Christ as their sin-bearer, Savior, and Lord. God promises them eternal life in heaven. In addition, God makes available to us as Christians the spiritual protection we need to protect our hearts, minds, and souls from the ever-threatening physical and spiritual dangers of this world. To come under God's spiritual protection, trust and obey Him. Be a devoted—never lukewarm—follower of the Lord Jesus Christ. Diligently study, trust, and obey God's Word above the wisdom of this world and even above your own thinking. Be a man or woman of serious prayer. Repent of any sins that are part of your life. Study earnestly to understand what it means in Ephesians 6 to "*be strong in the Lord and in His mighty power*" and to "*put on the full armor of God.*" If you are a Christian, your spiritual health (the condition of your heart, mind, and soul) depends upon these things.

Do not let this Book of the Law depart from your mouth; meditate on it day and night, so that you may be careful to do everything written in it. Then you will be prosperous and successful. Have I not commanded you? Be strong and courageous. Do not be terrified; do not be discouraged, for the LORD your God will be with you wherever you go."

Joshua 1:8–9

"As for God, his way is perfect; the word of the LORD is flawless. He is a shield for all who take refuge in him.

2 Samuel 22:31

**As for God,
his way is perfect;
the word of the LORD
is flawless.
He is a shield for all
who take refuge
in him.**

For the eyes of the Lord range throughout the earth to strengthen those whose hearts are fully committed to him.

2 Chronicles 16:9a

My shield is God Most High, who saves the upright in heart. God is a righteous judge, a God who expresses his wrath every day.

Psalm 7:10–11

In the Lord I take refuge. How then can you say to me: "Flee like a bird to your mountain. For look, the wicked bend their bows; they set their arrows against the strings to shoot from the shadows at the upright in heart. When the foundations are being destroyed, what can the righteous do?"

Psalm 11:1–3

I love you, O LORD, my strength. The LORD is my rock, my fortress and my deliverer; my God is my rock, in whom I take refuge. He is my shield and the horn of my salvation, my stronghold. I call to the LORD, who is worthy of praise, and I am saved from my enemies.

Psalm 18:1–3

As for God, his way is perfect; the word of the LORD is flawless. He is a shield for all who take refuge in him.

Psalm 18:30

In you, O LORD, I have taken refuge; let me never be put to shame; deliver me in your righteousness. Turn your ear to me, come quickly to my rescue; be my rock of refuge, a strong fortress to save me. Since you are my rock and my fortress, for the sake of your name lead and guide me. Free me from the trap that is set for me, for you are my refuge. Into your hands I commit my spirit; redeem me, O LORD, the God of truth.

Psalm 31:1–5

In you, O LORD, I have taken refuge; let me never be put to shame; deliver me in your righteousness.

How great is your goodness, which you have stored up for those who fear you, which you bestow in the sight of men on those who take refuge in you. In the shelter of your presence you hide them from the intrigues of men; in your dwelling you keep them safe from accusing tongues.

Psalm 31:19–20

God is our refuge and strength, an ever-present help in trouble. Therefore we will not fear, though the earth give way and the mountains fall into the heart of the sea,

Psalm 46:1–2

Find rest, O my soul, in God alone; my hope comes from him. He alone is my rock and my salvation; he is my fortress, I will not be shaken. My salvation and my honor depend on God; he is my mighty rock, my refuge. Trust in him at all times, O people; pour out your hearts to him, for God is our refuge.

Psalm 62:5–8

He who dwells in the shelter of the Most High will rest in the shadow of the Almighty. I will say of the LORD, "He is my refuge and my fortress, my God, in whom I trust."

Psalm 91:1–2

Unless the LORD watches over the city, the watchmen stand guard in vain.

How can a young man keep his way pure? By living according to your word. I seek you with all my heart; do not let me stray from your commands. I have hidden your word in my heart that I might not sin against you. Praise be to you, O LORD; teach me your decrees. With my lips I recount all the laws that come from your mouth. I rejoice in following your statutes as one rejoices in great riches. I meditate on your precepts and consider your ways. I delight in your decrees; I will not neglect your word.

Psalm 119:9–16

Unless the LORD builds the house, its builders labor in vain. Unless the LORD watches over the city, the watchmen stand guard in vain.

Psalm 127: 1

For the LORD gives wisdom, and from his mouth come knowledge and understanding. He holds victory in store for the upright, he is a shield to those whose walk is blameless, for he guards the course of the just and protects the way of his faithful ones.

Proverbs 2:6–8

Trust in the LORD with all your heart and lean not on your own understanding; in all your ways acknowledge him, and he will make your paths straight.

Proverbs 3:5–6

The name of the LORD is a strong tower; the righteous run to it and are safe.

Proverbs 18:10

The fear of the LORD leads to life: Then one rests content, untouched by trouble.

Proverbs 19:23

Trust in the LORD with all your heart and lean not on your own understanding; in all your ways acknowledge him, and he will make your paths straight.

"Every word of God is flawless; he is a shield to those who take refuge in him. Do not add to his words, or he will rebuke you and prove you a liar.

Proverbs 30:5–6

For the LORD is our judge, the LORD is our lawgiver, the LORD is our king; it is he who will save us.

Isaiah 33:22

For though we live in the world, we do not wage war as the world does. The weapons we fight with are not the weapons of the world. On the contrary, they have divine power to demolish strongholds. We demolish arguments and every pretension that sets itself up against the knowledge of God, and we take captive every thought to make it obedient to Christ.

2 Corinthians 10:3–5

Finally, be strong in the Lord and in his mighty power.

Finally, be strong in the Lord and in his mighty power. Put on the full armor of God so that you can take your stand against the devil's schemes. For our struggle is not against flesh and blood, but against the rulers, against the authorities, against the powers of this dark world and against the spiritual forces of evil in the heavenly realms.

Ephesians 6:10–12

Therefore put on the full armor of God, so that when the day of evil comes, you may be able to stand your ground, and after you have done everything, to stand. Stand firm then, with the belt of truth buckled around your waist, with the breastplate of righteousness in place, and with your feet fitted with the readiness that comes from the gospel of peace. In addition to all this, take up the shield of faith, with which you can extinguish all the flaming arrows of the evil one. Take the helmet of salvation and the sword of the Spirit, which is the word of God. And pray in the Spirit on all occasions with all kinds of prayers and requests. With this in mind, be alert and always keep on praying for all the saints.

Ephesians 6:13–18

Do not be anxious about anything, but in everything,
by prayer and petition, with thanksgiving, present your
requests to God. And the peace of God, which transcends
all understanding, will guard your hearts and your minds
in Christ Jesus.

Philippians 4:6–7

Finally, brothers, whatever is true, whatever is noble,
whatever is right, whatever is pure, whatever is lovely,
whatever is admirable—if anything is excellent or
praiseworthy—think about such things. Whatever you
have learned or received or heard from me, or seen in me—
put it into practice. And the God of peace will be with you.

Philippians 4:8–9

But since we belong to the day, let us be self-controlled,
putting on faith and love as a breastplate, and the hope
of salvation as a helmet. For God did not appoint us
to suffer wrath but to receive salvation through our
Lord Jesus Christ.

1 Thessalonians 5:8–9

Be joyful always; pray continually; give thanks in all
circumstances, for this is God's will for you in Christ Jesus.
Do not put out the Spirit's fire; do not treat prophecies
with contempt. Test everything. Hold on to the good.
Avoid every kind of evil.

1 Thessalonians 5:16–22

For God did not give us a spirit of timidity, but a spirit of
power, of love and of self-discipline.

2 Timothy 1:7

**Finally, brothers,
whatever is true,
whatever is noble,
whatever is right,
whatever is pure,
whatever is lovely,
whatever is admirable—
if anything is excellent
or praiseworthy—
think about
such things.**

Keep your lives free from the love of money and be content with what you have, because God has said, "Never will I leave you; never will I forsake you." So we say with confidence, "The Lord is my helper; I will not be afraid. What can man do to me?"

Hebrews 13:5–6

Therefore, dear friends, since you already know this, be on your guard so that you may not be carried away by the error of lawless men and fall from your secure position. But grow in the grace and knowledge of our Lord and Savior Jesus Christ. To him be glory both now and forever! Amen.

2 Peter 3:17–18

Who is it that overcomes the world? Only he who believes that Jesus is the Son of God.

for everyone born of God overcomes the world. This is the victory that has overcome the world, even our faith. Who is it that overcomes the world? Only he who believes that Jesus is the Son of God.

1 John 5:4–5

Chapter 27

God's Righteousness

**Righteous are you, O LORD, and your laws are right.
The statutes you have laid down are righteous; they are
fully trustworthy.**

Psalm 119:137–138

The Bible states that God is perfectly righteous (without guilt or sin; conforming to divine law; consistent with what is morally right). God alone is holy, and is uniquely qualified to determine what is righteous and what is not. He is able to see into every human heart and knows the consequences of every thought, word, and deed. God defines for us in the Bible what is right and wrong, what is moral and immoral, and what is good and evil. It is on these standards that He has established His laws for mankind. God speaks to us through the Bible about how we are to live. He calls us to pursue righteousness.

I, the LORD, speak the truth; I declare what is right. *Isaiah 45:19b*

Who is wise? He will realize these things. Who is discerning? He will understand them. The ways of the LORD are right; the righteous walk in them, but the rebellious stumble in them. *Hosea 14:9*

But you, man of God, flee from all this, and pursue righteousness, godliness, faith, love, endurance and gentleness. *1 Timothy 6:11*

As you read the verses in this chapter, notice how often the words *right*, *righteous*, *righteousness*, and *good* appear together with the words *truth* and *justice*. I believe God is telling us through these verses that these virtues are closely related. Can righteousness survive when truth and justice are abandoned? Can truth and justice survive when righteousness is abandoned? As we look at history and at our own lives, the answer to both of these questions is clearly "No." The lives of individuals, the health of families, and the paths of nations are significantly influenced by human decisions to either pursue or reject God's standards of righteousness.

He is the Rock, his works are perfect, and all his ways are just. A faithful God who does no wrong, upright and just is he.

Deuteronomy 32:4

I know, my God, that you test the heart and are pleased with integrity. . . .

1 Chronicles 29:17a

My shield is God Most High, who saves the upright in heart. God is a righteous judge, a God who expresses his wrath every day.

Psalm 7:10–11

**For the LORD
is righteous,
he loves justice;
upright men
will see his face.**

For the LORD is righteous, he loves justice; upright men will see his face.

Psalm 11:7

As for God, his way is perfect; the word of the LORD is flawless. He is a shield for all who take refuge in him.

Psalm 18:30

The law of the LORD is perfect, reviving the soul. The statutes of the LORD are trustworthy, making wise the simple. The precepts of the LORD are right, giving joy to the heart. The commands of the LORD are radiant, giving light to the eyes. The fear of the LORD is pure, enduring forever. The ordinances of the LORD are sure and altogether righteous.

Psalm 19:7–9

Good and upright is the LORD; therefore he instructs sinners in his ways. He guides the humble in what is right and teaches them his way.

Psalm 25:8–9

For the word of the Lord is right and true; he is faithful in all he does. The Lord loves righteousness and justice; the earth is full of his unfailing love.

Psalm 33:4–5

The eyes of the LORD are on the righteous and his ears are attentive to their cry; the face of the LORD is against those who do evil, to cut off the memory of them from the earth.

Psalm 34:15–16

Commit your way to the LORD; trust in him and he will do this: He will make your righteousness shine like the dawn, the justice of your cause like the noonday sun.

Psalm 37:5–6

Good and upright is the LORD; therefore he instructs sinners in his ways. He guides the humble in what is right and teaches them his way.

Turn from evil and do good; then you will dwell in the land forever. For the Lord loves the just and will not forsake his faithful ones. They will be protected forever, but the offspring of the wicked will be cut off; the righteous will inherit the land and dwell in it forever. The mouth of the righteous man utters wisdom, and his tongue speaks what is just. The law of his God is in his heart; his feet do not slip.

Psalm 37:27–31

The mouth of the righteous man utters wisdom, and his tongue speaks what is just. The law of his God is in his heart; his feet do not slip.

Psalm 37:30–31

Your righteousness reaches to the skies, O God, you who have done great things. Who, O God, is like you? Though you have made me see troubles, many and bitter, you will restore my life again; from the depths of the earth you will again bring me up. You will increase my honor and comfort me once again.

Psalm 71:19–21

Your righteousness is everlasting and your law is true.

Righteous are you, O LORD, and your laws are right. The statutes you have laid down are righteous; they are fully trustworthy.

Psalm 119:137–138

Your righteousness is everlasting and your law is true.

Psalm 119:142

Your statutes are forever right; give me understanding that I may live.

Psalm 119:144

All your words are true; all your righteous laws are eternal.

Psalm 119:160

The LORD is righteous in all his ways and loving toward all he has made.

Psalm 145:17

For the LORD gives wisdom, and from his mouth come knowledge and understanding. He holds victory in store for the upright, he is a shield to those whose walk is blameless, for he guards the course of the just and protects the way of his faithful ones. Then you will understand what is right and just and fair—every good path. For wisdom will enter your heart, and knowledge will be pleasant to your soul. Discretion will protect you, and understanding will guard you.

Proverbs 2:6–11

The LORD is righteous in all his ways and loving toward all he has made.

The path of the righteous is like the first gleam of dawn, shining ever brighter till the full light of day. But the way of the wicked is like deep darkness; they do not know what makes them stumble.

Proverbs 4:18–19

In the way of righteousness there is life; along that path is immortality.

Proverbs 12:28

The LORD detests the way of the wicked but he loves those who pursue righteousness.

Proverbs 15:9

To do what is right and just is more acceptable to the LORD than sacrifice.

Proverbs 21:3

So this is what the Sovereign LORD says: "See, I lay a stone in Zion, a tested stone, a precious cornerstone for a sure foundation; the one who trusts will never be dismayed. I will make justice the measuring line and righteousness the plumb line; hail will sweep away your refuge, the lie, and water will overflow your hiding place.

Isaiah 28:16–17

For this is what the LORD says—he who created the heavens, he is God; he who fashioned and made the earth, he founded it; he did not create it to be empty, but formed it to be inhabited—he says: "I am the LORD, and there is no other. I have not spoken in secret, from somewhere in a land of darkness; I have not said to Jacob's descendants, 'Seek me in vain.' I, the LORD, speak the truth; I declare what is right.

Isaiah 45:18–19

But my righteousness will last forever, my salvation through all generations."

"Hear me, you who know what is right, you people who have my law in your hearts: Do not fear the reproach of men or be terrified by their insults. For the moth will eat them up like a garment; the worm will devour them like wool. But my righteousness will last forever, my salvation through all generations."

Isaiah 51:7–8

So justice is driven back, and righteousness stands at a distance; truth has stumbled in the streets, honesty cannot enter. Truth is nowhere to be found, and whoever shuns evil becomes a prey. The LORD looked and was displeased that there was no justice.

Isaiah 59:14–15

He has showed you, O man, what is good. And what does the LORD require of you? To act justly and to love mercy and to walk humbly with your God.

Micah 6:8

Your eyes are too pure to look on evil; you cannot tolerate wrong. Why then do you tolerate the treacherous? Why are you silent while the wicked swallow up those more righteous than themselves?

Habakkuk 1:13

These are the things you are to do: Speak the truth to each other, and render true and sound judgment in your courts; do not plot evil against your neighbor, and do not love to swear falsely. I hate all this," declares the LORD.

Zechariah 8:16–17

Your eyes are too pure to look on evil; you cannot tolerate wrong.

I am not ashamed of the gospel, because it is the power of God for the salvation of everyone who believes: first for the Jew, then for the Gentile. For in the gospel a righteousness from God is revealed, a righteousness that is by faith from first to last, just as it is written: "The righteous will live by faith."

Romans 1:16–17

But because of your stubbornness and your unrepentant heart, you are storing up wrath against yourself for the day of God's wrath, when his righteous judgment will be revealed. God "will give to each person according to what he has done." To those who by persistence in doing good seek glory, honor and immortality, he will give eternal life. But for those who are self-seeking and who reject the truth and follow evil, there will be wrath and anger.

Romans 2:5–8

God made him who had no sin to be sin for us, so that in him we might become the righteousness of God.

This righteousness from God comes through faith in Jesus Christ to all who believe. There is no difference, for all have sinned and fall short of the glory of God, and are justified freely by his grace through the redemption that came by Christ Jesus.

Romans 3:22–24

For I can testify about them that they are zealous for God, but their zeal is not based on knowledge. Since they did not know the righteousness that comes from God and sought to establish their own, they did not submit to God's righteousness. Christ is the end of the law so that there may be righteousness for everyone who believes.

Romans 10:2–4

God made him who had no sin to be sin for us, so that in him we might become the righteousness of God.

2 Corinthians 5:21

But the fruit of the Spirit is love, joy, peace, patience, kindness, goodness, faithfulness, gentleness and self-control. Against such things there is no law. Those who belong to Christ Jesus have crucified the sinful nature with its passions and desires. Since we live by the Spirit, let us keep in step with the Spirit.

Galatians 5:22–25

Finally, brothers, whatever is true, whatever is noble, whatever is right, whatever is pure, whatever is lovely, whatever is admirable—if anything is excellent or praiseworthy—think about such things. Whatever you have learned or received or heard from me, or seen in me— put it into practice. And the God of peace will be with you.

Philippians 4:8–9

But the fruit of the Spirit is love, joy, peace, patience, kindness, goodness, faithfulness, gentleness and self-control.

Paul, a servant of God and an apostle of Jesus Christ for the faith of God's elect and the knowledge of the truth that leads to godliness—a faith and knowledge resting on the hope of eternal life, which God, who does not lie, promised before the beginning of time,

Titus 1:1–2

For the grace of God that brings salvation has appeared to all men. It teaches us to say "No" to ungodliness and worldly passions, and to live self-controlled, upright and godly lives in this present age, while we wait for the blessed hope—the glorious appearing of our great God and Savior, Jesus Christ, who gave himself for us to redeem us from all wickedness and to purify for himself a people that are his very own, eager to do what is good. These, then, are the things you should teach. Encourage and rebuke with all authority. Do not let anyone despise you.

Titus 2:11–15

But the wisdom that comes from heaven is first of all pure; then peace-loving, considerate, submissive, full of mercy and good fruit, impartial and sincere. Peacemakers who sow in peace raise a harvest of righteousness.

James 3:17–18

To this you were called, because Christ suffered for you, leaving you an example, that you should follow in his steps. "He committed no sin, and no deceit was found in his mouth."

1 Peter 2:21–22

God is light; in him there is no darkness at all.

For, "Whoever would love life and see good days must keep his tongue from evil and his lips from deceitful speech. He must turn from evil and do good; he must seek peace and pursue it. For the eyes of the Lord are on the righteous and his ears are attentive to their prayer, but the face of the Lord is against those who do evil."

1 Peter 3:10–12

This is the message we have heard from him and declare to you: God is light; in him there is no darkness at all. If we claim to have fellowship with him yet walk in the darkness, we lie and do not live by the truth. But if we walk in the light, as he is in the light, we have fellowship with one another, and the blood of Jesus, his Son, purifies us from all sin. If we claim to be without sin, we deceive ourselves and the truth is not in us. If we confess our sins, he is faithful and just and will forgive us our sins and purify us from all unrighteousness. If we claim we have not sinned, we make him out to be a liar and his word has no place in our lives.

1 John 1:5–10

300

Chapter 28

God's Warnings

If we deliberately keep on sinning after we have received the knowledge of the truth, no sacrifice for sins is left, but only a fearful expectation of judgment and of raging fire that will consume the enemies of God.

Hebrews 10:26–27

God's warnings are found throughout the Bible. Some Old Testament warnings were specific to a particular group of Jews living at a particular time. Other warnings from God speak to all of humanity across history. Regardless of whom the warning is intended for, all of God's warnings reflect His nature and character. Even when a specific warning is not aimed directly at us, it is able to teach us about God's character and about how seriously He views sin. Sin is the breaking of God's laws and every sin is a sin against God.

The Bible clearly presents God's character traits, His values, His standards, His commands, His wisdom, His love for us, and His desire for an eternal relationship with each one of us. The Bible explains God's only provision for forgiving us for our sins. That provision is that we place our faith in Jesus Christ, who paid the just penalty for our sins by incurring the full wrath of God against man's sin. The Bible clearly presents God's warnings for sinning against Him and for rejecting the Lordship of Jesus Christ in our lives. God's warnings are actually a reflection of His love for us, His patience with us, and His desire that no one be separated from Him for eternity.

God's warnings are a call for human beings to acknowledge Him, to submit to His Lordship, to repent of our sins, to trust in Him, and to obey Him. God's justice, judgment, wrath, and punishment await those to reject the God of the Bible. God's warnings are always motivated by His love for us and His desire for what is truly best for us. The warnings presented in this chapter can be a wake-up call for people to repent of their sins and believe in and follow the Lord Jesus Christ as their sin-bearer, Savior, and Lord. These warnings can also be a wake-up call for Christians to repent of their sins where they are disobeying and dishonoring God in their lives. May we all earnestly heed God's warnings.

"'But if you will not listen to me and carry out all these commands, and if you reject my decrees and abhor my laws and fail to carry out all my commands and so violate my covenant, then I will do this to you: I will bring upon you sudden terror, wasting diseases and fever that will destroy your sight and drain away your life. You will plant seed in vain, because your enemies will eat it. I will set my face against you so that you will be defeated by your enemies; those who hate you will rule over you, and you will flee even when no one is pursuing you. If after all this you will not listen to me, I will punish you for your sins seven times over. I will break down your stubborn pride and make the sky above you like iron and the ground beneath you like bronze. Your strength will be spent in vain, because your soil will not yield its crops, nor will the trees of the land yield their fruit.

Leviticus 26:14–20

Be careful that you do not forget the LORD your God,

Be careful that you do not forget the LORD your God, failing to observe his commands, his laws and his decrees that I am giving you this day. . . . But remember the LORD your God, for it is he who gives you the ability to produce wealth, and so confirms his covenant, which he swore to your forefathers, as it is today. If you ever forget the LORD your God and follow other gods and worship and bow down to them, I testify against you today that you will surely be destroyed. Like the nations the LORD destroyed before you, so you will be destroyed for not obeying the LORD your God.

Deuteronomy 8:11, 18–20

See, I set before you today life and prosperity, death and destruction. For I command you today to love the Lord your God, to walk in his ways, and to keep his commands, decrees and laws; then you will live and increase, and the Lord your God will bless you in the land you are entering to possess. But if your heart turns away and you are not obedient, and if you are drawn away to bow down to other gods and worship them, I declare to you this day that you will certainly be destroyed. You will not live long in the land you are crossing the Jordan to enter and possess.

Deuteronomy 30:15–18

Stern discipline awaits him who leaves the path; he who hates correction will die.

Proverbs 15:10

A false witness will not go unpunished, and he who pours out lies will not go free.

Proverbs 19:5

**Woe to those
who call evil good
and good evil,
who put darkness
for light
and light for darkness,**

A man who remains stiff-necked after many rebukes will suddenly be destroyed—without remedy.

Proverbs 29:1

Woe to those who call evil good and good evil, who put darkness for light and light for darkness, who put bitter for sweet and sweet for bitter.

Isaiah 5:20

Woe to those who are wise in their own eyes and clever in their own sight.

Isaiah 5:21

I will lead the blind by ways they have not known, along unfamiliar paths I will guide them; I will turn the darkness into light before them and make the rough places smooth. These are the things I will do; I will not forsake them. But those who trust in idols, who say to images, 'You are our gods,' will be turned back in utter shame.

Isaiah 42:16–17

And if at another time I announce that a nation or kingdom is to be built up and planted, and if it does evil in my sight and does not obey me, then I will reconsider the good I had intended to do for it.

Jeremiah 18:9–10

"I am against the prophets who wag their own tongues and yet declare, 'The Lord declares.'

"Therefore," declares the Lord, "I am against the prophets who steal from one another words supposedly from me. Yes," declares the Lord, "I am against the prophets who wag their own tongues and yet declare, 'The Lord declares.' Indeed, I am against those who prophesy false dreams," declares the Lord. "They tell them and lead my people astray with their reckless lies, yet I did not send or appoint them. They do not benefit these people in the least," declares the Lord.

Jeremiah 23:30–32

When I fed them, they were satisfied; when they were satisfied, they became proud; then they forgot me. So I will come upon them like a lion, like a leopard I will lurk by the path. Like a bear robbed of her cubs, I will attack them and rip them open. Like a lion I will devour them; a wild animal will tear them apart.

Hosea 13:6–8

"Be careful not to do your 'acts of righteousness' before men, to be seen by them. If you do, you will have no reward from your Father in heaven.

Matthew 6:1

"Whoever acknowledges me before men, I will also acknowledge him before my Father in heaven. But whoever disowns me before men, I will disown him before my Father in heaven.

Matthew 10:32–33

Jesus knew their thoughts and said to them, "Every kingdom divided against itself will be ruined, and every city or household divided against itself will not stand.

Matthew 12:25

But whoever disowns me before men, I will disown him before my Father in heaven.

And so I tell you, every sin and blasphemy will be forgiven men, but the blasphemy against the Spirit will not be forgiven. Anyone who speaks a word against the Son of Man will be forgiven, but anyone who speaks against the Holy Spirit will not be forgiven, either in this age or in the age to come.

Matthew 12:31–32

At that time the disciples came to Jesus and asked, "Who is the greatest in the kingdom of heaven?" He called a little child and had him stand among them. And he said: "I tell you the truth, unless you change and become like little children, you will never enter the kingdom of heaven. Therefore, whoever humbles himself like this child is the greatest in the kingdom of heaven. "And whoever welcomes a little child like this in my name welcomes me. But if anyone causes one of these little ones who believe in me to sin, it would be better for him to have a large millstone hung around his neck and to be drowned in the depths of the sea.

Matthew 18:1–6

Woe to the world because of the things that cause people to sin!

"Woe to the world because of the things that cause people to sin! Such things must come, but woe to the man through whom they come!

Matthew 18:7

I tell you the truth, all the sins and blasphemies of men will be forgiven them. But whoever blasphemes against the Holy Spirit will never be forgiven; he is guilty of an eternal sin."

Mark 3:28–29

The Son of Man will go just as it is written about him. But woe to that man who betrays the Son of Man! It would be better for him if he had not been born.

Mark 14:21

And everyone who speaks a word against the Son of Man will be forgiven, but anyone who blasphemes against the Holy Spirit will not be forgiven.

Luke 12:10

I tell you the truth, anyone who will not receive the kingdom of God like a little child will never enter it."

Luke 18:17

For the one whom God has sent speaks the words of God, for God gives the Spirit without limit. The Father loves the Son and has placed everything in his hands. Whoever believes in the Son has eternal life, but whoever rejects the Son will not see life, for God's wrath remains on him."

John 3:34–36

"I am the vine; you are the branches. If a man remains in me and I in him, he will bear much fruit; apart from me you can do nothing.

John 15:5

"Therefore since we are God's offspring, we should not think that the divine being is like gold or silver or stone—an image made by man's design and skill. In the past God overlooked such ignorance, but now he commands all people everywhere to repent. For he has set a day when he will judge the world with justice by the man he has appointed. He has given proof of this to all men by raising him from the dead."

Acts 17:29–31

I tell you the truth, anyone who will not receive the kingdom of God like a little child will never enter it."

But because of your stubbornness and your unrepentant heart, you are storing up wrath against yourself for the day of God's wrath, when his righteous judgment will be revealed. God "will give to each person according to what he has done." To those who by persistence in doing good seek glory, honor and immortality, he will give eternal life. But for those who are self-seeking and who reject the truth and follow evil, there will be wrath and anger.

Romans 2:5–8

But for those who are self-seeking and who reject the truth and follow evil, there will be wrath and anger.

Don't you know that you yourselves are God's temple and that God's Spirit lives in you? If anyone destroys God's temple, God will destroy him; for God's temple is sacred, and you are that temple.

1 Corinthians 3:16–17

Do you not know that the wicked will not inherit the kingdom of God? Do not be deceived: Neither the sexually immoral nor idolaters nor adulterers nor male prostitutes nor homosexual offenders nor thieves nor the greedy nor drunkards nor slanderers nor swindlers will inherit the kingdom of God. And that is what some of you were. But you were washed, you were sanctified, you were justified in the name of the Lord Jesus Christ and by the Spirit of our God.

1 Corinthians 6:9–11

Timothy, my son, I give you this instruction in keeping with the prophecies once made about you, so that by following them you may fight the good fight, holding on to faith and a good conscience. Some have rejected these and so have shipwrecked their faith.

1 Timothy 1:18–19

But mark this: There will be terrible times in the last days. People will be lovers of themselves, lovers of money, boastful, proud, abusive, disobedient to their parents, ungrateful, unholy, without love, unforgiving, slanderous, without self-control, brutal, not lovers of the good, treacherous, rash, conceited, lovers of pleasure rather than lovers of God—having a form of godliness but denying its power. Have nothing to do with them.

2 Timothy 3:1–5

It is impossible for those who have once been enlightened, who have tasted the heavenly gift, who have shared in the Holy Spirit, who have tasted the goodness of the word of God and the powers of the coming age, if they fall away, to be brought back to repentance, because to their loss they are crucifying the Son of God all over again and subjecting him to public disgrace.

Hebrews 6:4–6

If we deliberately keep on sinning after we have received the knowledge of the truth, no sacrifice for sins is left, but only a fearful expectation of judgment and of raging fire that will consume the enemies of God.

Hebrews 10:26–27

I warn everyone who hears the words of the prophecy of this book: If anyone adds anything to them, God will add to him the plagues described in this book. And if anyone takes words away from this book of prophecy, God will take away from him his share in the tree of life and in the holy city, which are described in this book.

Revelation 22:18–19

But mark this: There will be terrible times in the last days. People will be lovers of themselves, lovers of money, boastful, proud, abusive,

Chapter 29

God's Ways and Paths

Trust in the LORD with all your heart and lean not on your own understanding; in all your ways acknowledge him, and he will make your paths straight.

Proverbs 3:5–6

As human beings, our natural ways of thinking and the paths we naturally feel like following are often vastly different from God's ways and paths. God is always holy, righteous, truthful, and moral, and we are not. God is perfect in awareness and understanding of reality, and we are not. God knows the future, and we do not. God tells us in Isaiah 55:8–9: "'*For my thoughts are not your thoughts, neither are your ways my ways,' declares the LORD. 'As the heavens are higher than the earth, so are my ways higher than your ways and my thoughts than your thoughts.'*" To what extent do you really believe God's message in this verse—that His ways and thoughts are immeasurably higher than your ways and thoughts? The way you answer this question will reveal much about your view of God and the Bible.

As Christians, we are continually choosing to what extent we will follow God's ways and paths instead of the often attractive and comfortable ways and paths of this world. These choices involve our thought-life, what we fill our minds with, what we say, and what we do. The more faithfully we love, trust, and obey God the more He will guide our thinking and direct our paths. The more that we trust and follow the ways of this world the more that we will drift away from God's ways. Who do you want to direct your ways and paths? If you choose God, that means trusting the Bible—the Word of God—above the ways of this world and even above your own thinking. This is the path to spiritual maturity—thinking and living more like Jesus Christ and less like this world.

He is the Rock, his works are perfect, and all his ways are just. A faithful God who does no wrong, upright and just is he.

Deuteronomy 32:4

But be very careful to keep the commandment and the law that Moses the servant of the LORD gave you: to love the LORD your God, to walk in all his ways, to obey his commands, to hold fast to him and to serve him with all your heart and all your soul."

Joshua 22:5

He is the Rock, his works are perfect, and all his ways are just.

The law of the LORD is perfect, reviving the soul. The statutes of the LORD are trustworthy, making wise the simple. The precepts of the LORD are right, giving joy to the heart. The commands of the LORD are radiant, giving light to the eyes. The fear of the LORD is pure, enduring forever. The ordinances of the LORD are sure and altogether righteous. They are more precious than gold, than much pure gold; they are sweeter than honey, than honey from the comb. By them is your servant warned; in keeping them there is great reward.

Psalm 19:7–11

The LORD is my shepherd, I shall not be in want. He makes me lie down in green pastures, he leads me beside quiet waters, he restores my soul. He guides me in paths of righteousness for his name's sake. Even though I walk through the valley of the shadow of death, I will fear no evil, for you are with me; your rod and your staff, they comfort me. You prepare a table before me in the presence of my enemies. You anoint my head with oil; my cup overflows. Surely goodness and love will follow me all the days of my life, and I will dwell in the house of the LORD forever.

Psalm 23:1–6

To you, O LORD, I lift up my soul; in you I trust, O my God. Do not let me be put to shame, nor let my enemies triumph over me. No one whose hope is in you will ever be put to shame, but they will be put to shame who are treacherous without excuse. Show me your ways, O LORD, teach me your paths; guide me in your truth and teach me, for you are God my Savior, and my hope is in you all day long.

Psalm 25:1–5

**Show me your ways,
O LORD,
teach me your paths;
guide me in your truth
and teach me,
for you are
God my Savior,
and my hope
is in you
all day long.**

All the ways of the LORD are loving and faithful for those who keep the demands of his covenant.

Psalm 25:10

Commit your way to the LORD; trust in him and he will do this: He will make your righteousness shine like the dawn, the justice of your cause like the noonday sun.

Psalm 37:5–6

If the LORD delights in a man's way, he makes his steps firm; though he stumble, he will not fall, for the LORD upholds him with his hand.

Psalm 37:23–24

Teach me your way, O LORD, and I will walk in your truth; give me an undivided heart, that I may fear your name. I will praise you, O Lord my God, with all my heart; I will glorify your name forever. For great is your love toward me; you have delivered me from the depths of the grave.

Psalm 86:11–13

Blessed are they whose ways are blameless, who walk according to the law of the LORD. Blessed are they who keep his statutes and seek him with all their heart.

Psalm 119:1–2

How can a young man keep his way pure? By living according to your word.

How can a young man keep his way pure? By living according to your word. I seek you with all my heart; do not let me stray from your commands. I have hidden your word in my heart that I might not sin against you. Praise be to you, O LORD; teach me your decrees. With my lips I recount all the laws that come from your mouth. I rejoice in following your statutes as one rejoices in great riches. I meditate on your precepts and consider your ways. I delight in your decrees; I will not neglect your word.

Psalm 119:9–16

Teach me, O LORD, to follow your decrees; then I will keep them to the end. Give me understanding, and I will keep your law and obey it with all my heart. Direct me in the path of your commands, for there I find delight. Turn my heart toward your statutes and not toward selfish gain. Turn my eyes away from worthless things; preserve my life according to your word.

Psalm 119:33–37

Because I love your commands more than gold, more than pure gold, and because I consider all your precepts right, I hate every wrong path.

Psalm 119:127–128

The LORD is righteous in all his ways and loving toward all he has made.

Psalm 145:17

The LORD is righteous in all his ways and loving toward all he has made.

My son, if you accept my words and store up my commands within you, turning your ear to wisdom and applying your heart to understanding, and if you call out for insight and cry aloud for understanding, and if you look for it as for silver and search for it as for hidden treasure, then you will understand the fear of the LORD and find the knowledge of God. For the LORD gives wisdom, and from his mouth come knowledge and understanding. He holds victory in store for the upright, he is a shield to those whose walk is blameless, for he guards the course of the just and protects the way of his faithful ones. Then you will understand what is right and just and fair—every good path. For wisdom will enter your heart, and knowledge will be pleasant to your soul. Discretion will protect you, and understanding will guard you.

Proverbs 2:1–11

Trust in the LORD with all your heart and lean not on your own understanding; in all your ways acknowledge him, and he will make your paths straight.

Proverbs 3:5–6

Let your eyes look straight ahead, fix your gaze directly before you. Make level paths for your feet and take only ways that are firm. Do not swerve to the right or the left; keep your foot from evil.

Proverbs 4:25–27

Stern discipline awaits him who leaves the path; he who hates correction will die.

Proverbs 15:10

"I am the Lord your God, who teaches you what is best for you, who directs you in the way you should go.

I will lead the blind by ways they have not known, along unfamiliar paths I will guide them; I will turn the darkness into light before them and make the rough places smooth. These are the things I will do; I will not forsake them. But those who trust in idols, who say to images, 'You are our gods,' will be turned back in utter shame.

Isaiah 42:16–17

"Come near me and listen to this: "From the first announcement I have not spoken in secret; at the time it happens, I am there." And now the Sovereign Lord has sent me, with his Spirit. This is what the Lord says—your Redeemer, the Holy One of Israel: "I am the Lord your God, who teaches you what is best for you, who directs you in the way you should go. If only you had paid attention to my commands, your peace would have been like a river, your righteousness like the waves of the sea.

Isaiah 48:16–18

"For my thoughts are not your thoughts, neither are your ways my ways," declares the LORD. "As the heavens are higher than the earth, so are my ways higher than your ways and my thoughts than your thoughts.

Isaiah 55:8–9

This is what the LORD says: "Stand at the crossroads and look; ask for the ancient paths, ask where the good way is, and walk in it, and you will find rest for your souls. But you said, 'We will not walk in it.'

Jeremiah 6:16

Who is wise? He will realize these things. Who is discerning? He will understand them. The ways of the LORD are right; the righteous walk in them, but the rebellious stumble in them.

Hosea 14:9

"As the heavens are higher than the earth, so are my ways higher than your ways and my thoughts than your thoughts."

Oh, the depth of the riches of the wisdom and knowledge of God! How unsearchable his judgments, and his paths beyond tracing out!

Romans 11:33

Finally, brothers, whatever is true, whatever is noble, whatever is right, whatever is pure, whatever is lovely, whatever is admirable—if anything is excellent or praiseworthy—think about such things. Whatever you have learned or received or heard from me, or seen in me— put it into practice. And the God of peace will be with you.

Philippians 4:8–9

Chapter 30

What Displeases God

Woe to those who are wise in their own eyes and clever in their own sight.

Isaiah 5:21

Sin—the breaking of God's laws—is displeasing to God. God is displeased with anything that is evil, deceptive, or opposed to His values and laws. He is displeased when people have little or no interest in knowing Him for who He is and what He stands for. God is displeased whenever people choose to trust in and follow the philosophies and wisdom of man that contradict the Bible. He is displeased when people knowingly choose to disobey Him. These actions all reflect a lack of love and respect for God and a lack of trust in the Bible—the Word of God. These things are evidence of foolish, prideful hearts, and they ultimately result in harm to self and others. Throughout the Bible God clearly communicates the kinds of thoughts, words, and actions that are displeasing to Him.

God knows our hearts better than we do. He cares deeply about the thoughts, attitudes, and intents of your heart, because they determine your relationship with Him, to what extent your life will be glorifying to Him, and the quality of your life. God teaches us in the Bible that sinful living corrupts and damages lives. God earnestly urges us in Proverbs 4:23, "*Above all else, guard your heart, for it is the wellspring of life.*" How do you guard your heart? First, believe in and follow the Lord Jesus Christ as your sin-bearer, Savior, and Lord. Second, trust and obey the Word of God. Third, understand and take up the full armor of God (Ephesians 6:10–18). Fourth, do not fill your mind with, or dwell on, those things that are displeasing to God. If we truly love God, we will strive to glorify Him in our thought life and in how we live our lives. This means being diligent in obeying Him and turning away from those thoughts, words, and actions that are displeasing to Him. The verses in this chapter reveal to us the kinds of heart-attitudes and behaviors that offend and grieve our holy, righteous, and loving God.

And God spoke all these words: "I am the LORD your God, who brought you out of Egypt, out of the land of slavery.

Exodus 20:1–3

"You shall have no other gods before me.

Exodus 20:3

"You shall not make for yourself an idol in the form of anything in heaven above or on the earth beneath or in the waters below.

Exodus 20:4

"You shall not misuse the name of the LORD your God, for the LORD will not hold anyone guiltless who misuses his name.

Exodus 20:7

"You shall have no other gods before me.

"You shall not murder.

Exodus 20:13

"You shall not commit adultery.

Exodus 20:14

"You shall not steal.

Exodus 20:15

"You shall not give false testimony against your neighbor.

Exodus 20:16

"You shall not covet your neighbor's house. You shall not covet your neighbor's wife, or his manservant or maidservant, his ox or donkey, or anything that belongs to your neighbor."

Exodus 20:17

See, I set before you today life and prosperity, death and destruction. For I command you today to love the Lord your God, to walk in his ways, and to keep his commands, decrees and laws; then you will live and increase, and the Lord your God will bless you in the land you are entering to possess. But if your heart turns away and you are not obedient, and if you are drawn away to bow down to other gods and worship them, I declare to you this day that you will certainly be destroyed. You will not live long in the land you are crossing the Jordan to enter and possess.

Deuteronomy 30:15–18

You are not a God who takes pleasure in evil; with you the wicked cannot dwell.

You are not a God who takes pleasure in evil; with you the wicked cannot dwell. The arrogant cannot stand in your presence; you hate all who do wrong. You destroy those who tell lies; bloodthirsty and deceitful men the LORD abhors.

Psalm 5:4–6

There are six things the LORD hates, seven that are detestable to him: haughty eyes, a lying tongue, hands that shed innocent blood, a heart that devises wicked schemes, feet that are quick to rush into evil, a false witness who pours out lies and a man who stirs up dissension among brothers.

Proverbs 6:16–19

"To you, O men, I call out; I raise my voice to all mankind. You who are simple, gain prudence; you who are foolish, gain understanding. Listen, for I have worthy things to say; I open my lips to speak what is right. My mouth speaks what is true, for my lips detest wickedness. All the words of my mouth are just; none of them is crooked or perverse. To the discerning all of them are right; they are faultless to those who have knowledge. Choose my instruction instead of silver, knowledge rather than choice gold, for wisdom is more precious than rubies, and nothing you desire can compare with her.

Proverbs 8:4–11

The LORD detests lying lips, but he delights in men who are truthful.

To fear the LORD is to hate evil; I hate pride and arrogance, evil behavior and perverse speech.

Proverbs 8:13

The LORD abhors dishonest scales, but accurate weights are his delight.

Proverbs 11:1

The LORD detests men of perverse heart but he delights in those whose ways are blameless.

Proverbs 11:20

A good man obtains favor from the LORD, but the LORD condemns a crafty man.

Proverbs 12:2

The LORD detests lying lips, but he delights in men who are truthful.

Proverbs 12:22

The LORD detests the way of the wicked but he loves those who pursue righteousness.

Proverbs 15:9

The LORD detests the thoughts of the wicked, but those of the pure are pleasing to him.

Proverbs 15:26

The LORD detests all the proud of heart. Be sure of this: They will not go unpunished.

Proverbs 16:5

The LORD detests differing weights, and dishonest scales do not please him.

Proverbs 20:23

**Woe to those
who call evil good
and good evil,
who put darkness
for light
and light for darkness,**

Haughty eyes and a proud heart, the lamp of the wicked, are sin!

Proverbs 21:4

Woe to those who call evil good and good evil, who put darkness for light and light for darkness, who put bitter for sweet and sweet for bitter.

Isaiah 5:20

Woe to those who are wise in their own eyes and clever in their own sight.

Isaiah 5:21

So justice is driven back, and righteousness stands at a distance; truth has stumbled in the streets, honesty cannot enter. Truth is nowhere to be found, and whoever shuns evil becomes a prey. The LORD looked and was displeased that there was no justice.

Isaiah 59:14–15

"Therefore," declares the Lord, "I am against the prophets who steal from one another words supposedly from me. Yes," declares the Lord, "I am against the prophets who wag their own tongues and yet declare, 'The Lord declares.' Indeed, I am against those who prophesy false dreams," declares the Lord. "They tell them and lead my people astray with their reckless lies, yet I did not send or appoint them. They do not benefit these people in the least," declares the Lord.

Jeremiah 23:30–32

Your eyes are too pure to look on evil; you cannot tolerate wrong.

but they do not realize that I remember all their evil deeds. Their sins engulf them; they are always before me.

Hosea 7:2

Your eyes are too pure to look on evil; you cannot tolerate wrong. Why then do you tolerate the treacherous? Why are you silent while the wicked swallow up those more righteous than themselves?

Habakkuk 1:13

These are the things you are to do: Speak the truth to each other, and render true and sound judgment in your courts; do not plot evil against your neighbor, and do not love to swear falsely. I hate all this," declares the LORD.

Zechariah 8:16–17

"Woe to the world because of the things that cause people to sin! Such things must come, but woe to the man through whom they come!

Matthew 18:7

He said to them, "You are the ones who justify yourselves in the eyes of men, but God knows your hearts. What is highly valued among men is detestable in God's sight.

Luke 16:15

The wrath of God is being revealed from heaven against all the godlessness and wickedness of men who suppress the truth by their wickedness, since what may be known about God is plain to them, because God has made it plain to them. For since the creation of the world God's invisible qualities—his eternal power and divine nature—have been clearly seen, being understood from what has been made, so that men are without excuse.

Romans 1:18–20

Woe to the world because of the things that cause people to sin!

For although they knew God, they neither glorified him as God nor gave thanks to him, but their thinking became futile and their foolish hearts were darkened. Although they claimed to be wise, they became fools and exchanged the glory of the immortal God for images made to look like mortal man and birds and animals and reptiles.

Romans 1:21–23

They exchanged the truth of God for a lie, and worshiped and served created things rather than the Creator—who is forever praised. Amen. Because of this, God gave them over to shameful lusts. Even their women exchanged natural relations for unnatural ones. In the same way the men also abandoned natural relations with women and were inflamed with lust for one another. Men committed indecent acts with other men, and received in themselves the due penalty for their perversion.

Romans 1:25–27

They exchanged the truth of God for a lie,

Furthermore, since they did not think it worthwhile to retain the knowledge of God, he gave them over to a depraved mind, to do what ought not to be done. They have become filled with every kind of wickedness, evil, greed and depravity. They are full of envy, murder, strife, deceit and malice. They are gossips, slanderers, God-haters, insolent, arrogant and boastful; they invent ways of doing evil; they disobey their parents; they are senseless, faithless, heartless, ruthless. Although they know God's righteous decree that those who do such things deserve death, they not only continue to do these very things but also approve of those who practice them.

Romans 1:28–32

Those who live according to the sinful nature have their minds set on what that nature desires; but those who live in accordance with the Spirit have their minds set on what the Spirit desires. The mind of sinful man is death, but the mind controlled by the Spirit is life and peace; the sinful mind is hostile to God. It does not submit to God's law, nor can it do so. Those controlled by the sinful nature cannot please God.

Romans 8:5–8

Love is patient, love is kind. It does not envy, it does not boast, it is not proud. It is not rude, it is not self-seeking, it is not easily angered, it keeps no record of wrongs. Love does not delight in evil but rejoices with the truth. It always protects, always trusts, always hopes, always perseveres.

1 Corinthians 13:4–7

The acts of the sinful nature are obvious: sexual immorality, impurity and debauchery; idolatry and witchcraft; hatred, discord, jealousy, fits of rage, selfish ambition, dissensions, factions and envy; drunkenness, orgies, and the like. I warn you, as I did before, that those who live like this will not inherit the kingdom of God.

Galatians 5:19–21

But among you there must not be even a hint of sexual immorality, or of any kind of impurity, or of greed, because these are improper for God's holy people. Nor should there be obscenity, foolish talk or coarse joking, which are out of place, but rather thanksgiving. For of this you can be sure: No immoral, impure or greedy person—such a man is an idolater—has any inheritance in the kingdom of Christ and of God. Let no one deceive you with empty words, for because of such things God's wrath comes on those who are disobedient. Therefore do not be partners with them.

Ephesians 5:3–7

But among you there must not be even a hint of sexual immorality, or of any kind of impurity, or of greed, because these are improper for God's holy people.

327

Put to death, therefore, whatever belongs to your earthly nature: sexual immorality, impurity, lust, evil desires and greed, which is idolatry. Because of these, the wrath of God is coming. You used to walk in these ways, in the life you once lived. But now you must rid yourselves of all such things as these: anger, rage, malice, slander, and filthy language from your lips. Do not lie to each other, since you have taken off your old self with its practices and have put on the new self, which is being renewed in knowledge in the image of its Creator.

Colossians 3:5–10

Put to death, therefore, whatever belongs to your earthly nature: sexual immorality, impurity, lust, evil desires and greed, which is idolatry. Because of these, the wrath of God is coming.

How much more severely do you think a man deserves to be punished who has trampled the Son of God under foot, who has treated as an unholy thing the blood of the covenant that sanctified him, and who has insulted the Spirit of grace?

Hebrews 10:29

If any of you lacks wisdom, he should ask God, who gives generously to all without finding fault, and it will be given to him. But when he asks, he must believe and not doubt, because he who doubts is like a wave of the sea, blown and tossed by the wind. That man should not think he will receive anything from the Lord; he is a double-minded man, unstable in all he does.

James 1:5–8

We know that we have come to know him if we obey his commands. The man who says, "I know him," but does not do what he commands is a liar, and the truth is not in him. But if anyone obeys his word, God's love is truly made complete in him. This is how we know we are in him: Whoever claims to live in him must walk as Jesus did.

1 John 2:3–6

Do not love the world or anything in the world. If anyone loves the world, the love of the Father is not in him. For everything in the world—the cravings of sinful man, the lust of his eyes and the boasting of what he has and does—comes not from the Father but from the world. The world and its desires pass away, but the man who does the will of God lives forever.

1 John 2:15–17

Do not love the world or anything in the world. If anyone loves the world, the love of the Father is not in him.

I warn everyone who hears the words of the prophecy of this book: If anyone adds anything to them, God will add to him the plagues described in this book. And if anyone takes words away from this book of prophecy, God will take away from him his share in the tree of life and in the holy city, which are described in this book.

Revelation 22:18–19

Chapter 31

What Pleases God

It gave me great joy to have some brothers come and tell about your faithfulness to the truth and how you continue to walk in the truth. I have no greater joy than to hear that my children are walking in the truth.

3 John 3–4

What pleases God? God is pleased with anything that is consistent with His character, His values, and His laws. God is pleased when we truly love Him and one another.

Jesus replied: "'Love the Lord your God with all your heart and with all your soul and with all your mind.' This is the first and greatest commandment. And the second is like it: 'Love your neighbor as yourself.' *Matthew 22:37–39*

God is pleased when we choose to earnestly trust, obey, worship, and serve Him. He is pleased when we walk in humility, live according to His Word, and are faithful and obedient ambassadors for Jesus Christ. Living this way glorifies God and blesses others. Throughout the Bible God makes clear the kinds of thoughts, words, and actions that are pleasing to Him.

Part of becoming a faithful follower of Jesus Christ and knowing God more fully is to be continually growing in our understanding of His character, His values, His standards, and how He calls us to live. To grow in our understanding of God requires trusting the Bible—the Word of God, rather than the alternative philosophies and opinions of this world. Being diligent in studying the Bible will protect us from the danger of sincerely thinking that we are pleasing God when in reality we are displeasing Him. God gives us clear guidance on this in 2 Timothy 2:15: "*Do your best to present yourself to God as one approved, a workman who does not need to be ashamed and who correctly handles the word of truth.*" A committed follower of Jesus Christ is earnest about seeking to please God. May the verses in this chapter be helpful to you as you seek to accurately understand what pleases our holy, righteous, and loving God.

""Honor your father and your mother, so that you may live long in the land the LORD your God is giving you.

Exodus 20:12

See, I am setting before you today a blessing and a curse— the blessing if you obey the commands of the LORD your God that I am giving you today; the curse if you disobey the commands of the LORD your God and turn from the way that I command you today by following other gods, which you have not known.

Deuteronomy 11:26–28

"Honor your father and your mother,

Now what I am commanding you today is not too difficult for you or beyond your reach. It is not up in heaven, so that you have to ask, "Who will ascend into heaven to get it and proclaim it to us so we may obey it?" Nor is it beyond the sea, so that you have to ask, "Who will cross the sea to get it and proclaim it to us so we may obey it?" No, the word is very near you; it is in your mouth and in your heart so you may obey it.

Deuteronomy 30:11–14

See, I set before you today life and prosperity, death and destruction. For I command you today to love the Lord your God, to walk in his ways, and to keep his commands, decrees and laws; then you will live and increase, and the Lord your God will bless you in the land you are entering to possess. But if your heart turns away and you are not obedient, and if you are drawn away to bow down to other gods and worship them, I declare to you this day that you will certainly be destroyed. You will not live long in the land you are crossing the Jordan to enter and possess.

Deuteronomy 30:15–18

This day I call heaven and earth as witnesses against you that I have set before you life and death, blessings and curses. Now choose life, so that you and your children may live and that you may love the Lord your God, listen to his voice, and hold fast to him. For the Lord is your life, and he will give you many years in the land he swore to give to your fathers, Abraham, Isaac and Jacob.

Deuteronomy 30:19–20

I know, my God, that you test the heart and are pleased with integrity. . . .

1 Chronicles 29:17a

For the word of the Lord is right and true; he is faithful in all he does. The Lord loves righteousness and justice; the earth is full of his unfailing love.

Psalm 33:4–5

The Lord loves righteousness and justice;

Surely you desire truth in the inner parts; you teach me wisdom in the inmost place.

Psalm 51:6

Because I love your commands more than gold, more than pure gold, and because I consider all your precepts right, I hate every wrong path.

Psalm 119:127–128

I will bow down toward your holy temple and will praise your name for your love and your faithfulness, for you have exalted above all things your name and your word.

Psalm 138:2

The LORD is near to all who call on him, to all who call on him in truth.

Psalm 145:18

the LORD delights in those who fear him, who put their hope in his unfailing love.

Psalm 147:11

The LORD abhors dishonest scales, but accurate weights are his delight.

Proverbs 11:1

**The LORD is near
to all who call on him,
to all who call on him
in truth.**

The LORD detests men of perverse heart but he delights in those whose ways are blameless.

Proverbs 11:20

The LORD detests lying lips, but he delights in men who are truthful.

Proverbs 12:22

The LORD detests the way of the wicked but he loves those who pursue righteousness.

Proverbs 15:9

The LORD detests the thoughts of the wicked, but those of the pure are pleasing to him.

Proverbs 15:26

To do what is right and just is more acceptable to the LORD than sacrifice.

Proverbs 21:3

Has not my hand made all these things, and so they came
into being?" declares the LORD. "This is the one I esteem:
he who is humble and contrite in spirit, and trembles
at my word.

Isaiah 66:2

This is what the LORD says: "Let not the wise man boast
of his wisdom or the strong man boast of his strength or
the rich man boast of his riches, but let him who boasts
boast about this: that he understands and knows me,
that I am the LORD, who exercises kindness, justice and
righteousness on earth, for in these I delight," declares
the LORD.

Jeremiah 9:23–24

"The most important one," answered Jesus, "is this: 'Hear,
O Israel, the Lord our God, the Lord is one. Love the
Lord your God with all your heart and with all your soul
and with all your mind and with all your strength.' The
second is this: 'Love your neighbor as yourself.' There is no
commandment greater than these."

Mark 12:29–31

**"This is the one
I esteem:
he who is humble
and contrite in spirit,
and trembles
at my word.**

Yet a time is coming and has now come when the true
worshipers will worship the Father in spirit and truth,
for they are the kind of worshipers the Father seeks.
God is spirit, and his worshipers must worship in spirit
and in truth."

John 4:23–24

For I have come down from heaven not to do my will but to do the will of him who sent me. And this is the will of him who sent me, that I shall lose none of all that he has given me, but raise them up at the last day. For my Father's will is that everyone who looks to the Son and believes in him shall have eternal life, and I will raise him up at the last day."

John 6:38–40

Stop judging by mere appearances, and make a right judgment."

John 7:24

For my Father's will is that everyone who looks to the Son and believes in him shall have eternal life,

Whoever has my commands and obeys them, he is the one who loves me. He who loves me will be loved by my Father, and I too will love him and show myself to him."

John 14:21

"I am the vine; you are the branches. If a man remains in me and I in him, he will bear much fruit; apart from me you can do nothing. If anyone does not remain in me, he is like a branch that is thrown away and withers; such branches are picked up, thrown into the fire and burned. If you remain in me and my words remain in you, ask whatever you wish, and it will be given you. This is to my Father's glory, that you bear much fruit, showing yourselves to be my disciples.

John 15:5–8

"As the Father has loved me, so have I loved you. Now remain in my love. If you obey my commands, you will remain in my love, just as I have obeyed my Father's commands and remain in his love. I have told you this so that my joy may be in you and that your joy may be complete.

John 15:9–11

Love is patient, love is kind. It does not envy, it does not boast, it is not proud. It is not rude, it is not self-seeking, it is not easily angered, it keeps no record of wrongs. Love does not delight in evil but rejoices with the truth. It always protects, always trusts, always hopes, always perseveres.

1 Corinthians 13:4–7

If you obey my commands, you will remain in my love, just as I have obeyed my Father's commands and remain in his love.

But the fruit of the Spirit is love, joy, peace, patience, kindness, goodness, faithfulness, gentleness and self-control. Against such things there is no law. Those who belong to Christ Jesus have crucified the sinful nature with its passions and desires. Since we live by the Spirit, let us keep in step with the Spirit.

Galatians 5:22–25

Do not be deceived: God cannot be mocked. A man reaps what he sows. The one who sows to please his sinful nature, from that nature will reap destruction; the one who sows to please the Spirit, from the Spirit will reap eternal life. Let us not become weary in doing good, for at the proper time we will reap a harvest if we do not give up. Therefore, as we have opportunity, let us do good to all people, especially to those who belong to the family of believers.

Galatians 6:7–10

For you were once darkness, but now you are light in the Lord. Live as children of light for the fruit of the light consists in all goodness, righteousness and truth) and find out what pleases the Lord.

Ephesians 5:8–10

I urge, then, first of all, that requests, prayers, intercession and thanksgiving be made for everyone—for kings and all those in authority, that we may live peaceful and quiet lives in all godliness and holiness. This is good, and pleases God our Savior, who wants all men to be saved and to come to a knowledge of the truth. For there is one God and one mediator between God and men, the man Christ Jesus,

1 Timothy 2:1–5

This is good, and pleases God our Savior, who wants all men to be saved and to come to a knowledge of the truth.

Although I hope to come to you soon, I am writing you these instructions so that, if I am delayed, you will know how people ought to conduct themselves in God's household, which is the church of the living God, the pillar and foundation of the truth.

1 Timothy 3:14–15

Since an overseer is entrusted with God's work, he must be blameless—not overbearing, not quick-tempered, not given to drunkenness, not violent, not pursuing dishonest gain. Rather he must be hospitable, one who loves what is good, who is self-controlled, upright, holy and disciplined. He must hold firmly to the trustworthy message as it has been taught, so that he can encourage others by sound doctrine and refute those who oppose it.

Titus 1:7–9

Make every effort to live in peace with all men and to be
holy; without holiness no one will see the Lord. See to it
that no one misses the grace of God and that no bitter root
grows up to cause trouble and defile many.

Hebrews 12:14–15

But the wisdom that comes from heaven is first of all pure;
then peace-loving, considerate, submissive, full of mercy
and good fruit, impartial and sincere. Peacemakers who
sow in peace raise a harvest of righteousness.

James 3:17–18

For this very reason, make every effort to add to your
faith goodness; and to goodness, knowledge; and to
knowledge, self-control; and to self-control, perseverance;
and to perseverance, godliness; and to godliness, brotherly
kindness; and to brotherly kindness, love. For if you
possess these qualities in increasing measure, they will
keep you from being ineffective and unproductive in your
knowledge of our Lord Jesus Christ.

2 Peter 1:5–8

**He is patient with you,
not wanting anyone
to perish,
but everyone
to come to repentance.**

The Lord is not slow in keeping his promise, as some
understand slowness. He is patient with you, not wanting
anyone to perish, but everyone to come to repentance.

2 Peter 3:9

We know that we have come to know him if we obey his commands. The man who says, "I know him," but does not do what he commands is a liar, and the truth is not in him. But if anyone obeys his word, God's love is truly made complete in him. This is how we know we are in him: Whoever claims to live in him must walk as Jesus did.

1 John 2:3–6

It gave me great joy to have some brothers come and tell about your faithfulness to the truth and how you continue to walk in the truth. I have no greater joy than to hear that my children are walking in the truth.

3 John 3–4

But if anyone obeys his word, God's love is truly made complete in him.

Section 3

What the Bible Says About Human Beings

The Bible verses in the chapters of this section reveal to us God's foundational truths about human beings. It is on these truths that God wants us to base our understanding of ourselves, others, and our need for a right relationship with the Lord Jesus Christ. Through these foundational truths God speaks to us regarding the following:

1. How God has designed you
2. How God views you
3. The reality of sin in your life and its consequences
4. The personal relationship that God desires to have with you
5. Your free will and the importance of your choices
6. How God wants you to view and think about yourself
7. How God wants you to view, love, and care for others

May the Bible verses in these chapters help you to more accurately understand who you really are and why God created you.

Chapter 32

The Miracle of Human Life

For we are God's workmanship, created in Christ Jesus
to do good works, which God prepared in advance for
us to do.

Ephesians 2:10

The Bible is very clear that human beings are created by God. Our Creator has supernaturally designed us as living beings that are both physical and spiritual. He created us spiritually in His image in such a way that we can enter into a loving, personal relationship with Him for eternity. God also created us with the ability to enter into loving, committed, God-honoring relationships with each other. He has wonderfully designed human beings to be able to think rationally, feel emotions, make free-will choices, communicate both verbally and nonverbally, give and receive love, experience joy, appreciate beauty, be creative, and much more.

What makes our physical lives possible is God's power and order, which He is continually applying to sustain the universe, the earth, and all of life. God is in control of everything we need for life, from the physical laws that govern the universe down to the behavior of the smallest subatomic particles. God has masterfully designed the functioning of our DNA, our cells, and every biological system within our bodies. With every new discovery, scientists are amazed at the intricacy of these biological systems and how they work together. Had human sin not entered the world, the physical universe and every component of our human bodies would continue to function flawlessly for eternity according to God's original design.

Each of us is truly the product of supernatural design, both physically and spiritually. Everyone, regardless of one's sinful past, can choose to place his or her faith in the Lord Jesus Christ and be spiritually reborn. Each of us, regardless of our human talents and abilities, can greatly serve and glorify God when we choose to be totally given over to Him with all of our heart, soul, mind, and strength. This is God's desire.

Then God said, "Let us make man in our image, in our likeness, and let them rule over the fish of the sea and the birds of the air, over the livestock, over all the earth, and over all the creatures that move along the ground." So God created man in his own image, in the image of God he created him; male and female he created them.

Genesis 1:26–27

the LORD God formed the man from the dust of the ground and breathed into his nostrils the breath of life, and the man became a living being.

Genesis 2:7

So God created man in his own image, in the image of God he created him;

So the LORD God caused the man to fall into a deep sleep; and while he was sleeping, he took one of the man's ribs and closed up the place with flesh. Then the LORD God made a woman from the rib he had taken out of the man, and he brought her to the man. The man said, "This is now bone of my bones and flesh of my flesh; she shall be called 'woman,' for she was taken out of man." For this reason a man will leave his father and mother and be united to his wife, and they will become one flesh. The man and his wife were both naked, and they felt no shame.

Genesis 2:21–25

Know that the LORD is God. It is he who made us, and we are his; we are his people, the sheep of his pasture.

Psalm 100:3

Your hands made me and formed me; give me understanding to learn your commands.

Psalm 119:73

For you created my inmost being; you knit me together in my mother's womb. I praise you because I am fearfully and wonderfully made; your works are wonderful, I know that full well. My frame was not hidden from you when I was made in the secret place. When I was woven together in the depths of the earth, your eyes saw my unformed body. All the days ordained for me were written in your book before one of them came to be.

Psalm 139:13–16

Ears that hear and eyes that see—the LORD has made them both.

Proverbs 20:12

"This is what the LORD says—your Redeemer, who formed you in the womb: I am the LORD, who has made all things, who alone stretched out the heavens, who spread out the earth by myself,

Isaiah 44:24

"Before I formed you in the womb I knew you,

The word of the LORD came to me, saying, "Before I formed you in the womb I knew you, before you were born I set you apart; I appointed you as a prophet to the nations."

Jeremiah 1:4–5

"But at the beginning of creation God 'made them male and female.' 'For this reason a man will leave his father and mother and be united to his wife, and the two will become one flesh.' So they are no longer two, but one. Therefore what God has joined together, let man not separate."

Mark 10:6–9

But the angel said to him: "Do not be afraid, Zechariah; your prayer has been heard. Your wife Elizabeth will bear you a son, and you are to give him the name John. He will be a joy and delight to you, and many will rejoice because of his birth, for he will be great in the sight of the Lord. He is never to take wine or other fermented drink, and he will be filled with the Holy Spirit even from birth.

Luke 1:13–15

At that time Mary got ready and hurried to a town in the hill country of Judea, where she entered Zechariah's home and greeted Elizabeth. When Elizabeth heard Mary's greeting, the baby leaped in her womb, and Elizabeth was filled with the Holy Spirit.

Luke 1:39–41

For we are God's workmanship, created in Christ Jesus to do good works,

Jesus answered, "I tell you the truth, no one can enter the kingdom of God unless he is born of water and the Spirit. Flesh gives birth to flesh, but the Spirit gives birth to spirit. You should not be surprised at my saying, 'You must be born again.'

John 3:5–7

So it is written: "The first man Adam became a living being"; the last Adam, a life-giving spirit.

1 Corinthians 15:45

For it is by grace you have been saved, through faith—and this not from yourselves, it is the gift of God—not by works, so that no one can boast. For we are God's workmanship, created in Christ Jesus to do good works, which God prepared in advance for us to do.

Ephesians 2:8–10

346

Chapter 33

You Are a Physical and Spiritual Being

Do not be afraid of those who kill the body but cannot kill the soul. Rather, be afraid of the One who can destroy both soul and body in hell.

Matthew 10:28

We are more than physical matter organized and made alive by some evolved biochemical, electrical phenomenon. New discoveries in science continue to reveal that our bodies are highly sophisticated biological systems. In fact, the technology of our bodies is so advanced that science is not even close to fully understanding the workings of the cell, DNA, protein folding, the immune system, the human brain, and the list goes on. However, we are more than physical beings. We are beings who God has supernaturally designed and created to be both spiritual and physical. God tells us in the Bible that He is a spiritual being and that He created mankind in His image. It is the spiritual side of us that reflects God's image and enables us to experience loving, meaningful relationships with each other and with God.

The Bible speaks often about the human heart, soul, mind, and spirit. It is beyond our reach to scientifically study and fully understand the spiritual dimension of human beings and how our spiritual selves are integrated with our physical bodies. We have impressive technology that enables us to vastly extend our five senses and better understand the world we live in. However, we are still unable to directly observe and scientifically study our spiritual dimension. We currently have only one accurate and trustworthy window into the spiritual realm, and that window is the Word of God. The Bible tells you everything you need to know about the "spiritual you" and about God's provision through the Lord Jesus Christ for entering into a right relationship with Him.

May the verses in this chapter help you to grow in your confidence that you are wonderfully designed and created by God. The God of the Bible created you in His image to love Him, love others, serve Him, and live with Him for eternity. May this be your path.

But the LORD said to Samuel, "Do not consider his appearance or his height, for I have rejected him. The LORD does not look at the things man looks at. Man looks at the outward appearance, but the LORD looks at the heart."

1 Samuel 16:7

The LORD does not look at the things man looks at. Man looks at the outward appearance, but the LORD looks at the heart."

For you created my inmost being; you knit me together in my mother's womb. I praise you because I am fearfully and wonderfully made; your works are wonderful, I know that full well. My frame was not hidden from you when I was made in the secret place. When I was woven together in the depths of the earth, your eyes saw my unformed body. All the days ordained for me were written in your book before one of them came to be.

Psalm 139:13–16

Do not be wise in your own eyes; fear the LORD and shun evil. This will bring health to your body and nourishment to your bones.

Proverbs 3:7–8

My son, pay attention to what I say; listen closely to my words. Do not let them out of your sight, keep them within your heart; for they are life to those who find them and health to a man's whole body.

Proverbs 4:20–22

Above all else, guard your heart, for it is the wellspring of life.

Proverbs 4:23

A heart at peace gives life to the body, but envy
rots the bones.

Proverbs 14:30

A cheerful look brings joy to the heart, and good news gives
health to the bones.

Proverbs 15:30

A cheerful heart is good medicine, but a crushed spirit dries
up the bones.

Proverbs 17:22

A man's spirit sustains him in sickness, but a crushed spirit
who can bear?

Proverbs 18:14

**"Cursed is the one
who trusts in man,
who depends on flesh
for his strength
and whose heart turns
away from the LORD.**

He has made everything beautiful in its time. He has also
set eternity in the hearts of men; yet they cannot fathom
what God has done from beginning to end.

Ecclesiastes 3:11

This is what the LORD says: "Cursed is the one who trusts
in man, who depends on flesh for his strength and whose
heart turns away from the LORD.

Jeremiah 17:5

I will give them an undivided heart and put a new spirit in them; I will remove from them their heart of stone and give them a heart of flesh. Then they will follow my decrees and be careful to keep my laws. They will be my people, and I will be their God. But as for those whose hearts are devoted to their vile images and detestable idols, I will bring down on their own heads what they have done, declares the Sovereign LORD."

Ezekiel 11:19–21

**I will give you
a new heart and
put a new spirit in you;
I will remove from you
your heart of stone
and give you
a heart of flesh.**

I will give you a new heart and put a new spirit in you; I will remove from you your heart of stone and give you a heart of flesh. And I will put my Spirit in you and move you to follow my decrees and be careful to keep my laws.

Ezekiel 36:26–27

"Do not store up for yourselves treasures on earth, where moth and rust destroy, and where thieves break in and steal. But store up for yourselves treasures in heaven, where moth and rust do not destroy, and where thieves do not break in and steal. For where your treasure is, there your heart will be also.

Matthew 6:19–21

Do not be afraid of those who kill the body but cannot kill the soul. Rather, be afraid of the One who can destroy both soul and body in hell.

Matthew 10:28

"Come to me, all you who are weary and burdened, and I will give you rest. Take my yoke upon you and learn from me, for I am gentle and humble in heart, and you will find rest for your souls. For my yoke is easy and my burden is light."

Matthew 11:28–30

Then Jesus said to his disciples, "If anyone would come after me, he must deny himself and take up his cross and follow me. For whoever wants to save his life will lose it, but whoever loses his life for me will find it. What good will it be for a man if he gains the whole world, yet forfeits his soul? Or what can a man give in exchange for his soul?

Matthew 16:24–26

Jesus replied: '"Love the Lord your God with all your heart and with all your soul and with all your mind.' This is the first and greatest commandment. And the second is like it: 'Love your neighbor as yourself.'

Matthew 22:37–39

**Jesus replied:
'"Love the Lord
your God
with all your heart
and with all your soul
and with all your mind.'**

He said to them, "This is what I told you while I was still with you: Everything must be fulfilled that is written about me in the Law of Moses, the Prophets and the Psalms." Then he opened their minds so they could understand the Scriptures. He told them, "This is what is written: The Christ will suffer and rise from the dead on the third day, and repentance and forgiveness of sins will be preached in his name to all nations, beginning at Jerusalem. You are witnesses of these things. I am going to send you what my Father has promised; but stay in the city until you have been clothed with power from on high."

Luke 24:44–48

Jesus answered, "I tell you the truth, no one can enter the kingdom of God unless he is born of water and the Spirit. Flesh gives birth to flesh, but the Spirit gives birth to spirit. You should not be surprised at my saying, 'You must be born again.'

John 3:5–7

For the wages of sin is death, but the gift of God is eternal life in Christ Jesus our Lord.

Romans 6:23

Flesh gives birth to flesh, but the Spirit gives birth to spirit. You should not be surprised at my saying, 'You must be born again.'

I know that nothing good lives in me, that is, in my sinful nature. For I have the desire to do what is good, but I cannot carry it out. For what I do is not the good I want to do; no, the evil I do not want to do—this I keep on doing. Now if I do what I do not want to do, it is no longer I who do it, but it is sin living in me that does it. So I find this law at work: When I want to do good, evil is right there with me. For in my inner being I delight in God's law; but I see another law at work in the members of my body, waging war against the law of my mind and making me a prisoner of the law of sin at work within my members. What a wretched man I am! Who will rescue me from this body of death? Thanks be to God—through Jesus Christ our Lord! So then, I myself in my mind am a slave to God's law, but in the sinful nature a slave to the law of sin.

Romans 7:18–25

Those who live according to the sinful nature have their minds set on what that nature desires; but those who live in accordance with the Spirit have their minds set on what the Spirit desires. The mind of sinful man is death, but the mind controlled by the Spirit is life and peace; the sinful mind is hostile to God. It does not submit to God's law, nor can it do so. Those controlled by the sinful nature cannot please God.

Romans 8:5–8

You, however, are controlled not by the sinful nature but by the Spirit, if the Spirit of God lives in you. And if anyone does not have the Spirit of Christ, he does not belong to Christ. But if Christ is in you, your body is dead because of sin, yet your spirit is alive because of righteousness. And if the Spirit of him who raised Jesus from the dead is living in you, he who raised Christ from the dead will also give life to your mortal bodies through his Spirit, who lives in you.

Romans 8:9–11

And if the Spirit of him who raised Jesus from the dead is living in you, he who raised Christ from the dead will also give life to your mortal bodies through his Spirit, who lives in you.

Therefore, I urge you, brothers, in view of God's mercy, to offer your bodies as living sacrifices, holy and pleasing to God—this is your spiritual act of worship. Do not conform any longer to the pattern of this world, but be transformed by the renewing of your mind. Then you will be able to test and approve what God's will is—his good, pleasing and perfect will.

Romans 12:1–2

. . . The body is not meant for sexual immorality, but for the Lord, and the Lord for the body. By his power God raised the Lord from the dead, and he will raise us also. Do you not know that your bodies are members of Christ himself? Shall I then take the members of Christ and unite them with a prostitute? Never! Do you not know that he who unites himself with a prostitute is one with her in body? For it is said, "The two will become one flesh." But he who unites himself with the Lord is one with him in spirit.

1 Corinthians 6:13–17

**Though outwardly
we are wasting away,
yet inwardly
we are being renewed
day by day.**

For God, who said, "Let light shine out of darkness," made his light shine in our hearts to give us the light of the knowledge of the glory of God in the face of Christ. But we have this treasure in jars of clay to show that this all-surpassing power is from God and not from us.

2 Corinthians 4:6–7

Therefore we do not lose heart. Though outwardly we are wasting away, yet inwardly we are being renewed day by day. For our light and momentary troubles are achieving for us an eternal glory that far outweighs them all. So we fix our eyes not on what is seen, but on what is unseen. For what is seen is temporary, but what is unseen is eternal.

2 Corinthians 4: 16–18

Now we know that if the earthly tent we live in is destroyed, we have a building from God, an eternal house in heaven, not built by human hands. Meanwhile we groan, longing to be clothed with our heavenly dwelling,

2 Corinthians 5:1–2

Therefore we are always confident and know that as long as we are at home in the body we are away from the Lord. We live by faith, not by sight. We are confident, I say, and would prefer to be away from the body and at home with the Lord. So we make it our goal to please him, whether we are at home in the body or away from it.

2 Corinthians 5:6–9

For this reason I kneel before the Father, from whom his whole family in heaven and on earth derives its name. I pray that out of his glorious riches he may strengthen you with power through his Spirit in your inner being, so that Christ may dwell in your hearts through faith. And I pray that you, being rooted and established in love, may have power, together with all the saints, to grasp how wide and long and high and deep is the love of Christ, and to know this love that surpasses knowledge—that you may be filled to the measure of all the fullness of God.

Ephesians 3:14–19

I pray that out of his glorious riches he may strengthen you with power through his Spirit in your inner being, so that Christ may dwell in your hearts through faith.

But our citizenship is in heaven. And we eagerly await a Savior from there, the Lord Jesus Christ, who, by the power that enables him to bring everything under his control, will transform our lowly bodies so that they will be like his glorious body.

Philippians 3:20–21

Since, then, you have been raised with Christ, set your hearts on things above, where Christ is seated at the right hand of God. Set your minds on things above, not on earthly things.

Colossians 3:1–2

For the word of God is living and active. Sharper than any double-edged sword, it penetrates even to dividing soul and spirit, joints and marrow; it judges the thoughts and attitudes of the heart.

Hebrews 4:12

But when this priest had offered for all time one sacrifice for sins, he sat down at the right hand of God. Since that time he waits for his enemies to be made his footstool, because by one sacrifice he has made perfect forever those who are being made holy. The Holy Spirit also testifies to us about this. First he says: "This is the covenant I will make with them after that time, says the Lord. I will put my laws in their hearts, and I will write them on their minds." Then he adds: "Their sins and lawless acts I will remember no more." And where these have been forgiven, there is no longer any sacrifice for sin.

Hebrews 10:12–18

For you were like sheep going astray, but now you have returned to the Shepherd and Overseer of your souls.

When they hurled their insults at him, he did not retaliate; when he suffered, he made no threats. Instead, he entrusted himself to him who judges justly. He himself bore our sins in his body on the tree, so that we might die to sins and live for righteousness; by his wounds you have been healed. For you were like sheep going astray, but now you have returned to the Shepherd and Overseer of your souls.

1 Peter 2:23–25

Chapter 34

God Values All Human Life

**This is good, and pleases God our Savior, who wants all
men to be saved and to come to a knowledge of the truth.**
1 Timothy 2:3–4

God created human beings in His image. He desires a loving relationship with each one of us for eternity. He still desires this, even though we have all sinned (Romans 3:23). God calls all human beings to be responsive to His prompting, to choose to earnestly seek Him, to repent of sin, and then to believe in and follow Jesus Christ as Lord and Savior. God promises us in Jeremiah 29:13 *"You will seek me and find me when you seek me with all your heart."*

In addition to valuing human life, God also values righteousness and justice. God's holy nature requires that the just penalty for sin must be paid. The fact that God must execute perfect justice for those guilty of sin does not mean that He does not value human life. Out of love for human beings, God has provided a single way for the penalty for our sins to be paid and for us to be forgiven. John 14:6 tells us: *"Jesus answered, 'I am the way and the truth and the life. No one comes to the Father except through me."* God offers each of us His Son, Jesus Christ—the Lamb of God—as the perfect, sinless sacrifice to pay the full penalty for our sins. God's solution for our sins allows Him to have a personal, loving, and eternal relationship with human beings, while at the same time not compromising His holy justice. Whether or not one accepts God's offer is a personal choice every individual must make. To deny one's sinful nature and to refuse to repent of one's sins equals rejecting the Lord Jesus Christ and sentencing oneself to God's perfect justice and punishment for sin. That punishment is eternal separation from God in a place called hell. To accept God's offer of salvation means to repent of one's sins and to place one's faith in Jesus Christ. It also means to become an obedient follower of the Lord Jesus Christ. The fact that Jesus Christ came to be our sin-bearer, Savior, and Lord demonstrates how much God values and loves every human soul.

Then God said, "Let us make man in our image, in our likeness, and let them rule over the fish of the sea and the birds of the air, over the livestock, over all the earth, and over all the creatures that move along the ground." So God created man in his own image, in the image of God he created him; male and female he created them.

Genesis 1:26–27

But the LORD said to Samuel, "Do not consider his appearance or his height, for I have rejected him. The LORD does not look at the things man looks at. Man looks at the outward appearance, but the LORD looks at the heart."

1 Samuel 16:7

So God created man in his own image, in the image of God he created him; male and female he created them.

When I consider your heavens, the work of your fingers, the moon and the stars, which you have set in place, what is man that you are mindful of him, the son of man that you care for him? You made him a little lower than the heavenly beings and crowned him with glory and honor.

Psalm 8:3–5

Teach me your way, O LORD, and I will walk in your truth; give me an undivided heart, that I may fear your name. I will praise you, O Lord my God, with all my heart; I will glorify your name forever. For great is your love toward me; you have delivered me from the depths of the grave.

Psalm 86:11–13

Know that the LORD is God. It is he who made us, and we are his; we are his people, the sheep of his pasture.

Psalm 100:3

For you created my inmost being; you knit me together in my mother's womb. I praise you because I am fearfully and wonderfully made; your works are wonderful, I know that full well. My frame was not hidden from you when I was made in the secret place. When I was woven together in the depths of the earth, your eyes saw my unformed body. All the days ordained for me were written in your book before one of them came to be.

Psalm 139:13–16

This is what God the LORD says—he who created the heavens and stretched them out, who spread out the earth and all that comes out of it, who gives breath to its people, and life to those who walk on it:

Isaiah 42:5

I will sprinkle clean water on you, and you will be clean; I will cleanse you from all your impurities and from all your idols. I will give you a new heart and put a new spirit in you; I will remove from you your heart of stone and give you a heart of flesh. And I will put my Spirit in you and move you to follow my decrees and be careful to keep my laws.

Ezekiel 36:25–27

"Therefore I tell you, do not worry about your life, what you will eat or drink; or about your body, what you will wear. Is not life more important than food, and the body more important than clothes? Look at the birds of the air; they do not sow or reap or store away in barns, and yet your heavenly Father feeds them. Are you not much more valuable than they? Who of you by worrying can add a single hour to his life?

Matthew 6:25–27

For you created my inmost being; you knit me together in my mother's womb. I praise you because I am fearfully and wonderfully made;

359

"The King will reply, 'I tell you the truth, whatever you did for one of the least of these brothers of mine, you did for me.'

Matthew 25:40

"For God so loved the world that he gave his one and only Son, that whoever believes in him shall not perish but have eternal life. For God did not send his Son into the world to condemn the world, but to save the world through him. Whoever believes in him is not condemned, but whoever does not believe stands condemned already because he has not believed in the name of God's one and only Son.

John 3:16–18

**For God
so loved the world
that he gave
his one and only Son,
that whoever
believes in him
shall not perish
but have eternal life.**

When Jesus spoke again to the people, he said, "I am the light of the world. Whoever follows me will never walk in darkness, but will have the light of life."

John 8:12

Whoever has my commands and obeys them, he is the one who loves me. He who loves me will be loved by my Father, and I too will love him and show myself to him."

John 14:21

Jesus replied, "If anyone loves me, he will obey my teaching. My Father will love him, and we will come to him and make our home with him. He who does not love me will not obey my teaching. These words you hear are not my own; they belong to the Father who sent me.

John 14:23–24

"As the Father has loved me, so have I loved you. Now remain in my love. If you obey my commands, you will remain in my love, just as I have obeyed my Father's commands and remain in his love. I have told you this so that my joy may be in you and that your joy may be complete.

John 15:9–11

"The God who made the world and everything in it is the Lord of heaven and earth and does not live in temples built by hands. And he is not served by human hands, as if he needed anything, because he himself gives all men life and breath and everything else. From one man he made every nation of men, that they should inhabit the whole earth; and he determined the times set for them and the exact places where they should live. God did this so that men would seek him and perhaps reach out for him and find him, though he is not far from each one of us. 'For in him we live and move and have our being.' As some of your own poets have said, 'We are his offspring.'

Acts 17:24–28

> "Everyone who calls on the name of the Lord will be saved.

But God demonstrates his own love for us in this: While we were still sinners, Christ died for us.

Romans 5:8

For there is no difference between Jew and Gentile—the same Lord is Lord of all and richly blesses all who call on him, for, "Everyone who calls on the name of the Lord will be saved.

Romans 10:12–13

For this reason I kneel before the Father, from whom his whole family in heaven and on earth derives its name. I pray that out of his glorious riches he may strengthen you with power through his Spirit in your inner being, so that Christ may dwell in your hearts through faith. And I pray that you, being rooted and established in love, may have power, together with all the saints, to grasp how wide and long and high and deep is the love of Christ, and to know this love that surpasses knowledge—that you may be filled to the measure of all the fullness of God.

Ephesians 3:14–19

For there is one God and one mediator between God and men, the man Christ Jesus, who gave himself as a ransom for all men

This is good, and pleases God our Savior, who wants all men to be saved and to come to a knowledge of the truth. For there is one God and one mediator between God and men, the man Christ Jesus, who gave himself as a ransom for all men—the testimony given in its proper time. And for this purpose I was appointed a herald and an apostle—I am telling the truth, I am not lying—and a teacher of the true faith to the Gentiles.

1 Timothy 2:3–7

Your beauty should not come from outward adornment, such as braided hair and the wearing of gold jewelry and fine clothes. Instead, it should be that of your inner self, the unfading beauty of a gentle and quiet spirit, which is of great worth in God's sight.

1 Peter 3:3–4

The Lord is not slow in keeping his promise, as some understand slowness. He is patient with you, not wanting anyone to perish, but everyone to come to repentance.

2 Peter 3:9

This is how God showed his love among us: He sent his
one and only Son into the world that we might live through
him. This is love: not that we loved God, but that he
loved us and sent his Son as an atoning sacrifice for our sins.
Dear friends, since God so loved us, we also ought to
love one another.

1 John 4:9–11

And this is the testimony: God has given us eternal life, and
this life is in his Son. He who has the Son has life; he who
does not have the Son of God does not have life. I write
these things to you who believe in the name of the Son of
God so that you may know that you have eternal life.

1 John 5:11–13

**This is how God
showed his love
among us:
He sent
his one and only Son
into the world
that we might live
through him.**

Chapter 35

The Inner Person Matters Most to God

But the LORD said to Samuel, "Do not consider his appearance or his height, for I have rejected him. The LORD does not look at the things man looks at. Man looks at the outward appearance, but the LORD looks at the heart."

1 Samuel 16:7

God, who is spirit, created mankind in His image spiritually. This does not mean that we are exactly the same as God. However, it does mean that we are designed to be a reflection of the person of God. God has masterfully designed us to think, reason, make choices, feel emotions, communicate, love, be caring, experience joy, appreciate beauty, be creative, and much more. This begins to describe the "inner you" with whom God desires a personal relationship for eternity. God has also designed us to live and experience life as physical beings in this physical world. We therefore have been created as human beings who are both spiritual and physical.

Human beings often think that their physical appearance, talents, or accomplishments matter most to God. This is a wrong understanding. If a person's heart-attitude and motives are displeasing to God, then that person's words, actions, and accomplishments will not please God regardless of how righteous or impressive they may appear from a human perspective. What really matters to God are the values, desires, attitudes, thoughts, motives, and choices of your heart and mind. It is these that will determine how you will live your life moment-by-moment. May the verses in this chapter help you to realize what truly matters most to God regarding you and your life.

Love the LORD your God with all your heart and with all your soul and with all your strength. These commandments that I give you today are to be upon your hearts. Impress them on your children. Talk about them when you sit at home and when you walk along the road, when you lie down and when you get up.

Deuteronomy 6:5–7

But the LORD said to Samuel, "Do not consider his appearance or his height, for I have rejected him. The LORD does not look at the things man looks at. Man looks at the outward appearance, but the LORD looks at the heart."

1 Samuel 16:7

**Love the LORD
your God
with all your heart
and with all your soul
and with all your strength.**

Test me, O LORD, and try me, examine my heart and my mind; for your love is ever before me, and I walk continually in your truth.

Psalm 26:2–3

Teach me your way, O LORD, and I will walk in your truth; give me an undivided heart, that I may fear your name. I will praise you, O Lord my God, with all my heart; I will glorify your name forever. For great is your love toward me; you have delivered me from the depths of the grave.

Psalm 86:11–13

How can a young man keep his way pure? By living according to your word. I seek you with all my heart; do not let me stray from your commands. I have hidden your word in my heart that I might not sin against you.

Psalm 119:9–11

My son, if you accept my words and store up my commands within you, turning your ear to wisdom and applying your heart to understanding, and if you call out for insight and cry aloud for understanding, and if you look for it as for silver and search for it as for hidden treasure, then you will understand the fear of the LORD and find the knowledge of God.

Proverbs 2:1–5

Let love and faithfulness never leave you; bind them around your neck, write them on the tablet of your heart. Then you will win favor and a good name in the sight of God and man.

Proverbs 3:3–4

Trust in the LORD with all your heart and lean not on your own understanding; in all your ways acknowledge him, and he will make your paths straight.

Proverbs 3:5–6

Trust in the LORD with all your heart and lean not on your own understanding; in all your ways acknowledge him, and he will make your paths straight.

Above all else, guard your heart, for it is the wellspring of life.

Proverbs 4:23

Like a gold ring in a pig's snout is a beautiful woman who shows no discretion.

Proverbs 11:22

All a man's ways seem right to him, but the LORD weighs the heart.

Proverbs 21:2

A wife of noble character who can find? She is worth far more than rubies. Her husband has full confidence in her and lacks nothing of value. She brings him good, not harm, all the days of her life. . . . She speaks with wisdom, and faithful instruction is on her tongue. She watches over the affairs of her household and does not eat the bread of idleness. Her children arise and call her blessed; her husband also, and he praises her: "Many women do noble things, but you surpass them all."

Proverbs 31:10–12, 26–29

Charm is deceptive, and beauty is fleeting; but a woman who fears the LORD is to be praised.

Proverbs 31:30

The Lord says: "These people come near to me with their mouth and honor me with their lips, but their hearts are far from me.

The Lord says: "These people come near to me with their mouth and honor me with their lips, but their hearts are far from me. Their worship of me is made up only of rules taught by men. Therefore once more I will astound these people with wonder upon wonder; the wisdom of the wise will perish, the intelligence of the intelligent will vanish." Woe to those who go to great depths to hide their plans from the LORD, who do their work in darkness and think, "Who sees us? Who will know?" You turn things upside down, as if the potter were thought to be like the clay! Shall what is formed say to him who formed it, "He did not make me"? Can the pot say of the potter, "He knows nothing"?

Isaiah 29:13–16

For this is what the high and lofty One says—he who lives forever, whose name is holy: "I live in a high and holy place, but also with him who is contrite and lowly in spirit, to revive the spirit of the lowly and to revive the heart of the contrite.

Isaiah 57:15

This is what the LORD says: "Cursed is the one who trusts in man, who depends on flesh for his strength and whose heart turns away from the LORD.

Jeremiah 17:5

The heart is deceitful above all things and beyond cure. Who can understand it? "I the LORD search the heart and examine the mind, to reward a man according to his conduct, according to what his deeds deserve."

Jeremiah 17:9–10

> **"I the LORD search the heart and examine the mind, to reward a man according to his conduct, according to what his deeds deserve."**

You will seek me and find me when you seek me with all your heart.

Jeremiah 29:13

Your heart became proud on account of your beauty, and you corrupted your wisdom because of your splendor. . . .

Ezekiel 28:17

"But they refused to pay attention; stubbornly they turned their backs and stopped up their ears. They made their hearts as hard as flint and would not listen to the law or to the words that the LORD Almighty had sent by his Spirit through the earlier prophets. So the LORD Almighty was very angry. "'When I called, they did not listen; so when they called, I would not listen,' says the LORD Almighty.

Zechariah 7:11–13

But the things that come out of the mouth come from the heart, and these make a man 'unclean.' For out of the heart come evil thoughts, murder, adultery, sexual immorality, theft, false testimony, slander.

Matthew 15:18–19

**Jesus replied:
"'Love the Lord
your God
with all your heart
and with all your soul
and with all your mind.'**

Jesus replied: "'Love the Lord your God with all your heart and with all your soul and with all your mind.' This is the first and greatest commandment. And the second is like it: 'Love your neighbor as yourself.'

Matthew 22:37–39

He went on: "What comes out of a man is what makes him 'unclean.' For from within, out of men's hearts, come evil thoughts, sexual immorality, theft, murder, adultery, greed, malice, deceit, lewdness, envy, slander, arrogance and folly. All these evils come from inside and make a man 'unclean.'"

Mark 7:20–23

"The most important one," answered Jesus, "is this: 'Hear, O Israel, the Lord our God, the Lord is one. Love the Lord your God with all your heart and with all your soul and with all your mind and with all your strength.' The second is this: 'Love your neighbor as yourself.' There is no commandment greater than these."

Mark 12:29–31

He replied, "Blessed rather are those who hear the word of God and obey it."

Luke 11:28

He said to them, "You are the ones who justify yourselves in the eyes of men, but God knows your hearts. What is highly valued among men is detestable in God's sight.

Luke 16:15

"You are the ones who justify yourselves in the eyes of men, but God knows your hearts. What is highly valued among men is detestable in God's sight.

Jesus replied, "If anyone loves me, he will obey my teaching. My Father will love him, and we will come to him and make our home with him. He who does not love me will not obey my teaching. These words you hear are not my own; they belong to the Father who sent me.

John 14:23–24

The man without the Spirit does not accept the things that come from the Spirit of God, for they are foolishness to him, and he cannot understand them, because they are spiritually discerned.

1 Corinthians 2:14

As for those who seemed to be important—whatever they were makes no difference to me; God does not judge by external appearance—those men added nothing to my message.

Galatians 2:6

But the fruit of the Spirit is love, joy, peace, patience, kindness, goodness, faithfulness, gentleness and self-control. Against such things there is no law. Those who belong to Christ Jesus have crucified the sinful nature with its passions and desires. Since we live by the Spirit, let us keep in step with the Spirit.

Galatians 5:22–25

As for those who seemed to be important—whatever they were makes no difference to me; God does not judge by external appearance

For you were once darkness, but now you are light in the Lord. Live as children of light (for the fruit of the light consists in all goodness, righteousness and truth) and find out what pleases the Lord.

Ephesians 5:8–10

I also want women to dress modestly, with decency and propriety, not with braided hair or gold or pearls or expensive clothes, but with good deeds, appropriate for women who profess to worship God.

1 Timothy 2:9–10

Now that you have purified yourselves by obeying the truth so that you have sincere love for your brothers, love one another deeply, from the heart.

1 Peter 1:22

For you have been born again, not of perishable seed, but of imperishable, through the living and enduring word of God. For, "All men are like grass, and all their glory is like the flowers of the field; the grass withers and the flowers fall, but the word of the Lord stands forever." And this is the word that was preached to you.

1 Peter 1:23–25

Your beauty should not come from outward adornment, such as braided hair and the wearing of gold jewelry and fine clothes. Instead, it should be that of your inner self, the unfading beauty of a gentle and quiet spirit, which is of great worth in God's sight.

1 Peter 3:3–4

**Your beauty
should not come from
outward adornment,**

. . .

**Instead,
it should be that
of your inner self,**

Chapter 36

All Humans Are Born with a Sinful Nature

Surely I was sinful at birth, sinful from the time my mother conceived me.

Psalm 51:5

What is sin? Sin is the breaking of God's laws. The Bible tells us that we all have sinned against God (Romans 3:23). The alternative view held by this world is that people are basically good. Before I believed that God existed, I used to rationalize that I was a "good" person because I was not doing the really "bad" things that many others in this world were doing. I viewed myself as a good person because I believed that I had good intentions or felt that I was justified in what I was doing. In reality, this kind of thinking is evidence of a sinful heart because it seeks to justify what a prideful, self-centered person feels like doing.

In reality, every human being, with the exception of Jesus Christ, has inherited a sinful nature from Adam and Eve. Sin entered the human race when Adam and Eve chose to disobey God. The sinful nature within humans is evident when we observe how very young children naturally exhibit selfishness and resort to lying to get what they want. How one's sinful nature surfaces in one's life will vary depending upon one's unique personality and life experiences, but it always surfaces. Every sin is a sin against the holy God of the Bible. When we sin, we always harm ourselves spiritually and sometimes physically. Whether we realize it or not, our sin always influences other people's lives—sooner or later, undermines our personal relationships, and distances us from God.

Thankfully, God has provided a way for people to escape being slaves to sin during this life and incurring the just punishment of hell for sinning against Him. God sent Jesus Christ into this world to receive God's full wrath against sin, thereby paying the full penalty for our past, present, and future sins. For Jesus Christ's sacrifice to cover your sins, you must acknowledge that you have sinned against God, you must repent of your sins, and you must believe in and follow the Lord Jesus Christ as your sin-bearer, Savior, and Lord.

The Lord smelled the pleasing aroma and said in his heart: "Never again will I curse the ground because of man, even though every inclination of his heart is evil from childhood. And never again will I destroy all living creatures, as I have done.

Genesis 8:21

Who can discern his errors? Forgive my hidden faults. Keep your servant also from willful sins; may they not rule over me. Then will I be blameless, innocent of great transgression. May the words of my mouth and the meditation of my heart be pleasing in your sight, O LORD, my Rock and my Redeemer.

Psalm 19:12–14

Never again will I curse the ground because of man, even though every inclination of his heart is evil from childhood.

Surely I was sinful at birth, sinful from the time my mother conceived me.

Psalm 51:5

Who can say, "I have kept my heart pure; I am clean and without sin"?

Proverbs 20:9

There is not a righteous man on earth who does what is right and never sins.

Ecclesiastes 7:20

Surely he took up our infirmities and carried our sorrows,
yet we considered him stricken by God, smitten by him,
and afflicted. But he was pierced for our transgressions,
he was crushed for our iniquities; the punishment that
brought us peace was upon him, and by his wounds we are
healed. We all, like sheep, have gone astray, each of us has
turned to his own way; and the LORD has laid on him the
iniquity of us all.

Isaiah 53:4–6

Surely the arm of the LORD is not too short to save, nor
his ear too dull to hear. But your iniquities have separated
you from your God; your sins have hidden his face from
you, so that he will not hear.

Isaiah 59:1–2

The heart is deceitful above all things and beyond cure.
Who can understand it? "I the LORD search the heart
and examine the mind, to reward a man according to his
conduct, according to what his deeds deserve."

Jeremiah 17:9–10

The heart is deceitful above all things and beyond cure. Who can understand it?

He went on: "What comes out of a man is what makes him
'unclean.' For from within, out of men's hearts, come evil
thoughts, sexual immorality, theft, murder, adultery, greed,
malice, deceit, lewdness, envy, slander, arrogance and folly.
All these evils come from inside and make a man 'unclean.'"

Mark 7:20–23

This is the verdict: Light has come into the world, but men loved darkness instead of light because their deeds were evil. Everyone who does evil hates the light, and will not come into the light for fear that his deeds will be exposed. But whoever lives by the truth comes into the light, so that it may be seen plainly that what he has done has been done through God."

John 3:19–21

for all have sinned and fall short of the glory of God,

Romans 3:23

But God demonstrates his own love for us in this: While we were still sinners, Christ died for us.

Romans 5:8

**for all have sinned
and fall short
of the glory of God,**

I know that nothing good lives in me, that is, in my sinful nature. For I have the desire to do what is good, but I cannot carry it out. For what I do is not the good I want to do; no, the evil I do not want to do—this I keep on doing. Now if I do what I do not want to do, it is no longer I who do it, but it is sin living in me that does it. So I find this law at work: When I want to do good, evil is right there with me. For in my inner being I delight in God's law; but I see another law at work in the members of my body, waging war against the law of my mind and making me a prisoner of the law of sin at work within my members. What a wretched man I am! Who will rescue me from this body of death? Thanks be to God—through Jesus Christ our Lord! So then, I myself in my mind am a slave to God's law, but in the sinful nature a slave to the law of sin.

Romans 7:18–25

But the Scripture declares that the whole world is a prisoner of sin, so that what was promised, being given through faith in Jesus Christ, might be given to those who believe.

Galatians 3:22

Formerly, when you did not know God, you were slaves to those who by nature are not gods. But now that you know God—or rather are known by God—how is it that you are turning back to those weak and miserable principles? Do you wish to be enslaved by them all over again?

Galatians 4:8–9

So I say, live by the Spirit, and you will not gratify the desires of the sinful nature. For the sinful nature desires what is contrary to the Spirit, and the Spirit what is contrary to the sinful nature. They are in conflict with each other, so that you do not do what you want.

Galatians 5:16–17

The acts of the sinful nature are obvious: sexual immorality, impurity and debauchery; idolatry and witchcraft; hatred, discord, jealousy, fits of rage, selfish ambition, dissensions, factions and envy; drunkenness, orgies, and the like. I warn you, as I did before, that those who live like this will not inherit the kingdom of God.

Galatians 5:19–21

But the Scripture declares that the whole world is a prisoner of sin,

But the fruit of the Spirit is love, joy, peace, patience, kindness, goodness, faithfulness, gentleness and self-control. Against such things there is no law. Those who belong to Christ Jesus have crucified the sinful nature with its passions and desires. Since we live by the Spirit, let us keep in step with the Spirit.

Galatians 5:22–25

Those who belong to Christ Jesus have crucified the sinful nature with its passions and desires.

As for you, you were dead in your transgressions and sins, in which you used to live when you followed the ways of this world and of the ruler of the kingdom of the air, the spirit who is now at work in those who are disobedient. All of us also lived among them at one time, gratifying the cravings of our sinful nature and following its desires and thoughts. Like the rest, we were by nature objects of wrath. But because of his great love for us, God, who is rich in mercy, made us alive with Christ even when we were dead in transgressions—it is by grace you have been saved.

Ephesians 2:1–5

You, however, did not come to know Christ that way. Surely you heard of him and were taught in him in accordance with the truth that is in Jesus. You were taught, with regard to your former way of life, to put off your old self, which is being corrupted by its deceitful desires; to be made new in the attitude of your minds; and to put on the new self, created to be like God in true righteousness and holiness.

Ephesians 4:20–24

For he has rescued us from the dominion of darkness and brought us into the kingdom of the Son he loves, in whom we have redemption, the forgiveness of sins.

Colossians 1:13–14

Put to death, therefore, whatever belongs to your earthly nature: sexual immorality, impurity, lust, evil desires and greed, which is idolatry. Because of these, the wrath of God is coming. You used to walk in these ways, in the life you once lived. But now you must rid yourselves of all such things as these: anger, rage, malice, slander, and filthy language from your lips. Do not lie to each other, since you have taken off your old self with its practices and have put on the new self, which is being renewed in knowledge in the image of its Creator.

Colossians 3:5–10

But mark this: There will be terrible times in the last days. People will be lovers of themselves, lovers of money, boastful, proud, abusive, disobedient to their parents, ungrateful, unholy, without love, unforgiving, slanderous, without self-control, brutal, not lovers of the good, treacherous, rash, conceited, lovers of pleasure rather than lovers of God—having a form of godliness but denying its power. Have nothing to do with them.

2 Timothy 3:1–5

Put to death, therefore, whatever belongs to your earthly nature:

For the time will come when men will not put up with sound doctrine. Instead, to suit their own desires, they will gather around them a great number of teachers to say what their itching ears want to hear. They will turn their ears away from the truth and turn aside to myths.

2 Timothy 4:3–4

At one time we too were foolish, disobedient, deceived and enslaved by all kinds of passions and pleasures. We lived in malice and envy, being hated and hating one another. But when the kindness and love of God our Savior appeared, he saved us, not because of righteous things we had done, but because of his mercy. He saved us through the washing of rebirth and renewal by the Holy Spirit, whom he poured out on us generously through Jesus Christ our Savior, so that, having been justified by his grace, we might become heirs having the hope of eternal life. This is a trustworthy saying. And I want you to stress these things, so that those who have trusted in God may be careful to devote themselves to doing what is good. These things are excellent and profitable for everyone.

Titus 3:3–8

If we claim to be without sin, we deceive ourselves and the truth is not in us.

If we deliberately keep on sinning after we have received the knowledge of the truth, no sacrifice for sins is left, but only a fearful expectation of judgment and of raging fire that will consume the enemies of God.

Hebrews 10:26–27

If we claim to be without sin, we deceive ourselves and the truth is not in us. If we confess our sins, he is faithful and just and will forgive us our sins and purify us from all unrighteousness. If we claim we have not sinned, we make him out to be a liar and his word has no place in our lives.

1 John 1:8–10

My dear children, I write this to you so that you will not
sin. But if anybody does sin, we have one who speaks to the
Father in our defense—Jesus Christ, the Righteous One.
He is the atoning sacrifice for our sins, and not only for
ours but also for the sins of the whole world.

1 John 2:1–2

Everyone who sins breaks the law; in fact, sin is lawlessness.
But you know that he appeared so that he might take away
our sins. And in him is no sin. No one who lives in him
keeps on sinning. No one who continues to sin has either
seen him or known him.

1 John 3:4–6

Dear children, do not let anyone lead you astray. He who
does what is right is righteous, just as he is righteous. He
who does what is sinful is of the devil, because the devil
has been sinning from the beginning. The reason the Son
of God appeared was to destroy the devil's work. No one
who is born of God will continue to sin, because God's seed
remains in him; he cannot go on sinning, because he has
been born of God. This is how we know who the children
of God are and who the children of the devil are: Anyone
who does not do what is right is not a child of God; nor is
anyone who does not love his brother.

1 John 3:7–10

**But if anybody
does sin,
we have one who
speaks to the Father
in our defense—
Jesus Christ,
the Righteous One.**

This is how God showed his love among us: He sent his one
and only Son into the world that we might live through
him. This is love: not that we loved God, but that he loved
us and sent his Son as an atoning sacrifice for our sins. Dear
friends, since God so loved us, we also ought to love
one another.

1 John 4:9–11

Chapter 37

We Each Choose Where We Will Spend Eternity

Whoever believes in the Son has eternal life, but whoever rejects the Son will not see life, for God's wrath remains on him."

John 3:36

God has given human beings free will—the awesome power to choose our beliefs, values, and how we will live. Our free will also applies to how we will view and respond to the amazing wonders of this world we live in. God has given us more than enough rational reasons to believe that He exists and that the Bible is true. There is ample evidence everywhere in nature that clearly shows that this world is the product of amazing, intelligent design. The Bible proclaims in Romans 1:20 that God's creation reveals His eternal power and His divine nature. This passage also informs us that because of that revelation we are without excuse if we choose not to earnestly seek Him. Regarding the Bible, there is ample historical, documentary, and fulfilled-prophecy evidence to demonstrate its accuracy and reliability. Please see Appendix 5, item 10 for resources regarding the trustworthiness of the Bible.

Each of us must choose whether or not we will earnestly seek to know the truth about the God who designed and created us. If you sincerely pursue the truth about God with diligence and unbiased critical thinking, God will reveal to you the trustworthiness of the Bible and the reality of the Lord Jesus Christ. Then, one thing will remain: a choice to either reject Him or place your faith in Him. If you acknowledge that you have sinned against God, repent of your sins, and believe in and follow Jesus Christ as your sin-bearer, Savior, and Lord, then you will be spiritually reborn and live with Him in heaven for eternity. Every other alternative is a rejection of Jesus Christ. Rejecting Him leads to spending eternity separated from God in a place called hell. Because God knows our innermost thoughts and the true condition of our hearts, He will hold each one of us accountable for choosing or rejecting a right relationship with Jesus Christ. God has given you the awesome power to choose where you will spend eternity. May you choose wisely.

The LORD redeems his servants; no one will be condemned who takes refuge in him.

Psalm 34:22

"Not everyone who says to me, 'Lord, Lord,' will enter the kingdom of heaven, but only he who does the will of my Father who is in heaven.

Matthew 7:21

Then Jesus said to his disciples, "If anyone would come after me, he must deny himself and take up his cross and follow me. For whoever wants to save his life will lose it, but whoever loses his life for me will find it. What good will it be for a man if he gains the whole world, yet forfeits his soul? Or what can a man give in exchange for his soul?

Matthew 16:24–26

**For God
so loved the world
that he gave
his one and only Son,
that whoever
believes in him
shall not perish
but have eternal life.**

Just as Moses lifted up the snake in the desert, so the Son of Man must be lifted up, that everyone who believes in him may have eternal life.

John 3:14–15

"For God so loved the world that he gave his one and only Son, that whoever believes in him shall not perish but have eternal life. For God did not send his Son into the world to condemn the world, but to save the world through him. Whoever believes in him is not condemned, but whoever does not believe stands condemned already because he has not believed in the name of God's one and only Son.

John 3:16–18

For the one whom God has sent speaks the words of God, for God gives the Spirit without limit. The Father loves the Son and has placed everything in his hands. Whoever believes in the Son has eternal life, but whoever rejects the Son will not see life, for God's wrath remains on him."

John 3:34–36

"I tell you the truth, whoever hears my word and believes him who sent me has eternal life and will not be condemned; he has crossed over from death to life.

John 5:24

For I have come down from heaven not to do my will but to do the will of him who sent me. And this is the will of him who sent me, that I shall lose none of all that he has given me, but raise them up at the last day. For my Father's will is that everyone who looks to the Son and believes in him shall have eternal life, and I will raise him up at the last day."

John 6:38–40

Whoever believes in the Son has eternal life, but whoever rejects the Son will not see life, for God's wrath remains on him."

I tell you the truth, he who believes has everlasting life. I am the bread of life.

John 6:47–48

Jesus answered, "I did tell you, but you do not believe. The miracles I do in my Father's name speak for me, but you do not believe because you are not my sheep. My sheep listen to my voice; I know them, and they follow me. I give them eternal life, and they shall never perish; no one can snatch them out of my hand. My Father, who has given them to me, is greater than all; no one can snatch them out of my Father's hand. I and the Father are one."

John 10:25–30

Jesus said to her, "I am the resurrection and the life. He who believes in me will live, even though he dies; and whoever lives and believes in me will never die. Do you believe this?"

John 11:25–26

"As for the person who hears my words but does not keep them, I do not judge him. For I did not come to judge the world, but to save it. There is a judge for the one who rejects me and does not accept my words; that very word which I spoke will condemn him at the last day. For I did not speak of my own accord, but the Father who sent me commanded me what to say and how to say it. I know that his command leads to eternal life. So whatever I say is just what the Father has told me to say."

John 12:47–50

Jesus answered, "I am the way and the truth and the life. No one comes to the Father except through me.

Jesus answered, "I am the way and the truth and the life. No one comes to the Father except through me.

John 14:6

After Jesus said this, he looked toward heaven and prayed: "Father, the time has come. Glorify your Son, that your Son may glorify you. For you granted him authority over all people that he might give eternal life to all those you have given him. Now this is eternal life: that they may know you, the only true God, and Jesus Christ, whom you have sent.

John 17:1–3

But because of your stubbornness and your unrepentant heart, you are storing up wrath against yourself for the day of God's wrath, when his righteous judgment will be revealed. God "will give to each person according to what he has done." To those who by persistence in doing good seek glory, honor and immortality, he will give eternal life. But for those who are self-seeking and who reject the truth and follow evil, there will be wrath and anger.

Romans 2:5–8

For the wages of sin is death, but the gift of God is eternal life in Christ Jesus our Lord.

Romans 6:23

Those who live according to the sinful nature have their minds set on what that nature desires; but those who live in accordance with the Spirit have their minds set on what the Spirit desires. The mind of sinful man is death, but the mind controlled by the Spirit is life and peace; the sinful mind is hostile to God. It does not submit to God's law, nor can it do so. Those controlled by the sinful nature cannot please God.

Romans 8:5–8

But for those who are self-seeking and who reject the truth and follow evil, there will be wrath and anger.

You, however, are controlled not by the sinful nature but by the Spirit, if the Spirit of God lives in you. And if anyone does not have the Spirit of Christ, he does not belong to Christ. But if Christ is in you, your body is dead because of sin, yet your spirit is alive because of righteousness. And if the Spirit of him who raised Jesus from the dead is living in you, he who raised Christ from the dead will also give life to your mortal bodies through his Spirit, who lives in you.

Romans 8:9–11

That if you confess with your mouth, "Jesus is Lord," and believe in your heart that God raised him from the dead, you will be saved. For it is with your heart that you believe and are justified, and it is with your mouth that you confess and are saved. As the Scripture says, "Anyone who trusts in him will never be put to shame."

Romans 10:9–11

For there is no difference between Jew and Gentile—the same Lord is Lord of all and richly blesses all who call on him, for, "Everyone who calls on the name of the Lord will be saved.

Romans 10:12–13

"Everyone who calls on the name of the Lord will be saved.

However, as it is written: "No eye has seen, no ear has heard, no mind has conceived what God has prepared for those who love him"—

1 Corinthians 2:9

Now it is God who makes both us and you stand firm in Christ. He anointed us, set his seal of ownership on us, and put his Spirit in our hearts as a deposit, guaranteeing what is to come.

2 Corinthians 1:21–22

Therefore we do not lose heart. Though outwardly we are wasting away, yet inwardly we are being renewed day by day. For our light and momentary troubles are achieving for us an eternal glory that far outweighs them all. So we fix our eyes not on what is seen, but on what is unseen. For what is seen is temporary, but what is unseen is eternal.

2 Corinthians 4: 16–18

Do not be deceived: God cannot be mocked. A man reaps what he sows. The one who sows to please his sinful nature, from that nature will reap destruction; the one who sows to please the Spirit, from the Spirit will reap eternal life.

Galatians 6:7–8

But our citizenship is in heaven. And we eagerly await a Savior from there, the Lord Jesus Christ, who, by the power that enables him to bring everything under his control, will transform our lowly bodies so that they will be like his glorious body.

Philippians 3:20–21

Here is a trustworthy saying that deserves full acceptance: Christ Jesus came into the world to save sinners—of whom I am the worst. But for that very reason I was shown mercy so that in me, the worst of sinners, Christ Jesus might display his unlimited patience as an example for those who would believe on him and receive eternal life.

1 Timothy 1:15–16

Do not be deceived: God cannot be mocked. A man reaps what he sows.

So do not be ashamed to testify about our Lord, or ashamed of me his prisoner. But join with me in suffering for the gospel, by the power of God, who has saved us and called us to a holy life—not because of anything we have done but because of his own purpose and grace. This grace was given us in Christ Jesus before the beginning of time, but it has now been revealed through the appearing of our Savior, Christ Jesus, who has destroyed death and has brought life and immortality to light through the gospel.

2 Timothy 1:8–10

Praise be to the God and Father of our Lord Jesus Christ! In his great mercy he has given us new birth into a living hope through the resurrection of Jesus Christ from the dead, and into an inheritance that can never perish, spoil or fade—kept in heaven for you,

1 Peter 1:3–4

For you have been born again, not of perishable seed, but of imperishable, through the living and enduring word of God. For, "All men are like grass, and all their glory is like the flowers of the field; the grass withers and the flowers fall, but the word of the Lord stands forever." And this is the word that was preached to you.

1 Peter 1:23–25

Do not love the world or anything in the world. If anyone loves the world, the love of the Father is not in him.

Do not love the world or anything in the world. If anyone loves the world, the love of the Father is not in him. For everything in the world—the cravings of sinful man, the lust of his eyes and the boasting of what he has and does—comes not from the Father but from the world. The world and its desires pass away, but the man who does the will of God lives forever.

1 John 2:15–17

This is the one who came by water and blood—Jesus Christ. He did not come by water only, but by water and blood. And it is the Spirit who testifies, because the Spirit is the truth. For there are three that testify: the Spirit, the water and the blood; and the three are in agreement. We accept man's testimony, but God's testimony is greater because it is the testimony of God, which he has given about his Son. Anyone who believes in the Son of God has this testimony in his heart. Anyone who does not believe God has made him out to be a liar, because he has not believed the testimony God has given about his Son. And this is the testimony: God has given us eternal life, and this life is in his Son. He who has the Son has life; he who does not have the Son of God does not have life. I write these things to you who believe in the name of the Son of God so that you may know that you have eternal life.

1 John 5:6–13

We know that we are children of God, and that the whole world is under the control of the evil one. We know also that the Son of God has come and has given us understanding, so that we may know him who is true. And we are in him who is true—even in his Son Jesus Christ. He is the true God and eternal life.

1 John 5:19–20

He who has the Son has life; he who does not have the Son of God does not have life.

393

But, dear friends, remember what the apostles of our Lord Jesus Christ foretold. They said to you, "In the last times there will be scoffers who will follow their own ungodly desires." These are the men who divide you, who follow mere natural instincts and do not have the Spirit. But you, dear friends, build yourselves up in your most holy faith and pray in the Holy Spirit. Keep yourselves in God's love as you wait for the mercy of our Lord Jesus Christ to bring you to eternal life.

Jude 1:17–21

Nothing impure will ever enter it, nor will anyone who does what is shameful or deceitful, but only those whose names are written in the Lamb's book of life.

The twelve gates were twelve pearls, each gate made of a single pearl. The great street of the city was of pure gold, like transparent glass. I did not see a temple in the city, because the Lord God Almighty and the Lamb are its temple. The city does not need the sun or the moon to shine on it, for the glory of God gives it light, and the Lamb is its lamp. The nations will walk by its light, and the kings of the earth will bring their splendor into it. On no day will its gates ever be shut, for there will be no night there. The glory and honor of the nations will be brought into it. Nothing impure will ever enter it, nor will anyone who does what is shameful or deceitful, but only those whose names are written in the Lamb's book of life.

Revelation 21:21–27

Chapter 38

Your Heart

But the LORD said to Samuel, "Do not consider his appearance or his height, for I have rejected him. The LORD does not look at the things man looks at. Man looks at the outward appearance, but the LORD looks at the heart."

1 Samuel 16:7

What is a person's "spiritual heart"? From studying the Bible I believe that the heart is the center of a person's core values, desires, attitudes, thoughts, and will. God is telling us in the verse above and in many of the verses within this chapter that the condition of a person's heart is of primary importance to Him. The condition of your heart will determine your relationship with God, your character, your choices, your behavior, and the direction of your life. God, who designed and created us, tells us in Proverbs 4:23 that our hearts need to be carefully guarded: *"Above all else, guard your heart, for it is the wellspring of life."*

Some people claim that the God of the Bible does not exist. Other people try to redefine Him according to their own desires and preferences. Both groups of people have rejected God and what He stands for. Their hearts are far from Him. God holds every person accountable for the thoughts, attitudes, and choices of his or her spiritual heart. God calls you to seek Him, trust Him, and love Him with all your heart.

As you read and ponder the Bible verses in this chapter, I invite you to keep in mind the following questions:

1. What is the condition of everyone's spiritual heart at birth?
2. Which Bible verses describe heart attributes that are pleasing to God?
3. What is the current condition of your heart?
4. To what extent is your heart obedient to God's Word?
5. In what ways are you guarding your heart? Where are you failing to guard your heart?
6. Which Bible verses speak to changes that God wants to see in your heart?

The Lord saw how great man's wickedness on the earth had become, and that every inclination of the thoughts of his heart was only evil all the time. The Lord was grieved that he had made man on the earth, and his heart was filled with pain.

Genesis 6:5–6

The Lord smelled the pleasing aroma and said in his heart: "Never again will I curse the ground because of man, even though every inclination of his heart is evil from childhood. And never again will I destroy all living creatures, as I have done.

Genesis 8:21

**Love the LORD
your God
with all your heart
and with all your soul
and with all your strength.**

Love the LORD your God with all your heart and with all your soul and with all your strength. These commandments that I give you today are to be upon your hearts. Impress them on your children. Talk about them when you sit at home and when you walk along the road, when you lie down and when you get up.

Deuteronomy 6:5–7

But be very careful to keep the commandment and the law that Moses the servant of the LORD gave you: to love the LORD your God, to walk in all his ways, to obey his commands, to hold fast to him and to serve him with all your heart and all your soul."

Joshua 22:5

But the LORD said to Samuel, "Do not consider his appearance or his height, for I have rejected him. The LORD does not look at the things man looks at. Man looks at the outward appearance, but the LORD looks at the heart."

1 Samuel 16:7

And you, my son Solomon, acknowledge the God of your father, and serve him with wholehearted devotion and with a willing mind, for the LORD searches every heart and understands every motive behind the thoughts. If you seek him, he will be found by you; but if you forsake him, he will reject you forever.

1 Chronicles 28:9

I know, my God, that you test the heart and are pleased with integrity. . . .

1 Chronicles 29:17a

Man looks at the outward appearance, but the LORD looks at the heart."

I will praise you, O LORD, with all my heart; I will tell of all your wonders. I will be glad and rejoice in you; I will sing praise to your name, O Most High.

Psalm 9:1–2

I will praise the LORD, who counsels me; even at night my heart instructs me. I have set the LORD always before me. Because he is at my right hand, I will not be shaken.

Psalm 16:7–8

Who can discern his errors? Forgive my hidden faults. Keep your servant also from willful sins; may they not rule over me. Then will I be blameless, innocent of great transgression. May the words of my mouth and the meditation of my heart be pleasing in your sight, O LORD, my Rock and my Redeemer.

Psalm 19:12–14

Test me, O LORD, and try me, examine my heart and my mind; for your love is ever before me, and I walk continually in your truth.

Psalm 26:2–3

Create in me a pure heart, O God, and renew a steadfast spirit within me.

From heaven the LORD looks down and sees all mankind; from his dwelling place he watches all who live on earth— he who forms the hearts of all, who considers everything they do.

Psalm 33:13–15

The mouth of the righteous man utters wisdom, and his tongue speaks what is just. The law of his God is in his heart; his feet do not slip.

Psalm 37:30–31

Create in me a pure heart, O God, and renew a steadfast spirit within me. Do not cast me from your presence or take your Holy Spirit from me. Restore to me the joy of your salvation and grant me a willing spirit, to sustain me.

Psalm 51:10–12

My flesh and my heart may fail, but God is the strength of my heart and my portion forever.

Psalm 73:26

Teach me your way, O LORD, and I will walk in your truth; give me an undivided heart, that I may fear your name. I will praise you, O Lord my God, with all my heart; I will glorify your name forever. For great is your love toward me; you have delivered me from the depths of the grave.

Psalm 86:11–13

How can a young man keep his way pure? By living according to your word. I seek you with all my heart; do not let me stray from your commands. I have hidden your word in my heart that I might not sin against you.

Psalm 119:9–11

**I seek you
with all my heart;
do not let me stray
from your commands.**

May my heart be blameless toward your decrees, that I may not be put to shame.

Psalm 119:80

Your statutes are my heritage forever; they are the joy of my heart. My heart is set on keeping your decrees to the very end.

Psalm 119:111–112

Search me, O God, and know my heart; test me and know my anxious thoughts. See if there is any offensive way in me, and lead me in the way everlasting.

Psalm 139:23–24

My son, if you accept my words and store up my commands within you, turning your ear to wisdom and applying your heart to understanding, and if you call out for insight and cry aloud for understanding, and if you look for it as for silver and search for it as for hidden treasure, then you will understand the fear of the LORD and find the knowledge of God.

Proverbs 2:1–5

For the LORD gives wisdom, and from his mouth come knowledge and understanding. He holds victory in store for the upright, he is a shield to those whose walk is blameless, for he guards the course of the just and protects the way of his faithful ones. Then you will understand what is right and just and fair—every good path. For wisdom will enter your heart, and knowledge will be pleasant to your soul. Discretion will protect you, and understanding will guard you.

Proverbs 2:6–11

Trust in the LORD with all your heart and lean not on your own understanding;

Let love and faithfulness never leave you; bind them around your neck, write them on the tablet of your heart. Then you will win favor and a good name in the sight of God and man.

Proverbs 3:3–4

Trust in the LORD with all your heart and lean not on your own understanding; in all your ways acknowledge him, and he will make your paths straight.

Proverbs 3:5–6

My son, pay attention to what I say; listen closely to my words. Do not let them out of your sight, keep them within your heart; for they are life to those who find them and health to a man's whole body.

Proverbs 4:20–22

Above all else, guard your heart, for it is the wellspring of life.

Proverbs 4:23

An anxious heart weighs a man down, but a kind word cheers him up.

Proverbs 12:25

A heart at peace gives life to the body, but envy rots the bones.

Proverbs 14:30

Above all else, guard your heart, for it is the wellspring of life.

The lips of the wise spread knowledge; not so the hearts of fools.

Proverbs 15:7

A happy heart makes the face cheerful, but heartache crushes the spirit.

Proverbs 15:13

The discerning heart seeks knowledge, but the mouth of a fool feeds on folly.

Proverbs 15:14

The heart of the righteous weighs its answers, but the
mouth of the wicked gushes evil.

Proverbs 15:28

A cheerful look brings joy to the heart, and good news gives
health to the bones.

Proverbs 15:30

The crucible for silver and the furnace for gold, but the
LORD tests the heart.

Proverbs 17:3

**The crucible
for silver
and the furnace
for gold,
but the LORD
tests the heart.**

A man of perverse heart does not prosper; he whose tongue
is deceitful falls into trouble.

Proverbs 17:20

A cheerful heart is good medicine, but a crushed spirit dries
up the bones.

Proverbs 17:22

The heart of the discerning acquires knowledge; the ears of
the wise seek it out.

Proverbs 18:15

A man's own folly ruins his life, yet his heart rages against
the LORD.

Proverbs 19:3

Many are the plans in a man's heart, but it is the LORD's
purpose that prevails.

Proverbs 19:21

Who can say, "I have kept my heart pure; I am clean and without sin"?

Proverbs 20:9

All a man's ways seem right to him, but the LORD weighs the heart.

Proverbs 21:2

Folly is bound up in the heart of a child, but the rod of discipline will drive it far from him.

Proverbs 22:15

As water reflects a face, so a man's heart reflects the man.

Proverbs 27:19

Who can say, "I have kept my heart pure; I am clean and without sin"?

Blessed is the man who always fears the LORD, but he who hardens his heart falls into trouble.

Proverbs 28:14

He has made everything beautiful in its time. He has also set eternity in the hearts of men; yet they cannot fathom what God has done from beginning to end.

Ecclesiastes 3:11

The Lord says: "These people come near to me with their mouth and honor me with their lips, but their hearts are far from me. Their worship of me is made up only of rules taught by men. Therefore once more I will astound these people with wonder upon wonder; the wisdom of the wise will perish, the intelligence of the intelligent will vanish." Woe to those who go to great depths to hide their plans from the LORD, who do their work in darkness and think, "Who sees us? Who will know?" You turn things upside down, as if the potter were thought to be like the clay! Shall what is formed say to him who formed it, "He did not make me"? Can the pot say of the potter, "He knows nothing"?

Isaiah 29:13–16

The heart is deceitful above all things and beyond cure. Who can understand it?

For this is what the high and lofty One says—he who lives forever, whose name is holy: "I live in a high and holy place, but also with him who is contrite and lowly in spirit, to revive the spirit of the lowly and to revive the heart of the contrite.

Isaiah 57:15

This is what the LORD says: "Cursed is the one who trusts in man, who depends on flesh for his strength and whose heart turns away from the LORD.

Jeremiah 17:5

The heart is deceitful above all things and beyond cure. Who can understand it? "I the LORD search the heart and examine the mind, to reward a man according to his conduct, according to what his deeds deserve."

Jeremiah 17:9–10

You will seek me and find me when you seek me with
all your heart.

Jeremiah 29:13

"This is the covenant I will make with the house of Israel
after that time," declares the Lord. "I will put my law in
their minds and write it on their hearts. I will be their God,
and they will be my people.

Jeremiah 31:33

I will give them an undivided heart and put a new spirit in
them; I will remove from them their heart of stone and give
them a heart of flesh. Then they will follow my decrees and
be careful to keep my laws. They will be my people, and I
will be their God. But as for those whose hearts are devoted
to their vile images and detestable idols, I will bring down
on their own heads what they have done, declares the
Sovereign LORD."

Ezekiel 11:19–21

**You will seek me
and find me
when you seek me
with all your heart.**

I will give you a new heart and put a new spirit in you; I will
remove from you your heart of stone and give you a heart
of flesh. And I will put my Spirit in you and move you to
follow my decrees and be careful to keep my laws.

Ezekiel 36:26–27

"But they refused to pay attention; stubbornly they turned their backs and stopped up their ears. They made their hearts as hard as flint and would not listen to the law or to the words that the LORD Almighty had sent by his Spirit through the earlier prophets. So the LORD Almighty was very angry. "'When I called, they did not listen; so when they called, I would not listen,' says the LORD Almighty.

Zechariah 7:11–13

"Do not store up for yourselves treasures on earth, where moth and rust destroy, and where thieves break in and steal. But store up for yourselves treasures in heaven, where moth and rust do not destroy, and where thieves do not break in and steal. For where your treasure is, there your heart will be also.

Matthew 6:19–21

For out of the overflow of the heart the mouth speaks.

Knowing their thoughts, Jesus said, "Why do you entertain evil thoughts in your hearts?

Matthew 9:4

"Make a tree good and its fruit will be good, or make a tree bad and its fruit will be bad, for a tree is recognized by its fruit. You brood of vipers, how can you who are evil say anything good? For out of the overflow of the heart the mouth speaks.

Matthew 12:33–34

He replied, "The knowledge of the secrets of the kingdom of heaven has been given to you, but not to them. Whoever has will be given more, and he will have an abundance. Whoever does not have, even what he has will be taken from him. This is why I speak to them in parables: "Though seeing, they do not see; though hearing, they do not hear or understand. In them is fulfilled the prophecy of Isaiah: "'You will be ever hearing but never understanding; you will be ever seeing but never perceiving. For this people's heart has become calloused; they hardly hear with their ears, and they have closed their eyes. Otherwise they might see with their eyes, hear with their ears, understand with their hearts and turn, and I would heal them.'

Matthew 13:11–15

You hypocrites! Isaiah was right when he prophesied about you: "'These people honor me with their lips, but their hearts are far from me. They worship me in vain; their teachings are but rules taught by men.' "

Matthew 15:7–9

These people honor me with their lips, but their hearts are far from me.

But the things that come out of the mouth come from the heart, and these make a man 'unclean.' For out of the heart come evil thoughts, murder, adultery, sexual immorality, theft, false testimony, slander.

Matthew 15:18–19

Jesus replied: "'Love the Lord your God with all your heart and with all your soul and with all your mind.' This is the first and greatest commandment. And the second is like it: 'Love your neighbor as yourself.'

Matthew 22:37–39

He replied, "Isaiah was right when he prophesied about you hypocrites; as it is written: '"These people honor me with their lips, but their hearts are far from me. They worship me in vain; their teachings are but rules taught by men.' You have let go of the commands of God and are holding on to the traditions of men."

Mark 7:6–8

He went on: "What comes out of a man is what makes him 'unclean.' For from within, out of men's hearts, come evil thoughts, sexual immorality, theft, murder, adultery, greed, malice, deceit, lewdness, envy, slander, arrogance and folly. All these evils come from inside and make a man 'unclean.'"

Mark 7:20–23

**Love the Lord
your God
with all your heart
and with all your soul
and with all your mind
and with all your strength**

"The most important one," answered Jesus, "is this: 'Hear, O Israel, the Lord our God, the Lord is one. Love the Lord your God with all your heart and with all your soul and with all your mind and with all your strength.' The second is this: 'Love your neighbor as yourself.' There is no commandment greater than these."

Mark 12:29–31

"No good tree bears bad fruit, nor does a bad tree bear good fruit. Each tree is recognized by its own fruit. People do not pick figs from thornbushes, or grapes from briers. The good man brings good things out of the good stored up in his heart, and the evil man brings evil things out of the evil stored up in his heart. For out of the overflow of his heart his mouth speaks.

Luke 6:43–45

For where your treasure is, there your heart will be also.

Luke 12:34

He said to them, "You are the ones who justify yourselves in the eyes of men, but God knows your hearts. What is highly valued among men is detestable in God's sight.

Luke 16:15

Therefore, since we have been justified through faith, we have peace with God through our Lord Jesus Christ, through whom we have gained access by faith into this grace in which we now stand. And we rejoice in the hope of the glory of God. Not only so, but we also rejoice in our sufferings, because we know that suffering produces perseverance; perseverance, character; and character, hope. And hope does not disappoint us, because God has poured out his love into our hearts by the Holy Spirit, whom he has given us.

Romans 5:1–5

For where your treasure is, there your heart will be also.

That if you confess with your mouth, "Jesus is Lord," and believe in your heart that God raised him from the dead, you will be saved. For it is with your heart that you believe and are justified, and it is with your mouth that you confess and are saved. As the Scripture says, "Anyone who trusts in him will never be put to shame."

Romans 10:9–11

So then, men ought to regard us as servants of Christ and as those entrusted with the secret things of God. Now it is required that those who have been given a trust must prove faithful. I care very little if I am judged by you or by any human court; indeed, I do not even judge myself. My conscience is clear, but that does not make me innocent. It is the Lord who judges me. Therefore judge nothing before the appointed time; wait till the Lord comes. He will bring to light what is hidden in darkness and will expose the motives of men's hearts. At that time each will receive his praise from God.

1 Corinthians 4:1–5

He will bring to light what is hidden in darkness and will expose the motives of men's hearts.

Now it is God who makes both us and you stand firm in Christ. He anointed us, set his seal of ownership on us, and put his Spirit in our hearts as a deposit, guaranteeing what is to come.

2 Corinthians 1:21–22

For God, who said, "Let light shine out of darkness," made his light shine in our hearts to give us the light of the knowledge of the glory of God in the face of Christ. But we have this treasure in jars of clay to show that this all-surpassing power is from God and not from us.

2 Corinthians 4:6–7

For this reason I kneel before the Father, from whom his whole family in heaven and on earth derives its name. I pray that out of his glorious riches he may strengthen you with power through his Spirit in your inner being, so that Christ may dwell in your hearts through faith. And I pray that you, being rooted and established in love, may have power, together with all the saints, to grasp how wide and long and high and deep is the love of Christ, and to know this love that surpasses knowledge—that you may be filled to the measure of all the fullness of God.

Ephesians 3:14–19

So I tell you this, and insist on it in the Lord, that you must no longer live as the Gentiles do, in the futility of their thinking. They are darkened in their understanding and separated from the life of God because of the ignorance that is in them due to the hardening of their hearts. Having lost all sensitivity, they have given themselves over to sensuality so as to indulge in every kind of impurity, with a continual lust for more.

Ephesians 4:17–19

They are darkened in their understanding and separated from the life of God because of the ignorance that is in them due to the hardening of their hearts.

Slaves, obey your earthly masters with respect and fear, and with sincerity of heart, just as you would obey Christ. Obey them not only to win their favor when their eye is on you, but like slaves of Christ, doing the will of God from your heart. Serve wholeheartedly, as if you were serving the Lord, not men, because you know that the Lord will reward everyone for whatever good he does, whether he is slave or free. And masters, treat your slaves in the same way. Do not threaten them, since you know that he who is both their Master and yours is in heaven, and there is no favoritism with him.

Ephesians 6:5–9

Since, then, you have been raised with Christ, set your hearts on things above, where Christ is seated at the right hand of God. Set your minds on things above, not on earthly things.

Colossians 3:1–2

Let the peace of Christ rule in your hearts, since as members of one body you were called to peace. And be thankful. Let the word of Christ dwell in you richly as you teach and admonish one another with all wisdom, and as you sing Psalms, hymns and spiritual songs with gratitude in your hearts to God. And whatever you do, whether in word or deed, do it all in the name of the Lord Jesus, giving thanks to God the Father through him.

Colossians 3:15–17

set your hearts on things above, where Christ is seated at the right hand of God.

The goal of this command is love, which comes from a pure heart and a good conscience and a sincere faith. Some have wandered away from these and turned to meaningless talk. They want to be teachers of the law, but they do not know what they are talking about or what they so confidently affirm.

1 Timothy 1:5–7

Flee the evil desires of youth, and pursue righteousness, faith, love and peace, along with those who call on the Lord out of a pure heart.

2 Timothy 2:22

See to it, brothers, that none of you has a sinful, unbelieving heart that turns away from the living God. But encourage one another daily, as long as it is called Today, so that none of you may be hardened by sin's deceitfulness.

Hebrews 3:12–13

For the word of God is living and active. Sharper than any double-edged sword, it penetrates even to dividing soul and spirit, joints and marrow; it judges the thoughts and attitudes of the heart.

Hebrews 4:12

But when this priest had offered for all time one sacrifice for sins, he sat down at the right hand of God. Since that time he waits for his enemies to be made his footstool, because by one sacrifice he has made perfect forever those who are being made holy. The Holy Spirit also testifies to us about this. First he says: "This is the covenant I will make with them after that time, says the Lord. I will put my laws in their hearts, and I will write them on their minds." Then he adds: "Their sins and lawless acts I will remember no more." And where these have been forgiven, there is no longer any sacrifice for sin.

Hebrews 10:12–18

For the word of God is living and active.
. . .
it judges the thoughts and attitudes of the heart.

Submit yourselves, then, to God. Resist the devil, and he will flee from you. Come near to God and he will come near to you. Wash your hands, you sinners, and purify your hearts, you double-minded.

James 4:7–8

But in your hearts set apart Christ as Lord. Always be prepared to give an answer to everyone who asks you to give the reason for the hope that you have. But do this with gentleness and respect, keeping a clear conscience, so that those who speak maliciously against your good behavior in Christ may be ashamed of their slander.

1 Peter 3:15–16

Dear children, let us not love with words or tongue but with actions and in truth. This then is how we know that we belong to the truth, and how we set our hearts at rest in his presence whenever our hearts condemn us. For God is greater than our hearts, and he knows everything.

1 John 3:18–20

But in your hearts set apart Christ as Lord.

Chapter 39

Your Soul

Come to me, all you who are weary and burdened, and I will give you rest. Take my yoke upon you and learn from me, for I am gentle and humble in heart, and you will find rest for your souls. For my yoke is easy and my burden is light."

Matthew 11:28–30

What is the human soul? The Bible tells us that it is part of who we are as beings whom God created in His image. The Bible tells us that we each have a physical body, a spirit, a soul, a heart, and a mind. The Bible does not give us a detailed blueprint for how these are integrated and work together to enable us to experience life as human beings in this world. However, God does reveal to us in the Bible what we need to know about our heart, soul, and mind so that we may live our lives in the way that He knows is best for us.

In my search to better understand my soul, I looked to science and discovered that it is of little help in understanding the spiritual makeup of human beings. Our five senses, even when coupled with modern technology, still cannot see into the dimensions of the spiritual realm with any clarity. However, this limitation has not prevented the development of a hodgepodge of conflicting and ever-changing opinions and theories about the human mind and soul. Sadly, our culture uses these conjectures to guide people's lives. Only God truly understands the spiritual realm and the spiritual side of each of us. For this reason, only the Bible's teaching regarding human nature and behavior is fully accurate and trustworthy. This is why it is far wiser to trust the Bible for how to live life each day in a world that is both amazingly wonderful and yet is also troubled with widespread dangers, suffering, and death.

(Note: Some Bible verses found in this chapter do not contain the English word *soul* even though the Old Testament Hebrew word and the New Testament Greek word have traditionally been translated into English as *soul* or *life*. The New International Version translators sometimes use alternative English words that convey the same idea using language more widely used today. These particular verses use the words *you*, *yourselves*, *I*, *my life*, *me*, and *living being* to refer to the human soul.)

For the life of a creature is in the blood, and I have given it to you to make atonement for yourselves on the altar; it is the blood that makes atonement for one's life.

Leviticus 17:11

Love the LORD your God with all your heart and with all your soul and with all your strength. These commandments that I give you today are to be upon your hearts. Impress them on your children. Talk about them when you sit at home and when you walk along the road, when you lie down and when you get up.

Deuteronomy 6:5–7

The law of the LORD is perfect, reviving the soul.

But be very careful to keep the commandment and the law that Moses the servant of the LORD gave you: to love the LORD your God, to walk in all his ways, to obey his commands, to hold fast to him and to serve him with all your heart and all your soul."

Joshua 22:5

The law of the LORD is perfect, reviving the soul. The statutes of the LORD are trustworthy, making wise the simple. The precepts of the LORD are right, giving joy to the heart. The commands of the LORD are radiant, giving light to the eyes. The fear of the LORD is pure, enduring forever. The ordinances of the LORD are sure and altogether righteous.

Psalm 19:7–9

The LORD is my shepherd, I shall not be in want. He makes me lie down in green pastures, he leads me beside quiet waters, he restores my soul. He guides me in paths of righteousness for his name's sake. Even though I walk through the valley of the shadow of death, I will fear no evil, for you are with me; your rod and your staff, they comfort me. You prepare a table before me in the presence of my enemies. You anoint my head with oil; my cup overflows. Surely goodness and love will follow me all the days of my life, and I will dwell in the house of the LORD forever.

Psalm 23:1–6

To you, O LORD, I lift up my soul; in you I trust, O my God. Do not let me be put to shame, nor let my enemies triumph over me. No one whose hope is in you will ever be put to shame, but they will be put to shame who are treacherous without excuse. Show me your ways, O LORD, teach me your paths; guide me in your truth and teach me, for you are God my Savior, and my hope is in you all day long.

Psalm 25:1–5

The LORD is my shepherd, I shall not be in want. He makes me lie down in green pastures, he leads me beside quiet waters, he restores my soul.

Who, then, is the man that fears the LORD? He will instruct him in the way chosen for him. He will spend his days in prosperity, and his descendants will inherit the land. The LORD confides in those who fear him; he makes his covenant known to them.

Psalm 25:12–14

Evil will slay the wicked; the foes of the righteous will be condemned. The LORD redeems his servants; no one will be condemned who takes refuge in him.

Psalm 34:21–22

But God will redeem my life from the grave; he will surely take me to himself.

Psalm 49:15

Teach me your way, O LORD, and I will walk in your truth; give me an undivided heart, that I may fear your name. I will praise you, O Lord my God, with all my heart; I will glorify your name forever. For great is your love toward me; you have delivered me from the depths of the grave.

Psalm 86:11–13

My soul is weary with sorrow; strengthen me according to your word.

I am laid low in the dust; preserve my life according to your word. I recounted my ways and you answered me; teach me your decrees. Let me understand the teaching of your precepts; then I will meditate on your wonders. My soul is weary with sorrow; strengthen me according to your word. Keep me from deceitful ways; be gracious to me through your law. I have chosen the way of truth; I have set my heart on your laws. I hold fast to your statutes, O LORD; do not let me be put to shame. I run in the path of your commands, for you have set my heart free.

Psalm 119:25–32

Your statutes are wonderful; therefore I obey them.

Psalm 119:129

I wait for your salvation, O LORD, and I follow your commands. I obey your statutes, for I love them greatly. I obey your precepts and your statutes, for all my ways are known to you.

Psalm 119:166–168

For you created my inmost being; you knit me together in my mother's womb. I praise you because I am fearfully and wonderfully made; your works are wonderful, I know that full well. My frame was not hidden from you when I was made in the secret place. When I was woven together in the depths of the earth, your eyes saw my unformed body. All the days ordained for me were written in your book before one of them came to be.

Psalm 139:13–16

For the LORD gives wisdom, and from his mouth come knowledge and understanding. He holds victory in store for the upright, he is a shield to those whose walk is blameless, for he guards the course of the just and protects the way of his faithful ones. Then you will understand what is right and just and fair—every good path. For wisdom will enter your heart, and knowledge will be pleasant to your soul. Discretion will protect you, and understanding will guard you.

Proverbs 2:6–11

For the LORD gives wisdom, and from his mouth come knowledge and understanding.
. . .
For wisdom will enter your heart, and knowledge will be pleasant to your soul.

My son, preserve sound judgment and discernment, do not let them out of your sight; they will be life for you, an ornament to grace your neck. Then you will go on your way in safety, and your foot will not stumble; when you lie down, you will not be afraid; when you lie down, your sleep will be sweet. Have no fear of sudden disaster or of the ruin that overtakes the wicked, for the LORD will be your confidence and will keep your foot from being snared.

Proverbs 3:21–26

Do not be afraid of those who kill the body but cannot kill the soul. Rather, be afraid of the One who can destroy both soul and body in hell.

Matthew 10:28

"Come to me, all you who are weary and burdened, and I will give you rest. Take my yoke upon you and learn from me, for I am gentle and humble in heart, and you will find rest for your souls. For my yoke is easy and my burden is light."

Matthew 11:28–30

Jesus replied:
"'Love the Lord
your God
with all your heart
and with all your soul
and with all your mind.'

Then Jesus said to his disciples, "If anyone would come after me, he must deny himself and take up his cross and follow me. For whoever wants to save his life will lose it, but whoever loses his life for me will find it. What good will it be for a man if he gains the whole world, yet forfeits his soul? Or what can a man give in exchange for his soul?

Matthew 16:24–26

Jesus replied: "'Love the Lord your God with all your heart and with all your soul and with all your mind.' This is the first and greatest commandment. And the second is like it: 'Love your neighbor as yourself.'

Matthew 22:37–39

Then he called the crowd to him along with his disciples and said: "If anyone would come after me, he must deny himself and take up his cross and follow me. For whoever wants to save his life will lose it, but whoever loses his life for me and for the gospel will save it. What good is it for a man to gain the whole world, yet forfeit his soul? Or what can a man give in exchange for his soul?

Mark 8:34–37

So it is written: "The first man Adam became a living being"; the last Adam, a life-giving spirit.

1 Corinthians 15:45

May God himself, the God of peace, sanctify you through and through. May your whole spirit, soul and body be kept blameless at the coming of our Lord Jesus Christ.

1 Thessalonians 5:23

What good is it for a man to gain the whole world, yet forfeit his soul?

For the word of God is living and active. Sharper than any double-edged sword, it penetrates even to dividing soul and spirit, joints and marrow; it judges the thoughts and attitudes of the heart.

Hebrews 4:12

Therefore, get rid of all moral filth and the evil that is so prevalent and humbly accept the word planted in you, which can save you. Do not merely listen to the word, and so deceive yourselves. Do what it says.

James 1:21–22

Now that you have purified yourselves by obeying the truth so that you have sincere love for your brothers, love one another deeply, from the heart.

1 Peter 1:22

Dear friends, I urge you, as aliens and strangers in the world, to abstain from sinful desires, which war against your soul. Live such good lives among the pagans that, though they accuse you of doing wrong, they may see your good deeds and glorify God on the day he visits us.

1 Peter 2:11–12

**Dear friends,
I urge you,
as aliens and strangers
in the world,
to abstain
from sinful desires,
which war
against your soul.**

When they hurled their insults at him, he did not retaliate; when he suffered, he made no threats. Instead, he entrusted himself to him who judges justly. He himself bore our sins in his body on the tree, so that we might die to sins and live for righteousness; by his wounds you have been healed. For you were like sheep going astray, but now you have returned to the Shepherd and Overseer of your souls.

1 Peter 2:23–25

Chapter 40

Your Mind

**Jesus replied: "'Love the Lord your God with all your heart
and with all your soul and with all your mind.' This is the
first and greatest commandment. And the second is like it:
'Love your neighbor as yourself.'**

Matthew 22:37–39

What is your mind, and how should you use it? This is a challenging question because, although we each have a mind, we are unable to directly and precisely observe and study it. Scientists study the brain, observe behavior, and talk with people. Although these specialists have gathered much data and have developed a wide variety of theories regarding how the mind works and why people behave the way they do, the human mind remains a mystery to scientists.

Some definitions of the word *mind* state that the mind is the human consciousness that originates in the brain. This view seems to imply that thinking is the "natural result" of electrochemical activity within and between brain cells. This is an opinion and has not been proven by scientists. Science is able to demonstrate that the brain is involved in thinking, but it is unable to prove that human thinking originates in the brain. A more accurate statement would be to say that the human mind involves or utilizes the brain. This would be consistent both with what scientists observe and with what the Bible says.

The Bible tells us that human beings consist of body, soul, and spirit. The Bible also tells us that we have a spiritual heart and mind. It is a mystery to me how all of these are interrelated. I suspect that understanding exactly how these things work together requires an understanding of spiritual dimensions that are currently beyond our grasp.

What does the Bible say about the mind? God, the one who designed and created us, tells us in the Bible what we need to know about the human mind. God does not try to explain to you how He designed and engineered your mind. Rather, He tells you in the Bible how you should equip, protect, and use your mind to trust, obey, glorify, and serve Him. May the verses in this chapter guide and encourage you to use your mind wisely.

And you, my son Solomon, acknowledge the God of your father, and serve him with wholehearted devotion and with a willing mind, for the LORD searches every heart and understands every motive behind the thoughts. If you seek him, he will be found by you; but if you forsake him, he will reject you forever.

1 Chronicles 28:9

Test me, O LORD, and try me, examine my heart and my mind; for your love is ever before me, and I walk continually in your truth.

Psalm 26:2–3

You will keep in perfect peace him whose mind is steadfast, because he trusts in you.

You will keep in perfect peace him whose mind is steadfast, because he trusts in you. Trust in the LORD forever, for the LORD, the LORD, is the Rock eternal.

Isaiah 26:3–4

The heart is deceitful above all things and beyond cure. Who can understand it? "I the LORD search the heart and examine the mind, to reward a man according to his conduct, according to what his deeds deserve."

Jeremiah 17:9–10

"This is the covenant I will make with the house of Israel after that time," declares the Lord. "I will put my law in their minds and write it on their hearts. I will be their God, and they will be my people.

Jeremiah 31:33

Jesus replied: "'Love the Lord your God with all your heart and with all your soul and with all your mind.' This is the first and greatest commandment. And the second is like it: 'Love your neighbor as yourself.'

Matthew 22:37–39

Love the Lord your God with all your heart and with all your soul and with all your mind and with all your strength.' The second is this: 'Love your neighbor as yourself.' There is no commandment greater than these."

Mark 12:30–31

He said to them, "This is what I told you while I was still with you: Everything must be fulfilled that is written about me in the Law of Moses, the Prophets and the Psalms." Then he opened their minds so they could understand the Scriptures. He told them, "This is what is written: The Christ will suffer and rise from the dead on the third day, and repentance and forgiveness of sins will be preached in his name to all nations, beginning at Jerusalem. You are witnesses of these things. I am going to send you what my Father has promised; but stay in the city until you have been clothed with power from on high."

Luke 24:44–48

Jesus replied: "'Love the Lord your God with all your heart and with all your soul and with all your mind.'

So I find this law at work: When I want to do good, evil is right there with me. For in my inner being I delight in God's law; but I see another law at work in the members of my body, waging war against the law of my mind and making me a prisoner of the law of sin at work within my members.

Romans 7:21–23

What a wretched man I am! Who will rescue me from this body of death? Thanks be to God—through Jesus Christ our Lord! So then, I myself in my mind am a slave to God's law, but in the sinful nature a slave to the law of sin.

Romans 7:24–25

Those who live according to the sinful nature have their minds set on what that nature desires; but those who live in accordance with the Spirit have their minds set on what the Spirit desires. The mind of sinful man is death, but the mind controlled by the Spirit is life and peace; the sinful mind is hostile to God. It does not submit to God's law, nor can it do so. Those controlled by the sinful nature cannot please God.

Romans 8:5–8

The mind of sinful man is death,

but the mind controlled by the Spirit is life and peace;

the sinful mind is hostile to God.

Therefore, I urge you, brothers, in view of God's mercy, to offer your bodies as living sacrifices, holy and pleasing to God—this is your spiritual act of worship. Do not conform any longer to the pattern of this world, but be transformed by the renewing of your mind. Then you will be able to test and approve what God's will is—his good, pleasing and perfect will.

Romans 12:1–2

The night is nearly over; the day is almost here. So let us put aside the deeds of darkness and put on the armor of light. Let us behave decently, as in the daytime, not in orgies and drunkenness, not in sexual immorality and debauchery, not in dissension and jealousy. Rather, clothe yourselves with the Lord Jesus Christ, and do not think about how to gratify the desires of the sinful nature.

Romans 13:12–14

However, as it is written: "No eye has seen, no ear has heard, no mind has conceived what God has prepared for those who love him"—

1 Corinthians 2:9

The spiritual man makes judgments about all things, but he himself is not subject to any man's judgment: "For who has known the mind of the Lord that he may instruct him?" But we have the mind of Christ.

1 Corinthians 2:15–16

You, however, did not come to know Christ that way. Surely you heard of him and were taught in him in accordance with the truth that is in Jesus. You were taught, with regard to your former way of life, to put off your old self, which is being corrupted by its deceitful desires; to be made new in the attitude of your minds; and to put on the new self, created to be like God in true righteousness and holiness.

Ephesians 4:20–24

many live as enemies of the cross of Christ.

. . .

Their mind is on earthly things.

For, as I have often told you before and now say again even with tears, many live as enemies of the cross of Christ. Their destiny is destruction, their god is their stomach, and their glory is in their shame. Their mind is on earthly things.

Philippians 3:18–19

Once you were alienated from God and were enemies in your minds because of your evil behavior. But now he has reconciled you by Christ's physical body through death to present you holy in his sight, without blemish and free from accusation—if you continue in your faith, established and firm, not moved from the hope held out in the gospel. This is the gospel that you heard and that has been proclaimed to every creature under heaven, and of which I, Paul, have become a servant.

Colossians 1:21–23

Since, then, you have been raised with Christ, set your hearts on things above, where Christ is seated at the right hand of God. Set your minds on things above, not on earthly things.

Colossians 3:1–2

Set your minds on things above, not on earthly things.

For God did not give us a spirit of timidity, but a spirit of power, of love and of self-discipline.

2 Timothy 1:7

To the pure, all things are pure, but to those who are corrupted and do not believe, nothing is pure. In fact, both their minds and consciences are corrupted. They claim to know God, but by their actions they deny him. They are detestable, disobedient and unfit for doing anything good.

Titus 1:15–16

But when this priest had offered for all time one sacrifice for sins, he sat down at the right hand of God. Since that time he waits for his enemies to be made his footstool, because by one sacrifice he has made perfect forever those who are being made holy. The Holy Spirit also testifies to us about this. First he says: "This is the covenant I will make with them after that time, says the Lord. I will put my laws in their hearts, and I will write them on their minds." Then he adds: "Their sins and lawless acts I will remember no more." And where these have been forgiven, there is no longer any sacrifice for sin.

Hebrews 10:12–18

If any of you lacks wisdom, he should ask God, who gives generously to all without finding fault, and it will be given to him. But when he asks, he must believe and not doubt, because he who doubts is like a wave of the sea, blown and tossed by the wind. That man should not think he will receive anything from the Lord; he is a double-minded man, unstable in all he does.

James 1:5–8

**But when he asks,
he must believe
and not doubt,
because he who doubts
is like a wave of the sea,
blown and tossed
by the wind.**

· · ·

**he is a
double-minded man,
unstable in all he does.**

Chapter 41

The Holy Spirit Lives Within Christians

May the God of hope fill you with all joy and peace as you trust in him, so that you may overflow with hope by the power of the Holy Spirit.

Romans 15:13

You are supernaturally designed and created by God as a being who is both physical and spiritual. The physical side of you is an amazingly designed biological machine. The spiritual side of you includes your heart, soul, mind, and spirit. The Bible tells us that God made human beings in His image spiritually so they could enter into a perfect relationship with Him and with others for eternity. However, Adam and Eve chose to disobey God. This was the beginning of human sin—the breaking of God's laws. We all have inherited Adam's sinful nature and have sinned against God (Romans 3:23). God clearly warned Adam that the penalty for breaking His commandment was death—immediate spiritual death and eventual physical death. Spiritual death means spiritual separation from God. Unless we are saved through the sacrifice of Jesus Christ on the cross, this separation from God is for eternity.

Out of love for us, God chose to provide a way for us to be saved so that we may live with Him in heaven for eternity. God sent His Son, Jesus Christ, to receive the punishment of God's wrath against sin that we deserve. Jesus Christ went to the cross to pay the full penalty for our past, present, and future sins. However, for Jesus Christ's sacrifice to free us from the penalty for sinning against God, something is required of us. We must acknowledge that we have sinned against God and ask for His forgiveness. We must repent of our sins. We must truly believe in and follow the Lord Jesus Christ as our sin-bearer, Savior, and Lord. The Bible tells us that when this happens, the Holy Spirit supernaturally comes to reside within us. Although in this life we are not yet sinless, we are no longer slaves to sin. To the extent that we love, trust, and obey God, He will guide us and continue to transform us to become more Christ-like through the leading and empowering of the Holy Spirit living within us.

Jesus answered, "I tell you the truth, no one can enter the kingdom of God unless he is born of water and the Spirit. Flesh gives birth to flesh, but the Spirit gives birth to spirit. You should not be surprised at my saying, 'You must be born again.'

John 3:5–7

Yet a time is coming and has now come when the true worshipers will worship the Father in spirit and truth, for they are the kind of worshipers the Father seeks. God is spirit, and his worshipers must worship in spirit and in truth."

John 4:23–24

If you love me, you will obey what I command. And I will ask the Father, and he will give you another Counselor to be with you forever— the Spirit of truth.

On the last and greatest day of the Feast, Jesus stood and said in a loud voice, "If anyone is thirsty, let him come to me and drink. Whoever believes in me, as the Scripture has said, streams of living water will flow from within him." By this he meant the Spirit, whom those who believed in him were later to receive. Up to that time the Spirit had not been given, since Jesus had not yet been glorified.

John 7:37–39

"If you love me, you will obey what I command. And I will ask the Father, and he will give you another Counselor to be with you forever—the Spirit of truth. The world cannot accept him, because it neither sees him nor knows him. But you know him, for he lives with you and will be in you.

John 14:15–17

But the Counselor, the Holy Spirit, whom the Father will send in my name, will teach you all things and will remind you of everything I have said to you. Peace I leave with you; my peace I give you. I do not give to you as the world gives. Do not let your hearts be troubled and do not be afraid.

John 14:26–27

Not only so, but we also rejoice in our sufferings, because we know that suffering produces perseverance; perseverance, character; and character, hope. And hope does not disappoint us, because God has poured out his love into our hearts by the Holy Spirit, whom he has given us.

Romans 5:3–5

May the God of hope fill you with all joy and peace as you trust in him, so that you may overflow with hope by the power of the Holy Spirit.

You, however, are controlled not by the sinful nature but by the Spirit, if the Spirit of God lives in you. And if anyone does not have the Spirit of Christ, he does not belong to Christ. But if Christ is in you, your body is dead because of sin, yet your spirit is alive because of righteousness. And if the Spirit of him who raised Jesus from the dead is living in you, he who raised Christ from the dead will also give life to your mortal bodies through his Spirit, who lives in you.

Romans 8:9–11

May the God of hope fill you with all joy and peace as you trust in him, so that you may overflow with hope by the power of the Holy Spirit.

Romans 15:13

We have not received the spirit of the world but the Spirit who is from God, that we may understand what God has freely given us. This is what we speak, not in words taught us by human wisdom but in words taught by the Spirit, expressing spiritual truths in spiritual words.

1 Corinthians 2:12–13

Don't you know that you yourselves are God's temple and that God's Spirit lives in you? If anyone destroys God's temple, God will destroy him; for God's temple is sacred, and you are that temple.

1 Corinthians 3:16–17

Don't you know that you yourselves are God's temple and that God's Spirit lives in you?

Flee from sexual immorality. All other sins a man commits are outside his body, but he who sins sexually sins against his own body. Do you not know that your body is a temple of the Holy Spirit, who is in you, whom you have received from God? You are not your own; you were bought at a price. Therefore honor God with your body.

1 Corinthians 6:18–20

Now it is God who makes both us and you stand firm in Christ. He anointed us, set his seal of ownership on us, and put his Spirit in our hearts as a deposit, guaranteeing what is to come.

2 Corinthians 1:21–22

So from now on we regard no one from a worldly point of view. Though we once regarded Christ in this way, we do so no longer. Therefore, if anyone is in Christ, he is a new creation; the old has gone, the new has come!

2 Corinthians 5:16–17

But the fruit of the Spirit is love, joy, peace, patience, kindness, goodness, faithfulness, gentleness and self-control. Against such things there is no law. Those who belong to Christ Jesus have crucified the sinful nature with its passions and desires. Since we live by the Spirit, let us keep in step with the Spirit.

Galatians 5:22–25

And you also were included in Christ when you heard the word of truth, the gospel of your salvation. Having believed, you were marked in him with a seal, the promised Holy Spirit, who is a deposit guaranteeing our inheritance until the redemption of those who are God's possession—to the praise of his glory.

Ephesians 1:13–14

For this reason I kneel before the Father, from whom his whole family in heaven and on earth derives its name. I pray that out of his glorious riches he may strengthen you with power through his Spirit in your inner being, so that Christ may dwell in your hearts through faith. And I pray that you, being rooted and established in love, may have power, together with all the saints, to grasp how wide and long and high and deep is the love of Christ, and to know this love that surpasses knowledge—that you may be filled to the measure of all the fullness of God.

Ephesians 3:14–19

Having believed, you were marked in him with a seal, the promised Holy Spirit,

It is God's will that you should be sanctified: that you should avoid sexual immorality; that each of you should learn to control his own body in a way that is holy and honorable, not in passionate lust like the heathen, who do not know God; and that in this matter no one should wrong his brother or take advantage of him. The Lord will punish men for all such sins, as we have already told you and warned you. For God did not call us to be impure, but to live a holy life. Therefore, he who rejects this instruction does not reject man but God, who gives you his Holy Spirit.

1 Thessalonians 4:3–8

Guard the good deposit that was entrusted to you— guard it with the help of the Holy Spirit who lives in us.

For God did not give us a spirit of timidity, but a spirit of power, of love and of self-discipline.

2 Timothy 1:7

What you heard from me, keep as the pattern of sound teaching, with faith and love in Christ Jesus. Guard the good deposit that was entrusted to you—guard it with the help of the Holy Spirit who lives in us.

2 Timothy 1:13–14

At one time we too were foolish, disobedient, deceived and enslaved by all kinds of passions and pleasures. We lived in malice and envy, being hated and hating one another. But when the kindness and love of God our Savior appeared, he saved us, not because of righteous things we had done, but because of his mercy. He saved us through the washing of rebirth and renewal by the Holy Spirit, whom he poured out on us generously through Jesus Christ our Savior, so that, having been justified by his grace, we might become heirs having the hope of eternal life. This is a trustworthy saying. And I want you to stress these things, so that those who have trusted in God may be careful to devote themselves to doing what is good. These things are excellent and profitable for everyone.

Titus 3:3–8

He saved us through the washing of rebirth and renewal by the Holy Spirit, whom he poured out on us generously through Jesus Christ our Savior,

And this is his command: to believe in the name of his Son, Jesus Christ, and to love one another as he commanded us. Those who obey his commands live in him, and he in them. And this is how we know that he lives in us: We know it by the Spirit he gave us.

1 John 3:23–24

You, dear children, are from God and have overcome them, because the one who is in you is greater than the one who is in the world. They are from the world and therefore speak from the viewpoint of the world, and the world listens to them. We are from God, and whoever knows God listens to us; but whoever is not from God does not listen to us. This is how we recognize the Spirit of truth and the spirit of falsehood.

1 John 4:4–6

Appendix 1

What It Means to Equip Your Mind with the Word of God

What I Do Not Mean by Equipping Your Mind with the Word of God

What do I mean by the title of this book, *Equip Your Mind with the Word of God*? I do not mean simply acquiring academic knowledge about the contents of the Bible. There are many people who have studied the Bible this way and are very knowledgeable about the Bible as a religious, literary, or historical book. However, this book is not about gathering academic knowledge in the form of Bible verses. There are also people who have read the Bible along with other religious books and who view the Bible as simply one of many sources of spiritual wisdom. They collect only those Bible verses that mesh comfortably with their worldview or support what they feel like doing. Then there are people who are professing Christians, who attend church, who may be active in serving in their church, and who may even be familiar with much of the Bible. However, they do not believe what the Bible says about itself. Although they may believe that the Bible contains truth from God, they also believe that one cannot know for sure which verses come from God and which originate with man. These are all examples of what I do not mean by equipping one's mind with the Word of God.

Can Anyone Equip His or Her Mind with the Word of God?

The subject of equipping your mind with the Word of God primarily applies to Christians—spiritually reborn followers of Jesus Christ (I explain what I mean by the term *Christian* in the Introduction to this book). However, I do believe it is possible for someone who is not yet a spiritually reborn Christian to begin equipping his or her mind with the Word of God. Consider a person who is earnestly seeking to discover and know the true Creator God of the universe. Now suppose that he or she, as part of their commitment to an objective, diligent investigation, is willing to temporarily assume that the God of the Bible does exist, that the whole Bible is the supernatural Word of God as it claims to be, and that it is fully trustworthy. Given this scenario, if this person seriously ponders even a handful of key Bible verses during their sincere search to know God, I believe that the Holy Spirit will speak to that person's heart through Scripture. In my opinion, this person is beginning to equip his or her mind with the Word of God. He or she must then choose how to respond to what the Holy Spirit reveals through Scripture. If you are someone who is truly seeking to know God, then I encourage you to ponder the Bible verses in this book and ask God to speak to your heart through them.

What it Means to Equip Your Mind with the Word of God

For spiritually reborn followers of the Lord Jesus Christ, earnestly equipping your mind with the Word of God involves the following:

1. It means that you are regularly reading and studying the Bible because you trust that the Bible is in fact the Word of God, you deeply desire to know God better, and you want to know what He is saying to you. This requires studying the Bible diligently.

2. It means increasingly asking the question, "*What does the Bible say about this?*" You find yourself asking this question more frequently because you truly want to view God, this world, life's situations, other people, and yourself the way God calls you to in the Bible. A valuable exercise for an individual or for a small group would be to ask this question for each of the "Thirty Important Questions" listed in "Appendix 6: Trusting the Bible—A Self-Test for Christians."

3. It means that you are purposefully collecting Bible verses, physically or mentally, that are especially relevant to you. The Holy Spirit will reveal to you (through your conscience, the circumstances of life, or other Christians) which Bible verses are important for you to equip your mind with right now. These are verses that you need to trust and treasure in your heart to guide your thinking. My personal collection includes Bible verses that I have memorized as well as those verses that I am familiar with but have not memorized. Those verses that I have not memorized are located in places where I can easily view them or readily retrieve them when needed (they are underlined in my Bible, stored in my personal computer and handheld computer, printed on a folded sheet in my shirt pocket, posted on walls in my home, and printed in this book). These are all Scriptures that I trust, treasure, and rely on to guide my thinking.

4. It means meditating on and being prepared to apply to your life those Bible verses that make up your personal collection. Your motivation is not based on scholarly performance or earning your salvation. God's Word tells us that we cannot earn any portion of our salvation. Salvation is received only by faith in Jesus Christ according to the biblical Gospel. Your motivation is to grow closer to God and to glorify Him in your thoughts, words, and actions.

5. It means asking God to help you to correctly understand His Word and to properly apply it in your everyday living.

My Experience

I learned that even when I was equipped with only a few foundational verses, my view of the world and my thinking began to change in profound ways. The first Bible passage that I equipped my mind with was Proverbs 3:5–6. These verses continue to significantly influence my worldview and transform my life.

> Trust in the LORD with all your heart and lean not on your own understanding; in all your ways acknowledge him, and he will make your paths straight. *Proverbs 3:5–6*

Initially this was a huge pill for me to swallow because I did not like what it was saying. However, when I came to the point of trusting that this verse is truly the Word of God and realized that God says what He means and means what He says, I memorized it and allowed it to guide my thinking. This is when I began my journey of trusting the Bible above my own thinking and above the wisdom of this world on all matters about which the Bible speaks. I am far from perfect in living this out, but I am committed to this path. Trusting God's Word has enabled me to more effectively test my own thinking and the world around me for truth. Truth is that which accurately represents reality. The Bible is the only reliable foundation for understanding the truth about God, ourselves, this world, how life works, and what God desires for us and from us. Pursuing this path continues to be life-transforming for me.

The Right Time is Now

Do not be discouraged if you are new to the Bible and it seems overwhelming to you. Even if you are near the end of your life, don't think that it is too late for you to start. It is never too late to begin studying the Bible. It is also never too late to become more intentional about equipping your mind with the Word of God. God will use even one Bible verse to begin bringing about amazing changes in your life if you trust in Him and in His Word. A Christian who has treasured just one verse in his or her heart is better equipped with the Word of God than someone who can recite many verses and has academically studied the Bible for years but has not treasured them in his or her heart.

If you choose to be diligent in equipping your mind with the Word of God, you will be embarking on a path of discovery and transformation through God's truths found in the Bible. You will learn how God calls you to apply these truths in your own life. God's Word will become foundational to how you think and live. Your ability to discern truth from untruth will grow in a world that is full of deception. Your worldview will become more biblical, and you will see God, yourself, others, and this world more accurately. Your relationship with God will deepen. To the extent that you earnestly, prayerfully, and diligently follow this path, God will transform your life according to His plan.

This is not about your talents, abilities, or accomplishments. This is about trusting God, His wisdom, and His power. It is about submitting your life to the all-knowing, all-powerful, loving Creator of the universe so that He may accomplish in you what He knows is best for you—in this life and in the next.

Appendix 2

Why It Is Important to Equip Your Mind with the Word of God

1. God Communicates His Truths Through the Bible

Equipping your mind with the Word of God is important because the Word of God is the primary language-based way that God uses to communicate His truths to human beings. The Bible, when trusted and used properly, is a guidance system for Christian thinking that is of infinite value. God has given us the Bible to teach us how to rightly view Him, other people, this world, the circumstances of daily life, and ourselves. The Word of God teaches us about who God is, who we are, what this world is all about, and what happens when we physically die and leave this world. The Bible teaches us the truth about our sinful nature that separates us from God. The Bible teaches us the truth about Jesus Christ and how He alone can save us from the penalty for having sinned against God. Only through Jesus Christ can we enter into a right relationship with God for eternity. The Bible teaches us how to live our lives in ways that are pleasing to Him and spiritually fulfilling for us. The Word of God is the truth that teaches us the reality of all these things. The Lord Jesus Christ tells us in John 17:17 "*Sanctify them by the truth; your word is truth.*"

2. The Holy Spirit Speaks Through the Bible

Equipping your mind with the Word of God is important because the Holy Spirit often speaks through God's Word to communicate with and transform Christians. It is often when you are carefully reading and meditating on a Bible passage that the Holy Spirit reveals to you biblical truths, insights, and wisdom. The Holy Spirit also uses times when you are pondering Bible verses and applying them in your life to grow you spiritually.

But when he, the Spirit of truth, comes, he will guide you into all truth. He will not speak on his own; he will speak only what he hears, and he will tell you what is yet to come. He will bring glory to me by taking from what is mine and making it known to you. *John 16:13–14*

But the fruit of the Spirit is love, joy, peace, patience, kindness, goodness, faithfulness, gentleness and self-control. Against such things there is no law. Those who belong to Christ Jesus have crucified the sinful nature with its passions and desires. Since we live by the Spirit, let us keep in step with the Spirit. *Galatians 5:22–25*

On the other hand, if you spend little or no time reading, studying, and pondering the Word of God, then you are suppressing the work of the Holy Spirit in your life. To the extent that you are not regularly setting your mind on the Word of God, your mind will drift toward the desires of your sinful nature and worldly things. Equipping your mind with the Word of God helps protect you from this spiritual pitfall.

Those who live according to the sinful nature have their minds set on what that nature desires; but those who live in accordance with the Spirit have their minds set on what the Spirit desires. The mind of sinful man is death, but the mind controlled by the Spirit is life and peace; the sinful mind is hostile to God. It does not submit to God's law, nor can it do so. Those controlled by the sinful nature cannot please God. *Romans 8:5–8*

Since, then, you have been raised with Christ, set your hearts on things above, where Christ is seated at the right hand of God. Set your minds on things above, not on earthly things. *Colossians 3:1–2*

3. Applying God's Word Requires Knowing God's Word

Equipping your mind with the Word of God is important because it is essential to being able to accurately and consistently apply Scripture to how you think and live. What happens when our minds are not equipped with the Word of God? Our ability to discern truth from untruth, good from evil, right from wrong, and wise from foolish will be weak even though we sincerely wish to be faithful Christians. We will tend to think more like the world thinks and make worldly decisions. Our perspectives and choices will initially seem to be wise, but the results will often prove to be disappointing and sometimes harmful. Our relationship with God and our relationships with other people will suffer in spite of our desire for them to flourish.

4. Minds That Are Not Equipped with the Word of God Will Follow the Ways of this World

Equipping your mind with the Word of God is important because we humans have a tendency to want to go our own self-centered ways and justify whatever we feel like doing. Christians are not immune from this. If we are not continually equipping our minds with the Bible, then the Word of God will not be fresh in our minds and will have less influence on our moment-by-moment thinking. Instead, what will be fresher in our minds will be the myriad of messages and images continually coming our way from the world around us. Many of these messages and images are expertly designed to influence our thinking and appeal to our selfish desires. When our minds are not equipped with God's Word, we will lack discernment in many areas important to our lives. We will then be more likely to deceive ourselves and rationalize that an ungodly path is actually not a problem. The next self-deception is the human tendency to seek the approval of like-minded people whom we believe will agree with our selfish position. Christians who want to faithfully follow the Lord Jesus Christ must be equipped with the Word of God.

5. Knowing the Word of God is Essential to Putting on the Armor of God

Equipping your mind with the Word of God is important because it affects your ability to put on the full armor of God for spiritual protection (Ephesians 6:10–18). Spiritual protection means protecting your heart and mind from succumbing to such things as deception, doubts about God, doubts about the Bible, discouragement, distractions, pridefulness, unwillingness to forgive, bitterness, discontent, sinful lusts, greed, and selfishness. All around us and within us there is a great spiritual battle raging. The hearts and minds of human beings are the targets. This spiritual battle involves your heart and mind initially, but through your thinking and your choices this battle also affects your physical being as well as everyone within your sphere of influence. Your submission to the Lordship of Jesus Christ, your prayer life, and how well equipped you are with the Word of God will determine how protected you will be with the armor of God. When you are under spiritual attack, will you emerge from the battle standing firm for Jesus Christ, or will you instead be defeated? Will you be standing firm so that you will be able to help those you care about as they face spiritual battles of their own? Or, will you be deceived for lack of God's armor and then discover in retrospect that during many of the spiritual battles you had been manipulated by Satan's forces into furthering his cause? For Christians, there is no escaping this great spiritual battle. We need to be equipped with the Word of God to be able to stand firm for Jesus Christ in this fallen, deceptive world.

6. Christians Are Called to Make Choices Based on the Word of God

Equipping your mind with the Word of God is important because each day we face spiritual choices that are part of the great spiritual battle, whether we realize it or not. God calls us in the Bible to trust and obey Him above anyone or anything else. Each time we face a decision between following God's wisdom or following man's wisdom we are involved in the great spiritual battle between God and Satan. What we choose will affect our current spiritual life as well as the person we are in the process of becoming. As in physical-world battlefields, things that at first seem insignificant can turn out to be monumental. It is vital in both the physical and spiritual realms that we recognize the difference between what is significant and what is insignificant. Knowing and trusting what the Bible says is essential to being able to discern which personal choices could have serious consequences for our lives or for others. Christians who are not equipped with the Word of God have hearts and minds that are highly vulnerable to spiritual attacks by Satan, his forces, and those humans they manipulate.

7. The Word of God Is Foundational for Discerning Good from Evil, Right from Wrong, and Truth from Error

Equipping your mind with the Word of God is important because when we know and trust God's Word, the Holy Spirit uses it to expose evil and to warn us when we are heading down the wrong path. Equipping your mind with the Word of God will enable you to properly use the Bible to test your own thoughts and feelings, test the advice and wisdom of other people, and test all that you see and hear in the world around you. You will be better able to recognize your blind spots so that you can make God-honoring course corrections. God's Word will always be consistent with the Holy Spirit's leading and with sound, godly counsel from other Christians. If the Bible is at odds with an alleged leading of the Holy

Spirit, with the counsel of another Christian, or with your own thinking, God calls you to trust and obey the Bible instead. As a Christian, God calls you to trust and obey His Word even when you don't feel like it. Equipping your mind with the Word of God is part of God's plan to protect you from spiritual dangers, to bring spiritual blessings into your life, and to develop you into a mature, faithful disciple of the Lord Jesus Christ.

8. The Word of God is Essential to Being a Faithful Ambassador for Jesus Christ

Equipping your mind with the Word of God is important because it is essential if you are to be a faithful and fruitful ambassador for the Lord Jesus Christ. The Lord Jesus Christ commands Christians to make disciples:

> Then Jesus came to them and said, "All authority in heaven and on earth has been given to me. Therefore go and make disciples of all nations, baptizing them in the name of the Father and of the Son and of the Holy Spirit, and teaching them to obey everything I have commanded you. And surely I am with you always, to the very end of the age." *Matthew 28:18–20*

If our minds are not equipped with the Word of God, then our lives will not be consistent with the Word of God. If our lives are not consistent with the Word of God, then we will not properly reflect Jesus Christ to others. If we are not properly reflecting Jesus Christ, then we will be ineffective at being His ambassadors to this world and at making disciples of others. If you want to be a faithful and fruitful ambassador for the Lord Jesus Christ, then the Word of God must be central to your life.

9. Equipping Your Mind with the Word of God is an Essential Part of Renewing Your Mind and Being Transformed by God

God calls us in Romans 12:2 to be transformed: *"Do not conform any longer to the pattern of this world, but be transformed by the renewing of your mind. Then you will be able to test and approve what God's will is—his good, pleasing and perfect will."* Renewing your mind involves submitting your life to God, trusting in Him, and trusting the Word of God above the wisdom of this world. It involves viewing the world and our lives according to God's values, principles, and truths which He reveals to us in the Bible. Renewing your mind means setting your mind on things that are pleasing to God instead of on things that are displeasing to Him. All of these things are crucial for us as Christians who must still face life's troubles, temptations, the anti-God influences of our culture, and the attacks of Satan and those he controls. Satan's forces are continually working to deceive us, destroy our trust and confidence in the Bible, and undermine our faith in the Lord Jesus Christ. Standing firm against these influences and being transformed through the renewing of your mind requires having a mind that is equipped with the Word of God.

10. How You View and Treat the Bible Will Influence Every Area of Your Life

How you view and treat the Bible will determine how you think about God, view and relate to Jesus Christ, treat other people, view yourself, view this world, and think about truth. In addition, how you view and treat the Bible will determine what you believe about life, death, heaven, hell, and what is required for entrance into an eternal relationship with God. Finally, how you view and treat the Bible will determine your moral values, life priorities, daily priorities and what you think, say, and do each day. God cares deeply about your thoughts and attitudes in each of these areas. God knows that your thoughts and attitudes reflect the condition of your heart and will determine your words and actions.

God calls you to trust and obey Him—which means trusting in and obeying His Word. God tells us in the Bible how He wants us to view and treat His Word. Chapters 1–4 of Volume 1 of this book series presents how God calls us to view and treat the Bible. If the Bible is truly central to your life, God's principles and wisdom will be at home in your heart and will be reflected in your thoughts, words, and deeds. You will increasingly have what is called a *biblical worldview*. Developing a God-honoring biblical worldview and equipping your mind with the Word of God go hand in hand

The Bible is God's precious gift that He uses to teach us His truth, guide our thinking, and transform our lives. When the minds of Christians are well equipped with the Word of God, they are better able to discern God's truth and principles from man's contrary philosophies, myths, and deceptions. Equipping your mind with the Word of God is vitally important for developing a God-honoring biblical worldview and for growing in *spiritual maturity*—thinking and living more like Jesus Christ and less like this world.

Appendix 3

How to Equip Your Mind
with the Word of God

Appendix 1 deals with *what* it means to equip your mind with the Word of God. Appendix 2 deals with *why* it is important to equip your mind with the Word of God. Appendix 3 deals with *how* to equip your mind with the Word of God. So how do you equip your mind with the Word of God? The right answer is "God's way." Central to equipping your mind with the Word of God is viewing and treating the Bible the way God tells you to in the Bible. This appendix presents eighteen specific actions which I believe are important for equipping your mind with the Word of God.

Action 1: Be a Spiritually Reborn Follower of Jesus Christ.

If you are not sure what this means, please refer to the section in the Introduction titled: "What I Mean by the Term *Christian*." The Holy Spirit must be involved for anyone to equip his or her mind with the Word of God.

Action 2: Be Committed to Seeking Truth.

Base your life on what is true. Develop the skill of discernment—the ability to differentiate between what is true and what is not. Truth—that which accurately represents reality—is very important to God. Not pursuing truth, rejecting truth, and compromising truth all have serious spiritual (heart, mind, and soul) consequences sooner or later. Our attitude and approach toward truth will significantly influence how we view and treat the Bible. How we view and treat the Bible will determine how we view the Lord Jesus Christ, our values, our path through this life, and our place in eternity. God allows you to choose to what extent your life will be based on truth. Two of my favorite human quotes speak about truth:

There is but one straight course, and that is to seek truth and pursue it steadily. *George Washington*[1]

Truth is the first thing to go when people want to go their own way.
Frank Peretti[2]

Notice in the following Bible verses how the words *truth* and *true* are closely associated with the Lord Jesus Christ or with the Word of God. The Word of God is referred to in these verses by the terms: *words, laws, teaching,* and *doctrine*:

All your words are *true*; all your righteous laws are eternal. *Psalm 119:160*

To the Jews who had believed him, Jesus said, "If you hold to my teaching, you are really my disciples. Then you will know the *truth*, and the *truth* will set you free." *John 8:31–32*

Jesus answered, "I am the way and the *truth* and the life. No one comes to the Father except through me. *John 14:6*

After Jesus said this, he looked toward heaven and prayed: "Father, the time has come. Glorify your Son, that your Son may glorify you. . . . Sanctify them by the *truth*; your word is *truth*. *John 17:1, 17*

"You are a king, then!" said Pilate. Jesus answered, "You are right in saying I am a king. In fact, for this reason I was born, and for this I came into the world, to testify to the *truth*. Everyone on the side of *truth* listens to me." *John 18:37*

Do your best to present yourself to God as one approved, a workman who does not need to be ashamed and who correctly handles the word of *truth*. *2 Timothy 2:15*

For the time will come when men will not put up with sound doctrine. Instead, to suit their own desires, they will gather around them a great number of teachers to say what their itching ears want to hear. They will turn their ears away from the *truth* and turn aside to myths. *2 Timothy 4:3–4*

Seek to know what is true about God, the Bible, yourself, and this world. Base your life upon these truths.

Action 3: Believe, and Know Why You Believe, That the Bible Is in Fact the Word of God.

There is no way to equip your mind with the Word of God if you don't believe that the Bible is what it says it is (see Chapter 1). God calls Christians to trust that He has accurately preserved the Bible across the centuries, across languages, and across cultures. We are to trust the Bible. This means that when the Bible speaks about something, we are to trust what it says above the wisdom of this world. This also means trusting the Bible above your own thinking whenever your thinking is at odds with the Bible. Diligently test your ideas and the ideas of others for truth. Do not allow the foolish ideas of man to undermine your trust and confidence in the Bible.

God supernaturally used approximately forty different individuals over a period of more than 1,500 years to write the sixty-six books of the Bible. The Bible is an integrated message system that reflects miraculous consistency between its sixty-six books. The Bible continues to withstand the test of time as its historical accounts continue to be consistent with new archeological discoveries. The Bible is unique in its ability to accurately describe future events hundreds and even thousands of years before they come to pass, demonstrating God's foreknowledge. This is referred to as *predictive prophecy*. God, who is not limited in space and time as we are, uses these evidences to authenticate that He is the author of the Bible and that the Bible is truly supernatural in nature.

If this subject is difficult for you because you have doubts about the Bible as I did, make this a personal study project. Commit to doing some homework to understand the many evidences that support the Bible's reliability and trustworthiness. Appendix 5, item 10, points to several excellent resources to assist you in your investigation.

Action 4: Trust That God Has Protected the Bible Across Time.

The Bible is an integral part of God's eternal plan for communicating directly with human beings. God has protected His Word down through the ages so that we may have Bibles that accurately present the Word of God. The Bible has been under attack for thousands of years, and new attacks continue today. In spite of Satan's continual attempts to destroy or undermine the integrity of the Bible, God ensures its survival to accomplish His purposes throughout history.

Your word, O LORD, is eternal; it stands firm in the heavens. *Psalm 119:89*

The grass withers and the flowers fall, but the word of our God stands forever." *Isaiah 40:8*

Heaven and earth will pass away, but my words will never pass away. *Matthew 24:35*

Action 5: Be Prepared to Withstand the World's Attacks on the Reliability and Trustworthiness of the Bible.

Confidently viewing the Bible as the trustworthy Word of God is becoming increasingly unpopular in our culture and even in many churches and religious institutions. Some people believe that we cannot really know what the Word of God says because all we have are Bibles that are copies of copies of manuscripts from thousands of years ago. For this reason, some of them teach that we need to rely upon our own reasoning, feelings, experiences and worldly wisdom in order to know God better. This reflects our great capacity as human beings to rationalize doing what we feel like doing. Throughout history men have devised clever reasons for justifying why they need not trust what the Bible clearly states. In reality, the serious study of Bible manuscripts, Greek and Hebrew languages, archeology, history, and fulfilled Bible prophecy provides more than adequate evidence that the Bible is accurate and trustworthy. What we need to do is diligently check out the evidence, objectively test our and others' assumptions, and earnestly pursue the truth even if it is inconvenient or uncomfortable. Rejecting or resisting the truth—that which accurately represents reality—does not free one from the consequences of reality. This is especially true regarding the Word of God.

Many today, both outside and inside the church, claim that Darwin's theory of evolution provides more than enough scientific evidence to prove that the Genesis account of creation should not be taken seriously. If you hear this, beware! The theory of evolution is not based on empirical (relying on verification by observation and experiment) scientific evidence, but on opinions. Do not be misled as I was. Appendix 5 of this book deals specifically with Darwin's theory of evolution and the unscientific arguments that continue to defend it. I have included Appendix 5 because the unscientific theory of evolution continues to be widely used today to undermine people's trust and confidence in the Bible.

Satan employs a variety of clever undermining strategies to get people to doubt that the Bible really is the Word of God. One way for us to detect an attack against the Bible—which is in reality an attack against God—is to watch for teaching or behavior that promotes trusting the wisdom of this world above trusting the Bible. These attacks come in many forms: "*Science disproves the Bible. Secular psychotherapy is the best way to help people to cope with the problems of living. The Bible has changed over time and therefore is unreliable. The Bible is too old to be relevant for the 21st century. Whatever works to help us reach our Christian goals is fine with God. There is no absolute truth that we can know for sure. Truth is what makes sense and feels right to you. God wants you to satisfy the desires of your heart. The Bible is a living document that each generation must interpret for itself.*" These are all man-centered ideas that contradict the Bible. When you diligently test these and similar arguments by asking clarifying questions, requiring solid evidence, and testing the underlying assumptions for truth, you will discover that they are false.

Do not be misled by the following line of thinking which is becoming increasingly common today: "*Regarding the Bible, we have no way of knowing for sure which parts of the Bible are the words of God and which parts are just the words of men. Therefore, although we study and embrace the Bible, we must view the Bible through the lens of our own thinking, feelings, and experiences to discover God's truths for us. Only then will we truly experience God and begin to understand what it really means to be a Christian.*" Unfortunately many people in our day are choosing to accept foolish messages like this one. The reasons are many: these messages are smoothly presented by likable teachers, people are not reading the Bible for themselves, and people are simply not testing for truth what teachers and authors are saying. Do not just accept what you hear and read because it is proclaimed by a professing Christian. Find out for yourself if it is consistent with what the Bible says.

Do you truly want to know God better, grow in spiritual maturity, and increasingly honor Him with how you live your life? If so, then you must guard your heart and mind from worldly deceptions and self-deception. How do you do this? Pray for God's protection and leading. Pray that God would help you to properly understand the Bible. Then read and trust the Bible. When the Bible speaks about something, trust what it says above the wisdom of this world and even above your own ideas. Choose to be obedient to God's Word. Then God will do the rest.

Action 6: Use a Bible That Accurately Represents the Word of God

Be sure to use a Bible that is the result of diligent and reliable translations of the Hebrew and Greek Scriptures into English. There are many faithful, accurate translations of the Bible from which to choose. However, there are also a number of "Bibles" that have been corrupted with human ideas that are inconsistent with the Word of God. Some of these Bibles are modified by specific religious groups to support their preferred beliefs. Other so-called Bibles cannot be considered accurate English translations because they are the work of individuals who have rewritten the Bible to conform to their own personal opinions. Such paraphrase "Bibles" often convey different messages than those revealed in faithful versions of the Bible. Please note that these cases are quite different than a single Bible scholar who has simply updated a reliable Bible version by replacing archaic words with current English words. Such an updated version is still accurate and reliable. This can be readily verified by comparing the texts. The front section of a Bible should explain the translation approach used, the translation team involved, and the Greek and Hebrew source documents used to produce the Bible.

For those of you who may be asking which Bible you should use, I will share with you my perspective. About seven years ago I faced the same question and began to explore the subject of Bible versions. I learned that there are many good English translations of the Bible. I have become familiar with several of these and would not hesitate to use them as a devotional or study Bible. There are other good English Bibles, but I am uncomfortable recommending a Bible version that I am not personally familiar with. Given this, the English Bible versions that I am comfortable recommending include the following: Amplified®, English Standard Version®, King James 2000®, King James Version, New American Standard Bible®, New International Version®, New King James Version®, and the World English Bible®. I personally use more than one Bible version. For some passages the "idea for idea" translation approach used in some Bibles enables me to better understand what the Bible is saying. At other times referencing a Bible version that is based on a more "word for word" translation approach reveals insights that I did not see in my "idea for idea" Bible version. The introduction in the front of your Bible will explain which translation approach was used by the publisher. Once you have a solid Bible, it is vitally important that you use it.

Action 7: Believe What the Bible Says About Itself

As a Christian, it is of utmost importance that you believe what the Bible says about itself. Chapter 1 presents Bible verses that focus specifically on how God wants you to view the Bible. It is important that you trust the Bible above the wisdom and philosophies of this world. Your view of the Bible will determine your worldview, your relationship with the Lord Jesus Christ, your growth in spiritual maturity, how you relate to other people, your path through this life, and your place in eternity. May the Bible—the Word of God—be a lamp to your feet and a light to your path (from Psalm 119:105).

Action 8: Decide Up Front That You Will Be Obedient to God.

Before you begin reading, studying, or pondering Scripture, make up your mind that you will be obedient to God as He speaks to you through His Word. This shows your faithful submission to the Lordship of Jesus Christ.

God knows your heart. How do you think God views a person who approaches reading the Bible with the following wait-and-see attitude? *"Before I will obey this Bible passage, I must first see whether or not I like what it is saying. Then I will decide whether or not it is right for me."* God has already answered this question for us in the following three Bible verses and in hundreds of other verses throughout the Bible.

"If you love me, you will obey what I command. *John 14:15*

Whoever has my commands and obeys them, he is the one who loves me. He who loves me will be loved by my Father, and I too will love him and show myself to him." *John 14:21*

Do not merely listen to the word, and so deceive yourselves. Do what it says. *James 1:22*

Action 9: Make Studying the Bible One of Your Top Priorities.

Bible study options include topical studies, word studies, character studies, doctrinal studies, and verse-by-verse book studies. These are all beneficial. My recommendation is to always be involved in a verse-by-verse Bible-book study. This could be on your own or within a small-group setting. If your small group is studying the book of Genesis, then on your own you may also choose to study a topic such as "humility" or the "armor of God." If your small group is studying the word *love*, then I encourage you to concurrently be studying a book of the Bible on your own or with a second Bible-study group. This could be in person or via the Internet through organizations such as the Koinonia Institute[3]. Verse-by-verse Bible studies ensure that you don't miss important biblical truths and principles that may never be covered in your other studies.

Action 10: Pray for God to Help You to Understand the Bible.

As you study a Bible verse or passage, begin with prayer. It is the Holy Spirit that enables people to understand the Word of God beyond a superficial level. Ask God to guide your thinking and reveal to you the truths and insights within the Scriptures you are studying. Pray also for God to help you to properly and wisely apply the Word of God in your life. The Psalmist who penned Psalm 119 prayed for these very things:

> I am your servant; give me discernment that I may understand your statutes.
> *Psalm 119:125*

> Teach me, O LORD, to follow your decrees; then I will keep them to the end. Give me understanding, and I will keep your law and obey it with all my heart. Direct me in the path of your commands, for there I find delight. Turn my heart toward your statutes and not toward selfish gain. Turn my eyes away from worthless things; preserve my life according to your word.
> *Psalm 119:33–37*

> Your statutes are forever right; give me understanding that I may live.
> *Psalm 119:144*

Action 11: Be Committed to Accurately Understanding the Bible.

God calls us to live according to His Word. We cannot do that if we have a wrong understanding of what the Bible is saying. The first goal of studying a Bible passage should always be to accurately understand the meaning that God intended. This requires diligently studying the Bible. God wants us to revere His Word, know His Word, trust His Word, faithfully live according to His Word, and accurately teach His Word. When we do this we are honoring God and allowing the Holy Spirit to transform us. God cares deeply about the role that we allow the Bible to play in our lives. He cares deeply about how we view and treat His Word. These principles are revealed in the following Bible verses:

"Every word of God is flawless; he is a shield to those who take refuge in him. Do not add to his words, or he will rebuke you and prove you a liar. *Proverbs 30:5–6*

"Why do you call me, 'Lord, Lord,' and do not do what I say? I will show you what he is like who comes to me and hears my words and puts them into practice. He is like a man building a house, who dug down deep and laid the foundation on rock. When a flood came, the torrent struck that house but could not shake it, because it was well built. *Luke 6:46–48*

But the one who hears my words and does not put them into practice is like a man who built a house on the ground without a foundation. The moment the torrent struck that house, it collapsed and its destruction was complete." *Luke 6:49*

He replied, "Blessed rather are those who hear the word of God and obey it." *Luke 11:28*

Watch your life and doctrine closely. Persevere in them, because if you do, you will save both yourself and your hearers. *1 Timothy 4:16*

Do your best to present yourself to God as one approved, a workman who does not need to be ashamed and who correctly handles the word of truth. *2 Timothy 2:15*

In the presence of God and of Christ Jesus, who will judge the living and the dead, and in view of his appearing and his kingdom, I give you this charge: Preach the Word; be prepared in season and out of season; correct, rebuke and encourage—with great patience and careful instruction. *2 Timothy 4:1–2*

Do not merely listen to the word, and so deceive yourselves. Do what it says. *James 1:22*

Action 12: Interpret and Apply the Bible Correctly.

Follow a proven process for properly interpreting and applying Bible verses. The following six steps are representative of solid Bible-interpretation methods used by faithful Bible scholars. The order of these steps is very important.

1. Pray that God would help you to understand His meaning in the Bible verse or passage that you are about to study. Pray that God would help you to properly answer the following questions.

2. What does the text in the Bible verse or passage actually say?

3. What is the context surrounding the Bible verse or passage? Some Hebrew and Greek words and phrases have multiple meanings. The intended meaning is revealed by the context. Understand the specific situation and context to accurately understand what the author was actually saying.

4. What is the meaning of the verse or passage that the author—God—intended? The meaning you discover must be consistent with what the Bible teaches elsewhere. God's character and His Word are unchanging.

5. What, if anything, is implied in the verse or passage even though it is not specifically stated? If you believe that something is implied, it must be consistent with what the Bible teaches elsewhere.

6. What is the significance of this verse or passage for your life? Only after properly completing steps 1–5 should you focus on how to apply the Bible verse or passage to your life situation.

Action 13: Utilize Trustworthy Bible Study Resources.

Take advantage of the many excellent Bible study resources that are available via books, audio, video, and computer software. These include reliable Bible versions, Bible dictionaries, Bible commentaries, and teachings on how to accurately study and interpret the Bible. If you are new to studying the Bible, seek the counsel of biblical, spiritually mature Christians to help you select reliable Bible study resources.

There are many excellent Bible-study software programs available for both Windows and Mac OS X computers. Two excellent, free computer based resources are the web-based *Blue Letter Bible* (www.blueletterbible.org) and the Windows-based *e-Sword* Bible program (www.e-sword.net). The e-Sword program is free, as are many of the Bible versions, commentaries, dictionaries, and related resources that can be downloaded from the e-Sword website. In addition, links to several other Bible versions and study resources that work with e-Sword are available for purchase. Finally, there are many excellent Bible programs available for handheld computers.

Action 14: Properly Handle Difficult Bible Passages.

If you come across a difficult passage in the Bible, start a personal journal. Record in your journal the verses, the date, what you see as the difficulty, and your questions. Pray that God would teach you what He wants you to know about this Bible passage. Then continue on with your study of the Bible. Whenever you receive an answer to one of your recorded difficulties, record the answer and its supporting evidence in your journal. Your journal will become an encouraging record of past difficulties that God cleared up for you in His timing. I first heard about this idea from Bible teacher Chuck Missler in his briefing pack: *How to Study the Bible*[4].

There are some difficult verses in the Bible that remain a mystery even to Bible experts. However, these difficulties do not represent cases where the Bible has been proven to be wrong. In reality, the number and type of difficulties we find in Bible passages are like a grain of sand next to a mountain when compared to the difficulties that exist with man's ideas, philosophies, wisdom, and many so-called facts that are widely accepted. Some difficult Bible passages will remain mysteries until we get to heaven. Others will be resolved as we grow in our understanding of the Bible and as we learn how to properly apply it to our lives.

Action 15: Guard Your Heart.

Be discerning regarding what you fill your mind with and what you expose your mind to each day. If you are filling your mind with things that violate God's laws or that God considers foolish or worthless, your efforts to equip your mind with the Word of God will be greatly hampered. Choosing to set your mind on things that displease God will undermine your growth in spiritual maturity. First, it takes time away from activities that are pleasing to God and that are edifying for you. Second, it inhibits the Holy Spirit's work in your life. Christians should avoid those things that God considers worthless and that diminish the Holy Spirit's influence in their lives. The following Bible verses offer wise advice:

> Since, then, you have been raised with Christ, set your hearts on things above, where Christ is seated at the right hand of God. Set your minds on things above, not on earthly things. *Colossians 3:1–2*

Be joyful always; pray continually; give thanks in all circumstances, for this is God's will for you in Christ Jesus. Do not put out the Spirit's fire; do not treat prophecies with contempt. Test everything. Hold on to the good. Avoid every kind of evil. *1 Thessalonians 5:16–22*

Action 16: Stand Firm for Jesus Christ and Never Compromise Your Integrity.

Do not fall into the trap of trying to maintain opposing beliefs and values in different "compartments" within your mind. We humans can sometimes fool ourselves for a while, but we cannot fool God. His moral laws are always in effect. Their consequences cannot be circumvented or avoided. We will reap what we sow sooner or later. Compromising integrity is always damaging to the soul and leads to harming others.

Some Christians show great interest in biblical truths and wisdom, but at the same time are unwilling to give up their beliefs, ideas, values, or behaviors that are in conflict with the Bible. They try to maintain these conflicting beliefs in separate "compartments" within their minds. They choose to base their thinking and choices on either one compartment or another depending upon which one best supports what they feel like doing at the moment. Consider a man who professes to be a Christian and declares that the Bible is the Word of God. Suppose such a man treats his wife in ways that are in total opposition to what God tells us in the Bible. He may even seek a divorce without any biblical justification. Or, suppose this same man prides himself in being an honest man. What if he then justifies being deceptive in certain circumstances because his goal or cause is noble. The Bible calls such a man "double-minded." God never condones sin.

Submit yourselves, then, to God. Resist the devil, and he will flee from you. Come near to God and he will come near to you. Wash your hands, you sinners, and purify your hearts, you double-minded. *James 4:7–8*

This is not equipping one's mind with the Word of God. This is self-deception. Such thinking sets people up for internal spiritual and emotional problems and undermines their relationships with others. It also leads to a lack of discernment, being easily deceived, and having a confused and inconsistent faith in God. Following this path leads Christians away from a solid biblical worldview and undermines their growth in spiritual maturity.

God calls us to both purify our hearts and renew our minds by trusting and obeying Him.

> Therefore, I urge you, brothers, in view of God's mercy, to offer your bodies as living sacrifices, holy and pleasing to God—this is your spiritual act of worship. Do not conform any longer to the pattern of this world, but be transformed by the renewing of your mind. Then you will be able to test and approve what God's will is—his good, pleasing and perfect will.
> *Romans 12:1–2*

Place your trust in the Word of God above the wisdom of this world and even above your own ideas. Then God will help you to stand firm for Him, avoid the pitfall of double-minded thinking, and live with integrity.

Action 17: In Your Everyday Living, Make It a Habit of Asking Yourself: *"What Does the Bible Say?"*

- What does the Bible say about this idea?
- What does the Bible say about this situation?
- What does the Bible say about what I feel like doing right now?
- What does the Bible say about what I should be doing right now to glorify God?

Search for Scriptures that either directly or indirectly answer these questions. When you understand what the Bible says about your situation, honor God with your obedience. This reflects your love for God, your faithful submission to the Lordship of Jesus Christ, and your respect for the authority of the Word of God.

Action 18: Commit Bible Verses to Memory.

Memorize Bible verses that are particularly meaningful to you at this point in your life. Review them regularly and ponder their meaning and application to your current life. I regularly review my memory verses to keep them fresh in my mind. In your prayers, ask God to help you to properly apply each Bible verse that you have memorized. Just knowing a Bible verse is of little value if it is always overridden with worldly wisdom or personal preferences. If you already have a verse or passage in mind, start your memorizing there. If you are looking for suggestions, I recommend starting with one or two from the following list:

Teach me, O LORD, to follow your decrees; then I will keep them to the end. Give me understanding, and I will keep your law and obey it with all my heart. Direct me in the path of your commands, for there I find delight. Turn my heart toward your statutes and not toward selfish gain. Turn my eyes away from worthless things; preserve my life according to your word. *Psalm 119:33–37*

Your word is a lamp to my feet and a light for my path. *Psalm 119:105*

Trust in the Lord with all your heart and lean not on your own understanding; in all your ways acknowledge him, and he will make your paths straight. *Proverbs 3:5–6*

Above all else, guard your heart, for it is the wellspring of life. *Proverbs 4:23*

All a man's ways seem innocent to him, but motives are weighed by the Lord. *Proverbs 16:2*

He who answers before listening—that is his folly and his shame. *Proverbs 18:13*

"For my thoughts are not your thoughts, neither are your ways my ways," declares the Lord. "As the heavens are higher than the earth, so are my ways higher than your ways and my thoughts than your thoughts." *Isaiah 55:8–9*

You will seek me and find me when you seek me with all your heart. *Jeremiah 29:13*

But seek first his kingdom and his righteousness, and all these things will be given to you as well. Therefore do not worry about tomorrow, for tomorrow will worry about itself. Each day has enough trouble of its own. *Matthew 6:33–34*

Then Jesus said to his disciples, "If anyone would come after me, he must deny himself and take up his cross and follow me. *Matthew 16:24*

Love the Lord your God with all your heart and with all your soul and with all your mind and with all your strength.' The second is this: 'Love your neighbor as yourself.' There is no commandment greater than these." *Mark 12:30–31*

"For God so loved the world that he gave his one and only Son, that whoever believes in him shall not perish but have eternal life. *John 3:16*

When Jesus spoke again to the people, he said, "I am the light of the world. Whoever follows me will never walk in darkness, but will have the light of life." *John 8:12*

To the Jews who had believed him, Jesus said, "If you hold to my teaching, you are really my disciples. Then you will know the truth, and the truth will set you free." *John 8:31–32*

Jesus answered, "I am the way and the truth and the life. No one comes to the Father except through me. *John 14:6*

Do not conform any longer to the pattern of this world, but be transformed by the renewing of your mind. Then you will be able to test and approve what God's will is—his good, pleasing and perfect will. *Romans 12:2*

Be on your guard; stand firm in the faith; be men of courage; be strong. Do everything in love. *1 Corinthians 16:13–14*

. . . take captive every thought to make it obedient to Christ. *2 Corinthians 10:5b*

Since, then, you have been raised with Christ, set your hearts on things above, where Christ is seated at the right hand of God. Set your minds on things above, not on earthly things. *Colossians 3:1–2*

Am I now trying to win the approval of men, or of God? Or am I trying to please men? If I were still trying to please men, I would not be a servant of Christ. *Galatians 1:10*

But the fruit of the Spirit is love, joy, peace, patience, kindness, goodness, faithfulness, gentleness and self-control. Against such things there is no law. Those who belong to Christ Jesus have crucified the sinful nature with its passions and desires. Since we live by the Spirit, let us keep in step with the Spirit. *Galatians 5:22–24*

Do not let any unwholesome talk come out of your mouths, but only what is helpful for building others up according to their needs, that it may benefit those who listen. *Ephesians 4:29*

Be very careful, then, how you live—not as unwise but as wise, making the most of every opportunity, because the days are evil. Therefore do not be foolish, but understand what the Lord's will is. *Ephesians 5:15–17*

All Scripture is God-breathed and is useful for teaching, rebuking, correcting and training in righteousness, so that the man of God may be thoroughly equipped for every good work. *2 Timothy 3:16–17*

My dear brothers, take note of this: Everyone should be quick to listen, slow to speak and slow to become angry, for man's anger does not bring about the righteous life that God desires. *James 1:19–20*

His divine power has given us everything we need for life and godliness through our knowledge of him who called us by his own glory and goodness. *2 Peter 1:3*

Appendix 4

How the Word of God Can Teach You

The Word of God is a vital part of how God communicates with, teaches, and transforms Christians. If you are a Christian, the Holy Spirit is always ready to use the Word of God to work in your life in the following ways:

1. To guide your thinking in ways that are obedient and pleasing to God

2. To alert and correct you if you are being disobedient to God

3. To call you to repent of your sins

4. To teach you God's truths and train you in God's ways

5. To enable you to guard your heart and mind from spiritual dangers

6. To encourage you and broaden your perspective when you are discouraged

7. To give you courage and strength to faithfully serve and represent the Lord Jesus Christ in this world

8. To comfort you when you experience life's inevitable troubles, pain, suffering, and final days in this world

9. To help you to grow in spiritual maturity—thinking and living more like Jesus Christ and less like this world

10. To enable you to discern truth from untruth, good from evil, and right from wrong

Whenever you are faithfully and prayerfully reading, studying, pondering, memorizing, or applying God's Word in your life, you are inviting the Holy Spirit to work in your life in these ways. Every moment of every day Christians need the Holy Spirit to be working in their lives in one or more of these ten ways. Although the Holy Spirit knows exactly what we need, He will not force us to trust and obey the Word of God against our will. God desires that we love, trust, obey, and rely on Him moment-by-moment. He calls us to "pray continually" in 1 Thessalonians 5:16 because He wants us to be continually mindful of our dependence on Him, our need for His guidance, and our saving relationship with the Lord Jesus Christ. To the extent that you have this attitude, are a man or woman of prayer, and make the Bible central to your life, the Holy Spirit will use the the Word of God to produce spiritual fruit in your life.

> But the fruit of the Spirit is love, joy, peace, patience, kindness, goodness, faithfulness, gentleness and self-control. Against such things there is no law. Those who belong to Christ Jesus have crucified the sinful nature with its passions and desires. Since we live by the Spirit, let us keep in step with the Spirit. *Galatians 5:22–25*

If you are a Christian, you need to base your life on the Word of God in order to be the person whom God calls you to be and do what God wants you to do. The purpose of this book is to be a helpful resource for you as you seek to equip your mind with the Word of God. The remainder of this appendix demonstrates one of the ways that God teaches us through His Word. This is the approach used throughout this book.

As you diligently read the Bible and listen to sound Bible teaching, you will periodically recognize verses from different books of the Bible that seem to directly or indirectly illuminate a common theme. A few examples of the many themes found within the Bible are God's love for all human beings, the sinfulness of man, how to be forgiven by God, how Christians are to view and treat others, marriage, parenting, truth, false teachers, making wise choices, and God's plan for the end times. As you read Bible verses within the context of a theme, the Holy Spirit will begin revealing to you important biblical truths. Then, as you continue to ponder these Bible verses, the Holy Spirit will teach you about God's perspective, commands, and wisdom regarding this theme. He will guide you in how to properly apply these Bible verses in your life.

This appendix presents seven theme-based collections of Bible verses as examples of one way that God uses His Word to equip your mind with important biblical truths and principles. I have used a numbered list format for easy reference should you use this appendix as a resource in a Bible study with others. The following themes are based on chapters from the *Equip Your Mind with the Word of God* book series:

Bible Verses That Teach Us How God Wants Us to View and Treat the Bible:

1. Do not add to what I command you and do not subtract from it, but keep the commands of the LORD your God that I give you. *Deuteronomy 4:2*

2. "Every word of God is flawless; he is a shield to those who take refuge in him. Do not add to his words, or he will rebuke you and prove you a liar. *Proverbs 30:5–6*

3. The law of the LORD is perfect, reviving the soul. The statutes of the LORD are trustworthy, making wise the simple. The precepts of the LORD are right, giving joy to the heart. The commands of the LORD are radiant, giving light to the eyes. The fear of the LORD is pure, enduring forever. The ordinances of the LORD are sure and altogether righteous. *Psalm 19:7–9*

4. As for God, his way is perfect; the word of the LORD is flawless. He is a shield for all who take refuge in him. *Psalm 18:30*

5. In God, whose word I praise, in the LORD, whose word I praise—in God I trust; I will not be afraid. What can man do to me? *Psalm 56:10–11*

6. How can a young man keep his way pure? By living according to your word. I seek you with all my heart; do not let me stray from your commands. I have hidden your word in my heart that I might not sin against you. *Psalm 119:9–11*

7. Your statutes are my delight; they are my counselors. *Psalm 119:24*

8. Teach me, O LORD, to follow your decrees; then I will keep them to the end. Give me understanding, and I will keep your law and obey it with all my heart. Direct me in the path of your commands, for there I find delight. Turn my heart toward your statutes and not toward selfish gain. Turn my eyes away from worthless things; preserve my life according to your word. *Psalm 119:33–37*

9. The law from your mouth is more precious to me than thousands of pieces of silver and gold. *Psalm 119:72*

10. Oh, how I love your law! I meditate on it all day long. Your commands make me wiser than my enemies, for they are ever with me. I have more insight than all my teachers, for I meditate on your statutes. I have more understanding than the elders, for I obey your precepts. I have kept my feet from every evil path so that I might obey your word. I have not departed from your laws, for you yourself have taught me. How sweet are your words to my taste, sweeter than honey to my mouth! I gain understanding from your precepts; therefore I hate every wrong path. Your word is a lamp to my feet and a light for my path. *Psalm 119:97–105*

11. All your words are true; all your righteous laws are eternal. *Psalm 119:160*

12. My son, keep my words and store up my commands within you. Keep my commands and you will live; guard my teachings as the apple of your eye. Bind them on your fingers; write them on the tablet of your heart. *Proverbs 7:1–3*

13. Do your best to present yourself to God as one approved, a workman who does not need to be ashamed and who correctly handles the word of truth. *2 Timothy 2:15*

14. All Scripture is God-breathed and is useful for teaching, rebuking, correcting and training in righteousness, so that the man of God may be thoroughly equipped for every good work. *2 Timothy 3:16–17*

15. For the word of God is living and active. Sharper than any double-edged sword, it penetrates even to dividing soul and spirit, joints and marrow; it judges the thoughts and attitudes of the heart. *Hebrews 4:12*

16. Do not merely listen to the word, and so deceive yourselves. Do what it says. *James 1:22*

Bible Verses That Teach Us How God Wants Us to View and Relate to Him:

1. Trust in the LORD with all your heart and lean not on your own understanding; in all your ways acknowledge him, and he will make your paths straight. *Proverbs 3:5–6*

2. I will praise you, O LORD, with all my heart; I will tell of all your wonders. I will be glad and rejoice in you; I will sing praise to your name, O Most High. *Psalm 9:1–2*

3. I love you, O LORD, my strength. The LORD is my rock, my fortress and my deliverer; my God is my rock, in whom I take refuge. He is my shield and the horn of my salvation, my stronghold. *Psalm 18:1–2*

4. To you, O LORD, I lift up my soul; in you I trust, O my God. Do not let me be put to shame, nor let my enemies triumph over me. No one whose hope is in you will ever be put to shame, but they will be put to shame who are treacherous without excuse. Show me your ways, O LORD, teach me your paths; guide me in your truth and teach me, for you are God my Savior, and my hope is in you all day long. *Psalm 25:1–5*

5. Test me, O LORD, and try me, examine my heart and my mind; for your love is ever before me, and I walk continually in your truth. *Psalm 26:2–3*

6. Teach me your way, O LORD, and I will walk in your truth; give me an undivided heart, that I may fear your name. I will praise you, O Lord my God, with all my heart; I will glorify your name forever. For great is your love toward me; you have delivered me from the depths of the grave. *Psalm 86:11–13*

7. Yet a time is coming and has now come when the true worshipers will worship the Father in spirit and truth, for they are the kind of worshipers the Father seeks. God is spirit, and his worshipers must worship in spirit and in truth." *John 4:23–24*

8. Therefore, I urge you, brothers, in view of God's mercy, to offer your bodies as living sacrifices, holy and pleasing to God—this is your spiritual act of worship. Do not conform any longer to the pattern of this world, but be transformed by the renewing of your mind. Then you will be able to test and approve what God's will is—his good, pleasing and perfect will. *Romans 12:1–2*

9. Therefore, since we are receiving a kingdom that cannot be shaken, let us be thankful, and so worship God acceptably with reverence and awe, *Hebrews 12:28*

10. Jesus replied: "'Love the Lord your God with all your heart and with all your soul and with all your mind.' This is the first and greatest commandment. And the second is like it: 'Love your neighbor as yourself.' *Matthew 22:37–39*

Bible Verses That Teach Us About Jesus Christ:

1. As soon as Jesus was baptized, he went up out of the water. At that moment heaven was opened, and he saw the Spirit of God descending like a dove and lighting on him. And a voice from heaven said, "This is my Son, whom I love; with him I am well pleased." *Matthew 3:16–17*

2. "Come to me, all you who are weary and burdened, and I will give you rest. Take my yoke upon you and learn from me, for I am gentle and humble in heart, and you will find rest for your souls. For my yoke is easy and my burden is light." *Matthew 11:28–30*

3. Then Jesus came to them and said, "All authority in heaven and on earth has been given to me. Therefore go and make disciples of all nations, baptizing them in the name of the Father and of the Son and of the Holy Spirit, and teaching them to obey everything I have commanded you. And surely I am with you always, to the very end of the age." *Matthew 28:18–20*

4. The Word became flesh and made his dwelling among us. We have seen his glory, the glory of the One and Only, who came from the Father, full of grace and truth. *John 1:14*

5. The next day John saw Jesus coming toward him and said, "Look, the Lamb of God, who takes away the sin of the world! *John 1:29*

6. "For God so loved the world that he gave his one and only Son, that whoever believes in him shall not perish but have eternal life. For God did not send his Son into the world to condemn the world, but to save the world through him. Whoever believes in him is not condemned, but whoever does not believe stands condemned already because he has not believed in the name of God's one and only Son. *John 3:16–18*

7. For the one whom God has sent speaks the words of God, for God gives the Spirit without limit. The Father loves the Son and has placed everything in his hands. Whoever believes in the Son has eternal life, but whoever rejects the Son will not see life, for God's wrath remains on him." *John 3:34–36*

8. But he continued, "You are from below; I am from above. You are of this world; I am not of this world. I told you that you would die in your sins; if you do not believe that I am the one I claim to be, you will indeed die in your sins." "Who are you?" they asked. "Just what I have been claiming all along," Jesus replied. *John 8:23–25*

9. Jesus said to her, "I am the resurrection and the life. He who believes in me will live, even though he dies; and whoever lives and believes in me will never die. Do you believe this?" "Yes, Lord," she told him, "I believe that you are the Christ, the Son of God, who was to come into the world." *John 11:25–27*

10. Jesus answered, "I am the way and the truth and the life. No one comes to the Father except through me. *John 14:6*

11. But now a righteousness from God, apart from law, has been made known, to which the Law and the Prophets testify. This righteousness from God comes through faith in Jesus Christ to all who believe. There is no difference, for all have sinned and fall short of the glory of God, and are justified freely by his grace through the redemption that came by Christ Jesus. God presented him as a sacrifice of atonement, through faith in his blood. He did this to demonstrate his justice, because in his forbearance he had left the sins committed beforehand unpunished—he did it to demonstrate his justice at the present time, so as to be just and the one who justifies those who have faith in Jesus. *Romans 3:21–26*

12. Therefore, there is now no condemnation for those who are in Christ Jesus, because through Christ Jesus the law of the Spirit of life set me free from the law of sin and death. *Romans 8:1–2*

13. That if you confess with your mouth, "Jesus is Lord," and believe in your heart that God raised him from the dead, you will be saved. For it is with your heart that you believe and are justified, and it is with your mouth that you confess and are saved. As the Scripture says, "Anyone who trusts in him will never be put to shame." *Romans 10:9–11*

14. And this is his command: to believe in the name of his Son, Jesus Christ, and to love one another as he commanded us. Those who obey his commands live in him, and he in them. And this is how we know that he lives in us: We know it by the Spirit he gave us. *1 John 3:23–24*

15. Everyone who believes that Jesus is the Christ is born of God, and everyone who loves the father loves his child as well. This is how we know that we love the children of God: by loving God and carrying out his commands. This is love for God: to obey his commands. And his commands are not burdensome, *1 John 5:1–3*

Bible Verses That Teach Us About Faithfully Following Jesus Christ:

1. All men will hate you because of me, but he who stands firm to the end will be saved. *Matthew 10:22*

2. and anyone who does not take his cross and follow me is not worthy of me. Whoever finds his life will lose it, and whoever loses his life for my sake will find it. *Matthew 10:38–39*

3. Then Jesus said to his disciples, "If anyone would come after me, he must deny himself and take up his cross and follow me. *Matthew 16:24*

4. "I tell you, whoever acknowledges me before men, the Son of Man will also acknowledge him before the angels of God. But he who disowns me before men will be disowned before the angels of God. *Luke 12:8–9*

5. To the Jews who had believed him, Jesus said, "If you hold to my teaching, you are really my disciples. Then you will know the truth, and the truth will set you free." *John 8:31–32*

6. "If you love me, you will obey what I command. And I will ask the Father, and he will give you another Counselor to be with you forever—the Spirit of truth. The world cannot accept him, because it neither sees him nor knows him. But you know him, for he lives with you and will be in you. *John 14:15–17*

7. Jesus replied, "If anyone loves me, he will obey my teaching. My Father will love him, and we will come to him and make our home with him. He who does not love me will not obey my teaching. These words you hear are not my own; they belong to the Father who sent me. *John 14:23–24*

8. Am I now trying to win the approval of men, or of God? Or am I trying to please men? If I were still trying to please men, I would not be a servant of Christ. *Galatians 1:10*

9. I have been crucified with Christ and I no longer live, but Christ lives in me. The life I live in the body, I live by faith in the Son of God, who loved me and gave himself for me. *Galatians 2:20*

10. For this very reason, make every effort to add to your faith goodness; and to goodness, knowledge; and to knowledge, self-control; and to self-control, perseverance; and to perseverance, godliness; and to godliness, brotherly kindness; and to brotherly kindness, love. For if you possess these qualities in increasing measure, they will keep you from being ineffective and unproductive in your knowledge of our Lord Jesus Christ. But if anyone does not have them, he is nearsighted and blind, and has forgotten that he has been cleansed from his past sins. Therefore, my brothers, be all the more eager to make your calling and election sure. For if you do these things, you will never fall, and you will receive a rich welcome into the eternal kingdom of our Lord and Savior Jesus Christ. *2 Peter 1:5–11*

Bible Verses That Teach Us How God Wants Us to View and Treat Others:

1. Do not withhold good from those who deserve it, when it is in your power to act. Do not say to your neighbor, "Come back later; I'll give it tomorrow"—when you now have it with you. *Proverbs 3:27–28*

2. A friend loves at all times, and a brother is born for adversity. *Proverbs 17:17*

3. Do not say, "I'll do to him as he has done to me; I'll pay that man back for what he did." *Proverbs 24:29*

4. "You have heard that it was said, 'Love your neighbor and hate your enemy.' But I tell you: Love your enemies and pray for those who persecute you, *Matthew 5:43–44*

5. Jesus replied: "'Love the Lord your God with all your heart and with all your soul and with all your mind.' This is the first and greatest commandment. And the second is like it: 'Love your neighbor as yourself.' *Matthew 22:37–39*

6. But love your enemies, do good to them, and lend to them without expecting to get anything back. Then your reward will be great, and you will be sons of the Most High, because he is kind to the ungrateful and wicked. Be merciful, just as your Father is merciful. *Luke 6:35–36*

7. "A new command I give you: Love one another. As I have loved you, so you must love one another. By this all men will know that you are my disciples, if you love one another." *John 13:34–35*

8. Love must be sincere. Hate what is evil; cling to what is good. Be devoted to one another in brotherly love. Honor one another above yourselves. Never be lacking in zeal, but keep your spiritual fervor, serving the Lord. Be joyful in hope, patient in affliction, faithful in prayer. Share with God's people who are in need. Practice hospitality. *Romans 12:9–13*

9. Live in harmony with one another. Do not be proud, but be willing to associate with people of low position. Do not be conceited. *Romans 12:16*

10. Love is patient, love is kind. It does not envy, it does not boast, it is not proud. It is not rude, it is not self-seeking, it is not easily angered, it keeps no record of wrongs. Love does not delight in evil but rejoices with the truth. It always protects, always trusts, always hopes, always perseveres. Love never fails. *1 Corinthians 13:4–8a*

11. Praise be to the God and Father of our Lord Jesus Christ, the Father of compassion and the God of all comfort, who comforts us in all our troubles, so that we can comfort those in any trouble with the comfort we ourselves have received from God. *2 Corinthians 1:3–4*

12. The entire law is summed up in a single command: "Love your neighbor as yourself." *Galatians 5:14*

13. Carry each other's burdens, and in this way you will fulfill the law of Christ. *Galatians 6:2*

14. Therefore each of you must put off falsehood and speak truthfully to his neighbor, for we are all members of one body. *Ephesians 4:25*

15. Get rid of all bitterness, rage and anger, brawling and slander, along with every form of malice. Be kind and compassionate to one another, forgiving each other, just as in Christ God forgave you. *Ephesians 4:31–32*

16. Do nothing out of selfish ambition or vain conceit, but in humility consider others better than yourselves. Each of you should look not only to your own interests, but also to the interests of others. *Philippians 2:3–4*

17. Therefore, as God's chosen people, holy and dearly loved, clothe yourselves with compassion, kindness, humility, gentleness and patience. Bear with each other and forgive whatever grievances you may have against one another. Forgive as the Lord forgave you. And over all these virtues put on love, which binds them all together in perfect unity. *Colossians 3:12–14*

18. Do not rebuke an older man harshly, but exhort him as if he were your father. Treat younger men as brothers, older women as mothers, and younger women as sisters, with absolute purity. *1 Timothy 5:1–2*

19. Remind the people to be subject to rulers and authorities, to be obedient, to be ready to do whatever is good, to slander no one, to be peaceable and considerate, and to show true humility toward all men. *Titus 3:1–2*

20. Now that you have purified yourselves by obeying the truth so that you have sincere love for your brothers, love one another deeply, from the heart. *1 Peter 1:22*

Bible Verses That Warn Us Not to Set Our Hearts and Minds on Things That are Displeasing to God:

1. Do not bring a detestable thing into your house or you, like it, will be set apart for destruction. Utterly abhor and detest it, for it is set apart for destruction. *Deuteronomy 7:26*

2. When you enter the land the LORD your God is giving you, do not learn to imitate the detestable ways of the nations there. Let no one be found among you who sacrifices his son or daughter in the fire, who practices divination or sorcery, interprets omens, engages in witchcraft, or casts spells, or who is a medium or spiritist or who consults the dead. Anyone who does these things is detestable to the LORD, and because of these detestable practices the LORD your God will drive out those nations before you. *Deuteronomy 18:9–12*

3. I will set before my eyes no vile thing. The deeds of faithless men I hate; they will not cling to me. Men of perverse heart shall be far from me; I will have nothing to do with evil. *Psalm 101:3–4*

4. Teach me, O LORD, to follow your decrees; then I will keep them to the end. Give me understanding, and I will keep your law and obey it with all my heart. Direct me in the path of your commands, for there I find delight. Turn my heart toward your statutes and not toward selfish gain. Turn my eyes away from worthless things; preserve my life according to your word. *Psalm 119:33–37*

5. When men tell you to consult mediums and spiritists, who whisper and mutter, should not a people inquire of their God? Why consult the dead on behalf of the living? To the law and to the testimony! If they do not speak according to this word, they have no light of dawn. *Isaiah 8:19–20*

6. These wicked people, who refuse to listen to my words, who follow the stubbornness of their hearts and go after other gods to serve and worship them, will be like this belt—completely useless! *Jeremiah 13:10*

7. "Of what value is an idol, since a man has carved it? Or an image that teaches lies? For he who makes it trusts in his own creation; he makes idols that cannot speak. Woe to him who says to wood, 'Come to life!' Or to lifeless stone, 'Wake up!' Can it give guidance? It is covered with gold and silver; there is no breath in it. *Habakkuk 2:18–19*

8. They exchanged the truth of God for a lie, and worshiped and served created things rather than the Creator—who is forever praised. Amen. *Romans 1:25*

9. Those who live according to the sinful nature have their minds set on what that nature desires; but those who live in accordance with the Spirit have their minds set on what the Spirit desires. The mind of sinful man is death, but the mind controlled by the Spirit is life and peace; the sinful mind is hostile to God. It does not submit to God's law, nor can it do so. Those controlled by the sinful nature cannot please God. *Romans 8:5–8*

10. Do not deceive yourselves. If any one of you thinks he is wise by the standards of this age, he should become a "fool" so that he may become wise. For the wisdom of this world is foolishness in God's sight. As it is written: "He catches the wise in their craftiness"; *1 Corinthians 3:18–19*

11. For, as I have often told you before and now say again even with tears, many live as enemies of the cross of Christ. Their destiny is destruction, their god is their stomach, and their glory is in their shame. Their mind is on earthly things. *Philippians 3:18–19*

12. Since, then, you have been raised with Christ, set your hearts on things above, where Christ is seated at the right hand of God. Set your minds on things above, not on earthly things. *Colossians 3:1–2*

13. If anyone teaches false doctrines and does not agree to the sound instruction of our Lord Jesus Christ and to godly teaching, he is conceited and understands nothing. He has an unhealthy interest in controversies and quarrels about words that result in envy, strife, malicious talk, evil suspicions and constant friction between men of corrupt mind, who have been robbed of the truth and who think that godliness is a means to financial gain. *1 Timothy 6:3–5*

14. For the time will come when men will not put up with sound doctrine. Instead, to suit their own desires, they will gather around them a great number of teachers to say what their itching ears want to hear. They will turn their ears away from the truth and turn aside to myths. *2 Timothy 4:3–4*

15. Dear children, keep yourselves from idols. *1 John 5:21*

Bible Verses That Teach Us to Set Our Hearts and Minds on Things That are Pleasing to God:

1. How can a young man keep his way pure? By living according to your word. I seek you with all my heart; do not let me stray from your commands. I have hidden your word in my heart that I might not sin against you. *Psalm 119:9–11*

2. Your statutes are my delight; they are my counselors. *Psalm 119:24*

3. Oh, how I love your law! I meditate on it all day long. Your commands make me wiser than my enemies, for they are ever with me. I have more insight than all my teachers, for I meditate on your statutes. I have more understanding than the elders, for I obey your precepts. I have kept my feet from every evil path so that I might obey your word. I have not departed from your laws, for you yourself have taught me. How sweet are your words to my taste, sweeter than honey to my mouth! I gain understanding from your precepts; therefore I hate every wrong path. Your word is a lamp to my feet and a light for my path. *Psalm 119:97–105*

4. All your words are true; all your righteous laws are eternal. *Psalm 119:160*

5. My son, keep my words and store up my commands within you. Keep my commands and you will live; guard my teachings as the apple of your eye. Bind them on your fingers; write them on the tablet of your heart. *Proverbs 7:1–3*

6. Jesus replied: "'Love the Lord your God with all your heart and with all your soul and with all your mind.' *Matthew 22:37*

7. Since, then, you have been raised with Christ, set your hearts on things above, where Christ is seated at the right hand of God. Set your minds on things above, not on earthly things. *Colossians 3:1–2*

8. Finally, brothers, whatever is true, whatever is noble, whatever is right, whatever is pure, whatever is lovely, whatever is admirable—if anything is excellent or praiseworthy—think about such things. Whatever you have learned or received or heard from me, or seen in me—put it into practice. And the God of peace will be with you. *Philippians 4:8–9*

9. All Scripture is God-breathed and is useful for teaching, rebuking, correcting and training in righteousness, so that the man of God may be thoroughly equipped for every good work. *2 Timothy 3:16–17*

10. Let us fix our eyes on Jesus, the author and perfecter of our faith, who for the joy set before him endured the cross, scorning its shame, and sat down at the right hand of the throne of God. Consider him who endured such opposition from sinful men, so that you will not grow weary and lose heart. *Hebrews 12:2–3*

Appendix 5

Do Not Be Misled
by Darwin's Theory of Evolution

Why would I include a discussion on the theory of evolution in a Bible-verse reference book? The reason is because Darwin's theory of evolution has been effectively used since 1859 to undermine people's confidence in the Bible. This theory and its foundational assumptions are in reality nothing more than a popular set of opinions that are based on weak scientific evidence. In spite of this, the theory of evolution is widely treated in our culture as if it were a fact and a foundational truth of science. This is wrong. Until real scientific evidence can be presented and verified, the theory of evolution is merely conjecture. Intellectual and scientific integrity demand that it be treated as such. The theory of evolution conflicts with what the Bible says and is inconsistent with much of the physical evidence discovered to date. People who do not understand this will be misled.

When people believe the theory of evolution to be true, they conclude that the Bible's creation account in the book of Genesis must be wrong or doesn't mean what it says. Many will then reason that if the Bible can't be trusted when it speaks about creation, then it can't really be trusted when it speaks about other topics. They will view and treat the Bible as simply one of many ancient books authored by men, and they will not trust the Bible to be the Word of God. When professing Christians believe that the book of Genesis is wrong about creation, their willingness to trust the God of the Bible and be obedient to the authority of Scripture will be inconsistent. Their growth in spiritual maturity and in a biblical worldview will be undermined. When people believe in the theory of evolution, it weakens or destroys their trust and confidence in what the Bible says. This leads to serious consequences in their spiritual lives (their heart, mind, and soul) as well as in the lives of those within their sphere of influence.

The widespread teaching and promotion of the theory of evolution in our culture today is not justified on scientific grounds. The vast majority of our public schools and colleges teach that the process of evolution correctly explains the origin of the wide variety of plants and animals that inhabit the earth, including man. They treat and promote the theory of evolution as a foundational scientific truth, but they do so without the necessary scientific evidence. These institutions claim that scientific evidence fully supports the idea that life originated by chance from nonlife and then over hundreds of millions of years evolved into the wide variety of life that we see in our world. The theory of evolution is also widely supported and promoted in many museums, nature documentaries, science journals, nature magazines, and zoos. Because these institutions in America used to be known for their factual and objective presentation of information, people tend to trust them to present information that is accurate and scientifically sound. This is no longer a safe assumption. In our culture we need to test everything for truth. We need to be asking, *"Does this line up with reality?"* The evidence that evolutionists use to justify the theory of evolution does not stand up to true scientific scrutiny because it does not line up with reality.

True scientists don't accept impressively packaged claims without testing them to determine if they really represent reality. True scientists rely on real evidence. Although the evidence supporting the theory of evolution is weak, devoted evolutionists boldly claim that the evidence is strong enough to justify suppressing the competing theory of intelligent design. They continue to claim that the scientific evidence overwhelmingly supports the idea that life arose from nonlife and then over millions of years evolved into the wide variety of life forms found on earth. Although these evolutionists may start with the real physical evidence, they unscientifically interpret the evidence to reach their unscientific conclusions and conjectures. When packaged within a polished video, museum display, or authoritative textbook, the theory of evolution appears to be true. If you don't want to be deceived and manipulated, you need to diligently test everything for truth—that which accurately represents reality.

These are my opinions regarding the theory of evolution. Please do not simply accept or reject them based on whether or not they are consistent with your beliefs. I encourage you to critically test my assertions, reasoning, and conclusions to see if they are sound. What we should desire and earnestly be seeking is an understanding regarding the origin of life that fully matches reality.

It is my hope that this appendix will encourage, equip, and help you to diligently test for truth all that you see and hear regarding the origin of life issue. To this end I have organized this appendix into the following subtopics:

1. What Is Meant by the Term *Evolution*?

2. Empirical Science vs. Historical Science

1. What Is Meant by the Term *Evolution*?

At this point it is important to define what I mean when I use the word *evolution*. Two terms, *macroevolution* and *microevolution*, have been created to improve the accuracy of communications regarding the subject of the theory of evolution. When I speak of evolution or the theory of evolution in this book, I am referring to **macroevolution**—the transformation of one kind of animal or plant into another kind of animal or plant. Examples of *macroevolution* would be apes evolving into human beings, reptiles evolving into birds or mammals, and land mammals evolving into whales. Reliable evidence for *macroevolution*, including these three examples which are often presented in textbooks as if they were facts, is still missing.

When I use the term *evolution* in this appendix, I am not speaking of **microevolution**—the variation of traits within one kind of animal through the process of natural selection in the wild or the process of selective breeding under man's direction. An example of *microevolution* would be the wide variety of domestic dogs that man has produced through selective breeding. Another example would be the climate-induced variation in bill size and thickness among some Galapagos Island finches. There is ample observable evidence to prove that *microevolution* and natural selection are valid processes that can lead to variations within a single kind of animal or plant. It is important to keep in mind that *macroevolution* and *microevolution* are two very different concepts.

A word of caution is needed. Do not be deceived by arguments that claim that the theory of evolution (*macroevolution*) is true, but then use *microevolution* examples as evidence. Such arguments are not scientific. In *microevolution*, natural selection is able to favor certain traits over others as environmental pressures on a breeding population change. This is because the breeding population already has within its DNA pool the genetic information for the traits that are advantageous for survival under new environmental pressures. *Microevolution* results in variations within a single kind of animal, not new kinds of animals. What would scientists need to discover to be able to scientifically say that *macroevolution* is the process by which new kinds of plants and animals come into being? They would need observable evidence that natural selection in conjunction with random mutations were able to produce new genetic information that wasn't present before in the population's DNA. The introduction of such new genetic information needed for transforming one kind of organism into another has never been observed. One can choose to believe that this *macroevolution* conjecture is true; however this belief is based on faith and not on science. Using *microevolution* examples to support the conjecture of *macroevolution* is logically invalid and unscientific. Do not be misled.

2. Empirical Science vs. Historical Science

When discussing the evolution vs. creation controversy, it is important to understand two categories of science: *empirical science* and *historical science*. Proponents of the theory of evolution have gained unearned credibility for their theory by riding on the coattails of those scientists who practice true **empirical science**—understanding the physical world through verifiable, repeatable observations and experiments. *Empirical science* (sometimes called observational science) involves carefully investigating events and processes. *Empirical science* leads to applied science, engineering, and the resulting advanced technology of our age. However, the theory of evolution (macroevolution) that explains the origin of life and the origin of the many kinds of plants and animals falls into the realm of **historical science**—making assumptions and developing explanations regarding events and processes that happened in the past. *Historical science* is speculative because one cannot empirically observe the original event. It is important when investigating the scientific case for the theory of evolution (macroevolution) to understand that it falls into the realm of *historical science*, not *empirical science*.

When working in the realm of *historical science*, scientists base their understanding of past events and processes on a system of assumptions, observable evidence, proven scientific principles, and logic. How they interpret the physical evidence will be determined by the particular set of foundational assumptions that they have chosen. Origin of life scientists work with the same physical evidence. However, because of their differing starting assumptions they often interpret the evidence very differently and come to opposing conclusions regarding past events and processes. For this reason it is very important to understand and test the foundational assumptions being used by scientists investigating the origin of life.

Neither the theory of evolution nor the theory of intelligent design can be proven by empirical science because the origin of life and the origin of the many kinds of life forms on earth are past events. Although one cannot recreate the exact past environment to empirically test these *historical science* theories, one can look for physical evidence in the present that is either consistent or inconsistent with a given theory. If a theory is in fact the correct explanation for what happened in the past, then the physical evidence will be consistent with that theory. If there is significant physical evidence that is inconsistent with a *historical science* theory, then that theory has serious problems. With the latest advancements in technologies that enhance scientific investigation, the theory of evolution is becoming increasingly inconsistent with the physical evidence. Not only is the theory of evolution an opinion within the realm of *historical science*, it is an opinion requiring much faith to overcome its great inconsistencies with the observable, physical evidence.

3. Evolution—The Privileged Theory

The theory of evolution is a privileged theory in our world today. It has wrongly been granted immunity from standard scientific examination. This has allowed the theory of evolution to be taught and promoted across our culture as a foundational scientific truth. Only by compromising the proven scientific method and scientific integrity could this happen. The continued treatment of the theory of evolution as a "scientific fact" requires diligently protecting it and its underlying assumptions from serious scientific scrutiny. Every student of true science should be asking, "*Why is this happening?*"

The theory of evolution is a scientifically weak theory that has been carefully packaged and promoted to convince people that it should be treated as a fact. If competent science was prevailing over the origin of life issue, the current challenges to the Darwinian theory of evolution would be welcomed and encouraged. Challenging existing theories through diligent scientific testing is an important part of true science. However, that is not what we are seeing today regarding the evolution vs. intelligent design debate. In our public institutions, employees who challenge the theory of evolution on scientific grounds or who present the theory of intelligent design for serious scientific scrutiny are increasingly being reprimanded or persecuted. If these challenges to the theory of evolution were scientifically incompetent or baseless, then the time-proven scientific method would have exposed them rather quickly based on verifiable evidence and sound arguments. This has not happened. It is clear that the theory of evolution has a special, protected status that is not based on science.

To date, the arguments defending the theory of evolution are not scientific. Rather, the efforts to eliminate the scientific challenges have been based on legal action (claiming that the theory of intelligent design is nothing more than religion disguised as science), biased media coverage, and career intimidation. In the public arena, the theory of evolution is being heavily promoted as a "fact" and is being uniquely protected from critical scientific evaluation. Real science does not operate this way. In true science, every theory is fair game for competent, scientific scrutiny. This is because the purpose of true science is the pursuit of an accurate understanding of reality regarding our physical universe.

Why is the theory of evolution being so widely promoted and protected in our public institutions while the theory of intelligent design is being so adamantly attacked? Is this really a scientific controversy? It should be, but it is not. The intelligent design proponents continue to present observable evidence and challenging questions that call for scientific responses. The evolutionists respond with unscientific opinions, political arguments, lawsuits, job terminations, and cancellation of research grants. Their successes in discrediting the theory of intelligent design are based on lawsuits claiming that teaching this theory violates a separation of church and state principle (which is in reality a misapplication of Thomas Jefferson's writings). They have diverted the discussion away from science and made it into a legal and political issue. I believe that they have done this because they know that they do not have the scientific evidence and arguments needed to stand up to true scientific scrutiny. The proven scientific method, when diligently followed, is fully capable of challenging any scientific theory and testing it for validity. What is happening in America today is the unscientific shielding of the theory of evolution from normal and proper scientific scrutiny. We see widespread intolerance of any scientific investigation that may expose the major flaws in the theory of evolution. We also see widespread discrediting and suppression of the alternative explanation for the origin and diversity of life—the theory of intelligent design. From these observations it is clear that this is not really about two origin of life theories challenging each other scientifically. Rather, this is a worldview conflict.

4. Evolution Wrongly Rides on the Coattails of True Science

Some scientists who diligently apply scientific thinking and responsibly prepare precise, accurate documentation in other areas of scientific study fail to do the same when it comes to the theory of evolution. They make the mistake of allowing their presumptions, their preferences, research funding, or political pressure to bias their work or their stated positions regarding the subject of the origin and diversity of life. Such scientists then make unwarranted statements declaring or implying that the theory of evolution is a scientific truth. Their truly scientific accomplishments and credentials in other areas of research wrongly give false credibility to the theory of evolution. This results in many people falsely assuming that the theory of evolution is based on irrefutable evidence and has been upheld by the same scientific standards found within true empirical science. The end result is that many people are being deceived into believing that these assertions regarding the origin and diversity of life are proven facts, when in reality they are mere conjectures. I was one of these misguided people for many years. Do not be misled as I was. Do not let your confidence in the Bible be undermined as was mine.

5. How Important Is Scientific Integrity?

This arena of origin-of-life science is one where both biblical truth and critical thinking have been seriously compromised both in the culture and in many churches. The message of this culture is that the Bible's teaching about the physical world and the history of man is wrong because it is at odds with modern science. The assumption implied in this message is that this so-called modern science is based on true scientific evidence that is empirical—verified by observation and experiment. This is a false assumption. When members of the scientific community boldly state that the big bang was the beginning of our physical universe, that life came from non-life, and that the diverse kinds of plants and animals evolved from simpler life forms as if these were scientific truths, they are stepping outside of the realm of science. None of these statements has been validated empirically. These statements are, in reality, mere opinions and unproven theories. They are not scientific facts. There is nothing inherently wrong with scientists having personal opinions that are not empirically verifiable. However, it is wrong when mere opinions and conjectures about the origin of life are packaged and presented to the public as scientific truths in classrooms, in textbooks, in television documentaries, in museums, and elsewhere. Presenting these opinions to the public as if they are scientific truths lacks scientific integrity and is a disgrace to true science. A position that would reflect scientific integrity regarding this matter would look something like the following:

> *"We know very little about the processes that led to the origin of the universe, to the origin of life, and to the origin of the many kinds of life-forms found on earth. We were not there to observe what happened, and we have yet to observe any process by which life arises from nonlife. We do not even have an explanation for a process whereby a living cell could be formed from nonliving chemicals. We also have never observed one kind of animal evolving into another kind of animal. We do not even have conclusive fossil evidence showing the existence of necessary transitional forms needed to support our theory of evolution. We have our opinions and we have formulated several variations of Darwin's theory of evolution, but right now that's all we can say from a scientific perspective. However, we will keep searching for evidence to support our theories because we believe in them. We admit that our trust in the theory of evolution is based upon our faith that life on earth formed without any kind of intelligent design. Our trust in the theory of evolution is also based on our faith that someday we will be able to empirically show how one kind of animal (or plant) could change into another kind of animal (or plant). Here is the evidence that we have acquired to date, which we believe supports our theory. In addition, here is the evidence that we are aware of to date that is inconsistent with our theory. We do hope that in the future our theory will prove to be correct based upon newly discovered evidence. Until then, scientific integrity demands that other theories be objectively explored as long as established scientific principles and methodologies are followed. Regardless of how this turns out, our goal as a scientific community is to rigorously pursue truth in order to more accurately understand the physical world we live in."*

We should commend and support those scientists, textbook publishers, teachers, journal editors, and museum directors who reflect this kind of scientific integrity. We should encourage the rest to never compromise scientific integrity.

6. What About the Theory of Intelligent Design?

First, it is important to accurately understand what is meant by the *theory of intelligent design*. The following definition, along with many other useful resources on this topic, can be found at the Discovery Institute—Center for Science & Culture website on intelligent design (www.intelligentdesign.org).

> "*The scientific theory of intelligent design holds that certain features of the universe and of living things are best explained by an intelligent cause, not an undirected process such as natural selection.*"[1]

In this section I will share my perspective on the theory of intelligent design. Science was my favorite subject all through school. I was fascinated with the natural world, had a deep respect for the scientific method, and admired science's devotion to discovering the truth about the physical world. Up until the age of forty I believed that simple life originated by chance from non-life. I further believed that the first living thing evolved into increasingly more complex life forms. These in turn evolved over long periods of time into the amazing variety of plants and animals that we observe on earth today. This is what I was taught in school, saw on TV, learned at the local science museum, and read in books and nature magazines. All other ideas were treated as quaint religious stories that were not intended to be taken literally. It never occurred to me that there might be a credible alternative to the theory of evolution.

My unquestioning belief in the theory of evolution was challenged when I first became aware of what appeared to be solid evidence for an alternative explanation for the origin of life. This troubled me greatly for three reasons. First, I did not, and do not now, want to believe in something that is not true. Second, scientific integrity was, and still is, very important to me. Third, the subject of the origin of life has profound implications for how a person views the Bible. What a person believes about the Bible will determine their view of God and their relationship with the Lord Jesus Christ. This began my deeper investigation into the evidence for and against the theory of evolution. This adventure introduced me to the theory of intelligent design and to the great controversy between these two conflicting theories for the origin and diversity of life.

One of my early discoveries was the lack of scientific evidence supporting the theory of evolution (macroevolution). Evolutionary scientists continue to work diligently in hopes of finding solid evidence to support their theory. In the meantime, some evolutionists are adamantly fighting to discredit and suppress an alternative origin of life explanation—the theory of intelligent design. What is revealing is that although these attacks consist of authoritative claims sprinkled with scientific terminology, they do not rely on sound scientific evidence and arguments. What these evolutionists don't want you to know is that the needed scientific evidence to solidly support their theory is still missing.

Many devoted evolutionists fear that people will discover that the theory of intelligent design is already scientifically more credible than the theory of evolution. What many of them find unacceptable is that the theory of intelligent design is consistent with the existence of a Creator God. They have a close-minded attachment to the theory of evolution because it explains the miracle of life solely by random chance over long periods of time. The last thing that many devoted evolutionists want is for people to discover that the physical evidence in the world around us is actually consistent with the existence of an intelligent designer. Although the observable, verifiable evidence is consistent with an intelligent designer, it does not empirically prove that the God of the Bible is real. However, it does mean that true science is not in conflict with the existence of a Creator God. For this reason, the scientific theory of intelligent design is a grave threat to many die-hard evolutionists.

The fact that the theory of intelligent design is often championed by Christians has been cleverly used by those who are determined to protect the theory of evolution at all costs. They attack the theory of intelligent design not by challenging its scientific merits on scientific grounds, but by diverting the public debate away from the realm of science. They claim that the theory of intelligent design is really about religion and therefore should be banned from scientific discussions in our schools. Scientifically, the fact that the theory of intelligent design is consistent with what the Bible teaches is irrelevant. True scientists of integrity are not concerned that Christians use the theory of intelligent design as evidence that supports their faith. Rather, true scientists focus their attention on better understanding the physical world we live in through observation, experimentation, and accurate thinking. Those who are working hard to discredit the theory of intelligent design by claiming it is an extension of religion do so because they are unable to challenge it scientifically.

If evolutionists actually had sound scientific evidence on their side, they could have easily disposed of the theory of intelligent design years ago. In reality, they do not have such scientific evidence. Die-hard evolutionists must instead rely on misleading arguments, misinterpretation of evidence, and impressive packaging to create the illusion of scientific credibility. However, if illuminating questions are allowed to be asked regarding the existence of supporting empirical evidence, nothing substantial is left but conjectures and opinions. The theory of intelligent design is a valid scientific theory on its own, and it is consistent with the physical evidence that we observe in the world around us.

Critics seeking to discredit and suppress the theory of intelligent design utilize two primary strategies. The first is to convince a judge and jury that the theory of intelligent design is really about religion. They then argue that it is unconstitutional to teach religion in the science classroom. The theory of intelligent design, as presented by those scientists who favor it, does not deal with God or religion. It deals with evidence and implications of that evidence that are scientifically relevant. The critic's first strategy only wins when a judge and jury either ignore this fact or make their decisions based on preconceptions. The evolutionist's second primary strategy is to claim that the theory of intelligent design is not supported by evidence. They may use impressive scientific terminology as they express their opinions, however, they do not scientifically deal with the intelligent design evidence presented. Challenges to the theory of intelligent design should be based on solid scientific evidence, not on clever debating techniques and lawsuits based on religions implications. Since evolutionists don't have the former, they rely on the latter.

Some critics of the theory of intelligent design point out that some scientists are Christians. They then claim that this disqualifies intelligent design as a valid scientific investigation. From a scientific perspective, the religious beliefs of a scientist are irrelevant. In true science, the merits of a theory are based on how that theory stands up to objective scientific testing. True scientists consistently seek to better understand reality. True scientists never misrepresent reality to promote their personal preferences or agenda. True scientists are men and women of truth and integrity.

If knowing and sharing the truth is important to you, what should you do? I encourage you to explore the resources listed in Section 10 of this Appendix. I also encourage you to see the movie documentary *Expelled: No Intelligence Allowed*[2], in which Ben Stein investigates this very topic. Ask penetrating questions such as those listed in Section 9 of this Appendix. Don't accept evasive or superficial answers just because they are eloquent or come from a so-called expert. I encourage you to follow this timeless wisdom from George Washington: "*There is but one straight course, and that is to seek truth and pursue it steadily.*"[3] The *Truth Toolkit*, a free document available at www.mindequip.com, is designed to help you to test for truth in any area of life. It can be a helpful resource for pursuing the truth regarding the theory of evolution, the theory of intelligent design, and the biblical account of creation.

7. Believing in Biblical Creation Requires Faith

The more diligently you investigate this subject, the more you will discover that the Bible is consistent with the physical evidence of our world. The Bible does not speak about every detail of the physical world we live in, but what it does comment on it has proven to be accurate and reliable. Contrary to many claims, the biblical account of creation has not been proven wrong using empirical science. One is not forced to choose between believing the Bible and believing in science. Because they are consistent with each other, one can believe in both without compromising intellectual integrity. However, it is also important to realize that empirical science has not proven the Bible's account of creation to be true. This is why, as Christians, we admit that our belief in the biblical account of creation requires faith. However, it is an intellectually reasonable faith because the Bible continues to be consistent with what we see and experience in the world around us.

8. Believing in Darwin's Theory of Evolution Requires Faith

In reality, belief in any explanation for the origin of the universe and the origin of life requires faith. This includes the big bang theory regarding the origin of the universe, chemical evolution regarding the origin of living things from nonliving molecules, and Darwin's theory of evolution and its variations regarding the transformation of one kind of living thing into another. Because these events and processes occurred in the distant past, empirical science cannot prove these origin theories to be true. Believing in these theories is just as faith-based as believing in the biblical account of creation. In the case of the theories of chemical and biological evolution, the scientific discoveries over the past hundred years in the fields of biochemistry, microbiology, and information science continue to reveal great inconsistencies with these theories. In addition, reliable fossil evidence needed to support the theory of evolution is still missing.

The fossil record should be full of transitional forms, but it is not. Trusting in the theory of evolution for the origin and diversity of life requires an enormous faith that must ignore many scientific inconsistencies.

In the absence of needed, verifiable, observable evidence to support the theory of evolution, the following kinds of weak reasons are what remain:

- *"Evolution must be true because that is what is widely accepted by our culture."* Since when does a majority opinion determine what is true?

- *"Evolution must be true because that is what I learned in K-12 school, in college, and continue to learn from TV, science journals, and museums. How can all these institutions be wrong?"* History is full of examples where the beliefs of the major institutions of the day were later proven to be wrong. A classic example is the belief that the sun rotated around the earth.

- *"Evolution must be true because there is no other naturalistic explanation."* A "naturalistic explanation" is one that can be *currently* explained through empirically verifiable natural laws and processes. Forcing this "naturalistic explanation" constraint on the modern definition of science does not reflect true science. True science is the pursuit of truth regarding our physical universe using proven scientific principles and methodologies. On many occasions in history the established and accepted natural laws and processes had to be updated. Question: Were undiscovered physical world realities of the past actually untrue before they were discovered and accepted by the scientific community? The answer is "No!" *Example*: The earth did in fact revolve around the sun even before the scientific community would accept Galileo's teaching on this. *Example*: Nuclear radiation did in fact exist before it was detected by scientists. A scientific mindset that refuses to consider new ideas simply because they may imply a causal factor beyond what can be directly observed in the present using currently available instrumentation reflects mental rigidity or a protected special interest.

  Many scientific discoveries have been made in the past as a result of developing new research tools and exploring outside of the comfortable paradigms of the day. Those discoveries resulted in the scientific community expanding its paradigm boundaries to include the newly discovered realities. True science is the pursuit of truth about our physical world wherever it may lead, as long as that pursuit follows the time-proven scientific method.

Appendix 5

9. Questions for Discovering the Truth Regarding the Origin of Life

The right questions can be powerful tools for helping us to discern to what extent a truth claim is based on scientific evidence, unsupported assumptions, or personal preferences. It is important for those who seek to live according to truth to be able to distinguish between proven scientific facts and unproven opinions that are based on faith or personal preferences. Presenting unproven opinions or mere conjectures as if they were facts misleads people and is a warning sign that something dangerous is happening. Unfortunately this is commonplace today in how the theory of evolution is presented to the public. In our culture today, as throughout history, it is vitally important to be diligent in testing everything for truth. This is essential if we are to avoid making important life choices based upon wrong or misleading information.

The following kinds of questions can be helpful for distinguishing between mere conjectures and proven facts in many areas of life. I encourage you to employ these questions as you test what you read and hear regarding the various explanations for the origin of the universe, the earth, life, and human beings:

1. What specifically is being stated?

2. What is being implied by these statements?

3. Is this idea being presented as a fact, as the only viable theory, or as one of several theories being explored?

4. What is the verifiable, observable evidence supporting these ideas and assertions?

5. What are the underlying assumptions on which these ideas are based?

6. What is the empirical evidence, if any, supporting these underlying assumptions?

7. Which, if any, of these underlying assumptions are in reality unproven opinions or conjectures?

8. Are these ideas and assertions being presented to the public in a way that clearly distinguishes between proven facts, reasonable theories, and mere conjectures?

As Christians, we do not have to become scientists to defend our faith in God and the Bible. However, we do need to do enough homework to recognize that the theory of evolution is not founded on sound, empirical science. Many Christians already view the theory of evolution as mere conjecture and as an idea that is out of touch with reality. For those individuals this is not an issue. Others struggle, as I once did, with abandoning the theory of evolution because it is so firmly ingrained in their minds. For such individuals, resolving this issue is of utmost importance because it undermines their ability to trust the Bible.

If the theory of evolution has been ingrained in your mind as it was in mine, then you may view the ideas presented in this appendix to be counterintuitive and perhaps even absurd. The idea that the theory of evolution might not be scientifically sound might seem foolish to you. All I ask is that you arm yourself with the above questions and do some probing. We should test for truth all new ideas that have important implications, including the theory of intelligent design. Our questioning and testing should be both objective and thorough. However, we should not limit our diligent testing to new ideas. We also need to be testing any ideas that we have accepted in the past but have never really tested for truth. If you have never tested the theory of evolution using the above questions, I encourage you to do so. Some of you have been taught to believe that the Bible is inaccurate and unreliable when it speaks about the physical universe, the origin of life, and the diversity of life. If this applies to you, please use these questions to test the arguments and evidence used to persuade you.

We should not accept any ideas that truly matter in life without diligently evaluating them. God calls us to use our minds wisely and to test everything. If you want to be a man or woman whose life is built on the foundation of reality, you must not allow your personal preferences to determine what you are willing to test. Every idea that impacts people's lives should be tested for truth.

10. Resources That Provide Evidence That Supports the Trustworthiness of the Bible

The biblical Christian faith is a reasonable faith. It is logical and consistent with the reality we see around us. Although the Bible contains many mysteries and unanswered questions that we cannot currently explain in terms of human perception and experience, it has never been proven to be wrong. Sophisticated conjectures and opinions that discredit the Bible do not constitute proof that the Bible is in error. Proof requires solid evidence that has been properly verified.

Christians do not need to become experts in science and ancient history to have a strong faith in God and the Bible. However, Christians living in the 21st-century would be wise to become familiar with the existence of the solid evidence that supports the accuracy and reliability of the Bible. This evidence is found in the areas of documented history, archeology, predictive-prophecy, scientific-foreknowledge, and the study of Bible manuscripts. As Christians, we need to know that these evidences exist so that when we are being challenged with so-called facts that allegedly discredit the Bible we will not be shaken or deceived. In addition, we should be familiar with these evidences so that we can guide others to them when they are struggling with doubt or disbelief regarding the Bible. This is important for every Christian. It is especially important for young Christians considering how public schools and the media treat the Bible.

To learn about the historical and documentary reliability of the Bible, I recommend the books on these topics by both Josh McDowell and Norman Geisler. For reliable information and excellent resources explaining how the Bible is consistent with the physical evidence we see in the world around us, I recommend the following ministries:

- *Answers in Genesis* (www.answersingenesis.org)
- *Center for Scientific Creation* (www.creationscience.com)
- *Institute for Creation Research* (www.icr.org)
- *Koinonia House* (www.khouse.org)

In addition, the resources available through these organizations will help you to sharpen your critical-thinking and discernment skills. If you are unfamiliar with the evidences supporting the trustworthiness of the Bible, I encourage you to invest some time exploring these resources. Having an appreciation for what they offer will enable you to quickly find answers if and when you need them.

It is amazing that with just a few books and videos one can begin to see the holes in the so-called facts of the theory of evolution. It is also interesting to note that those who attack the trustworthiness of the Bible typically fail to present openly and clearly their foundational assumptions (which are often faith-based conjectures) that must be valid for their theories to be viable. True critical thinking and integrity-based scientific investigation always involve challenging an idea's underlying assumptions. Beware of any presentation of so-called facts where there is unwillingness to also present and expose to scrutiny the position's foundational assumptions.

11. What About the Idea that God Used Evolution (Macroevolution) to Produce Life on Earth?

Some Christians believe, as I once did, that the theory of evolution makes sense. They assume that since the theory of evolution is so widely taught in our culture that it must be true. They conclude that God somehow used evolution to create the wide variety of life we see on earth, including man. However, if they read their Bibles carefully they will discover many inconsistencies between what the Bible clearly says and what evolutionists teach. When Christians come to this realization they must choose one of two paths. The first is to conclude that the theory of evolution is wrong. The second is to conclude that the Bible is wrong or that it does not mean what it says. Those that take the second path must then reinterpret Bible passages that speak about creation in order to accommodate the theory of evolution. Reinterpreting Scripture to conform to human ideas or personal preferences is often called "Scripture twisting". It is dishonoring to God and it is dangerous for those who practice it. The twisted meanings assigned to these Bible passages then conflict with many other Bible passages from both the Old and New Testaments. Not only is the theory of evolution weak scientifically, but it is inconsistent with the clear teaching of the Bible.

There are two serious problems with trying to believe in both the theory of evolution and in biblical Christianity. The first problem is that it does not represent a viable integration of empirical (observational) science with a Bible-based Christian faith. It is based on faith that random chance, energy, and matter over long periods of time somehow formed into living things. This faith goes on to believe that life evolved into the amazing diversity of plant and animal life we see on earth—life that clearly displays sophisticated biotechnology far beyond human capabilities. Even with our advanced technology mankind is unable to understand many of the processes of life, much less duplicate them. In fact, the theory of evolution violates the scientific laws of biogenesis (life only comes from life) and the second law of thermodynamics (things move from a state of order to increasing disorder apart from the application of information). In reality, the theory of evolution is based on faith rather than on fact. Believing that the God of the Bible used macroevolution to develop life on earth represents an attempt to integrate two opposing and incompatible faiths. This is not reasonable.

The second problem with trying to believe in both the theory of evolution and biblical Christianity is that it conflicts with the Word of God. The theory of evolution is inconsistent with the Bible's teachings in both the Old and New

Testaments. The Genesis account of creation leaves no room for a Darwinian evolutionary process. In the New Testament, Jesus Christ and several of the Apostles spoke of people and events in the Old Testament as if they were real people and actual events. They spoke of the creation account in Genesis as being true, of Adam and Eve as real people, of Noah as a real person, and of the worldwide flood as a real event. The theory of evolution is totally inconsistent with what the Bible teaches.

We each must choose to what extent we will trust the Bible above the theory of evolution. Will we believe the creation account in the Old Testament and what Jesus and the Apostles clearly stated in the New Testament? It would be inconsistent for a Christian to say that he or she believes what Jesus and the Apostles said about salvation and heaven, but then reject what they said about the creation and the flood. Jesus Christ warned us about this in John 5:46-47: *"If you believed Moses, you would believe me, for he wrote about me. But since you do not believe what he wrote, how are you going to believe what I say?"*

Trying to believe in biblical Christianity along with the theory of evolution eventually undermines one's confidence in the trustworthiness of the Bible. Why should I believe what the Bible clearly says about God's character, His standards, His view of sin, His judgment, His love, His grace, His mercy, Jesus Christ's mission to save us from our sins, how to obtain salvation through faith in Jesus Christ, and what follows physical death if I do not believe what the Bible clearly says about how God created life on earth? What you believe about the origin of life on earth will influence how you view and treat the Bible.

Please note that I am not implying that in order to become a Christian one must first reject the idea that God used evolution. All Christians are on a lifelong path that involves growing in discernment and replacing false notions with truths. However, it is my opinion that Christians who continue to believe in the theory of evolution are holding beliefs that work to undermine their trust and confidence in the Bible. This always has serious consequences.

12. Trusting the Bible Is Vitally Important for Christians

Throughout the Bible's history it has been under attack by those who claim that it is not the Word of God, that it is full of errors, that it has been intentionally corrupted over time, or that we simply can't know for sure which parts of the Bible are from God. These attacks on the Bible all send the same message—that one cannot know for sure that the Bible is true and trustworthy.

Christians must be prepared to detect and defend against a variety of clever attacks against the Bible. We need to acquire at least a basic awareness and understanding of the solid evidence supporting why the Bible is in fact the Word of God and is fully trustworthy. Any weakness in our confidence in the Bible is an opportunity for Satan, his forces, or his pawns to deceive us.

Since Darwin's book on the origin of species was published in 1859, the undermining of people's confidence in the Bible using the theory of evolution has been very effective. How can Christians stand up to attacks against the Bible that declare that evolution proves that the Bible cannot be fully trusted?

- First, we must read and study the Bible. Then we must trust God and what He says in the Bible more than we trust the wisdom of this world.

- Second, we must pray for God's protection from being deceived.

- Third, we must diligently, wisely, and critically test everything for truth.

- Fourth, we must reject the teachings of the world when they are contrary to the plain teaching of God's Word.

- Fifth, we must think about science scientifically. True science is a proven process. It is to be followed diligently and documented responsibly regardless of a scientist's preferences or biases. True science is not automatically defined by a science textbook, by a university degree, by a research grant, by a group of science professionals expressing their opinions, by a museum exhibit, or by a television documentary. True science is about exploration, experimentation, observation, evidence, testing, and integrity. The theory of evolution is merely an outdated origin of life conjecture. It is scientifically weak and is unable to disprove the accuracy of the Bible.

Those Christians who try to maintain their belief in the theory of evolution will struggle with trusting the Word of God. Their ability to accurately understand portions of the Bible will be impaired. Their ability to take up the full armor of God (Ephesians 6:10-18) for spiritual protection will be diminished. They will then be more vulnerable to spiritual attacks such as deception, moral confusion, fears, worrying, discouragement, despair, temptation, pridefulness, doubts about God, and distractions from serving God. Their growth in spiritual maturity will be hampered. Their ability to discern God's truth from the false ideas of man will be weakened. When we as Christians have diligently studied the Bible and find that it speaks clearly about a subject, we need to trust it even if it appears to us to be counterintuitive. Many things in life that initially appear to be counterintuitive to us turn out in reality to be true. In the following two Bible verses God clearly calls us to trust Him—and that also means His Word—above the wisdom of man:

> "For my thoughts are not your thoughts, neither are your ways my ways," declares the LORD. "As the heavens are higher than the earth, so are my ways higher than your ways and my thoughts than your thoughts. *Isaiah 55:8-9*

> Trust in the LORD with all your heart and lean not on your own understanding; in all your ways acknowledge him, and he will make your paths straight. *Proverbs 3:5-6*

Some will say that the evolution issue is not important. I believe that any issue that leads a person to doubt the trustworthiness of the Bible is vitally important. Believing in the theory of evolution rather than in the biblical account of creation will have an undermining effect on how you view the Word of God. How you choose to view and treat the Bible will significantly influence each of the following areas of your Christian life:

1. Your understanding of the Bible

2. Your understanding of God

3. Your trust in God

4. Your relationship with Jesus Christ

5. Your submission and obedience to Jesus Christ

6. Your service to Jesus Christ

7. Your understanding of this world we live in

8. Your understanding of human nature

9. How you view and treat other people

10. Your ability to discern truth from error, right from wrong, good from evil

11. Your ability to trust and benefit from God's wisdom in the Bible

Trusting in man-centered ideas and wisdom above the Bible's teaching undermines a person's confidence and trust in the God of the Bible. This is a serious issue for all who profess to be followers of the Lord Jesus Christ. To what extent do you really trust the Bible? To help you find out, I invite you to carefully ponder *Appendix 6: Trusting the Bible—A Self-Test for Christians.*

Appendix 5

Appendix 6

Trusting the Bible— A Self-Test for Christians

To what extent do you trust the Bible? As Christians it is easy for us to say that we believe and trust the Bible. But what do we really mean when we say that we trust the Bible? "Trusting the Bible—A Self-Test for Christians" has two purposes. The first is to help us to better understand to what extent we are really trusting and relying on the Word of God in our everyday living. The second is to encourage us to discover and trust what the Bible says regarding thirty important questions that are vitally important to every human being. **Before answering the "Thirty Important Questions" that follow, consider what God says about trusting the Bible:**

1. The God of the Bible calls people to believe that the Bible is in fact the Word of God.

    All Scripture is God-breathed and is useful for teaching, rebuking, correcting and training in righteousness, so that the man of God may be thoroughly equipped for every good work. *2 Timothy 3:16–17*

2. The Bible teaches that although the Bible was penned by men it was authored by the Holy Spirit.

    Above all, you must understand that no prophecy of Scripture came about by the prophet's own interpretation. For prophecy never had its origin in the will of man, but men spoke from God as they were carried along by the Holy Spirit. *2 Peter 1:20–21*

3. God tells us that His Word is at work within everyone who believes that the Bible is the Word of God.

    And we also thank God continually because, when you received the word of God, which you heard from us, you accepted it not as the word of men, but as it actually is, the word of God, which is at work in you who believe. 1 *Thessalonians 2:13*

4. God calls us to trust in Him above our own understanding and to be obedient to Him.

> Trust in the LORD with all your heart and lean not on your own understanding; in all your ways acknowledge him, and he will make your paths straight. *Proverbs 3:5–6*

5. The Lord Jesus Christ warns us that not knowing what the Bible says or not appreciating how powerful God is leads to error—wrong thinking.

> Jesus replied, "You are in error because you do not know the Scriptures or the power of God. Matthew 22:29

6. The Lord Jesus Christ calls us to hear and obey the Word of God.

> He replied, "Blessed rather are those who hear the word of God and obey it." Luke 11:28

7. God tells us that His Word is truth. If we really believe that Jesus Christ is the Son of God, the Messiah, and the "King of Kings and Lord of Lords", then we must trust Him when He declares that God's Word is truth.

> After Jesus said this, he looked toward heaven and prayed: "Father, the time has come. Glorify your Son, that your Son may glorify you. . . . Sanctify them by the truth; your word is truth. John 17:1, 17

As Christians we are continually faced with choosing between following the wisdom of this world or trusting what the Bible says. The wisdom of this world refers to man's ideas, reasonings, and speculations that conflict with God's principles, ways, and wisdom. God calls us to trust the Bible—the Word of God. This means that when the Word of God is in conflict with what the world says or with what we think, we are to trust and obey God's Word.

> Do not deceive yourselves. If any one of you thinks he is wise by the standards of this age, he should become a "fool" so that he may become wise. For the wisdom of this world is foolishness in God's sight. 1 Corinthians 3:18–19a

It is my hope that this "Self-Test" will help you to grow in your confidence that the Bible is fully trustworthy and is far wiser than the wisdom of this world. Ask God to help you to discover, trust, and rightly apply what the Bible says regarding each of the following "Thirty Important Questions":

Thirty Important Questions

Perspective 1—*To what extent do you trust and rely on the Bible for answering each of the following thirty questions?*

Perspective 2—*What does the Bible say regarding each of the following thirty questions?*

1. What should I believe about the Bible?

2. Who is God, and what are His attributes?

3. God calls us to love Him. What does this mean? What should this look like in my life?

4. God calls us to love other people. What does this mean? What should this look like in my life?

5. Who is Jesus Christ, and what are His attributes?

6. What does Jesus Christ want of me?

7. What does it mean to love Jesus Christ?

8. What does it mean to follow Jesus Christ?

9. What is truth and how important is it to God?

10. How should I decide whether something is right or wrong, good or evil, moral or immoral?

11. What should I do when I become aware that God considers something in my life to be sinful?

12. How should I prepare my heart and mind each day so that when I am faced with temptations, troubles, and decisions I will choose obedience to the Lord Jesus Christ?

13. How should I use my time, talents, and resources?

14. What should I do when I am faced with troubles, disappointments, frustrations, suffering, or fears?

Thirty Important Questions

15. What criteria should I use in deciding what my life priorities and goals should be?

16. How should I evaluate what appear to be new opportunities?

17. If I have children, how should I view and relate to them?

18. If I have children, how and what should I teach them?

19. If I am married, how should I view and relate to my spouse?

20. How should I view and relate to my parents?

21. How should I view and relate to all other people?

22. What is the ultimate source of a human being's value?

23. To what extent is my value as a person determined by another's opinion?

24. How should I view myself when my life is in turmoil, stress-filled, or doesn't measure up to my expectations or the expectations of others?

25. How should I view myself when I feel in control, when things are going my way, and when others praise me for being successful?

26. How should I make sense of the world around me considering all of its wonders, beauty, and blessings, as well as its dangers, disappointments, tragedies, suffering, and death?

27. What should I believe regarding the origin of the universe and the earth?

28. What should I believe regarding the origin of life and human beings?

29. What do human beings really consist of? Are we really just highly "evolved" physical matter and energy that somehow interact to produce consciousness, reasoning, love, and creativity as much of our culture would have us believe? Or, did God create us as beings consisting of body, soul, and spirit who, through Christ, are able to enter into a relationship with Him for eternity?

30. What will happen to me when my physical body dies?

Notes

Introduction

1. *Noah Webster's 1828 First Edition of the American Dictionary of the English Language*, Public Domain. Many websites offer free online access to this dictionary (search on: *"Webster's 1828 Dictionary"*).

2. *Treasury of Scriptural Knowledge* by Canne, Browne, Blayney, Scott, and others about 1880, with introduction by R. A. Torrey, Public Domain. Many websites offer free online access to this dictionary (search on: *"Treasury of Scriptural Knowledge"*).

Chapter 18   God's Holiness

1. *Noah Webster's 1828 First Edition of the American Dictionary of the English Language*, Public Domain. Many websites offer free online access to this dictionary (search on: "Webster's 1828 Dictionary").

Appendix 3   How to Equip Your Mind with the Word of God

1. Quote from George Washington to Edmund Randolph in a letter dated July 31, 1795.

2. Quote from Frank Peretti's presentation entitled *The Chart*, published by Compass International (This presentation is available at www.compass.org).

3. Koinonia Institute information is available at www.studycenter.com

4. *How to Study the Bible* by Chuck Missler, Copyright 2006, published by Koinonia House (www.khouse.org).

Appendix 5   Do Not Be Misled by Darwin's Theory of Evolution

1. Discovery Institute Center for Science and Culture, *Top Questions*, September 8, 2005 (www.intelligentdesign.org).

2. The Movie: *Expelled: No Intelligence Allowed* (www.expelledthemovie.com).

3. Quote from George Washington to Edmund Randolph in a letter dated July 31, 1795.

If you would like to send me your comments regarding this book, please go to my website below and select the *Contact* tab near the top of the screen.

Thank you.
Barney Browne

MindEquip
www.mindequip.com

Notes

Notes

Notes

Notes

Contents

Section 1   The Bible

Section 2   What the Bible Says About God

Section 3   What the Bible Says About Human Beings

Appendices